CREATION *and* DESTRUCTION

Creation and Destruction
A Reappraisal of the *Chaoskampf* Theory in the Old Testament

David Toshio Tsumura

Winona Lake, Indiana
EISENBRAUNS
2005

Library of Congress Cataloging-in-Publication Data

Tsumura, David Toshio.
  Creation and destruction : a reappraisal of the chaoskampf theory in
    the Old Testament / David Toshio Tsumura.
        p.   cm.
    Rev. and expanded ed. of: The earth and the waters in Genesis 1
      and 2.
    ISBN 1-57506-106-6 (hardcover : alk. paper)
    1. Creation—Biblical teaching.   2. Water in the Bible.
  3. Earth in the Bible.   4. Bible. O.T. Genesis I–II—Criticism,
  interpretation, etc.   5. Bible. O.T. Genesis I–II—Language, style.
  I. Tsumura, David Toshio. Earth and the waters in Genesis 1 and 2.
  II. Title.
    BS1199.C73T78   2005
    222′.1106—dc22
                                                        2005009506

The paper used in this publication meets the minimum requirements of the American
National Standard for Information Sciences—Permanence of Paper for Printed
Library Materials, ANSI Z39.48-1984. ∞™

Dedicated to

Susan

and her parents

Ked and Betty Martin

Contents

Preface   ix

Abbreviations   xi

Introduction   1

PART 1
Creation Narratives in Genesis

1. The Earth in Genesis 1   9
    Etymology of *THW   10
    Etymology of *BHW   13
    Tōhû wābōhû and Ugaritic *tu-a-bi-*[*ú*]   15
    Uses of *tōhû* and *tōhû wābōhû*   22
    Tōhû wābōhû in the Framework of Genesis 1   33

2. The Waters in Genesis 1   36
    Babylonian Background   36
    Canaanite Background   41
    Etymology of *THM   42
    Uses of *THM   44
    *tihām- and *yamm-   49
    Excursus: A "Canaanite" Dragon Myth in Genesis 1:2?   53

3. The Earth-Waters-*rûaḥ* in Genesis 1   58
    The "Hyponymous" Word Pair *ʾrṣ–thm*(*t*)   58
    "Heaven" – "Earth" – "Sea":
        A Tripartite Division of the World   63
    "Heaven" – "Earth":
        A Bipartite Division of the World   65
    A Flooding of the Subterranean Waters?   69
    Excursus: Structure of *Enuma elish* I 1–9   72
    Exegetical Problems of *rûaḥ ʾĕlōhîm*   74

4. The Earth in Genesis 2   77
    The Earth in a Bare State   77
    Structure of Genesis 2:5–6   78
    "Earth," "Field," and "Land"   80
    No Vegetation   82
    No Man to "Till" the Land   83

5. The Waters in Genesis 2 85
    Rain and ʾēd   85
    Etymology of ʾēd   87
    Summary and Conclusions   106

6. The Earth-Waters Relationship in Genesis 2 107
    A Flooding of the Subterranean Waters   107
    Etymology of Eden   112
    Excursus: Etymology of Tigris and Euphrates   125
    Summary   127

7. God and the Waters 128
    God as a Rain-Giver   128
    Watery Beginning   129
    Conclusion   139

PART 2
The Chaoskampf *Motif in Poetic Texts*

8. Canaanite Myths and Hebrew Poetry 143
    The *"Chaoskampf* Myth"   143
    Methodological Principles   146
    Psalm 18 // 2 Samuel 22—Adaptation?   149
    Psalm 29: A Canaanite Hymn?   152

9. A Creation Motif in Psalm 46? 156
    The Relationship between Verses 2–3 and Verse 6   156
    The Relationship between Verses 2c–3 and Verse 4   160

10. A Destruction Motif in Habakkuk 3 164
    Yahweh versus the Sea (Verses 8 and 15)   164
    Yahweh's Bow and Mace (Verse 9)   168
    Yahweh's Destruction of the Evil One (Verse 13b)   174

11. Metaphor in Poetry 182
    War and Storm Imageries   184
    Destruction Motif   187
    Personification and Metaphor   191

Conclusions 196

Indexes 199
    Index of Authors   199
    Index of Scripture   204
    Index of Ancient Texts   208
    Index of Ancient Terms   210

Preface

This book is the outcome of my research during the past three decades. My interest in this topic was first kindled by Dr. D. F. Kinlaw during my seminary education, then cultivated by Dr. C. H. Gordon in graduate school and supported by Profs. D. J. Wiseman, K. A. Kitchen, and A. R. Millard. The first edition, part 1 of the present work, was completed during my stay at Tyndale House, Cambridge, England, as a research fellow for the "Genesis 1–11 Project" during 1986–88 and published as a monograph in 1989. For this edition, I have revised part 1 and added part 2.

In this book, I try to set the Genesis creation stories and some of the poetic texts of the Bible in the literary and mythological context of the ancient Near East to elucidate similarities and differences between the biblical creation tradition and the extrabiblical traditions. For this purpose, I checked primary sources in their original languages whenever I could.

The earlier edition of this book, *The Earth and the Waters in Genesis 1 and 2: A Linguistic Investigation* (JSOTSup 83; Sheffield: Sheffield Academic Press, 1989), was well accepted by scholars in this field but went out of print in less than three years. After its publication, the book was reviewed, mostly favorably, in the major scholarly journals, such as *BL* (1990), *ExTim* (1990), *ETR* (1990), *TLZ* (1990), *ZAW* (1990), *CBQ* (1991), *JBL* (1991), *JTS* (1991), *RB* (1991), *BZ* (1992), *VT* (1992), *EvQ* (1994), and *BO* (1995), and noted in commentaries and scholarly articles.

Various factors prevented me from revising and republishing it. Meanwhile, a number of significant works on the subject have appeared. Additionally, Prof. J. C. L. Gibson's request in *BL* (1990) for "another book," one on the *Chaoskampf* motif in the poetic books of the Old Testament, motivated me to write several chapters, if not a book, on this problem while revising the chapters on Genesis. I hope this new edition will make a modest contribution to the hotly debated issue of the "chaos" theory in the Old Testament.

I would like to express my deep appreciation to those who helped me on this project: besides the above-mentioned mentors, to Prof. W. G. Lambert and to Drs. R. S. Hess and B. K. Winter for various useful comments and encouragement; to Jim Eisenbraun and his staff, particularly Beverly McCoy; finally, but not least, to my wife, Susan, for her unfailing support, comments, and encouragement. To her and her parents I dedicate this book with love.

Gloria sola Deo!

Abbreviations

General

AH	*Atra-Ḫasīs epic*
Akk.	Akkadian
AO	Tablets in the collections of the Musée du Louvre
Arab.	Arabic
Aram.	Aramaic
ASV	American Standard Version
B.	Tractate of Babylonian Talmud
CH	Code of Hammurabi
DN	Divine name
EA	El-Amarna tablets
Ebla.	Eblaite
Ee	*Enuma elish*
Eg.	Egyptian
ET	English translation
fem.	Feminine
Gilg.	*Epic of Gilgamesh*
Gk.	Greek
Heb.	Hebrew
Hur.	Hurrian
imperf.	Imperfect
intrans.	Intransitive verb
JB	Jerusalem Bible
JPSV	Jewish Publication Society Version of the Old Testament
K.	Tablets in the Kouyunjik collection of the British Museum
KH	Kode d. Hammurabi
KJV	King James Version
LB	Late Babylonian
LXX	Septuagint
MA (mA)	Middle Assyrian
masc.	Masculine
MB (mB)	Middle Babylonian
MH	Mishnaic Hebrew
MT	Masoretic Text
NA	Neo-Assyrian

NAB	New American Bible
NASB	New American Standard Bible
NEB	New English Bible
NIV	New International Version
NRSV	New Revised Standard Version
OA	Old Assyrian
OAkk	Old Akkadian
OB	Old Babylonian
obv.	Obverse
Phoen.	Phoenician
pl.	Plate, plural
PN	Personal name
REB	Revised English Bible
rev.	Reverse
RS	Ras Shamra text
RSV	Revised Standard Version
SB	Standard Babylonian
Senn.	Sennacherib
sing.	Singular
Sum.	Sumerian
Syr.	Syriac
TM	Tablets from Tell Mardikh–Ebla
Ug.	Ugaritic
UET	Ur excavations, texts
Vulg.	Vulgate
VAT	Tablets in the collections of the Staatliche Museen, Berlin

Reference Works

AB	Anchor Bible
ABZ	R. Borger. *Assyrisch-babylonische Zeichenliste*. Kevelaer: Butzon & Bercker / Neukirchen-Vluyn: Neukirchener Verlag, 1978
Ach	C. Virolleaud. *L'Astrologie chaldéenne: Le livre intitulé "Enuma (Anu) ilu Bêl."* 3 vols. Paris: Geuthner, 1905–12
AEL	E. W. Lane. *An Arabic-English Lexicon*. London, 1863. Repr. Beirut: Librairie du Liban, 1968
AfO	*Archiv für Orientforschung*
AFw	H. Zimmern. *Akkadische Fremdwörter als Beweis für babylonischen Kultureinfluss*. Leipzig: Hinrichs, 1915
AG	K. Tallqvist. *Akkadische Götterepitheta*. Studia Orientalia 7. Helsinki: Societas Orientalis Fennica, 1938

AH	W. G. Lambert and A. R. Millard. *Atra-Ḫasīs: The Babylonian Story of the Flood.* Oxford, 1969. Repr. Winona Lake, Ind.: Eisenbrauns, 1999
AHw	W. von Soden. *Akkadisches Handwörterbuch.* Wiesbaden: Harrassowitz, 1965–81
AIA	S. A. Kaufman. *The Akkadian Influences on Aramaic.* Chicago: University of Chicago Press, 1974
AJBI	*Annual of the Japanese Biblical Institute*
AKA	E. A. W. Budge and L. W. King. *Annals of the Kings of Assyria.* London: British Museum, 1902–
AnBib	Analecta Biblica
AnOr	Analecta Orientalia
ANEP	J. B. Pritchard (ed.). *The Ancient Near East in Pictures Relating to the Old Testament.* Princeton: Princeton University Press, 1954
ANET	J. B. Pritchard (ed.). *Ancient Near Eastern Texts Relating to the Old Testament.* 3rd ed. Princeton: Princeton University Press, 1969
AOAT	Alter Orient und Altes Testament
ARET	Archivi reali di Ebla, Testi
ARM	Archives Royales de Mari
AS	Assyriological Studies
ASKT	P. Haupt. *Akkadische und sumerische Keilschrifttexte.* Leipzig: Hinrichs, 1881–82
ASN	*Annali della scuola normale, superiore di Pisa*
AuOr	*Aula Orientalis*
AUSS	*Andrews University Seminary Studies*
BA	*Biblical Archaeologist*
BaE	L. Cagni (ed.). *Il bilinguismo a Ebla.* Napels: Istituto universitario orientale, Departimento di studi asiatici, 1984
BASOR	*Bulletin of the American Schools of Oriental Research*
BBSt.	L. W. King (ed.). *Babylonian Boundary-Stones and Memorial-Tablets in the British Museum.* London: British Museum, 1912
BBVO	Berliner Beiträge zum Vorderen Orient
BDB	F. Brown, S. R. Driver, and C. A. Briggs. *A Hebrew and English Lexicon of the Old Testament.* Oxford: Clarendon, 1907
BG	A. Heidel. *The Babylonian Genesis: The Story of the Creation.* 2nd ed. Chicago: University of Chicago Press, 1951 [3rd ed., 1963]
BHS	Biblia Hebraica Stuttgartensia
Bib	*Biblica*
BibInt	*Biblical Interpretation*
BKAT	Biblischer Kommentar Altes Testament

BL   *Book List* (Society for Old Testament Study)
BMECCJ   *Bulletin of the Middle Eastern Culture Center in Japan*
BMS   L. W. King. *Babylonian Magic and Sorcery: Being "The Prayers of the Lifting of the Hand."* York Beach, Me.: Weiser, 2000
BN   *Biblische Notizen*
BO   *Bibliotheca Orientalis*
Borger Esarh. R. Borger, *Die Inschriften Asarhaddons, Königs von Assyrien.* AfO Beiheft 9. Osnabrück: Biblio-Verlag, 1967
BSac   *Bibliotheca Sacra*
BSOAS   *Bulletin of the School of Oriental and African Studies*
BWL   W. G. Lambert. *Babylonian Wisdom Literature.* Oxford, 1960. Repr. Winona Lake, Ind.: Eisenbrauns, 1996
BZ   *Biblische Zeitschrift*
BZAW   Beihefte zur *ZAW*
CAD   *Chicago Assyrian Dictionary of the Oriental Institute of the University of Chicago.* Chicago: University of Chicago Press, 1956–
CBQ   *Catholic Biblical Quarterly*
CML   G. R. Driver (ed.). *Canaanite Myths and Legends.* Edinburgh: T. & T. Clark, 1956
CML²   J. C. L. Gibson (ed.). *Canaanite Myths and Legends.* 2nd ed. Edinburgh: T. & T. Clark, 1978
CS   W. W. Hallo (ed.). *The Context of Scripture.* 3 vols. Leiden: Brill, 1997–2002
CT   Cuneiform Texts from Babylonian Tablets in the British Museum
CTA   A. Herdner (ed.). *Corpus des tablettes en cunéiformes alphabétiques.* 2 vols. Mission de Ras Shamra 10. Paris: Imprimérie nationale, 1963
DANE   P. Bienkowski and A. Millard (eds.). *Dictionary of the Ancient Near East.* London: British Museum, 2000
DCH   D. J. A. Clines. *The Dictionary of Classical Hebrew.* Sheffield: Sheffield Academic Press, 1993–
DDD   K. van der Toorn, B. Becking, and P. W. van der Horst (eds.). *Dictionary of Deities and Demons in the Bible.* Leiden: Brill, 1995
DOTT   D. W. Thomas (ed.). *Documents from Old Testament Times.* London: Thomas Nelson, 1958
ESP   J. J. M. Roberts. *The Earliest Semitic Pantheon: A Study of the Semitic Deities Attested in Mesopotamia before Ur III.* Baltimore: Johns Hopkins University Press, 1972
ETR   *Études théologiques et religieuses*
ExTim   *Expository Times*

EvQ	*Evangelical Quarterly*
GAG	W. von Soden. *Grundriss der akkadischen Grammatik.* 2nd ed. AnOr 33. Rome: Pontifical Biblical Institute, 1969
HAL	L. Koehler, W. Baumgartner, J. J. Stamm, and B. Hartmann. *Hebräisches und aramäisches Lexikon zum Alten Testament.* Fascicles 1–5. KB 3. Leiden: Brill, 1967–95
HALOT	L. Koehler, W. Baumgartner, J. J. Stamm, B. Hartmann, and M. E. J. Richardson. *The Hebrew and Aramaic Lexicon of the Old Testament.* 5 vols. Leiden: Brill, 1994–2000
HAR	*Hebrew Annual Review*
HSM	Harvard Semitic Monographs
HSS	Harvard Semitic Studies
HTR	*Harvard Theological Review*
ICC	International Critical Commentary
ICK	Inscriptions cunéiformes du Kültépe
IDB	G. A. Buttrick (ed.). *Interpreter's Dictionary of the Bible.* 4 vols. New York: Abingdon, 1962
JANES	*Journal of the Ancient Near Eastern Society of Columbia University*
JAOS	*Journal of the American Oriental Society*
JBL	*Journal of Biblical Literature*
JCS	*Journal of Cuneiform Studies*
JNES	*Journal of Near Eastern Studies*
JQR	*Jewish Quarterly Review*
JSOT	*Journal for the Study of the Old Testament*
JSOTSup	Journal for the Study of the Old Testament Supplements
JSS	*Journal of Semitic Studies*
JTS	*Journal of Theological Studies*
KAI	H. Donner and W. Röllig. *Kanaanäische und aramäische Inschriften.* 3 vols. Wiesbaden: Harrassowitz, 1962–68
KAR	Keilschrifttexte aus Assur religiösen Inhalts
KAV	Keilschrifttexte aus Assur verschiedenen Inhalts
KB	L. Koehler and W. Baumgartner. *Lexicon in Veteris Testamenti Libros.* Leiden: Brill, 1953
KTU	M. Dietrich, O. Loretz, and J. Sanmartín. *Die keilalphabetischen Texte aus Ugarit.* Neukirchen-Vluyn, 1976. *The Cuneiform Alphabetic Texts from Ugarit, Ras Ibn Hani, and Other Places.* 2nd, enlarged ed. Münster: Ugarit-Verlag, 1995
KUB	Keilschrifturkunden aus Boghazköi
LAPO	Littératures anciennes du Proche-Orient
LdE	L. Cagni (ed.). *La lingua di Ebla.* Naples: Istituto universitario orientale, Seminario di studi asiatici, 1981

LKA	E. Ebeling. *Literarische Keilschrifttexte aus Assur.* Berlin: Academie, 1953
LSS	Leipziger semitische Studien
Lyon Sar.	D. G. Lyon. *Keilschrifttexte Sargon's Königs von Assyrien 722–705 v. Chr.* Assyriologische Bibliothek 5. Leipzig: Zentralantiquariat, 1977
MAD	Materials for the Assyrian Dictionary
MARI	*Mari: Annales de recherches interdisciplinaires*
MEE	Materiali epigrafici di Ebla
MIOF	*Mitteilungen des Instituts für Orientforschung*
MLC	G. del Olmo Lete. *Mitos y leyendas de Canaan.* Madrid: Ediciones Cristiandad, 1981
MMEW	A. Livingstone. *Mystical and Mythological Explanatory Works of Assyrian and Babylonian Scholars.* Oxford: Clarendon, 1986
MRS	Mission de Ras Shamra
MSL	Materialien zum sumerischen Lexikon
MTZ	*Münchener theologische Zeitschrift*
NABU	*Nouvelles assyriologiques brèves et utilitaires*
NDBT	T. D. Alexander and B. S. Rosner (eds.). *New Dictionary of Biblical Theology.* Leicester: Inter-Varsity, 2000
NICOT	The New International Commentary on the Old Testament
NIDOTTE	W. A. VanGemeren (ed.). *New International Dictionary of Old Testament Theology and Exegesis.* 5 vols. Grand Rapids: Zondervan, 1997
NUS	*Newsletter for Ugaritic Studies*
OIP	Oriental Institute Publications
Or	*Orientalia*
OTA	*Old Testament Abstracts*
OTL	Old Testament Library
OTWSA	*Ou-Testamentiese Werkgemeenskap in Suid-Afrika*
PEQ	*Palestine Exploration Quarterly*
PLMU	C. H. Gordon. "Poetic Legends and Myths from Ugarit." *Berytus* 25 (1977), 5–133
PSBA	Proceedings of the Society of Biblical Archaeology
R	H. C. Rawlinson. *The Cuneifrom Inscriptions of Western Asia.* London: British Museum, n.d.
RA	*Revue d'assyriologie et d'archéologie orientale*
Racc.	F. Thureau-Dangin, *Rituels accadiens.* Paris, 1921
RB	*Revue biblique*
RGTC	Répertoire géographique des textes cunéiformes
RHA	*Revue hittite et asianique*

RlA	E. Ebeling et al. *Reallexikon der Assyriologie*. Berlin: de Gruyter, 1928–
RSP	*Ras Shamra Parallels*
SBH	F. I. Andersen. *The Sentence in Biblical Hebrew*. The Hague: Mouton, 1974
SBLDS	Society of Biblical Literature Dissertation Series
SBTS	Sources for Biblical and Theological Study
SD	Å. W. Sjöberg (ed.). *The Sumerian Dictionary*. Philadelphia: Babylonian Section of the University Museum, 1984–
SEb	*Studi Eblaiti*
SEL	*Studi epigrafici e linguistici sul vicino Oriente Antico*
SEM	E. Chiera. *Sumerian Epics and Myths*. OIP 15. Chicago: University of Chicago Press, 1934
SLE	P. Fronzaroli (ed.). *Studies on the Language of Ebla*. Florence: Istituto di linguistica e di lingue orientali, Università di Firenze, 1984
SLOBA	S. J. Lieberman. *The Sumerian Loanwords in Old-Babylonian Akkadian*. Vol. 1. Missoula, Mont.: Scholars Press for Harvard Semitic Museum, 1977
SLOCG	E. Lipiński. *Semitic Languages: Outline of a Comparative Grammar*. Leuven: Peeters, 1997
SPUMB	J. C. de Moor. *The Seasonal Pattern in the Ugaritic Myth of Baʿlu*. Kevelaer: Butzon & Bercker, 1971
ST	*Studia Theologica*
STC	L. W. King (ed.). *The Seven Tablets of Creation, or, The Babylonian and Assyrian Legends concerning the Creation of the World and of Mankind*. 2 vols. Repr., New York: AMS, 1976
Streck Asb.	M. Streck. *Assurbanipal und die letzten assyrischen könige bis zum untergange Niniveh's*. VAB 7. Leipzig: Hinrichs, 1916
TIT	T. Jacobsen. *Toward the Image of Tammuz and Other Essays on Mesopotamian History and Culture*. Ed. W. L. Moran. Cambridge: Harvard University Press, 1970
TCL	Textes cunéiformes. Musée du Louvre
TDOT	G. J. Botterweck and H. Ringgren (eds.). *Theological Dictionary of the Old Testament*. Grand Rapids: Eerdmans, 1974–
TJ	*Trinity Journal*
TLZ	*Theologische Literaturzeitung*
TO	A. Caquot, M. Sznycer, and A. Herdner. *Textes ougaritiques*. Vol. 1. Paris: Cerf, 1974
TOTC	Tyndale Old Testament Commentary
TRE	G. Krause and G. Müller. *Theologische Realenzyklopädie*. 17 vols. Berlin: de Gruyter, 1977–98

TuL	E. Ebeling. *Tod und Leben nach den Vorstellungen der Babylonier.* Berlin: de Gruyter, 1931–
TynBul	*Tyndale Bulletin*
UBL	Ugaritisch-biblische Literatur
UF	*Ugarit-Forschungen*
Ug.	*Ugaritica*
UT	C. H. Gordon. *Ugaritic Textbook.* AnOr 38. Rome: Pontifical Biblical Institute, 1965
UTS	C. H. Gordon. *Ugaritic Textbook, Supplement.* AnOr 38B. Rome: Pontifical Biblical Institute, 1967
UVST	J. Huehnergard. *Ugaritic Vocabulary in Syllabic Transcription.* Atlanta: Scholars Press, 1987
VAB	Vorderasiatische Bibliothek
VE	"Vocabulary of Ebla." Pp. 115–343 in G. Pettinato, *Testi lessicali bilingui della biblioteca L. 2769, parte 1.* MEE 4. Naples: Università Orientale di Napoli, 1982
VT	*Vetus Testamentum*
VTSup	Supplements to Vetus Testamentum
WäS	A. Erman and H. Grapow. *Wörterbuch der ägyptischen Sprache.* 5 vols. Berlin, 1926–31. Repr. Berlin: Akademie, 1953
WBC	Word Biblical Commentary
YOS	Yale Oriental Series
ZA	*Zeitschrift für Assyriologie*
ZAH	*Zeitschrift für Althebräistik*
ZAW	*Zeitschrift für die alttestamentliche Wissenschaft*
ZDMG	*Zeitschrift der deutschen morgenlandischen Gesellschaft*

Introduction

In human experience, water occupies a crucial place, both positive and negative. Water is one of the basic necessities for the existence of living things and is thus beneficial when controlled properly; however, it can be destructive when uncontrolled.[1]

In the biblical creation traditions, the water is an entity created by Yahweh, the Creator of the total cosmos, "the heavens and the earth" (Gen 1:1). It does not create anything by itself; the earth simply came out of it (Gen 1:9–10) as a result of divine fiat. In the Babylonian "creation" myth *Enuma elish*, however, all things, including the generations of deities, emanated from two pre-existent primordial waters, the divine pair Apsu and Tiamat.[2] Furthermore, in Sumerian mythology, An-ki ("undivided Heaven-Earth") was produced by Nammu, the mother goddess of primeval water.[3]

There is a popular hypothesis that the Chaoskampf motif of *Enuma elish*, the battle between Tiamat and Marduk, is behind the biblical idea of creation, especially in the background of Gen 1:2, and hence it has been assumed that the basic pattern of the biblical creation motif is "order out of chaos," as a result of the victory over the chaos waters, which symbolize the enemy of a creator god.

Because water imagery in the poetic texts of the Old Testament is often negative and even destructive, many scholars have taken such destructive images as a sign of "creation" (e.g., Ps 46; see ch. 9). This, however, is due to a misunderstanding of the nature of the imagery. Such a hypothesis does not work for the Genesis creation story (see part 1). Neither does it work for individual poetic texts when they are carefully interpreted on their own merits (see part 2).

---

1. See D. T. Tsumura, "Water," *NDBT*, 840–41. For ordinary Egyptian life, the annual flooding of the Nile River was very important. While low inundation causes famine, high inundation can bring destruction to buildings, crops, and irrigation works. See J. R. Huddlestun, " 'Who Is This That Rises like the Nile?': Some Egyptian Texts on the Inundation and a Prophetic Trope," in *Fortunate the Eyes That See: Essays in Honor of David Noel Freedman in Celebration of His Seventieth Birthday* (ed. A. B. Beck et al.; Grand Rapids: Eerdmans, 1995), 338–63.
2. Tsumura, "Water," 840.
3. F. Stolz, "Sea," *DDD*, 1392; F. Wiggerman, "Mythological Foundations of Nature," *Natural Phenomena* (1992), 293.

1

There are still questions about the meanings of key expressions in Gen 1:2 such as *tōhû wābōhû* and *tĕhôm,* as well as the nature of the earth-waters relationship. B. S. Childs, who like many other scholars accepts a mythological background for these expressions, explains Gen 1:2 as describing "the mystery of a primordial threat against creation, uncreated without form and void, which God strove to overcome."[4] He had expressed this view in more theological terms a quarter of century earlier: "the Old Testament writer struggles to contrast the creation, not with a background of empty neutrality, but with an active chaos standing in opposition to the will of God. . . . The chaos is a reality rejected by God."[5]

Anderson reasserted the same view, saying "God created out of chaos (not *ex nihilo*), as shown by the prefatory verse that portrays the earth as once being a chaotic waste: stygian darkness, turbulent waters, utter disorder."[6] B. Otzen also accepts this conventional view, saying, "Few would deny that elements of a description of chaos are present in v. 2."[7] This chaos theory was first advocated more than a century ago by H. Gunkel, who viewed the "chaos" in Gen 1:2 as the precosmic status of the world, that is, the world before the creation.[8] Recently, T. E. Fretheim has held that this verse refers to

---

4. B. S. Childs, *Old Testament Theology in a Canonical Context* (London: SCM, 1985), 223–24. It is well known that K. Barth treats this problem under the topic of *das Nichtige,* "nothingness," in his *Church Dogmatics,* vol. 3/3: *The Doctrine of Creation* (Edinburgh: T. & T. Clark, 1960), 289–368 (§50), esp. 352, where he says: "in Gen. 1:2 . . . there is a reference to the chaos which the Creator has already rejected, negated, passed over and abandoned even before He utters His first creative Word. . . . Chaos is the unwilled and uncreated reality which constitutes as it were the periphery of His creation and creature." Barth's view was deeply influenced by the view that has been accepted in Old Testament scholarship ever since H. Gunkel.

5. B. S. Childs, *Myth and Reality in the Old Testament* (London: SCM, 1960), 42.

6. B. W. Anderson, "Mythopoetic and Theological Dimensions of Biblical Creation Faith," in *Creation in the Old Testament* (ed. B. W. Anderson; Issues in Religion and Theology 6; Philadelphia: Fortress, 1984), 15.

7. B. Otzen, "The Use of Myth in Genesis," in *Myths in the Old Testament* (ed. B. Otzen, H. Gottlieb, and K. Jeppesen; London: SCM, 1980), 32.

8. H. Gunkel, "Influence of Babylonian Mythology upon the Biblical Creation Story," in *Creation in the Old Testament* (ed. B. W. Anderson; Issues in Religion and Theology 6; Philadelphia: Fortress, 1984), 25–52 [= an abridged English edition of *Schöpfung und Chaos in Urzeit und Endzeit* (1895), 3–120]; now also *Genesis: Translated and Interpreted* (Macon, Ga.: Mercer University Press, 1997 [orig. ed., 1910]), 104–6. See T. Podella, "Der 'Chaoskampf-mythos' im Alten Testament: Eine Problemanzeige," in *Mesopotamica-Ugaritica-Biblica: Festschrift für Kurt Bergerhof zur Vollendung seines 70. Lebensjahres am 7. Mai 1992* (ed. M. Dietrich and O. Loretz; AOAT 232; Neukirchen-Vluyn: Neukirchener Verlag, 1993), 285. In fact, the term *chaos* is a key word in (post-)modern society as well as in scientific theory.

the "pre-ordering situation" and that God's creative activity in vv. 3ff. was "the ordering of already existing reality." He rejects a specific link between the "deep" in v. 2 and Babylonian Tiamat as well as the negative connotation of "chaos."[9] However, this view deserves scrutiny. Does Gen 1:2 describe a "watery chaos" that existed before creation? In other words, do the terms *tōhû wābōhû* and *tĕhôm* in v. 2 really signify a chaotic state of the earth in waters and hence "a primordial threat against creation"?

There are also questions about the biblical view of the role of waters in relation to the earth in the two creation accounts. For example, it is often suggested that the nature of the "earth-waters" relationship in Gen 1 is totally different from that in Gen 2. G. von Rad in his commentary explains the initial states of the cosmos as follows:

> Whereas in ch. 1 creation moves from the chaos to the cosmos of the entire world, our account of creation [in Gen 2] sketches the original state as a desert in contrast to the sown.... [The] cosmological ideas [of J] ... are thus very unlike those [of P]. ... Water is here the assisting element of creation. In P and in some psalms it was the enemy of creation.[10]

A similar view is expressed by B. S. Childs, who refers to "the completely different atmosphere prevailing in 1.1–2.4a in comparison with 2.4bff."[11] B. W. Anderson also holds that "in this [J's] story the contrast is not between cosmos and chaos but between a well-watered oasis and the surrounding wilderness."[12] W. H. Schmidt similarly recognizes the contrast between the watery cosmogony of Gen 1:2 and the "steppe or desert lacking vegetation in the time of drought prior to rainfall" in 2:5.[13] On the other hand, some commentators (e.g., Gunkel, Driver, Zimmerli, Schmidt) have interpreted this dry earth in 2:5 as a dry chaos, "J's equivalent of P's watery chaos in 1:2."[14] It is

---

9. T. E. Fretheim, "The Book of Genesis," in *The New Interpreter's Bible* (Nashville: Abingdon, 1994), 342–43, 356.

10. G. von Rad, *Genesis* (OTL; Philadelphia: Westminster, 1961–72), 76–77. This view was already expressed in Gunkel, *Genesis*, 4: "There [Gen 1] water is the enemy, here [Gen 2] the friend." In his recent article, Otzen also contrasts the waters of "malevolence and danger" in Gen 1:2 and the "life-conferring" waters in Gen 2:6; see Otzen, "The Use of Myth in Genesis," 40–41.

11. Childs, *Myth and Reality*, 31.

12. B. W. Anderson, *Creation versus Chaos: The Reinterpretation of Mythical Symbolism in the Bible* (Philadelphia: Fortress, 1967 [1987, repr. with postscript]), 40.

13. W. H. Schmidt, *Die Schöpfungsgeschichte der Priesterschrift: Zur Überlieferungsgeschichte von Genesis 1:1–2:4a und 2:4b–3:24*, vol. 2: *Überarbeitete und erweiterte Auflage* (Neukirchen-Vluyn: Neukirchener Verlag, 1967), 196 ("vegetationlosen Steppe oder Wüste in der Trockenzeit vor dem Regenfall").

14. Cf. G. J. Wenham, *Genesis 1–15* (WBC 1; Waco, Tex.: Word, 1987), 57.

clear that the general situation described in Gen 2:5–6 is that of a "not yet productive" earth and an "assisting" water, ʾēd, though the etymology and meaning of ʾēd are still hotly debated.

However, does Gen 2:5–6 also describe a similar chaotic state of the earth, though a "dry chaos"? Is there any similarity between the "earth-waters" relationship in Gen 1 and in Gen 2? If so, in what sense are they similar? What is the function and meaning of the term ʾēd in Gen 2:6? How are the waters such as "rain-water," " ʾēd-water," and "river-waters" related to Eden and the Garden of Eden? The purpose of part 1 of this book is to clarify the initial state of the "earth" in its relation to the "waters" in Gen 1 and 2 by answering these questions.

Part 1 presents a linguistic analysis of some key terms related to the initial situation of the earth and its relationship with the waters in Gen 1:2 and Gen 2:5ff. Hence the scope of this study is limited: it includes neither discussions of terms such as ḥōšek and ʾĕlōhîm in Gen 1:2 nor a detailed analysis of the Eden story. However, the etymological studies are supplemented by a literary analysis and discourse-grammatical investigation of the text in which these key terms appear.

Emphasis is given to the etymological investigation of various key terms and expressions in light of cognate languages such as Ugaritic, Akkadian, Eblaite, and Arabic. Though methodologically a synchronic and structural study should have priority over a diachronic and comparative one, in the present study more emphasis is given to the etymological investigations, not because they have the last word in determining the meaning of disputed terms, but because many of the errors made in interpreting the biblical text we are dealing with stem from faulty etymology.

The present work does not intend to give a comprehensive literary analysis of the biblical creation stories; nor does it aim to solve all the theological problems related to the creation.

In part 2, the so-called *Chaoskampf*-motif in Psalms and other poetic passages is treated, though not comprehensively, following J. C. L. Gibson's suggestion.[15] Among the questions asked are the following: What are the

---

15. In his review of the earlier version of this monograph, J. C. L. Gibson commented: "Dr Tsumura's argument is thus far clear and convincing and ought in my view to be accepted by future commentators on Genesis. But do his findings, as he thinks they do, necessitate writing out all trace of menace in the early verses of Gen. 1? And if they do, where does that leave the *Chaoskampf*-motif in the Psalms, Job, and other poetic books, a motif which is closely connected with the themes of creation and providence? Are there two creation theologies in the Old Testament, one in which there is no lurking Leviathan in his created world with which God has to deal, and one in which there is? And if there are, which

functions of "waters" and "flood" in biblical poetry? Do the so-called chaos dragons such as Leviathan, Rahab, and Yam have anything to do with the creation motif in the biblical tradition? What is the relationship between these poetic texts and the Ugaritic myths of the Baal-Yam conflict? Are Pss 18 and 29 "adaptations" of Canaanite hymns, as suggested by some scholars? Selected passages where such questions arise, such as Ps 46 and Hab 3, will be handled, giving special consideration to methodological issues in the comparative study of the Old Testament and Ugaritic myths. I will investigate the metaphorical use of terms such as "sea," "storm," and "flood" in the final chapter in order to elucidate special features of poetic texts in the context of the ancient Near Eastern literary traditions.

Biblical citations in this book follow the standard chapter and verse schema found in English Bible translations.

---

of the two is more relevant for today's thinking on creation? Having whetted our appetites with this stimulating study, Dr Tsumura owes us another book" (*BL* [1990], 94).

PART 1

Creation Narratives in Genesis

1

The Earth in Genesis 1

The initial state of the earth is described in Gen 1:2 as *tōhû wābōhû*. This expression is traditionally translated into English as "vain within and void" (Wycliff); "void and empty" (Tyndale); "without form, and void" (KJV); "waste and void" (ASV 1901); "without form and void" (RSV 1971; NEB 1970); or "formless and empty" (NIV); "unformed and void" (JPSV 1985), and so on. The most recent translations are represented by "a formless void" (NRSV 1989) and "a vast waste" (REB 1989).

The idea of "formlessness"[1] has been accepted in translations such as the KJV, RSV, NEB, NIV, JPSV, and NRSV, while the REB recently changed "without form" of the NEB to "waste." The former position is recognizable already in Augustine, who says:

> The earth was invisible and unorganized, and darkness was over the abyss. Formlessness is suggested by these words. (*Confessions* 12.22)[2]

His view is based on the LXX's ἀόρατος καὶ ἀκατασκεύαστος "invisible and unformed" and was probably influenced, though indirectly, by Plato's *Timaeus*, which describes substance as "invisible and unshaped" (*Timaeus*, 51), "void of all the forms" (50–51).[3]

Greek translations other than the LXX are: κένωμα καὶ οὐθέν "an emptiness and a nothing" (Aquila); θὲν καὶ οὐθέν "a nothing and a nothing"

---

1. See BDB, 1062: "formlessness of the primaeval earth." It lists "formlessness," "confusion," "unreality," and "emptiness" as meanings of *tōhû wābōhû*, though stating "primary meaning difficult to seize."

2. See A. Louth (ed.), *Genesis 1–11* (Ancient Christian Commentary on Scripture, Old Testament 1; Downers Grove, Ill.: InterVarsity Press, 2001), 4.

3. Plato, *Timaeus, etc.*, with an English translation by R. G. Bury (Loeb Classical Library 234; Cambridge: Harvard University Press, 1929), 119. C. E. Gunton detects "a real echo of the *Timaeus*" in Augustine's remark: "In sum, first of all God creates 'a kind of intellectual creature' and only then the manifestly inferior material world (12.9)"; see Colin E. Gunton, *The Triune Creator: A Historical and Systematic Study* (Edinburgh Studies in Constructive Theology; Edinburgh: Edinburgh University Press, 1998), 78. "Augustin continued to be marked by the scars of the Manichaeism" (Gunton, p. 79).

(Theodotion); (ἐγένετο) ἀργὸν καὶ ἀδιάκριτον "(became) unworked and indistinguishable" (Symmachus).[4] In all these phrases we can detect the roots of modern translations that usually render it in an abstract sense, though the Hebrew expression seems to have had a concrete sense originally.[5]

Etymology of *THW

The term *tōhû* probably means "desert" or "waste" in Deut 32:10, where it appears parallel to *'ereṣ midbār* "a desert land."

yimṣā'ēhû bě'ereṣ midbār	In a desert land he found him,
ûb(ě)tōhû yělēl yěšîmōn	in a barren and howling waste. (NIV)

Until recently, its etymology had been explained in light of Arabic *t'h*, which Lane defined as "desert or waterless desert in which one loses his way."[6] This Arabic term as well as *tûh* ("desert"),[7] with a second weak consonant, might be a variant form of *thw, in light of two variant names such as *Tōhû* (1 Sam 1:1) and *Tôaḥ* (1 Chr 6:19). However, the Ugaritic term *thw* might be a better candidate for a cognate of Hebrew *tōhû*.

Ugaritic

The term *thw* appears in the following Ugaritic text:

[14])*p np.š . npš . lbim* [15])*thw .*	And my appetite is an appetite of
	the lion(s) in/of the desert(s)
hm . brlt . anḫr [16])*b ym .*	or a desire of the dolphin(?) in the sea.
	(KTU 1.5 [UT 67]:I:14–16)[8]

The same phrase appears in one of the mythological texts published in *Ug.* 5, 559–60: *lbim thw* (Text 4, lines 3–4).

A. Caquot, M. Sznycer, and A. Herdner (1974) explain *thw* in light of Hebrew *tōhû* and Arabic *t'h* "desert,"[9] following R. Dussaud, C. H. Gordon, H. L. Ginsberg, and U. Cassuto.[10] On the other hand, E. L. Greenstein (1973),

---

4. J. W. Wevers, *Septuaginta: Genesis* (Göttingen: Vandenhoeck & Ruprecht, 1974), 75.

5. See below.

6. Lane, *AEL*, 326.

7. Ibid., 323. Cf. W. F. Albright, "Contributions to Biblical Archaeology and Philology," *JBL* 43 (1924), 365, who also cites Aram. *twh* "be distracted."

8. In this monograph, Ugaritic texts are cited by *KTU* text number with Gordon's *UT* text number in square brackets.

9. Caquot, Sznycer, and Herdner, *TO*, 241, note *m*.

10. Also Gibson, *CML²*, 68 and 159: "waste."

W. Johnstone (1978), J. C. de Moor (1979), and R. J. Clifford (1987)[11] follow
W. F. Albright, T. H. Gaster, G. R. Driver, J. Gray, J. Aistleitner, and A. Jirku,
who connect the term *thw* with Arabic *hawiya* "to desire" and analyze it as a
verbal form.

However, Dietrich, Loretz, and Sanmartín (1975) read *thwt* instead of *thw*
for *Ug.* 5, 559–60:

[1])*w y'ny . bn* [2])*ilm . mt .*
npšm [3])*npš . lbim* [4])*thwt .*
w npš [5])*anḫr b ym .*   (KTU 1.133[604]:2–5)

The authors take both *thw* and *thwt* as nouns from *hwy (// Heb. *'wh) and
translate *thwt* as "Gier, Verlangen" like Hebrew *ta'ăwâ* "desire, appetite."[12]
They are certainly right to hold that the form *thwt* cannot be a verbal form
from *hwy. Yet their view that *hm brlt* is a gloss to *thw* in KTU 1.5:15 and
corresponds to *wnpš* in KTU 1.133:4, also a gloss, is not convincing. The par-
ticles *hm* and *w* should be taken as indicating the beginning of the second
colon and as introducing the terms *brlt* and *npš*, which correspond to those in
the first colon: *npš* or *npš.*[13]

Based on *KTU*'s reading, B. Margalit (1980) and G. del Olmo Lete (1981,
1982) explained *thwt* (KTU 1.133[UT 604]:4) as a variant form of *thw*, that
is, a feminine or plural form of *thw*, and again supported the view that Ugaritic *thw* is a cognate of Hebrew *tōhû*.[14]

Contextually, *lbim thw(t)* "the lion(s) in/of the desert(s)" corresponds well
to *anḫr b ym* "the dolphin(?) in the sea," since *npš* and *brlt* are a well-known
idiomatic pair (e.g., KTU 1.18:IV:25, 36–37, 1.19:II:38–39, 43–44). As for

---

11. E. L. Greenstein, "Another Attestation of Initial *h* > ' in West Semitic," *JANES* 5
(1973), 157–64; W. Johnstone, "Lexical and Comparative Philological Contributions to
Ugaritic of Mythological Texts of the 24th Campaign at Ras Shamra," *Ug* 7 (1978), 117;
J. C. de Moor, "Contributions to the Ugaritic Lexicon," *UF* 11 (1979), 640; R. J. Clifford,
"Mot Invites Baal to a Feast: Observations on a Difficult Ugaritic Text (CTA 5.i = KTU
1.5.1)," in *"Working with No Data": Semitic and Egyptian Studies Presented to Thomas O.
Lambdin* (ed. D. M. Golomb; Winona Lake, Ind.: Eisenbrauns, 1987), 57 n. 6.

12. M. Dietrich, O. Loretz, J. Sanmartín, "Beiträge zur Ugaritischen Textgeschichte
(II): Textologische Probleme in RS 24.293 = UG. 5, S. 559, NR. 4 und CTA 5 I 11*–22*,"
UF 7 (1975), 537 follows Greenstein, "Another Attestation of Initial *h* > ' in West Semitic,"
160 n. 20, who suggested a possible interchange of '/*h* in Hebrew '*wh* and Ugaritic *hwy*.

13. See Clifford, "Mot Invites Baal to a Feast," 58–59, for a recent discussion of the
'*p . . . hm . . .*' structure in lines 3–10.

14. B. Margalit, *A Matter of "Life" and "Death": A Study of the Baal-Mot Epic (CTA
4-5-6)* (Neukirchen-Vluyn: Neukirchener Verlag, 1980), 97; del Olmo Lete, *MLC*, 635;
idem, "Notes on Ugaritic Semantics V," *UF* 14 (1982), 60.

the image of hungry animals, it is interesting to compare it with the image in Jer 5:6, where *'aryēh miyya'ar* "a lion from the forest" corresponds to *zĕ'ēb 'ărābôt* "a wolf of the desert" in parallelism. In the Ugaritic texts, the land animal, *lbim thw(t)*, and the sea animal, *anḫr b ym*,[15] seem to constitute a merismatic pair[16] and express the comprehensiveness of the voracious appetite of the god Mot in the Ugaritic mythology.[17]

In light of the above, it is probable that Ugaritic *thw* is a cognate of Hebrew *tōhû* and that they have the common meaning of "a desert."[18] If so, they are probably ⟨qutl-⟩ pattern nouns (< */tuhwu/) from the common (West) Semitic root *thw.[19]

"Chaos"?

Since earliest times, many translators have felt that the meaning "desert" is unsatisfactory for the context of Gen 1:2, as reflected in the various Greek versions. Hence, English translations such as "formlessness," "confusion," "unreality," "emptiness" (BDB),[20] or "nothingness" have been suggested on a contextual basis. And it has been asserted that the term *tōhû* "should, according to all analogies, mean something like 'chaos'."[21]

Though Albright's etymological explanation that *tōhû* should be regarded as "a blend between *bōhû* and *tĕhôm*, from which the initial *t* was borrowed" is no longer tenable, his conclusion that the phrase *tōhû wābōhû* signifies a "chaos" and *tōhû* refers to "chaos as a watery deep, or tehom, in the Mesopotamian sense,"[22] is shared by many modern scholars. For example, Cassuto thinks that the phrase *tōhû wābōhû* refers to the "terrestrial state" in which "the whole material was an undifferentiated, unorganized, confused and lifeless agglomeration." He assumes in Gen 1:2 existence of a watery chaos in

---

15. Cf. Akk. *nāḫiru* "whale" as a "sea-horse" (*sîsâ ša tâmti*) in *CAD* N/1 137. Also note that in a certain text, VAT 8917 rev. 11–13, *ilibu* (anše.a.ab.ba [lit., 'horse of the sea']) "dromedary" is identified with the ghost of Tiāmat (*eṭemmu tiāmat*) and appears in parallel with *serrēmu* (anše.eden.na [lit., 'horse of the plain']) "wild ass," the ghost of Enlil; cf. Livingstone, *MMEW*, 82.

16. Del Olmo Lete, *MLC*, 635 notes that *thw* "estepa, desierto" is antonymous to *ym*.

17. Habakkuk 2:5. See A. Cooper, "Divine Names and Epithets in the Ugaritic Texts," *RSP* 3 (1981), 395.

18. Or, "wasteland" (Pardee, in *CS*, 1.265).

19. Huehnergard, *UVST*, 287 and 84: "*/tuhwu/ 'wasteland'."

20. Cf. *HALOT*, 1689, which now lists meanings: (1) "wilderness, wasteland, emptiness"; (2) "desert, emptiness, nothing." See below.

21. Albright, "Contributions to Biblical Archaeology," 365; also. F. M. Cross, *Canaanite Myth and Hebrew Epic: Essays in the History of the Religion of Israel* (Cambridge: Harvard University Press, 1973), 323.

22. Albright, "Contributions to Biblical Archaeology," 366.

which "water [was] above and solid matter beneath, and the whole a chaotic mass, without order or life."[23] Thus, the expression *tōhû wābōhû* in v. 2 is taken as signifying the primordial "chaos," which means not simply "emptiness"[24] but also "disorder" or "disorganization" and stands in direct opposition to "creation."

Before discussing the biblical usages of the term *tōhû*, in the following sections I will discuss the etymology of the term *bōhû* and a possible extrabiblical usage of *tōhû wābōhû*.

*Etymology of *BHW*

Arabic

The Hebrew term *bōhû* occurs only three times in the Bible, always with *tōhû*. Its etymology has been explained by the Arabic *bahiya* "to be empty" (BDB).[25] This Arabic term is used to describe the "empty" or "vacant" state of a tent or house that contains nothing or little furniture or goods.[26] Thus, it has basically a concrete meaning rather than an abstract meaning such as "nothingness" or "emptiness."

Akkadian

Albright suggested that the Akkadian term *bûbûtu* "emptiness, hunger" came from **buhbuhtu* and is a possible cognate of Hebrew *bōhû*.[27] However, *CAD* B 301–2 does not list "emptiness" as the meaning of *bubūtu* A, only giving the translations "famine, starvation, want"; "hunger"; and "sustenance" for the term. *AHw*, 135 suggests simply "hunger" for the meaning of *bubūtu*.

---

23. U. Cassuto, *From Adam to Noah* [part 1 of *A Commentary on the Book of Genesis*] (Jerusalem: Magnes, 1961), 23. B. K. Waltke, "The Creation Account in Genesis 1:1–3, Part III: The Initial Chaos Theory and the Precreation Chaos Theory," *BSac* 132 (1975), 225–28 interprets the phrase *tōhû wābōhû* as referring to "the chaotic state . . . before the creation." Also Wenham, *Genesis 1–15*, 16: "the dreadfulness of the situation before the divine word brought order out of chaos is underlined."

24. Note that Gk. Χάος "chaos" means "empty space" and derives etymologically from Χαίνειν (or Χασκω) "gape, yawn" (cf. the Norse *Ginunga Gap*). Cf. Albright, "Contributions to Biblical Archaeology," 366. For the meanings of Χάος, Liddell and Scott, p. 1976 lists (1) "chaos, the first state of the universe," "infinite space," "unformed matter"; (2) "space, the expanse of air"; (3) "the nether abyss, infinite darkness"; (4) any vast gulf or chasm"; "the gaping jaws [of the crocodile]"; (5) "one." "The modern sense of the word [chaos], i.e., 'disorder', developed only slowly and is not attested before the later Imperial Period" (van der Horst, "Chaos," *DDD*, 354).

25. *HALOT*, 111; Lane, *AEL*, 260.

26. Ibid., *AEL*, 269–70.

27. Albright, "Contributions to Biblical Archaeology," 366.

For a different term *bubu'tu*, the root of which is *bw⁽ rather than *bhw, *CAD* B 300 gives the meanings "inflammation, boil, pustule."[28] Neither of these Akkadian terms is a cognate of the Hebrew *bōhû*.

Phoenician

It has been suggested that the term *bōhû* is associated with the Phoenician divine name Βάαυ, the goddess of "night,"[29] which is mentioned by Philo of Byblos. According to Albright, the divine name Βάαυ "shows that the original form of the noun was *bắhu, like Arab. *bahw*; *buhw* has changed *a* to *u* under the influence of the labials."[30] Cassuto admits this possibility.[31] Certainly it is phonologically possible to posit an original "Canaanite" form */báhwu/ for both Hebrew *bōhû*[32] and Phoenician */bah(a)wu/, which was apparently represented in Greek script as *ba-a-u*. However, there is no evidence that the Hebrew term had any connection with the Phoenician divine name, except for their possible common derivation from the root *bhw.

Egyptian

If, as recent studies show,[33] the material for Philo's cosmogony originated in Egypt, the divine name Βάαυ might have come from an Egyptian word such as *bꜣ.w*.[34] However, even if this were the case, it is not likely that the Hebrew term *bōhû*, with the consonant /h/, is related to these Egyptian terms.

Recently, Görg suggested that *tōhû* and *bōhû* should be explained by other Egyptian terms, *thꜣ* "abweichen," "verfehlen," and *bhꜣ* "kopflos fliehen."[35] However, his etymological argument is almost purely speculative. For one thing, there is no evidence for the existence of the nominal forms *t(e/u)hꜣāw.t* or *b(e/u)hꜣāw.t*. Moreover, the suggested meanings of these nonexistent forms, "Ziellosigkeit," "Vergeblichkeit," and "Flüchtigkeit," "Nichtigkeit," are

---

28. Cf. A. R. Millard, "עלץ 'To exult'," *JTS* 26 (1975), 89 comparing Akkadian *bubu'tu* with *bû⁽ā'*, *bû⁽ātā'*, "abscess" (< *bûă⁽* "to swell, to rejoice").

29. As E. Ebeling noted more than half a century ago, this DN and Heb. *bōhû* have nothing to do with the Sum. goddess Ba'u; cf. Ebeling, "Ba'u," *RlA* 1.432. See also Albright, "Contributions to Biblical Archaeology," 366 n. 7; Cassuto, *From Adam to Noah*, 22.

30. Albright, "Contributions to Biblical Archaeology," 366.

31. Cassuto, *From Adam to Noah*, 21–22.

32. Cf. */báhwu/ > /búhwu/ > /búhuu/ > /búhū/ > /bṓhû/.

33. R. A. Oden, Jr., "Philo of Byblos and Hellenistic Historiography," *PEQ* (1978), 126.

34. J. Ebach's position that Βάαυ comes from the plural form of Egyptian Ba (*bꜣ.w*) is rejected on a phonological basis by Görg, who suggests that "Bāu" should be connected with Egyptian *bjꜣ* "heaven" or *bjꜣ.w*; cf. M. Görg, "*Tohû wabohû*: Ein Deutungsvorschlag," *ZAW* 92 (1980), 431–34. However, *bjꜣ* is no better than *bꜣ.w*.

35. Ibid., 433–34; idem, "'Chaos' und 'Chaosmächte' im Alten Testament," *BN* 70 (1993), 58–59. See on Ugaritic *tu-a-bi-[ú]* below.

pure guesses, especially "Vergeblichkeit" and "Nichtigkeit." Furthermore, no hendiadys using these two words is attested in Egyptian. So it is highly speculative to think that the pair "haltlos und gestaltlos" refers to negative attributes of the Hermopolitan Chaos ("Negativeigenschaften des hermopolitanischen Chaos").

Hebrew

Westermann recognizes only a stylistic variation between *tōhû* and *tōhû wābōhû*. According to him, "בהו is added only by way of alliteration," and "when תהו and בהו occur together there is no real difference in meaning."[36] However, if *bōhû* were added simply as an "alliteration" to *tōhû*, it would be difficult to explain why the conjunction *wā* was used to connect these two terms. Moreover, *tōhû* and *bōhû* seems to be a traditional word pair that can appear either as a parallel word pair (A//B), as in Isa 34:11, or as a juxtaposed phrase (A and B), as in Gen 1:2 and Jer 4:23.[37]

Thus, in light of the above discussion, Hebrew *bōhû*, though still lacking definite etymology, seems to be a Semitic term based on the root *bhw, possibly a cognate of Arabic *bahiya* "to be empty."

Tōhû wābōhû and Ugaritic tu-a-bi-[ú][38]

The expression *tōhû wābōhû* appears twice in the Bible, in Gen 1:2 and Jer 4:23, though *tōhû* and *bōhû* appear once as a parallel word pair in Isa 34:11. A Ugaritic counterpart of it has been suggested in one of the *vocabulaires polyglottes* that were published by J. Nougayrol in 1968 (*Ug.* 5, 137:II:23′):[39]

BAL *na-bal-ku-tum tap-šu-ḫu-[u]m-me*[40] *tu-a-bi-[ú(?)]*

---

36. C. Westermann, *Genesis*, vol. 1: *Genesis 1–11* (BKAT 1/1; Neukirchen-Vluyn: Neukirchener Verlag, 1974), 143 [ET 103].

37. On word pairs, see W. G. E. Watson, *Classical Hebrew Poetry: A Guide to Its Techniques* (JSOTSup 26; Sheffield: JSOT Press, 1984), 128–44; *Traditional Techniques in Classical Hebrew Verse* (JSOTSup 170; Sheffield: Sheffield Academic Press, 1994), 262–312.

38. An earlier version of this section was published in my "*Nabalkutu, tu-a-bi-[ú]* and *tōhû wābōhû,*" *UF* 19 (1987), 309–15. The view presented now is an improved one that takes into consideration W. G. Lambert's response to the earlier version: W. G. Lambert, "A Further Note on *tōhû wābōhû,*" *UF* 20 (1988), 135. This improvement was already made in the first edition (1989) of this book. However, M. Görg, "'Chaos' und 'Chaosmächte' im Alten Testament," 58 n. 28, missed the improvement.

39. *Ug.* 5, 242–43 [RS 20.123].

40. Laroche discusses this term under *tapš- "bas"* as *tapšuḫ- "abaisser, abattre"* in his Hurrian glossary, noting the following two lists in multilingual vocabularies:

137 II 15: Sum. SIG = Hur. *tap-ša-ḫal-še* = Ug. *maška [nu]*
homme de basse classe, pauvre (cf. Akk. *muškênu?*).

For this line, Nougayrol gives the translation "renverser, bouleversement" on the basis of Akkadian *nabalkutum*, and he calls scholars' attention, though with reservation, to the similarity between Ugaritic *tu-a-bi-[ú(?)]* and Hebrew *tōhû wābōhû*. De Moor also took note of this and said, "It may well be that the Ugaritians knew the equivalent of the Hebrew תהו ובהו (Gn 1:2)."[41]

I should like to investigate this interesting proposal, made by two prominent scholars, both morphologically and semantically.

Morphological Correspondence

tu-a-bi-[ú(?)]

Assuming Nougayrol's reconstruction *tu-a-bi-[ú(?)]* to be correct, the morphological correspondence of the Ugaritic *tu-a-bi-[ú(?)]* and the Hebrew expression *tōhû wābōhû* can be explained as follows:

a. The first half of the syllabic spelling, *tu-a*, probably stands for /tuha/, since the grapheme ⟨a⟩ in the syllabic spelling of Ugaritic terms can be used for the syllable /ha/, as in *ta-a-ma-tu₄* /tahāmatu/,[42] whose alphabetic spelling would be *thmt*.

b. The second half of the syllabic spelling, *bi-[ú]*, if the second sign is correctly restored, may stand for /bihu/, since the grapheme ⟨ú⟩ of the syllabic spelling is used for the syllable /hu/, as in *ṭu-ú-ru* (137:II:1′) /ṭuhuru/ "pure (gem)" and *ú-wa* (137:II:28′) /huwa/ "he," whose alphabetic spellings are *ṭhr* and *hw*.

c. In the light of Ugaritic *thw*, /túhwu/, one might postulate the older form of *tu-a-bi-ú* /tuha bihu/ as */túhwu wa-bíhwu/*, which experienced the following change:

*/túhwu wa-bíhwu/ > */túhwu ua-bíhwu/ > /túhwabíhwu/ > /túhʷabíhʷu/ > /tuhabihu/ : tu-a-bi-ú*

The Hebrew form *tōhû wābōhû* might be explained as having developed from the same original form as follows:

---

137 II 23: Sum. BAL = Akk. *nabalkutum* = Hur. *tap-šu-ḫu-um-me* renverser, abattre.

Cf. E. Laroche, *Glossaire de la langue hourrite deuxième partie (M–Z, Index)* (= *RHA* 35 [1977]), 256. Also cf. *Ug.* 5, 457, 461. However, his translation of *tapšuḫumme* as "renverser, abattre" is deeply influenced by the interpretation of Akk. *nabalkutu* and Ug. *tu-a-bi-[ú]*(?). See below, p. 21.

41. J. C. de Moor, "El, the Creator," in *The Bible World: Essays in Honor of Cyrus H. Gordon* (ed. G. Rendsburg et al.; New York: KTAV, 1980), 183 and n. 58.

42. See below, p. 43, on this term.

*/túhwu wa-bíhwu/ > /túhwu wa-búhwu/ > /túh<u>uu</u> wa-búh<u>uu</u>/ > /túhā wa-búhā/ > /tóhā wā-bóhā/: *tōhû wābōhû*

Thus, it is certainly not impossible, though there is still uncertainty about the final *ú* sign, that Ugaritic *tu-a-bi-*[*ú*(?)] and Hebrew *tōhû wābōhû* are two versions of the same idiomatic expression in West Semitic.

tu-a-pí-[*ku*(?)]

However, another possibility is to read the infinitive form *tu-a-pí-*[*ku*] for the Ugaritic column on the basis of Akkadian *nabalkutum* and Hurrian[43] *tap-šuḫumme*.[44] Because the verbal form *hpk* is identified in the Ugaritic alphabetical texts,[45] this suggestion is attractive.

However, there seems to be a morphological difficulty. The form, which can be normalized as /tuhap(p)iku/, is hard to explain as a Ugaritic tD infinitive of "to be upset" (Huehnergard), for if it were a tD infinitive, we would expect, in light of Arabic forms, something like /tahappaku/ or /tahappiku/, for active, and /tuhuppiku/, for passive.[46] Huehnergard himself accepts this difficulty, saying, "A possible difficulty with our proposal is that the form *tuqattil* for the tD infinitive, in view of *quttal* for the D, is rather unexpected."[47] Moreover, his acceptance ("perhaps") of *ta-ga-bi-ra*(-*yv*) as the tD verbal noun /tagabbir-/[48] works against his proposal.

On the other hand, the bilingual vocabulary from Ebla might support this proposal, as Lambert notes.[49] In this vocabulary, M. Krebernik detects two examples of a tD infinitive /tuPaRRis/ form, *du-za-li-um* /tuZalliHum/ and *du-ša-ne-u₄* /tu<u>d</u>anniHu(m)/.[50] Therefore, the proposed reading, /tuhap(p)i-ku/,

---

43. For -*umme* as the infinitive ending, see M. Dietrich and W. Mayer, "Beiträge zum Hurritischen (I): Einzelfragen zu Grammatik und Lexikon des Mitanni-Briefs," *UF* 23 (1991), 125–26.

44. J. Huehnergard, "Northwest Semitic Vocabulary in Akkadian Texts," *JAOS* 107 (1987), 723; *UVST*, 84, 121, 315, 322; Lambert, "A Further Note on *tōhû wābōhû*," 135.

45. Cf. *UT* 19.788: "to upset."

46. Cf. Gordon, *UT*, 81; S. Segert, *A Basic Grammar of the Ugaritic Language* (Berkeley: University of California Press, 1984), 67.

47. *UVST*, 84; cf. also J. Huehnergard, "A Dt Stem in Ugaritic?" *UF* 17 (1986), 402; *UVST*, 271: /tuhappiku/ is against "the existence of a vowel harmony rule around gutturals."

48. *UVST*, 322.

49. Lambert, "A Further Note on *tōhû wābōhû*," 135, though his argument lacks morphological precision. For one thing, the form *tuptarrisum* would not support the existence of "an infinitive *tuparrisu* in Ugaritic."

50. M. Krebernik, "Verbalnomina mit Prä- und Infigiertem t in Ebla," *SEb* 7 (1984), 208. Cf. K. Hecker, "Doppelt T-erweiterte Formen oder: Der Eblaitische Infinitive," *BaE*, 221; and B. Kienast, "Nomina mit T-präfix und T-infix in der Sprache von Ebla und ihre

might be morphologically supported, though this form is still rare in Eblaite and exceptional in Ugaritic.

Thus, both readings, *tu-a-bi-*[*ú(?)*] and *tu-a-pí-*[*ku(?)*], are possible from phonological and morphological points of view, though there is some difficulty with the latter. Nevertheless, one should remember that arguments based on reconstruction remain hypotheical. However, even if the reading *tu-a-bi-*[*ú(?)*] is correct, the meaning of the Akkadian counterpart, *nabalkutu*, is highly disputed.

Semantic Investigations

De Moor assumes that the Ugaritic phrase *tu-a-bi-*[*ú(?)*] signifies "the state of chaos"[51] in light of Akkadian *nabalkutu* as well as Hebrew *tōhû wābōhû*. However, while it is possible to render *nabalkutu* as "renverser, bouleversement" ("reversal, upheaval") in certain contexts, as Nougayrol does, neither *CAD* nor *AHw* lists this as a common meaning.[52] Furthermore, it is not certain that the common meaning of *nabalkutu* is "to turn over" or "to upset," let alone Huehnergard's "to jump, rebel."[53]

For now, let us suppose that Ugaritic *tu-a-bi-*[*ú(?)*] is equivalent to Hebrew *tōhû wābōhû*. Since *tōhû wābōhû* is always used for describing the state of the "earth" (Gen 1:2, Jer 4:23) or the "land" of Edom (Isa 34:11), it might be profitable in a semantic discussion of this Ugaritic phrase to analyze the parallel Akkadian term *nabalkutu* when it appears with a word like *erṣetu*.

Atra-Ḫasīs Epic

S iv 49 [54]

[*l*]*i-bal-kat erṣetu re-em-šá*	Let the earth's womb be . . . ,
šam-mu ia ú-ṣa-a šu-ú ia i-im-ru	Let no vegetables shoot up,
	no cereals grow.

S iv 58b–59 [55]

ib-bal-kat erṣetu re-em-šá	Earth's womb was . . . ,
šam-mu ul ú-ṣa-a šu-ú ul i'-ru	No vegetables shot up,
	no cereals grew.

---

sumerischen Äquivalente," *BaE*, 239; which list the forms /tuptarrisum/ and its variants as Dt infinitives.

51. De Moor, "El, the Creator," 183.

52. *CAD* N/1 11–12: "1) to cross over . . . ; 2) to slip out of place . . . ; 3) to turn over . . ."; *AHw*, 694–95: "überschreiten."

53. *UVST*, 83.

54. W. G. Lambert and A. R. Millard, *Atra-Ḫasîs: The Babylonian Story of the Flood* (Oxford: Clarendon, 1969), 108–9 [Repr. Winona Lake, Ind.: Eisenbrauns, 1999].

55. Ibid., 110–11.

The Chicago Assyrian Dictionary N/1 14, following Lambert and Millard, who translate *nabalkutu* in this context as "to rebel," classifies the text under the meaning "1. c) 'to rebel against authority.'" However *nabalkutu* with the meaning "to rebel" usually appears with "land or country" (*mātu*), "city" (*ālu*), "man" (*awīlū*), or people as its subject.[56] Since it is the "womb" (*rēmu*) that is the real "subject" of the (intrans.) verbs *libbalkat* and *ibbalkat* in the present text, the text seems to describe a womb that does not do its ordinary work—that is, it is barren or unproductive. Hence the verb might be translated "to be out of order."[57]

It should be noted that three lines later the "constriction" of the "womb" (*rēmu*) of the peoples is mentioned together with its subsequent state of "no child," meaning barrenness:

r[ēm]u (ARḪUŠ) *lu ku-ṣur-ma ia ú-še-šèr šèr-ra*
That the womb may be constricted and give birth to no child

(S iv 51)[58]

rēmu (ARḪUŠ) *ku-ṣur-ma ul ú-še-šèr šèr-ra*
So that the womb was constricted and gave birth to no child.

(S iv 61)[59]

Therefore, "the disfunction of the earth's womb" (S iv 49a, 58b) is mentioned parallel with the state of "no vegetables, no cereals" (S iv 49b, 59), that is, barrenness or unproductiveness, just as the "constriction of the human womb" (S iv 51a, 61a) is mentioned alongside the state of "no childbirth" (S iv 51b, 61b).

Moreover, this interpretation is confirmed by a parallel text in the Old Babylonian version of this epic, AH II iv 4–6:[60]

ú-ul ul-da er-ṣe-tum re-e[m-ša]
ša-am-mu ú-ul ú-ṣi-a [. .] ni-šu ú-ul am-ra-[tu4]

The womb of earth did not bear,
Vegetation did not sprout [. .]. People were not seen [. .].

---

56. Cf. *CAD* N/1 13–14, 19 (4.d: "to cause [someone] to rebel").

57. Cf. *CAD*'s meaning "2. a) 'to slip out of place, to become displaced, to turn upside down (said of parts of the human body, of the exta, and of the moon)'" in *CAD* N/1 16. See also *nabalkutu* used to describe the anomalous shape of a liver in hepatoscopy; cf. J.-W. Meyer, *Untersuchungen zu den Tonlebermodellen aus dem Alter Orient* (AOAT 39; Neukirchen-Vluyn: Neukirchener Verlag, 1987), 111–12, 135, 179–80.

58. Lambert and Millard, *AH*, 108–9.

59. Ibid., 110–11.

60. Ibid., 78–79.

The phrase *ú-ul ul-da* in this older version is replaced in the Assyrian version with *ib-bal-kat.*

This shows that one of the meanings of *nabalkutu* did correspond to that of *ul ūlda.* It may be surmised therefore that, diachronically, the Neo-Assyrian phrase *rēmu ibbalkat* "the womb is out of order (lit.)" had experienced its semantic development to become equivalent to and to replace the older phrase *rēmu ul ūlda* "the womb does not bear." Or, synchronically, *rēmu ibbalkat* "the womb is out of order" became an idiom meaning "the womb is unproductive." In either case, the term *nabalkutu* may have developed the meaning "to be unproductive," first with "the womb" as its subject and then without it in the process of idiomatization and may have become able to refer to the state of the unproductiveness of the earth (*erṣetu*).[61] Thus,

(1) *rēmu ibbalkat*
the womb is out of order → the womb is unproductive
(2) *erṣetu* [*rēmu ibbalkat*] → *erṣetu*[62] *rēmša ibbalkat*
the earth's womb is unproductive
(3) *erṣetu ibbalkat*
the earth is unproductive

The passages in the *Atra-Ḫasīs* epic should be translated:

Let the earth's womb be out of order,
    Let no vegetables shoot up, no cereals be seen.

Earth's womb was out of order,
    No vegetables shot up, no cereals were seen.

The Ritual of Kalû

This meaning, "to be unproductive," fits in another text, the Kalû ritual, line 16.

AO 6472:16 [63]

šumma erṣetu inūš tīb nakri šubat māti ul ikân : šumma erṣetu ibbalkit (BAL-*it*) *ina māti kalama lā kittu* (NU.GI.NA) *ibašši ṭēm māti išanni*

---

61. Compare the earth's womb "producing": *rēm-ša* [= *erṣetu*] + (*w*)*alādu* and *ṣēru pal-ku-ú ú-li-id id-ra-na* (AH S iv 58) "The broad plain produced salt" (ibid., 110–11).

62. The term *erṣetu* here is a *casus pendens*, i.e., "topicalization."

63. F. Thureau-Dangin, *Rituels Accadiens* (Paris: Leroux, 1921), 34–35. He translates line 16 as follows:

Si le sol tremble, surrection de l'ennemi,
    l'assiette du pays ne sera pas stable.
Si le sol se déplace, dans tout le pays il y aura instabilité,
    le pays perdra la raison.

Here, the three parts of the second half basically correspond to the three of the first half.[64]

(1) *erṣetu inūš*   = *erṣetu ibbalkit*
     the earth shakes   the earth is out of order (i.e.,
                               unproductive)
(2) *tīb nakri*   = *ina māti kalama lā kittu ibašši*
     attack of the enemy   there will be falsehood everywhere
                               in the country[65]
(3) *šubat māti ul ikân*   = *ṭēm māti išanni*
     the foundation of the   the status quo of the country changes[66]
     country is not stable

The expression *erṣetu ibbalkit* in this text has been explained as signifying the rolling "of the tremor of an earthquake."[67] However, the fact of simple correspondence should not be taken as a sign of synonymity. Thus, it is not justifiable to suggest that *nabalkutu* means "to roll" or "sich umwenden" on the basis of the *inūš* = *ibbalkit* correspondence, as *CAD* and *AHw* seem to do,[68] since the second is not an exact translation of the first. Correspondences (2) and (3), rather, suggest that the relationship between the first and second halves is that of cause and effect. If this is the case, the sentence *erṣetu ibbalkit* refers to some state of the earth caused by the "instability" of the earth.[69]

In light of the above discussion, Ugaritic *tu-a-bi-[ú(?)]* would be better compared with Akkadian *nabalkutu* "to be out of order," which acquires an idiomatic meaning of "to be unproductive" when it is in collocation with *erṣetu*, rather than with *nabalkutu* translated as "renverser, bouleversement" or "to turn over, upset." The meaning "to be unproductive" fits in line 23 of the *vocabulaires polyglottes*, where its Hurrian counterpart, *tapšuḫumme*, probably means "to be poor" rather than "to be low,"[70] in light of the other line,

---

64. This correspondence is also supported by the presence of a *Glossenkeil* (:) between the two halves. These three parts may correspond to the three prime gods, Anu, Enlil, and Ea, to whom worshipers are ordered to sacrifice in the following section, lines 17–19, of this text.

65. *CAD* K 469.

66. Cf. Lambert, *BWL*, 112–13, line 6; for this idiom, see *AHw*, 1166, 1386.

67. *CAD* N/1 18.

68. *AHw*, 695: "sich umwenden": "von der Erde bei Beben," cites AH S iv 49, 58 (see above, p. 18) as well as the present text.

69. In my interpretation, the disastrous state of the country (*mātu*) is mentioned in (2) and (3), and the verbal form *nabalkutu* in (1) takes as its subject "the earth (*erṣetu*)," not "the land/country" (*mātu*).

70. Cf. Huehnergard, *UVST*, 84, 80.

Ug. 5, 137:II:15: Sum. SIG = Hur. *tapšaḫalše* = Ug. *maška[nu]*.[71] Hence, this idiomatic meaning of *nabalkutu* has nothing to do with "the state of chaos."

On the other hand, if the Ugaritic column should be read *tu-a-pí-[ku(?)]* /tuhappiku/ "to be upset, to be turned over," as Lambert and Huehnergard suggest, this term has nothing to do with the biblical phrase *tōhû wābōhû*. Hence, the argument that the initial state in Gen 1:2 was "the state of chaos" loses another support. For the usages of the Hebrew terms *tōhû* "desert" and *bōhû* "emptiness" and the idiomatic phrase *tōhû wābōhû*, we now turn to the study of the biblical text itself.

Uses of tōhû and tōhû wābōhû

Tōhû

The term *tōhû* occurs 20 times in the Old Testament, 11 of which are in Isaiah. According to Westermann, the uses of the term can be classified into three groups: from the concrete meaning "desert" to the abstract, "emptiness." They are:[72]

1. "desert": "the grim desert waste that brings destruction"
    —Deut 32:10; Job 6:18, 12:24 = Ps 107:40
2. "a desert or devastation that is threatened"
    (*eine Öde oder Verwüstung, die angerichtet wird*)
    —Isa 24:10, 34:11, 40:23;[73] Jer 4:23
    "the state that is opposed to and precedes creation"
    —Gen 1:2, Isa 45:18, Job 26:7
3. "nothingness"[74]
    —1 Sam 12:21 (twice); Isa 29:21, 40:17, 41:29[!], 44:9, 45:19,[75]
    49:4,[76] 59:4
    Cf. *'yš thw* "a man of emptiness"—1QH 7:27

---

71. Note that Sum. SIG is explained in Akk. as *enšu ša muš[kēni*] "the weak, said of the poor" (Antagal E b 18ff.)—cited by *CAD* E 170; M/2 273 and now published in A. Cavigneaux, H. G. Güterbock, and M. T. Roth (eds.), *The Series Erim-ḫuš* = a n a n t u *and Anta-gál* = š a q û (MSL 17; Rome: Pontifical Biblical Institute, 1985), 211—and corresponds to Ug. *dl* /dallu/ "poor" in the polyglot text *S*ᵃ (cf. Huehnergard, *UVST*, 79) and that *muškēnu* "the poor man" and *enšu* "the weak" appear parallel to each other in *BWL*, 119, lines 11–12. Cf. also *AHw*, 684, 1193. The latter page lists *muškēnu u šarû* "the poor and the rich" (KAR 26.29).

72. Westermann, *Genesis*, 1.142–43 [ET 102–3].

73. Isaiah 40:23 should be classified as (3), just as Isa 40:17 is.

74. "It should be noted that in none of these passages does 'nothing' or 'nothingness' indicate the existence of a material 'nothing'; it is contrasted rather with meaningful existence" (Westermann, *Genesis*, 1.143 [ET 103]).

75. Isaiah 45:19 should be classified as (2). See below, pp. 26ff., for a detailed discussion.

76. Not in ET but in the German original.

"Desert"

The first group of texts (1) certainly describes *tōhû*, which is synonymous with "a desert land" (Deut 32:10), as a "wasteland" where caravans perish (Job 6:18) and as a "trackless waste" where people wander (Job 12:24, Ps 107:40). Thus, the term refers to the actual desert as "a waste land."

"Emptiness"

As for the third group (3), the term *tōhû* seems to refer to a situation that lacks something abstract that should be there, such as worth, purpose, truth, profit, or integrity. In some passages it appears parallel with other abstract nouns, such as *ʾayin* (or *ʾāyin*) in Isa 40:17 and 23,[77] *rîq* "empty" in 49:4, and *ʾepes* "nothing" in 41:29. Similarly, in 1 Sam 12:21 and Isa 44:9, the idols and the idol-makers are also condemned as *tōhû*, which is parallel with the phrase *lōʾ-yôʿîlû* or *bal-yôʿîlû* "unprofitable, worthless."[78] In two passages, the term *tōhû* refers to the words of the unrighteous, that is, "false testimony"[79] in Isa 29:21 and "empty argument" (NIV) in 59:4. In a Qumran text (1QH 7:27) the phrase *ʾyš thw* "a man of emptiness" also appears.[80]

In this regard, the passages in this category would be better understood as referring to "a lack" or "emptiness" rather than to "nothingness." Moreover, it should be noted here that this abstract use of *tōhû* seems to be typical of Isaiah and that the only other usage in this sense is 1 Sam 12:21, which refers to idols in a similar fashion to Isa 44:9. Furthermore, it is significant to note that the term in this sense is never used with nouns such as "earth" (*ʾereṣ*) and "city"(*ʿîr*).

"Desert-Like State"

In all of the passages belonging to Westermann's group (2),[81] the term *tōhû* is used for describing the situation or condition of places such as earth, land, or city. Let us examine each passage in detail.

---

77. Westermann classifies this verse as belonging to the second group (2), as noted above.

78. E. J. Young translates *tōhû* in Isa 44:9 as "unreality" and explains that the word "suggests an absence of all life and power," *The Book of Isaiah* (NICOT; Grand Rapids: Eerdmans, 1972), 3.172.

79. Idem, *The Book of Isaiah* (NICOT; Grand Rapids: Eerdmans, 1969), 2.322: "deceit." He explains that תֹּהוּ probably signifies "lies and falsehoods, anything that is vanity and not based upon truth" (p. 329).

80. *DCH*, I, 229.

81. Isaiah 40:23 really belongs to the third group, as noted above.

Isaiah 24:10
nišbĕrâ qiryat-tōhû
suggar kol-bayit mibbôʾ

The city of chaos is broken down,
   every house is shut up so that none can enter. (NRSV)

The ruined city lies desolate;
   the entrance to every house is barred. (NIV)

The entire chapter of Isa 24 talks about the Lord's devastation of the earth. The beginning and the end of the opening section, vv. 1–3a, refer to the earth, which will be "completely laid waste" (*YHWH bôqēq hāʾāreṣ // hibbôq tibbôq hāʾāreṣ*) and thus constitute an inclusio. In v. 12, "desolation (*šammâ*) is left in the city (*ʿîr*), the gates are battered into ruins" (NRSV), while in v. 10 the "desert-like" (or "desolate") state of a city, *qiryâ, resulting from its destruction (*šbr), is described using *tōhû*.[82] Thus, *tōhû* is almost equivalent to *šammâ*.[83] The JPSV translation is better than the NRSV or NIV:[84]

Towns are broken, empty;
   Every house is shut, none enters (JPSV)

Job 26:7
nōṭeh ṣāpôn ʿal- tōhû
tōleh ʾereṣ ʿal-bĕlî-mâ

He stretches out the north over the void,
   and hangs the earth upon nothing. (RSV)

He spreads out the northern "skies"[85] over empty space;
   he suspends the earth over nothing. (NIV)

Westermann thinks that the term *tōhû* here is "the direct opposite of creation," though he avoids translating *tōhû* as "chaos" here. However, the two verbal forms from *nth "to stretch, spread" and *tlh "to hang, suspend" seem to require concrete objects. Because the term *tōhû* is parallel with "a place where there is nothing" (*bĕlî-mâ*), not with the abstract concept "nothing" or "noth-

---

82. D. T. Tsumura, "'Chaos' in Genesis 1:2," in *Seisho no Shishin to Dentatsu: Collected Essays for Prof. Masao Sekine on His Seventy-Seventh Birthday* (Tokyo, 1989), 19 [Japanese]. Irwin also interprets this construction as a construct followed by a genitive of result; see W. H. Irwin, "The City of Chaos in Isa 24,10 and the Genitive of Result," *Bib* 75 (1994), 401–3.

83. See below, p. 31, on *šĕmāmâ* (Jer 4:27).

84. The translation "the deserted city" or "the empty city" of *HALOT*, 1689, does not correspond to the syntactical structure of the verse.

85. Cf. Isa 40:22: "He stretches out the heavens like a canopy" (NIV).

ingness" as in the case of the third group (above), one would expect it to have a concrete meaning. Hence, a translation like "a desert-like place" or "an empty place" might be suggested for *tōhû* in this context.

If the term *ṣāpôn* (cf. Isa 14:13) was indeed originally the place-name "Za-phon,"[86] it may stand for a high mountain like Ugaritic *spn*[87] in this context. Then the idea that the Lord stretches out the high mountains, that is, the high places of the earth,[88] over an empty place could correspond to the Lord's sus-pending the earth over a place where there is nothing (*bělî-mâ*), an empty place. Thus, the following translation might be suggested:

> He stretches out the high mountains over an empty place,
> he suspends the earth over a place where there is nothing.

Isaiah 45:18

lō'-tōhû běrā'â	he did not create it a chaos,
lāšebet yěṣārâ	he formed it to be inhabited. (RSV)[89]
	he did not create it to be empty,
	but formed it to be inhabited (NIV)

Taking *tōhû* as "chaos," Westermann explains that *tōhû* here is "the direct op-posite of creation."[90] However, *tōhû* here is contrasted with *lāšebet* in the par-allelism and seems to refer rather to a place that has no habitation, like the term *šěmāmâ* "desolation"(cf. Jer 4:27; Isa 24:12), *hārēb* "waste, desolate,"[91] and *ʿăzûbâ* "deserted."[92] There is nothing in this passage that would suggest a chaotic state of the earth "which is opposed to and precedes creation."[93] Thus, the term *tōhû* here too signifies "a desert-like place" and refers to "an unin-habited place." The verse might be better translated as follows:

> He created it not to be a desert-like place;
> he formed it to be inhabited.

---

86. M. H. Pope, *Job* (3rd ed.; AB 15; New York: Doubleday, 1973), 180; cf. J. J. M. Roberts, "Ṣāpon in Job 26:7," *Bib* 56 (1975), 554–57.

87. Cf. *Ug.* 5, 44 on RS 20.24, where *huršan hazi* "Mount Hazzi" corresponds to *spn* in the alphabetic divine list (KTU 1.118:4; cf. 14).

88. Cf. N. H. Tur-Sinai, *The Book of Job: A New Commentary* (Jerusalem: Kirjath-Sepher, 1967), 380–81: "the floating land."

89. "He did not create it a waste, But formed it for habitation" (JPSV).

90. Westermann, *Genesis*, 1.142 [ET 103].

91. Note the Akkadian cognate, *harbu* "wasteland," and its verbal use in the following passage: *erṣetu šî iharrumma ana arkat āmē uššab* "that land will become waste but it will be (re-)inhabited thereafter" (CT 39, 21:168, SB Alu—cited by *CAD* H 87). Also Ezek 28:19.

92. See below, p. 31, on Jer 4:23ff. for these terms.

93. Westermann, *Genesis*, 1.142 [ET 103].

It should be noted that *lōʾ-tōhû* here is a resultative object, referring to the purpose of God's creative action. In other words, this verse explains that God did not create the earth so that it might stay desert-like, but to be inhabited. So this verse does not contradict Gen 1:2, where God created the earth to be productive and inhabited, though it "was" still *tōhû wābōhû* in the initial state.[94]

Isaiah 45:19
lōʾ bassēter dibbartî
  bimqôm ʾereṣ ḥōšek
lōʾ ʾāmartî lĕzeraʿ yaʿăqōb
  tōhû baqqĕšûnî

The term *tōhû* here has been interpreted in basically two ways: in a concrete (locative) sense and in an abstract sense. For example, "seek me in chaos" (RSV); "look for me in the empty void" (NEB); "in a wasteland" (JPSV); "Look for me in an empty waste" (NAB). On the other hand, the NIV translates *tōhû* as "in vain," thus suggesting an abstract sense. A similar interpretation has been given by Westermann, who translates *tōhû* as in "im Öden (oder im Nichtigen)" and explains, "*Tōhū*, meaning nothingness, that which is empty, can also have the sense of 'futile' ('das Sinnlose')—the meaning would then be, 'Seek me in vain' ('Umsonst suchet mich')."[95]

All of them understand the syntax in the same way, following MT's punctuation and taking *tōhû* as an adverbial phrase that modifies the verbal phrase *baqqĕšûnî*, thus as part of the direct speech. The LXX similarly takes *tōhû* as a part of the direct speech. On the other hand, Symmachus's translation leaves some ambiguity in its understanding of the syntax of *tōhû*.[96]

Those who take the term *tōhû* in an abstract sense assume that *tōhû* corresponds to *bassēter* "in secret" (or "secretly") and hence means "in vain" or the like. *BHS*'s suggestion of reading בַתֹהוּ here seems to take this position. However, the term *tōhû* usually has such an abstract meaning only when it appears in parallelism with abstract nouns with a similar meaning, such as "nothing" or "emptiness," as noted above.

It may be that *tōhû* is just a part of the sarcastic expression *tōhû baqqĕšûnî* "In vain seek me!" (cf. NIV) and has no grammatical correspondence with any preceding phrase. However, since the two verbal phrases *dibbartî* and *ʾāmartî*

---

94. See below, pp. 33–35.

95. C. Westermann, *Das Buch Jesaja: Kapitel 40–66* (Göttingen, 1966), 140 [ET: *Isaiah 40–66* (London, 1969), 173]. Cf. also Young, *The Book of Isaiah*, 3.210: "In vain seek ye me"; M. Dijkstra, "Zur Deutung von Jesaja 45,15ff.," *ZAW* 89 (1977), 221: "Suchet mich vergebens."

96. For a detailed discussion, see my "*Tōhû* in Isa. xlv 19," *VT* 38 (1988), 361–64.

correspond to each other, *tōhû baqqĕšûnî* "In vain seek me!" could be taken as a direct object of *dibbartî* too. Thus, "Not in secret I spoke . . . 'In vain seek me!'" However, such an understanding is the least suitable to the context.

The most natural explanation structurally would be to say that *tōhû* is parallel to *bimqôm*[97] *'ereṣ ḥōšek* "in a land of darkness." In other words, *tōhû* without a preposition directly corresponds either to *'ereṣ ḥōšek* or to *ḥōšek* and, in the last colon, an element corresponding to *bimqôm* or *bimqôm 'ereṣ* is ellipsized. The former may be supported by the fact that *tōhû* basically means "desert." On the other hand, the latter might be supported by the similar expressions, though in reverse order, *tōhû wābōhû* // *ḥōšek* (Gen 1:2) and *tōhû wābōhû* // *'ên 'ôr* "no light" (Jer 4:23) as well as *tōhû* // *ḥōšek* (Job 12:24–25).[98] In this case, the term *tōhû*, corresponding directly to *ḥōšek* "darkness," probably means "desolation."

It is thus probably correct that the term *tōhû* is not to be included in the direct speech, since the verbal phrase *dibbartî*, like *'āmartî*, seems to take *lĕzera' ya'ăqōb* as an indirect object and *baqqĕšûnî* as a direct object, that is, direct speech. If *dibbartî* should take *tōhû baqqĕšûnî* as a direct object, the term *tōhû* would become a redundant element in a structure such as "I did not speak . . . in a land of darkness, 'In a wasteland / in a land of desolation (*tōhû*) seek me!'"

Our new translation would be as follows:

> I did not speak in secret,
>   in a land of darkness,
> I did not say to Jacob's descendants
>   (in a land of) desolation,[99] "Seek me!"

---

97. *Bimqôm* "in (lit., in the place of)" here functions almost as a compound preposition like *bĕtôk* or *ba'ăšer*. Also compare with *bimqôm 'ăšer* in Hos 2:1, 2 Sam 15:21, etc.

98. Note that vv. 24a–25b constitute the so-called "AXYB Pattern," in which v. 24a and v. 25b are in a distant parallelism, while v. 24b and v. 25a constitute an "inserted" bicolon; cf. my "'Inserted Bicolon,' the AXYB Pattern, in Amos I 5 and Psalm IX 7," *VT* 38 (1988), 234–36. In this structure, it is clear that *tōhû* and *ḥōšek* are a parallel word pair. This has never been noticed by commentators: e.g., Tur-Sinai, *The Book of Job*, 218–19; Pope, *Job*, 95; S. R. Driver and G. B. Gray, *A Critical and Exegetical Commentary on the Book of Job* (ICC; Edinburgh: T. & T. Clark, 1921), 120; E. Dhorme, *A Commentary on the Book of Job* (London: Thomas Nelson, 1967), 180; R. Gordis, *The Book of Job* (New York: Jewish Theological Seminary, 1978), 141; J. E. Hartley, *The Book of Job* (NICOT; Grand Rapids: Eerdmans, 1988), 212.

99. Or "(in) a desolate place."

Tōhû wābōhû

Jeremiah 4:23–26
rā'îtî 'et-hā'āreṣ wěhinnēh-tōhû wābōhû
wě'el-haššāmayim wě'ên 'ôrām
rā'îtî hehārîm wěhinnēh rō'ăšîm
wěkol-haggěbā'ôt hitqalqālû
rā'îtî wěhinnēh 'ên hā'ādām
wěkol-'ôp haššāmayim nādādû
rā'îtî wěhinnēh hakkarmel hammidbār
wěkol-'ārâw nittěṣû
mippěnê YHWH mippěnê ḥărôn 'appô

It is often asserted that Jer 4:23–26 pictures a return to the primeval chaos. For example, Bright says that "the story of Genesis 1 has been reversed: men, beasts, and growing things are gone, the dry land itself totters, the heavens cease to give their light, and primeval chaos returns. It is as if the earth had been 'uncreated.'"[100] McKane expresses a similar view in his recent commentary. He thinks that this signifies the "return to the chaos which prevailed before the world was ordered by Yahweh's creative acts."[101] He even says that "according to v. 23 there has been a collapse of cosmic order and an invasion by the power of chaos."[102]

However, this view is greatly influenced by the interpretation of the phrase tōhû wābōhû as "chaos" in Gen 1:2 and is not based on contextual analysis of Jer 4:23ff. itself.

There is certainly no question about the similarity in the terms and phrases between Jer 4:23ff. and Gen 1:2ff. However, it is not as certain as some scholars assume that the former is patterned after or "modeled on" the latter.

For example, Fishbane[103] finds in Jer 4:23–26 the same order of creation as in Gen 1:1–2:4a and assumes a "recovered use of the creation pattern" in this Jeremiah passage. According to him, the order of creation reflected in Jer 4:23–26 is as follows: tōhû wābōhû – "light" – "heavens" – "earth" (: "mountains,"

---

100. J. Bright, *Jeremiah* (AB 21; New York: Doubleday, 1965), 33.

101. W. McKane, *A Critical and Exegetical Commentary on Jeremiah* (ICC; Edinburgh: T. & T. Clark, 1986), 1.106. Cf. also B. S. Childs, *Myth and Reality in the Old Testament* (London: SCM, 1960), 42, 76; H. Wildberger, *Jesaja*, vol. 2: *Jesaja 13–27* (BKAT 10/2; Neukirchen-Vluyn: Neukirchener Verlag, 1978), 920; R. P. Carroll, *Jeremiah* (London: SCM, 1986), 168.

102. McKane, *Jeremiah*, 1.107.

103. M. Fishbane, "Jeremiah IV 23–26 and Job III 3–13: A Recovered Use of the Creation Pattern," *VT* 21 (1971), 152.

"hills") – "bird" – "man" – "his fierce anger." However, the actual order of terms and phrases mentioned in Jer 4:23ff. is as follows: "earth" as *tōhû wābōhû* – "heavens" without "light" – "mountains" and "hills" – "man" and "bird" – "fruitful land" and "desert" – "towns." Fishbane thinks that the difference in "the order of creation" in the cases of "earth" → "heavens" and "man" → "bird" in Jer 4:23ff. does not disprove his case, because "the synthetic parallelism progresses from below to above in all cases," and "there is no one fixed order to these traditional pairs."

However, it should be noted that not all the terms of the Jeremiah passage appear in the Genesis passage. Moreover, the order is not the same in both passages, despite Fishbane's explanation. For one thing, the "earth" in Jer 4:23 should be compared with the "earth" in Gen 1:2, since both are described by the same phrase, *tōhû wābōhû*. If this is the case, his suggestion to reverse the order of "earth" → "heavens" to "heavens" → "earth" so that the order might be the same as the order of Gen 1:3ff. is without support.

Also, Fishbane thinks that *'ôr* "light" in Jer 4:23 should, rather, be connected with *'ôr*, which was created on the first day in the Genesis account. However, "light" in Jer 4:23 refers to the light of the "heavens," and it should instead be compared with the "luminaries" (*mĕ'ōrōt*) of the sky in Gen 1:14, as McKane explains.[104] Holladay takes *'ôr* (Jer 4:23) as "light" rather than "the light-giving sun and moon and stars" but says: "In Genesis 1:3–5 the creation of light is not associated specifically with the heavens but is thoroughly appropriate here."[105] Thus he notes the difference between Gen 1:3–5 and Jer 4:23.

Kselman remarks that "the chiastic *thw wbhw // ḥšk* [in Gen 1:2] is echoed in Jer 4:23 (*thw wbhw // 'yn 'wrm*), a poem modelled on Gen 1."[106] Thus, he also takes the similarity in the two parallel pairs as a result of the direct relationship between the two documents. However, the similarity between Gen 1:2 and Jer 4:23 exists only in the similar phrases, "darkness" *ḥōšek* in Gen 1:2, and its *negated antonym*,[107] "no light" *'ên 'ôrām* in Jer 4:23, as well as *tōhû wābōhû* in both,[108] but the passages are not similar in subject matter. In

---

104. Cf. McKane, *Jeremiah*, 1.107.

105. W. L. Holladay, *Jeremiah 1: A Commentary on the Book of the Prophet Jeremiah Chapters 1–25* (Philadelphia: Fortress, 1986), 165.

106. J. S. Kselman, "The Recovery of Poetic Fragments from the Pentateuchal Priestly Source," *JBL* 97 (1978), 164 n. 13: "a poem modelled on Gen 1; cf. M. Fishbane, *VT* 21 (1971), 151–67."

107. See my "Exegetical Consideration on Hab 2:4a," *Tojo* 15 (1985), 1–26 [Japanese]; R. E. Longacre, *The Grammar of Discourse* (New York: Plenum, 1983), 116–19.

108. See above, p. 27, on the word pair *tōhû* and *ḥōšek* in Isa 45:19 and Job 12:24–25.

other words, in the Genesis passage it is "earth" // *tĕhôm* that is described; in Jeremiah, "earth" // "heavens."

Moreover, the nature of the word-pair relationship in Gen 1:2 is different from that in Jer 4:23. In the latter it is merismatic, or contrastive; in the former it is hyponymous.[109] While in Gen 1:2 only the "earth," which was totally covered with *tĕhôm*-waters, is the subject matter, in Jer 4:23 the whole universe, "the heavens and the earth," is the topic of concern. In light of the above discussion, it is rather difficult to assume that Jer 4:23–26 is patterned after or "modeled on" the creation story in Gen 1:1–2:4a.

Let us place Jer 4:23–26 in a wider literary context and view it in connection with vv. 27–28, where Yahweh's speech is reported.[110] For one thing, what Jeremiah saw in vv. 23–26 should be closely related to what Yahweh said in vv. 27–28.

> 27.   *kî-kōh ʾāmar YHWH*
>   *šĕmāmâ tihyeh kol-hāʾāreṣ*
>   *wĕkālâ lōʾ ʾeʿĕśeh*
> 28.   *ʿal-zōʾt teʾĕbal hāʾāreṣ*
>   *wĕqādĕrû haššāmayim mimmāʿal*
>   *ʿal kî-dibbartî zammōtî*
>   *wĕlōʾ niḥamtî wĕlōʾ-ʾāšûb mimmennâ*

> 27.   For thus says the LORD:
>   The whole land shall be a desolation;
>   yet I will not make a full end.
> 28.   Because of this the earth shall mourn,
>   and the heavens above grow black;
>   for I have spoken, I have purposed;
>   I have not relented nor will I turn back. (NRSV)

Holladay rightly notes that v. 28 corresponds with v. 23 and says, "Here the expression nicely dovetails with the extinguishing of the light of the heavens in v. 23. In a way the whole cosmos is in mourning for itself."[111] Thus, he notes the correspondence between *ʾên ʾôrām* (v. 23) and *qdr* "to be dark" (v. 28). However, he does not discuss the other correspondence—that is, *tōhû wābōhû* and *ʾbl* "to dry up," with regard to the "earth" in these verses.

---

109. See below, pp. 58–63, for a detailed discussion of a hyponymous relation between the "earth" and *tĕhôm*.

110. Wildberger, *Jesaja*, 2.920 treats Jer 4:23–28 as closely related to Isa 24:4, which mentions the "earth" that "dries up" (*ʾābĕlâ*) and the "whole world" that "withers" (*ʾumlĕlâ*).

111. Holladay, *Jeremiah* 1.168.

From a structural analysis of vv. 23–28 as a whole, it is noteworthy that the word pair "the earth" (*hāʾāreṣ*) and "the heavens" (*haššāmayim*) appears in this order both in the beginning (v. 23) and at the end (v. 28) of this section, thus functioning as an inclusio or a "frame" for the section. In other words, "(the earth is) *tōhû wābōhû*" // "(the heavens) are without light" in v. 23 corresponds to "(the earth) will dry up" (*ʾbl) // "(the heavens) will be dark" (*qdr) in v. 28. Here, the phrase *tōhû wābōhû* corresponds to the verbal phrase "to dry up"[112] and suggests the "aridness or unproductiveness" of the earth. This is in keeping with v. 27, which mentions that "the whole earth will become a desolation"[113] (*šĕmāmâ tihyeh kol-hāʾāreṣ*).

Regarding the second half of v. 27, *wĕkālâ lōʾ ʾeʿĕśeh*, various suggestions have been made. Most recently, it has been translated "and I will make its destruction complete" (McKane)[114] or "and none of it shall I (re)make" (Holladay),[115] by slightly changing the MT reading. On the other hand, Bright has translated the MT as it is: "though I'll make no full end,"[116] thus taking *kālâ* as "full end."[117] However, *kālâ* here as well as in Nah 1:8[118] seems to refer to "total destruction," that is, destruction brought about by a flood, like the *gamertu* which was brought about by *abūbu* "a flood" in the Babylonian Flood story.[119] Thus, the Jeremiah passage refers to a destruction brought about by the lack of water, not by the flood water. This is in keeping with my explanation, which takes *tōhû wābōhû* as signifying "aridness or unproductiveness" of the earth.

Because without v. 23 there would be no reason to compare the Jeremiah passage with the Genesis creation story,[120] we should conclude that the two

---

112. Cf. *HALOT*, 7: II ʾbl "to dry up," Jer 12:4, 23:10; Amos 1:2 and *CAD* A/1 29–30: *abālu* B "to dry up, dry out"; *AHw*, 3: *abālu* "(aus)trocknen," which is sometimes used for *šadû* and *eqlu*.

113. Cf. Exod 23:29, Isa 1:7. Note that the term *šĕmāmâ* "desolation" has the synonymous variants *ḥārēb* "waste, desolate" (Jer 33:10; cf. 32:43) and *ʿăzûbâ* "deserted" (Zeph 2:4, Isa 62:4, Jer 4:29; cf. 4:27). For Zeph 2:4, see L. Zalcman, "Ambiguity and Assonance at Zephaniah II 4," *VT* 36 (1986), 368.

114. McKane, *Jeremiah*, 1.108.

115. Holladay, *Jeremiah 1*, 166.

116. Bright, *Jeremiah*, 33. Bright adds the following comment: "the land will indeed be a waste, but it will not be the 'full end' described in vss. 23–26."

117. Compare with "complete destruction" (BDB, 478).

118. For this verse, see my article "Janus Parallelism in Nah 1:8," *JBL* 102 (1983), 109–11.

119. AH III v 42–44; cf. II viii 34 and III iii 38. Cf. Lambert and Millard, *AH*, 158 [a note on II viii 34]. See on Ps 29 (below).

120. Carroll thinks that "the poem could be a meditation on the creation story," and rejects Fishbane's view. See Carroll, *Jeremiah*, 169.

single verses, Jer 4:23 and Gen 1:2, simply share a common literary tradition in their use of *tōhû wābōhû*, which, according to the Jeremiah context, refers to a "desert-like" state of the "earth."

Isaiah 34:11
wĕnāṭâ ʿālêhā qaw-tōhû
wĕʾabnê-bōhû

And He shall stretch over it the line of desolation
And the plumb line of emptiness. (NASB)

The motif of "desolation" or *Verlassenheit*[121] can be also found in Isa 34:11, where *tōhû* and *bōhû* appear in parallel expressions: "the line of *thw*" (*qaw-tōhû*) // "the stones of *bhw*" (*ʾabnê-bōhû*). This text has been again connected with Gen 1:2, and it is often explained, for example, as "Yahweh had reduced the country for ever to a place just like chaos, to a real *tōhū-wābōhū* (cf. Gen. 1.2)."[122] However, as Wildberger rightly says, "But as the passage in the book of Jeremiah indicates, the creation story in Gen 1 need not be presupposed,"[123] Isa 34:11 simply means that "the land will become a desolation and waste so that it can no more receive inhabitants."[124] From the context of the Isaiah passage, it is rather difficult to see any direct connection with the Genesis creation story. It seems that Isaiah inherited the same literary tradition as Jer 4:23 and Gen 1:2 in describing the desolateness of the earth or land as *tōhû* and *bōhû*.

Let us summarize what we have concluded in the above discussion: the term *tōhû* means (1) "desert," (2) "a desert-like place," that is, "a desolate or empty place" or "an uninhabited place" or (3) "emptiness"; the phrase *tōhû wābōhû* has a similar meaning and refers to a state of "aridness or unproductiveness" (Jer 4:23) or "desolation" (Isa 34:11).

Having studied the etymology and biblical usages of the term *tōhû* as well as the expression *tōhû wābōhû,* it is now time to place this expression in the Genesis context.

---

121. H. Wildberger, *Jesaja,* vol. 3: *Jesaja 28–39* (BKAT 10/3; Neukirchen-Vluyn: Neukirchener Verlag, 1982), 1346.

122. O. Kaiser, *Isaiah 13–39: A Commentary* (London: SCM, 1974), 359.

123. Wildberger, *Jesaja,* 3.1346: "Aber wie die Stelle aus dem Jeremiabuch zeigt, braucht die Schöpfungserzählung von Gn 1 nicht vorausgesetzt zu sein." Here he changes his previous view on the Jeremiah passage. Cf. *Jesaja,* 2.920.

124. Young, *Isaiah,* 2.438, however, holds that the prophet Isaiah took language from Gen 1:2.

Tōhû wābōhû in the Framework of Genesis 1

Meaning of Term

In light of the above, it would be very reasonable to understand the phrase *tōhû wābōhû* in Gen 1:2 as also describing a state of "desolation and emptiness,"[125] though the context suggests that this was the initial state of the created earth rather than a state brought about as a result of God's judgment on the earth or land (cf. Jer 4:23, Isa 34:11). In this regard, the earth that "was"[126] (*hāyětâ*) *tōhû wābōhû* signifies the earth in a "bare" state, without vegetation and animals as well as without man. The author's intention in describing the earth in its initial state as *tōhû wābōhû* was not to present the earth as "the terrible, eerie, deserted wilderness"[127] but to introduce the earth as being "not yet" normal.

Discourse Analysis of Passage

This interpretation of *tōhû wābōhû* (lit., "desert-like and empty") as describing a bare state, a "desolate and uninhabited" state, of the earth fits the literary structure of the entire chapter.

According to a discourse analysis[128] of Gen 1:1–3, the first two verses constitute the SETTING for the EVENT that begins in v. 3, since the *wayqtl* (*waw* consecutive + imperf.), the narrative "tense," first appears in the phrase "and

---

125. See also Tur-Sinai, *The Book of Job*, 381: "in Gen 1:2 . . . [*tōhû*] describes the barrenness of the earth before anything grew on it."

126. Andersen, *SBH*, 85, thinks that Gen 1:2a means "the earth had become (or had come to be)," as a circumstance prior to the first fiat recorded in Gen 1:3.

127. *HALOT*, 1689.

128. That is, a linguistic analysis of supra-sentential units. In the fourth edition of *Davidson's Introductory Hebrew Grammar: Syntax* (Edinburgh: T. & T. Clark, 1994), J. Gibson describes it as the following:

> The narrative usually opens with a statement of circumstances, the subj. coming first, or a statement of time, with or without an impersonal וַיְהִי. . . . The story line begins thereafter with *Vav* cons. YIQTOL and is continued with other *Vav* cons. YIQTOLs, identifying the main successive events. (§80)

See ch. 4, pp. 77–78. Since the first edition (1989) of this monograph, more books have been written on Hebrew discourse analysis; for example, P. Cotterell and M. Turner, *Linguistics and Biblical Interpretation* (Downers Grove, Ill.: InterVarsity Press, 1989); R. D. Bergen (ed.), *Biblical Hebrew and Discourse Linguistics* (Dallas: Summer Institute of Linguistics, 1994); D. A. Dawson, *Text-Linguistics and Biblical Hebrew* (JSOTSup 177; Sheffield: Sheffield Academic Press, 1994); W. R. Bodine (ed.), *Discourse Analysis of Biblical Literature: What It Is and What It Offers* (SBL Semeia Studies; Atlanta: Scholars Press, 1995). See also Y. Endo, *The Verbal System of Classical Hebrew in the Joseph Story: An Approach from Discourse Analysis* (Assen: Van Gorcum, 1996).

God said" (*wayyō'mer 'ĕlōhîm*). After the summary statement "in the beginning God created the heavens and the earth" (v. 1), in v. 2a the author focuses
not on the "heavens" but on the "earth" where the audience stands, and, in
preparation for what is to come, presents the "earth" as "still" not being the
earth that they all are familiar with. Unlike the SETTING in 2:5–6 ("no shrub
. . . no plant . . . no rain . . . no man"),[129] 1:2 uses the grammatically positive
form *tōhû wābōhû* "desolate and empty."

The earth that they are familiar with has vegetation, animals, and man.
Therefore, in the following verses, the author will describe their coming into
existence through God's creation: vegetation on the third day and animals and
man on the sixth day. Both the third and the sixth day are set as climaxes in
the framework of this creation story, with the creation of man on the sixth day
as the grand climax.[130]

This literary structure[131] can be expressed as follows:

Gen 1:2   the *earth* as <u>desolate</u> and <u>empty</u> (*tōhû wābōhû*)

[day 1]	light and darkness	[day 4]	"sun" and "moon"
[day 2]	two waters	[day 5]	fish and birds
[day 3]	*earth* and seas	[day 6]	<u>animals</u> and <u>man</u>
	<u>vegetation</u>		on the *earth*

Thus, the "not-yet-productive" earth becomes productive when God says,
tadšē' hā'āreṣ deše' "let the land produce vegetation" (v. 11) on the third day
and *tôṣē' hā'āreṣ nepeš ḥayyâ* "let the land produce living creatures" (v. 24)
on the sixth day. Then, the "not-yet-inhabited" earth becomes inhabited when
God says, *na'ă'śeh 'ādām běṣalmēnû kidmûtēnû* "let us make man as our image, in our likeness" (v. 26). Thus, it is by God's fiats that the unproductive
and uninhabited earth becomes productive with vegetation and animals and
inhabited by man.[132] The story of creation in Gen 1:1–2:3 thus tells us that it

---

129. See ch. 4 (below).

130. Cf. Wenham, *Genesis 1–15*, 6; B. W. Anderson, *Creation versus Chaos: The Reinterpretation of Mythical Symbolism in the Bible* (Philadelphia: Fortress, 1967 [1987, reprint with postscript]), 187–88, and 191. Young notes that the definite article is used only
with the ordinal number "6" in this chapter; see E. J. Young, *Studies in Genesis One* (Philadelphia: Presbyterian and Reformed, 1964), 99.

131. Wenham, *Genesis 1–15*, 6–7; I. M. Kikawada and A. Quinn, *Before Abraham
Was: The Unity of Genesis 1–11* (Nashville: Abingdon, 1985), 78, suggest that the first three
days (regions) correspond to the second three days (corresponding inhabitants).

132. B. Otzen, "The Use of Myth in Genesis," in *Myths in the Old Testament* (ed.
B. Otzen, H. Gottlieb, and K. Jeppesen; London: SCM, 1980), 39, thinks that "the background of [Gen 1:11f.] is the ancient mythological idea of the 'Earth Mother' who 'gives
birth' to the products of the soil." It should be noted, however, that in Gen 1 animals are also

is God who created mankind "as his image" and provided for him an inhabitable and productive earth.

Therefore, v. 2 is, as Perry notes, a "prelude" to v. 3, where the first of God's creative actions begins with his utterance "let there be light!" It thus "'sets the scene' by portraying a universal state of readiness, pictured most vividly by God's spirit hovering in anticipation."[133] The narrator's concern, however, is *not* to argue whether the "earth" and the "water" in v. 2 had existed before the light or not; *nor* to declare positively that there was a "desolate and empty" earth in the beginning. Rather, he simply provides the audience with the preparatory information that the "earth" was *not yet normal*—that is, "not yet" the earth as it was known to them. This is not the same as describing what Perry holds is "absent or not yet there." It is a matter of explaining that the earth was "not yet normal," rather than an ontological problem of what was "not yet there."

In conclusion, the phrase *tōhû wābōhû* in Gen 1:2, which is traditionally translated into English "without form and void" (RSV) or the like, simply means "emptiness" and refers to the earth, which was a desolate and empty place, "an unproductive and uninhabited place." As Westermann notes, "creation and the world are to be understood always from the viewpoint of or in the context of human existence."[134] In other words, to communicate the subject of creation meaningfully to human beings, one must use the language and literary forms known to them. In order to give the background information to the audience in this verse, the author uses experiential language, explaining the initial situation of the earth as "not yet."

---

the products of the earth and that the existence of both plant life and animal life on the earth is the result of divine fiats. Note also that there is no single myth in the ancient Near East that treats both plants and animals as the products of the earth.

133. T. A. Perry, "A Poetics of Absence: The Structure and Meaning of Genesis 1:2," *JSOT* 58 (1993), 3–11.

134. Westermann, *Genesis*, 1.145 [ET 104]; also O. Kaiser, *Die mythische Bedeutung des Meeres in Ägypten, Ugarit und Israel* (BZAW 78; Berlin: Alfred Töpelmann, 1959), 13; W. H. Schmidt, *Die Schöpfungsgeschichte der Priesterschrift: Zur Überlieferungsgeschichte von Genesis 1:1–2:4a und 2:4b–3:24*, vol. 2: *Überarbeitete und erweiterte Auflage* (Neukirchen-Vluyn: Neukirchener Verlag, 1967), 86 n. 3.

2

The Waters in Genesis 1

Babylonian Background

H. Gunkel in his famous book *Schöpfung und Chaos in Urzeit und Endzeit* (1895) discussed the Babylonian background of *tĕhôm* in Gen 1:2.[1] He believed that the word derived directly from Tiamat,[2] the goddess of the primeval ocean of *Enuma elish*. Ever since, many biblical scholars have assumed some kind of direct or indirect connection between the Babylonian Tiamat and the Hebrew *tĕhôm*.[3] For example, B. W. Anderson holds that,

> as in the *Enuma elish* myth, Genesis 1 begins by portraying a precreation condition of watery chaos. Indeed, the Hebrew word for *deep* (Gen. 1:2: *Tehom*) appears here without the definite article (elsewhere it is in the feminine gender), as though it were a distant echo of the mythical battle with Tiamat, the female personification of the powers of chaos.[4]

Lexical Borrowing

The earlier scholars who followed Gunkel usually held that the author of Genesis had borrowed the Babylonian proper name Tiamat and demythologized it. However, if the Hebrew *tĕhôm* were an Akkadian loanword,[5] there should be a closer phonetic similarity to *ti'āmat*. The expected Hebrew form

---

1. An abridged English edition of pp. 3–120 is now available as H. Gunkel, "Influence of Babylonian Mythology upon the Biblical Creation Story," in *Creation in the Old Testament* (ed. B. W. Anderson; Issues in Religion and Theology 6; Philadelphia: Fortress, 1984), 25–52.

2. For a useful summary, see B. Alster, "Tiamat," *DDD*, 1634–39.

3. E.g., B. S. Childs, *Myth and Reality in the Old Testament* (London: SCM, 1960), 36; B. W. Anderson, *Creation versus Chaos: The Reinterpretation of Mythical Symbolism in the Bible* (Philadelphia: Fortress, 1967 [1987, reprint with postscript]), 15–40, esp. 39–40; M. K. Wakeman, *God's Battle with the Monster: A Study in Biblical Imagery* (Leiden: Brill, 1973), 86ff.

4. Anderson, *Creation versus Chaos*, 39; see Gunkel, "Influence of Babylonian Mythology," 42, 45.

5. Cf. Zimmern, *AFw*, 44.

would be something like *tiʾámat > tiʾṓmat > tĕʾōmát. This could have been subsequently changed to *tĕʾomấ(h), with a loss of the final /t/, but never to *tĕhôm*, with a loss of the entire feminine morpheme /-at/.[6]

Moreover, because the second consonant of Tiamat is /ʾ/, a glottal stop, which often disappears in the intervocalic position, so that the resultant vowel cluster experiences so-called vowel *sandhi*[7] in Akkadian as tiʾāmtum > tiāmtum > tâmtum, it is very unlikely that a West Semitic speaker would represent the second consonant as a fricative [h]. In fact, there is no example of West Semitic borrowing Akkadian /ʾ/ as /h/, except Akkadian *ilku* "duty" as *hlkʾ* (Aram.) with the word-initial /h/.[8] It is almost impossible to conclude that Akkadian *Tiamat* was borrowed by Hebrew as *tĕhôm* with an intervocalic /h/, for the latter also tends to disappear in Hebrew (e.g., /h/ in the definite article /ha-/ in the intervocalic position).[9]

However, some scholars still presume that there is a mythological connection,[10] though indirect and remote, between *tĕhôm* and Tiamat and hold that diachronically the term *tĕhôm* was originally a Babylonian proper noun. For example, Wakeman says that, "in view of the accepted etymological relation of the word to Tiamat . . . and given the conservative nature of poetry, we might expect to find echoes of the myth in the poetic clichés or formulas associated with *tĕhôm*."[11] She thus sees "vestiges of personality" in idiomatic expressions such as *tĕhôm rabbâ*.[12] At the same time, she thinks that, "though

---

6. An Akk. term could be borrowed into West Semitic either with or without the final /t/: e.g., *askupp/atu* (Akk.) "threshold" > *ʾskwpt* (Syr.), *maddattu* (Akk.) "tribute" > *mndh* or *mdh* (Bib. Aram.) and *mdʾt* (Syr.); cf. *egirtu* (Akk.) "letter" > *ʾ(y)grh/t(ʾ)*. See Kaufman, *AIA*, 37, 67; cf. 48; cf. Zimmern, *AFw*, 9.

7. D. T. Tsumura, "Vowel sandhi in Biblical Hebrew," *ZAW* 109 (1997), 575–88; "Vowel sandhi in Ugaritic," *Near Eastern Studies Dedicated to H. I. H. Prince Takahito Mikasa on the Occasion of His Seventy-Fifth Birthday* (BMECCJ 5; Wiesbaden: Harrassowitz, 1991), 427–35.

8. *AHw*, 371; Zimmern, *AFw*, 10; Kaufman, *AIA*, 58; cf. 27.

9. Cf. Heidel, BG³, 90, 100 n. 58; O. Kaiser, *Die mythische Bedeutung des Meeres in Ägypten, Ugarit und Israel* (BZAW 78; Berlin: Alfred Töpelmann, 1959), 115; W. H. Schmidt, *Die Schöpfungsgeschichte der Priesterschrift: Zur Überlieferungsgeschichte von Genesis 1:1–2:4a und 2:4b–3:24, 2. Überarbeitete und erweiterte Auflage* (Neukirchen-Vluyn: Neukirchener Verlag, 1967), 80 n. 5; C. Westermann, *Genesis*, vol. 1: *Genesis 1–11* (BKAT 1/1; Neukirchen-Vluyn: Neukirchener Verlag, 1974), 146 [ET: 105]; J. Day, *God's Conflict with the Dragon and the Sea: Echoes of a Canaanite Myth in the Old Testament* (Cambridge: Cambridge University Press, 1985), 50.

10. E.g., B. Otzen, "The Use of Myth in Genesis," in *Myths in the Old Testament* (ed. B. Otzen, H. Gottlieb, and K. Jeppesen; London: SCM, 1980), 32, 40.

11. Wakeman, *God's Battle with the Monster*, 86–87.

12. Ibid., 87–88.

תהום may be related etymologically to Tiamat, it is nowhere personified in the Bible. However, . . . the idea was in the process of being depersonalized."[13]

Here a certain confusion seems to exist in the use of the term *etymological* by some scholars. When one says that *těhôm* is etymologically related to Tiamat, no clear distinction is made between the fact that *těhôm* and Tiamat are cognate, sharing the common Semitic root *thm, and the popular supposition that *těhôm* is a loanword from the Akkadian divine name Tiamat, hence implying a mythological relationship. Because the latter is phonologically impossible, the idea that the Akkadian Tiamat was borrowed and subsequently demythologized is mistaken and should not be used as an argument in a lexicographical discussion of Hebrew *těhôm*. It should be pointed out that the Akkadian term *ti'āmtum > tâmtum* normally means "sea" or "ocean" in an ordinary sense and is sometimes *personified* as a divine being in mythological contexts.[14] Therefore, the fact that *těhôm* is etymologically related to Tiamat as a cognate should not be taken as evidence for the mythological dependence of the former on the latter.

Western "Origin"?

While the majority of biblical scholars assume the Babylonian background of *těhôm* (Gen 1:2), some Assyriologists have been questioning the alleged connection between Gen 1 and *Enuma elish*.[15] Lambert, Jacobsen, and Sjöberg are "extremely careful when dealing with influences from Mesopotamia on the mythological and religious concepts of the peoples living along the Mediterranean coast, and see instead a strong influence from that region on Mesopotamia."[16]

For example, in 1965, W. G. Lambert said, "there is no proof that the conflict of a deity with the sea is of Mesopotamian origin" and suggested as a possibility that the Amorites introduced the idea into Mesopotamia.[17] Jacobsen also argues that "the story of the battle between the god of thunderstorm and the sea originated on the coast of the Mediterranean and wandered east-

---

13. Idem, "Chaos," *IDB Supplement* (ed. K. Crim; Nashville: Abingdon, 1976), 144; idem, *God's Battle with the Monster*, 86ff.

14. Cf. *AHw*, 1353–54. See below, pp. 47–49, for further discussion on this matter.

15. For example, see J. V. K. Wilson, "The Epic of Creation," in *DOTT*, 14: "it seems very probable that the epic has no connections of any kind or at any point with Genesis."

16. Å. W. Sjöberg, "Eve and the Chameleon," in *In the Shelter of Elyon: Essays on Ancient Palestinian Life and Literature in Honor of G. W. Ahlström* (ed. W. B. Barrick and J. R. Spencer; JSOTSup 31; Sheffield: JSOT Press, 1984), 218.

17. W. G. Lambert, "A New Look at the Babylonian Background of Genesis," *JTS* 16 (1965), 295–96. For the relationship between *Enuma elish* and Gen 1, see also idem, "Babylonien und Israel," *TRE* 5.71–72.

ward from there to Babylon."[18] However, Lambert has revised his earlier position and now holds that the motif of the storm-god's conflict with the sea in *Enuma elish* came from northern Mesopotamian traditions.[19] One certainly has to adjust to the recent advance in the knowledge of the ancient Near East, especially of northern Mesopotamia, during the past two decades. In fact, one of the Mari documents mentions a battle between Addu of Aleppo and the sea-goddess Têmtum.[20] However, this is not enough grounds for assuming that *těhôm* (Gen 1:2) has a northern Mesopotamian background.

It should be noted that *Enuma elish* itself incorporates much older Mesopotamian traditions.[21] For example, according to Lambert, "not only was Enūma Eliš consciously based on Anzû, but other items of Ninurta mythology were deliberately worked in so as to present Marduk as Ninurta redivivus."[22] As for Tiamat, an Old Akkadian school tablet of the 22nd century B.C. that predates *Enuma elish* by a millennium mentions Tišpak, "steward of Tiamat"[23] (*abarak*[24] *tiāmtim*),[25] and the form *tiāmtim* appears in an Old Assyrian

---

18. T. Jacobsen, "The Battle between Marduk and Tiamat," *JAOS* 88 (1968), 107.

19. See W. G. Lambert, "Postscript," added to the reprinted article "A New Look at the Babylonian Background of Genesis," *JTS* 16 (1965), 287–300, in H.-P. Müller (ed.), *Babylonien und Israel: Historische, religiöse und sprachliche Beziehungen* (Darmstadt: Wissenschaftliche, 1991), 113; also his "Second Postscript" to the reprint of the article in R. S. Hess and D. T. Tsumura (eds.), *"I Studied Inscriptions from before the Flood": Ancient Near Eastern, Literary, and Linguistic Approaches to Genesis 1–11* (SBTS 4; Winona Lake, Ind.: Eisenbrauns, 1994), 111.

20. See J.-M. Durand, "Le Mythologeme du combat entre le Dieu de l'orage et la Mer en Mésopotamie," *MARI* 7 (1993), 41–61. But note Lambert's comment on Durand's "Pan-Amoritism" in "Second Postscript," 111. See below and part 2.

21. There is some disagreement on the dating of *Enuma elish* among Assyriologists. Lambert dates it around 1100 B.C., or the second half of the second millennium at the earliest. Cf. W. G. Lambert, "The Reign of Nebuchadnezzar I: A Turning Point in the History of Ancient Mesopotamian Religion," in *The Seed of Wisdom: Essays in Honour of T. J. Meek* (ed. W. S. McCullough; Toronto: University of Toronto Press, 1964), 6; also Alster, "Tiamat," *DDD*, 1636. Jacobsen dates it earlier. Jacobsen suggests that Marduk's victory over Tiʾāmat represents the conquest of the Sealand and its unification with Babylon and the North under Ulamburiash [ca. 1400 B.C.] (T. Jacobsen, *The Treasures of Darkness: A History of Mesopotamian Religion* [New Haven: Yale University Press, 1976], 189–90).

22. W. G. Lambert, "Ninurta Mythology in the Babylonian Epic of Creation," in *Keilschriftliche Literaturen: Ausgewählte Vorträge der XXXII. Rencontre Assyriologique Internationale* (ed. K. Hecker and W. Sommerfeld; BBVO 6; Berlin: Reimer, 1986), 56. See also idem, "The Theology of Death," in *Death in Mesopotamia* (ed. B. Alter; Mesopotamia 8; Copenhagen: Akademisk, 1980), 64–65 for the highly composite nature of *Enuma elish*.

23. See idem, "Postscript," 112–13; also "Second Postscript," 110–11.

24. On Durand's reinterpretation of this term, see Lambert's criticism in "Second Postscript," 111–13.

25. In Akkadian the god Sea is usually written as *tiāmtu* or *tâmtu*, and the writing *ti-amat* (GÉME) appears only once in a gloss. The most common phonetic spellings are *ti-à-wa-ti* and

personal name, Puzur-Tiāmtim, "Protected-by-Tiāmat."[26] Thus, the sea was personified as a divine being beginning with the earliest period of written history in Mesopotamia. In fact, it is obvious that the myth had a long oral stage before it was set down in writing.[27]

On the other hand, in some later creation narratives in Mesopotamia, the sea is not personified and has nothing to do with the conflict theme. In these traditions, the creation of the world or cosmos is not connected with the death of a dragon, as in *Enuma elish*. For example, a bilingual version of the *Creation of the World by Marduk* from the Neo-Babylonian period describes the creation of cosmos without a conflict theme. In this myth, the initial situation of the world is simply described: "All the land was sea." There the waters alone existed before the creation of the world.[28] However, the nonpersonified use of the sea (*tâmtum*) in this myth is not a result of depersonifying of the divine name.[29]

In light of the above, Westermann's statement that "the similarity between תהום and Tiamat would go back to a stage in the history of the creation narrative when the story of the struggles between the gods had *not yet*[30] been linked with creation"[31] needs revision. Because some narratives never associated the creation of cosmos with the conflict theme, there is no reason to assume that the older stage without the conflict-creation connection necessarily developed to a stage with this connection. Clearly, more than one creation tradition existed in ancient Mesopotamia, and *Enuma elish* inherited some of the older Mesopotamian mythological traditions about the storm-god as well as about the conflict of a deity with the sea.[32]

---

ta-à-wa-ti and the spelling *ta-ma-*[*tú*] also appears in a gloss (from oral communication with Prof. W. G. Lambert).

26. Cf. A. Westenholz, "Old Akkadian School Texts: Some Goals of Sargonic Scribal Education," *AfO* 25 (1974/77), 102.

27. T. C. Mitchell reminds us that "no inscriptional evidence is available earlier than the invention of writing in about 3000 B.C., whereas the account of creation presumably dates from a very much earlier period." See his review of the first edition of this book in *EvQ* 66 (1994), 257–59. Lambert holds that the Babylonian Tiamat and West Semitic Yam go back to a common "prehistoric" tradition that "spread very widely from the Indus Valley to the Aegean." See "Second Postscript," 111.

28. See below, p. 72; cf. Heidel, *BG*[3], 62; J. Bottéro, *Mythes et Rites de Babylone* (Geneva: Slatkine / Paris: Champion, 1985), 303. Thus, even in a myth related to Marduk's creative activity, the motif of *Chaoskampf* is not a prerequisite of creation.

29. See below, pp. 47–48, on this subject.

30. Emphasis mine.

31. Westermann, *Genesis*, 1.146–47 [ET: 106].

32. While Marduk certainly exhibited storm-god attributes in his combat with Tiamat, it is not correct to treat him as a storm-god as such. See below, pp. 122–123, on storm-gods. See W. Heimpel, "Mythologie, A.I: In Mesopotamien," *RlA* 8.558–60.

It should be noted, however, that it is the motif of a conflict of a storm-god with the sea, not the motif of creation by conflict, that Lambert and Jacobsen have suggested as originating in the west. Hence, Jacobsen's assumption does not necessarily support the view that the "primordial struggle in connection with the creation" existed in Ugaritic myth.[33] While in *Enuma elish* the motif of the conflict of a deity with the sea is integrated into the story of the creation of the cosmos, in Ugaritic the Baal-Yam conflict is not related to a "primordial struggle in connection with the creation" at all, as the following section will explain.

Canaanite Background

Since the discovery of Ugaritic myths, a Canaanite background has been widely accepted for the conflict between Yahweh and the sea dragons, Leviathan, Rahab, and others in poetic passages of the Old Testament, such as Pss 74:13–14, 89:10, 104:26; Isa 27:1, 51:9, etc.[34] The "Canaanite" conflict motif in these biblical passages, where the conflict is considered to be related to "creation,"[35] is held to be "a missing link" for positing an alleged *Chaoskampf* in Gen 1:2. Thus, the theme of *Chaoskampf* reflected both in the Babylonian *Enuma elish* and in the Ugaritic Baal myth tends to be taken as a required element in any cosmogonic story in the ancient Near East.

Creation of Cosmos?

However, scholars have noted that the myth of a Baal–Yam conflict in the extant Ugaritic texts has nothing to do with the creation of the cosmos as such,[36] and the storm-god Baal is not a creator-god, as is Marduk in *Enuma elish*. Hence, some Ugaritic scholars have assumed the existence of an earlier cosmogonic myth in the missing first column of KTU 1.1 or the broken section of 1.2,[37] which they think gives the "missing account" of the victories

---

33. Cf. de Moor, *SPUMB*, 41 n. 31.

34. See part 2 (chs. 8–11) below. Cf. A. Cooper, "Divine Names and Epithets in the Ugaritic Texts," in *RSP* 3.369–83 (on Ym//Nhr) and 388–91 (on Ltn).

35. On this topic, see C. Kloos, *Yhwh's Combat with the Sea: A Canaanite Tradition in the Religion of Ancient Israel* (Leiden: Brill, 1986), 70–86; Day, *God's Conflict with the Dragon and the Sea*, 18–49.

36. See M. S. Smith, "Interpreting the Baal Cycle," *UF* 18 (1986), 319–20; idem, *The Ugaritic Baal Cycle*, vol. 1: *Introduction with Text, Translation and Commentary of KTU 1.1–1.2* (VTSup 55; Leiden: Brill, 1994), 82–83; J. H. Grønbæk, "Baal's Battle with Yam: A Canaanite Creation Fight," *JSOT* 33 (1985), 27–44.

37. Day, *God's Conflict with the Dragon and the Sea*, 13: "a primordial battle associated with the creation of the world"; cf. also de Moor, *SPUMB*, 41 n. 31. However, in their review article of Day's book, Korpel and de Moor question Day's assumption that "there

over Yam, Nahar, the "dragon" (*tnn*),[38] the "crooked serpent" (*bṯn . ʿqltn*), and so on, claimed by Anat in 1.3:III:38ff. and the victory of Baal over *ltn* referred to in 1.5:I:1ff.[39] This is, Gibson believes, "what . . . comprised Ugaritic mythology's primordial battle of the good god with the powers of chaos so well known to us from the Mesopotamian and biblical parallels."[40]

J. Day suggests that the term *tĕhôm* can be traced back to the earlier Canaanite dragon myth that he, like Gibson, thinks is related to the creation theme. He says, "In so far as *tĕhôm*'s mythological background is concerned this is not Babylonian at all, but rather Canaanite, as the Old Testament dragon passages show, a point which some scholars still have not properly grasped."[41] Then he argues circularly that "the divine conflict with the dragon and the sea underwent a process of demythologization and the control of the waters simply became regarded as a job or work. This is found especially in Gen 1 . . . (Gen 1's) traditions are ultimately Canaanite."[42] The term *tĕhôm* in Gen 1:2 is hence understood as a depersonification of the original mythological divine name in Canaanite, though he holds that "both *tĕhôm* and Tiamat are derived from a common Semitic root."[43]

However, is there any reason to think that a term used as a common noun is the depersonification of a divine name, when both can go back to their original common noun? In our case, what is the etymology of the Hebrew term *tĕhôm*? Is there any direct connection between etymological and mythological similarity?

Etymology of *THM

Morphologically, Hebrew *tĕhôm* corresponds to Ugaritic *thm* rather than to the Akkadian divine name ᵈTiamat with a feminine ending /-at/. Ugaritic also

---

existed a different Canaanite myth in which the victor over Sea became the creator." M. C. A. Korpel and J. C. de Moor, "A Review of J. Day, *God's Conflict with the Dragon and the Sea: Echoes of a Canaanite Myth in the Old Testament,* 1985," *JSS* 31 (1986), 244.

38. Read /tunnanu/ (*Ug.* 5, 137:I:8′); cf. Huehnergard, *UVST,* 185–86.

39. For a useful summary and discussion on the narrative continuity of the Baal Cycle (KTU 1.1–1.6), see Smith, "Interpreting the Baal Cycle," 324–39. Note also his comment: "The comparative method has perhaps been abused in the case of the Baal cycle, in attempts to fill in the cycle's lacunae according to ideas about what 'should' be in the cycle. An early example of this procedure was to fill the gaps with an account of creation" (p. 328).

40. J. C. L. Gibson, "The Theology of the Ugaritic Baal Cycle," *Or* 53 (1984), 211.

41. Day, *God's Conflict with the Dragon and the Sea,* 50–51 and n. 141. However, what Lambert and Jacobsen pointed out is not the Canaanite background of the term *tĕhôm* but the "Canaanite" origin of the storm-sea conflict motif (see above, pp. 38–41).

42. Ibid., 61.

43. Ibid., 50.

has a feminine form, *thmt*, which is spelled syllabically as *ta-a-ma-tu$_4$* /tahā-matu/[44] (*Ug.* 5, 137:III:34″) for the name of an ocean-goddess. This spelling suggests that the Ugaritic term *thm* was probably read as /tahāmu/.

Akkadian *tiāmtum* or *tâmtum*, Arabic *tihāmat*, and Eblaite *ti-ʾà-ma-tum* /tihām(a)tum/,[45] together with the above-cited forms in Ugaritic and Hebrew, indicate that all these forms are reflections of a common Semitic term *tihām-. Thus Hebrew *tĕhôm* is simply a reflection of the common Semitic term *tihām.[46] And, as far as the first vowel is concerned, the Hebrew form *tĕhôm* reflects a stage of development from Proto-Semitic *tihām- that is older than the Ugaritic form *thm* /tahāmu/, the first vowel of which, /a/, is the result of vowel harmony: *tihām- > *tahāmu.

This etymological investigation shows that phonetic similarity is no proof of direct or indirect "borrowing."[47] In other words, the fact that the Hebrew term *tĕhôm* is related etymologically to the Akkadian divine name Tiamat and Ugaritic Tahāmu does not support the theory that the Hebrew term is the depersonification of an original divine name. The same can be said for the Hebrew term *šemeš* "sun," which is related etymologically to the Akkadian divine name *Šamaš*[48] and the Ugaritic divine name *Špš* /Šapšu/. Just as the Akkadian common noun *šamšu* is not a depersonification of the DN *Šamaš*, so Hebrew *šemeš* is not the depersonification of an original divine name.[49]

---

44. Rainey reads the last sign *tu$_4$* instead of *tum* (*Ug.* 5, 246) and explains that "the vocalization *ta-a-ma-tu$_4$* for *thmt* is due to vowel harmony." Cf. A. F. Rainey, "A New Grammar of Ugaritic," *Or* 56 (1987), 393; also J. Huehnergard, "Northwest Semitic Vocabulary in Akkadian Texts," *JAOS* 107 (1987), 725; *UVST*, 184–85, 247, 271. Note that in this multilingual vocabulary text, *Ug.* 5, 137, the Akkadian sign *a* ⟨a⟩ stands for either /ˀa/ or /ˁa/ or /ha/: e.g., *ma-a-du-ma* /maˀaduma/ (137:II:36′), *ba-a-lu* /baˁalu/ (137:IVb:17?), *tu-a-bi-ú* /tuhabihu/ ⟨ /túhwu wa bíhwu/ (137:II:23′) (see above p. 16), but not for /ā/. Since the alphabetic spelling is most likely *thmt*, the sign *a* in *ta-a-ma-tu$_4$* should be read as /ha/. Hence, Nougayrol's reading *tâmatum* (*Ug.* 5, 58) is not correct.

45. The sign *ʾà* (É) is used for etymological /ha/ or /ḥa/ in the Eblaite syllabary. Cf. M. Krebernik, "Zu Syllabar und Orthographie der lexikalischen Texte aus Ebla, Teil 1," *ZA* 72 (1982), 219–20; J. Krecher, "Sumerische und nichtsumerische Schicht in der Schriftkultur von Ebla," in *BaE*, 157. Thus, Gelb's view on the Old Akkadian sign *ʾà* (É) is supported by the Eblaite evidence; cf. I. J. Gelb, *Old Akkadian Writing and Grammar* (MAD 2; Chicago: University of Chicago Press, 1952), 34. See also E. Sollberger, *Administrative Texts Chiefly concerning Textiles (L. 2752)* (ARET 8; Rome: Missione Archeologica Italiana in Siria, 1986), 3.

46. See also Heidel, *BG*[2], 100; Schmidt, *Die Schöpfungsgeschichte der Priesterschrift*, 80 n. 5; now see *HALOT*, 1690.

47. Ibid., "as such it is not a loanword from Akkadian!"

48. See my "שמש—sun," in *NIDOTTE*, 4.185–90. For the early attestation of this DN, see J. J. M. Roberts, *The Earliest Semitic Pantheon: A Study of the Semitic Deities Attested in Mesopotamia before Ur III* (Baltimore: Johns Hopkins University Press, 1972), 51–52.

49. See below, pp. 50–51, on the common noun *ym* "sea" in Ugaritic.

Uses of *THM

Nonpersonified Use

Ugaritic

The Ugaritic counterpart of Hebrew *těhôm* appears both with a feminine
ending *-t* and without it. The shorter form, *thm*, appears twice in the alphabetic
texts. Though it appears once as a proper noun, constituting part of a compound divine name, "Heaven-and-Ocean" *šmm-w-thm* (KTU 1.100 [607]:1),
it also appears as a common noun, without any personification, parallel with
another common noun, *ym* "sea,"[50] in 1.23 [52]:30:

] *gp . ym*	. . . . the shore of the sea
wyṣġd . gp . thm	And roams the shore of the ocean.

The longer form with the feminine-singular ending *-t* can be recognized in the
divine name *ta-a-ma-tu₄* (= *thmt*), which corresponds to the Sumerian ANTU
in a multilingual vocabulary list (*Ug.* 5, 137:III:34″), as well as in the dual
form *thmtm* /tahāmat-āmi/.[51]

The plural form *thmt* /tahāmātu/ appears in 1.3 ['nt]:III:25 [22] (cf.
[130]:19, 1.17 [2Aqht]:VI:12), where the common nouns "heavens," "earth,"
"oceans," and "stars" are all used metaphorically.[52] Also in 1.92 [2001]:5:
wtglṭ thmt "she roils[53] the oceans," the plural form *thmt* has an ordinary sense

---

50. The term *yamm-* is a typical Northwest Semitic term for "sea" and corresponds to
Akkadian *tiāmtum, tâmtum.* The term *yamu* in an Akkadian plant list, the Uruanna text, is
a West Semitic word; cf. *CAD* I/J 322. In Amarna Akkadian, the sea is always referred to
by forms of the word *ayabba* (EA 74:20, 89:47, 105:13, 114:19, 151:42, 288:33, 340:6),
never spelled *ta-am-tu* (except in the *Adapa* text [356:50, 51], which is written in a standard Akkadian). I owe this information to Dr. R. S. Hess; see A. Malamat, "The Sacred
Sea," *Mari and the Bible* (Studies in the History and Culture of the Ancient Near East 12;
Leiden: Brill, 1998), 26 and nn. 10–11. See also *CAD* A/1 221 (also in Mari and SB literary
texts); *AHw,* 23; W. F. Albright and W. L. Moran, "Rib-Adda of Byblos and the Affairs of
Tyre (EA 89)," *JCS* 4 (1950), 167; cf. J. A. Knudtzon, *Die El-Amarna-Tafeln: Mit Einlei-
tung und Erläuterungen* (Aalen: Zeller, 1915), 2.1528 on *tâmtu.* It might be postulated that
the Sumerian loanword *ayabba* (← a-ab-ba) in West Semitic experienced the following
phonological change: a-ab-ba → *ayabba* → (a)yabba – (nasalization) → (a)yamba – (assimilation) → yamm- → *yām.* Cf. Akk. *ṣumbu < ṣubbu.* See D. O. Edzard, "Meer. A," in
RlA 8.1. For EA 89, see W. L. Moran, *Les Lettres d'El-Amarna: Correspondance diplomatique du pharaon* (LAPO 13; Paris: Cerf, 1987), 277–78. For the earliest equation of Sumerogram A.AB.BA and *a(y)yabba* in an OB bilingual hymn from southern Babylonia, see
Malamat, "The Sacred Sea," 27 and n. 13.

51. Singular stem + dual ending; cf. Huehnergard, *UVST,* 185.

52. See below, pp. 59–63, for this text.

53. See below, pp. 121ff., for a detailed discussion of this term. Note the expression
"(the gods) confused Tiamat" (*CAD* E 379) in Ee I 22.

without any personification.

In 1.4 [51]:IV:22, 1.6:I:34 [49:I:6], 1.17 [2Aqht]:VI:48, 1.3 ['nt]:V:7 [15], 1.2:III [129]:4 (cf. 1.5 [67]:VI:1). For example, the term *thmtm* /tahāmatāmi/ is a dual form, and these dual forms as well as the singular *thm* (1.23 [52]:30) refer to the waters near El's abode.

idk . l ttn . pnm	Then she surely sets face
'm . il . mbk . nhrm	Toward El at the sources of the two rivers
qrb . apq . thmtm	In the midst of the streams of the two oceans.

(1.4 [51]:IV:20–22)

and also 1.100 [607]:3:

'm . ³⁾il . mbk . nhrm	Toward El at the sources of the two rivers
b'dt . thmtm	In the assembly of the two oceans.

(cf. Gordon, *UTS*, 554)

In these mythological contexts, the term *thm(t)* is a common noun, "ocean (-waters)," without any personification. Also in KTU 1.19 [1Aqht]:I:45, the term *thmtm* is dual in form.[54] Here too it is used without personification.

Thus, Ugaritic *thm(t)* normally appears as a common noun in mythological texts. There is no reason for us to think that these nonpersonified uses of Ugaritic *thm(t)* are the result of *depersonification* of an original proper noun. If we do not think that other terms such as *ym, arṣ,* and *šmm* are depersonifications of the original divine entities,[55] we should not treat the term *thm* any differently.

Akkadian

Akkadian *tiāmtum* or *tâmtum* also appears in nonmythological texts, predating *Enuma elish* from earliest times, with the ordinary meaning "sea/ocean."[56] For example, in an Old Akkadian text the term *tiāmtim* is used in the ordinary sense as a geographical term, as in Sumerian a-ab-ba:[57]

---

54. See below, pp. 122–123.

55. In Ugaritic, *ym* is often "personified" and refers to a divine entity, the sea-god Yam. However, this term is also used as a common noun without any divine personification even in mythological contexts, as in the cases of *ym* (// *thm*) in 1.23 [52]:30, an expression "fish from the sea" *dg bym* (1.23 [52]:62–63), and a divine epithet *rbt aṯrt ym* "Lady 'Aṯirat of the sea" (1.4 [51]:I:13–14 [14–15], 21 [22]; III:25, 28–29, 34; 1.6:I:44, 45, 47, 53 [49:I:16, 17, 19, 25]). Cf. Albright's interpretation of *aṯrt ym* as "She Who Treads on the (dragon) Sea": W. F. Albright, *Yahweh and the Gods of Canaan* (London: Athlone, 1968 [repr. Winona Lake, Ind.: Eisenbrauns, 1990]), 166. However, compare the phrase *aṯrt ṣrm* "'Aṯirat of the Tyrians" (*UT* 19.428).

56. See Edzard, "Meer. A," *RlA* 8.1–3.

57. For Sumerian examples, see *SD* A/2 136–37.

Lagaš^{ki} *atima tiāmtim in'ar* (SAG.GIŠ.RA)
kakkī (^{giš}TUKUL-*gi*)-*su in tiāmtim imassī*[58]
he vanquished Lagaš as far as the sea.
He washed his weapons in the sea.

In an Old Babylonian letter which reports that "the sea,[59] the river, and the canal are low" (*tâmtum nārum u ḫirītum maṭā*), the term *tâmtum* appears as a common noun.[60] In the Old Babylonian Flood Story, *Atra-Ḫasīs* epic I i 15, the expression "the bar of the sea" (*naḫbalu tiāmtim*) appears. It is repeated six times (AH x rev. i 6, 10; x rev. ii 4, 11, 18, 34) in the Neo-Babylonian version, where another phrase, "the guards of the sea" (*maṣṣāru tâmti*; AH x rev. ii 24, 40), appears also without any personification of *tiāmtim, tâmti* "ocean." Also in the *Atra-Ḫasīs* epic III iv 6, *tiāmta* "sea" is in parallelism with *nāram* "river," both terms with ordinary meanings.[61]

Even in certain mythological contexts that mention the creation of the cosmos the term *tâmtum* appears without personification—for example, in the bilingual version of the *Creation of the World by Marduk* noted above.

Eblaite

In Eblaite, a language related to Old Akkadian, *ti-ʾà-ma-tum* appears also with the ordinary meaning, "sea, ocean": for example, *a-bar-rí-Iš ti-ʾà-ma-dím* (ARET 5, 6:VII:1–2, 3) /ʿabāriš tihām(a)tim/"jenseits des Meeres; Übersee."[62] Also it is clear from its context that *ti-ʾà-ma-tum* (ARET 5, 6:X:4) means the ordinary "sea."[63] In the Sumerian–Eblaite bilingual vocabulary

---

58. Sargon b 1, obv. col. 2: 49–55; b 6, obv. col. 8: 32–38 in H. Hirsch, "Die Inschriften Sargons," *AfO* 20 (1963), 35, 42; also E. Sollberger and J.-R. Kupper, *Inscriptions Royales Sumériennes et Akkadiennes* (LAPO 3; Paris: Cerf, 1971), 97. This practice of "washing of weapons in the sea" continued until the Neo-Assyrian period; cf. *CAD* K 52. See also A. Malamat, "Campaigns to the Mediterranean by Iahdunlim and Other Early Mesopotamian Rulers," *Studies in Honor of Benno Landsberger on His Seventy-Fifth Birthday, April 21, 1965* (AS 16; Chicago: University of Chicago Press, 1965), 365–73, esp. 365–67 (on "Sargon of Akkad"); idem, "Das Heilige Meer," in *"Wer ist wie du, Herr, unter den Göttern?" Studien zur Theologie und Religionsgeschichte Israels für Otto Kaiser zum 70. Geburtstag* (Göttingen: Vandenhoeck & Ruprecht, 1994), 66–67.
59. Or "lake"; cf. *CAD* Ḫ 198.
60. Also *AHw*, 1353–54 lists a number of nonmythological and nonpersonified uses of this term in Akkadian texts.
61. Lambert and Millard, *AH*, 96.
62. D. O. Edzard, *Hymnen, Beschwörungen und Verwandtes* (ARET 5; Rome: Missione Archeologica Italiana in Siria, 1984), 30. Note the Akkadian counterpart: *ēbir tiāmti* (VAB 4, 134, 45) cited in *AHw*, 1353. Also Edzard, "Meer. A," *RlA* 8.2.
63. Another example *ti-à-ma-du* in ARET 5, 4:I:6 may also refer to "sea" /tihāmatum/. Or "das Durcheinanderwimmeln" [tilḫam(a)tum] (Edzard, *Hymnen, Beschwörungen und*

text (MEE 4, 79:rev.III:8′–9′), the Sumerian ab-a is identified with *ti-ʾà-ma-tum* /tihām(a)tum/"sea."[64]

Hebrew

Thus, Ugaritic *thm(t)*, Akkadian *tiāmtum*, *tâmtum*, and Eblaite *ti-ʾà-ma-tum* all appear as a common noun, "sea" or "ocean," from their earliest attestation. If all these cognate terms can mean "sea" or "ocean" in the ordinary sense, there is no reason to think that Proto-Semitic *thm was not a common noun "sea/ocean." In light of the above, the Hebrew term *těhôm* also should normally be taken as a common noun.

Personification

This common noun, *tihām-* "ocean," is of course sometimes personified to become a divine name, as are nouns referring to other natural phenomena.

Akkadian

The term *tâmtu* is personified, if not deified, in the following Sumerian-Akkadian bilingual phrases:

a-ab-ba ama-dingir-re-e-ne-ke₄
ta-am-tu₂ um-mi DINGIR.MEŠ

the Sea, the mother of the gods. (von Weiher, Uruk 2, no. 5:7)[65]

However, "Tiamat" in *Enuma elish* is not simply a *personification* of the common noun *tiʾāmtu, tâmtu* "sea or ocean" but also a *deification* of the sea, morphologically "the absolute state of the noun."[66] Scholars such as H. Zimmern, though he took the Hebrew term *těhôm* as an Akkadian loanword, explained that *Tiamat* was a "mythische Personifikation" of *tiʾāmtu, tâmtu* "Meer."[67] It is reasonable to think with T. Jacobsen that the name Tiamat is an example of "common nouns used as proper names,"[68] being a personification

---

Verwandtes, 24–25) *ti-ʾà-ma-tum* (MEE 4, 12:V:10), which Pettinato, Dahood, and Zurro read as /tihāmat-um/, should be read as /tilʾam(a)-tum/. See M. Krebernik, "Zu Syllabar und Orthographie der lexikalischen Texte aus Ebla, Teil 2 (Glossar)," *ZA* 73 (1983), 3; Krecher, "Sumerische und nichtsumerische Schicht," 154. Cf. G. Pettinato, "I vocabolari bilingui di Ebla," in *LdE*, 270; E. Zurro, "La voz y la palabra," in *El Misterio de la Palabra: Homenaje de sus alumnos al profesor D. Luis Alonso Schökel* (ed. V. Collado and E. Zurro; Madrid: Ediciones Cristiandad, 1983), 34ff., esp. n. 84.

64. Cf. Krebernik, "Zu Syllabar und Orthographie . . . (Glossar)," 43; P. Fronzaroli, "The Eblaic Lexicon: Problems and Appraisal," in *SLE*, 151.

65. See *SD* A/2 141.

66. Alster, "Tiamat," *DDD*, 1635.

67. Zimmern, *AFw*, 44.

68. Jacobsen, "The Battle between Marduk and Tiamat," 105.

of the sea and its powers. The same position is taken by *AHw*, which lists
"Meer, See" as the ordinary meaning of this term.[69]

Ugaritic

In Ugaritic, *thm*, usually a common noun as noted above, appears also as a
divine name, once with a feminine ending -*t* and once without it, as *Thm* or
Thmt.[70] The ordinary word for sea, *yam,* is also used as the divine name Yam
in the myths.

A. Malamat observed that, "already in the Mari period (and possibly earlier), the Mediterranean Sea was conceived as a divinity." He explains that
"the cosmic force of the raging waters" was personified as Yam; this personification "originated in the nature and characteristics of the Mediterranean
Sea."[71] What Malamat argued is that the Northwest Semitic term *yamm* can
refer to the Mediterranean Sea, with personification and deification.

Rendsburg holds[72] that the differentiation between "sun" as an astronomi-
cal body and Sun as a deity might not be relevant to an ancient Near East-
erner. Be that as it may, these two were certainly distinguished as linguistic
entities in Akkadian, that is, *šamšu* and *Šamaš,* even though they might have
been coreferential. The ancients were certainly able to distinguish linguistically between nonpersonified and personified usage. There is no reason for us
to take the common noun *thm* as the result of the depersonification of the divine name *Tahām(at)u.*

Hebrew

In Hebrew, too, some common nouns are used metaphorically with personification in poetic texts. Sometimes they constitute a part of an idiom, as in
the case of the term *těhôm* in the phrase *těhôm rabbâ* "the great deep," which
is treated almost as a definite noun without an article (e.g., Gen 7:11, Isa
51:10, Amos 7:4).

It should be noted that several common nouns are used without the definite
article in Gen 1: for example, *těhôm, ḥošek, ʾôr, yôm, laylâ, rāqîă^ʿ,* and *šāmayim* (v. 8); others appear with the definite article: for example, *haššā-*

69. See also Edzard, "Meer. A," in *RlA* 8.1–3.
70. See below (p. 54). For new evidence (RS 1992.2004:29) of a divine *Thmt* in Ugaritic, see Alster, "Tiamat," *DDD,* 1637.
71. A. Malamat, "The Divine Nature of the Mediterranean Sea in the Foundation Inscription of Yahdunlim," in *Mari in Retrospect: Fifty Years of Mari and Mari Studies* (ed.
G. D. Young; Winona Lake, Ind.: Eisenbrauns, 1992), 211–15.
72. G. A. Rendsburg, "(A Review of) D. T. Tsumura, *The Earth and the Waters in
Genesis 1 and 2: A Linguistic Investigation* (JSOTSS 83). Sheffield: Sheffield Academic
Press, 1989," *JBL* 110 (1990), 138.

mayim, hāʾāreṣ (v. 1), *hāʾāreṣ* (v. 2), *hammāyim* (referring to *tĕhôm*), *hāʾôr* and *haḥōšek* (vv. 4–5), *hammāyim* (v. 6), and *hārāqîăʿ* (vv. 7–8). It should also be noted that the Hebrew article is sometimes omitted where one might expect it: for example, Gen 2:4, 14:19.[73] Thus, the lack of the definite article with *tĕhôm* is no proof of personification.[74] Furthermore, *tĕhôm* without the article appears either as part of an idiomatic expression or in poetic texts, which often omit the article.[75] The very existence of its plural form, *tĕhômôt* (or *tĕhōmôt, tĕhōmōt*) and its articular usage in Isa 63:13 and Ps 106:9 suggest that the term is a common noun in Hebrew, just as in Ugaritic, Akkadian, and Eblaite.

Finally, the term *tĕhôm* is not always a feminine noun, as some[76] assume in light of Akkadian Tiamat. In fact, it appears as a masculine noun with personification in Hab 3:10, a chapter where many scholars allege the existence of the so-called chaos motif.[77]

Thus, the lack of the definite article for *tĕhôm* in Gen 1:2 has nothing to do with personification or depersonification of the original term.

*tihām- and *yam-

While the common Semitic term *tihām- appears in West Semitic languages as Ugaritic *thm(t)* and Hebrew *tĕhôm(ôt)*, it is the term *ym* or *yām* that regularly denotes the sea in these languages. And *yamm- is typically a Northwest Semitic term (e.g., Ugaritic, Hebrew, Phoenician, Aramaic)[78] that appears in Akkadian only in the case of such borrowed words as *kusa-yāmi* (*AHw*, 514), though it has been borrowed into Egyptian as *ym*.[79]

---

73. See B. K. Waltke and M. O'Connor, *An Introduction to Biblical Hebrew Syntax* (Winona Lake, Ind.: Eisenbrauns, 1990), 250–51.

74. J. Skinner, *A Critical and Exegetical Commentary on Genesis* (2nd ed.; ICC; Edinburgh: T. & T. Clark, 1930), 17: "The invariable absence of the article (except with pl. in Ps 106:9, Isa 63:13) proves that it is a proper name."

75. See also Kaiser, *Die mythische Bedeutung des Meeres*, 115; Schmidt, *Die Schöpfungsgeschichte der Priesterschrift*, 81 n. 5.

76. E.g., Anderson, *Creation versus Chaos*, 39.

77. See below (ch. 10).

78. W. G. Lambert notes that "Yam 'Sea', Baal's enemy at Ras Shamra, does not so far appear in Eblaite documents under that name"; see "Old Testament Mythology in Its Ancient Near Eastern Context," *Congress Volume: Jerusalem, 1986* (VTSup 40; Leiden: Brill, 1988), 132.

79. A. Gardiner, *Egyptian Grammar* (2nd ed.; London: Oxford University Press, 1927, 1950), 422; *WÄS*, 1.78.

Hebrew *těhôm(ôt)* and *yām*

In Hebrew, *těhôm(ôt)* never appears as a term for the third element of the "heaven/earth/sea" structure of the universe. In this tripartite framework, expressed in Exod 20:11; Ps 146:6; Hag 2:6; Ps 96:11, 69:35, 135:6 (cf. Exod 20:4, Deut 5:8), it is *yām* "sea," not *těhôm*, that constitutes the third part. Likewise, it should be noted that in passages where the creatures in three divisions are mentioned—(1) "sea" – "heaven" – "earth" (or "field") in Gen 1:26, 28; Ezek 38:20; (2) "earth" (or "field") – "heaven" – "sea" in Gen 9:2, Hos 4:3, (Zeph 1:3), Ps 8:8–9, that is, "birds," "animals," and "fish"—the term for "sea" is always *yām*, never *těhôm(ôt)*.

These characteristics of *yām* correspond to those of Akkadian *apsû*, which constitutes the third part of the "three-decker universe," that is, heaven–earth–Apsû, represented by Anu, Enlil, and Ea (Enki) in the *Atra-Ḫasīs* epic (I i 7–18).[80]

At the same time, *yām* is used for the "sea" when it is contrasted with the "land" (*ʾereṣ*) in Gen 1:10 and other passages. In this regard, Hebrew *yām* corresponds to Akkadian *tiāmtum*, *tâmtum* "sea" as contrasted with *šadû* "land."[81] Thus, *yām* corresponds to *tiāmtu* as well as to *apsû* in the Akkadian language and means "sea" in a general sense.

On the other hand, in the relationship with the term *ʾereṣ* "earth," Hebrew *těhôm(ôt)* is hyponymous (Ps 71:20, 148:7; Prov 3:19–20; Gen 1:2) and, hence, what *těhôm(ôt)* refers to is included in what *ʾereṣ* refers to—that is, the *těhôm*-water is part of the earth.[82] Hebrew *těhôm(ôt)*, therefore, normally refers to the subterranean water, corresponding to Apsû of the Babylonian three earths, upper, middle, and lower, that is, the "abode of men–Apsû–underworld,"[83] though it can also refer to the "flood" caused by an overflow of the underground water (cf. *ʾēd* in Gen 2:6) as well as to a huge mass of waters, such as *těhôm* in Gen 1:2.

Ugaritic *thm(t)* and *ym*

In Ugaritic as well, the terms *thm* and *thmt* seem to have more specific meanings than *ym*, for, when paired with other terms, they always appear as

---

80. Cf. Lambert and Millard, *AH*, 166; W. G. Lambert, "The Cosmology of Sumer and Babylon," in *Ancient Cosmologies* (ed. C. Blacker and M. Loewe; London: Allen & Unwin, 1975), 58. Note that the Akkadian expression "the fish of the Apsû" (*nūnē apsî*) (*CAD* A/2 194–95) refers to the fish in lakes and rivers rather than the fish of the sea.

81. Cf. *AHw*, 1353–54.

82. See below, ch. 3, for a detailed discussion.

83. Lambert and Millard, *AH*, 166; Lambert, "The Cosmology of Sumer and Babylon," 59; Livingstone, *MMEW*, 87.

the second element. For example, *thm* appears in the word pair *ym – thm* (1.23 [52]:30), which denotes the waters, "sea" // "*thm*-water," near the abode of the god El. The same watery abode of El is described again by *nhrm – thmtm* (1.4 [51]:IV:22, 1.6:I:34 [49:I:6], 1.17 [2Aqht]:VI:48, 1.3 [ʿnt]:V:7 [15], 1.2:III [129]:4, 1.100 [607]:3): "(two) rivers" // "two *thmt*-waters." Finally, the term *thmt* signifies a watery area *on* or *in* the earth in *arṣ – thmt* (1.3 [ʿnt]:III:25 [22]), in which *thmt* is in hyponymous relation to *arṣ*.[84]

On the other hand, Ugaritic *ym* seems to have a meaning similar to Hebrew *yām* "sea" in a general sense. Its meaning seems to correspond to Sumerian a-ab-ba "body of water," which can stand for "lake" as well as for "sea,"[85] since its divine personification, Yam, is identified with ᵈA.AB.BA in the Akkadian pantheon list (RS 20.24) from Ugarit. This also suggests that Ugaritic *ym* has a much wider semantic field than *thm(t)*.

Akkadian *tiāmtum, tâmtum*

In *Enuma elish* the goddess Tiamat represents "sea" in contrast to the subterranean water-god Apsû, and these two waters, male and female, are described as being "intermingled as one" (line 5).[86] In the *Atra-Ḫasīs* epic, I i 15, S v 1, x rev. i 6, etc., Enki (Ea), the god of the sweet-water Apsû, is mentioned as having "the bolt, the bar of the sea" (*šigaru naḫbalu tiʾāmtim*).[87] This "bolt" may have kept Tiam(a)t(um) out—that is, kept its waters from mixing with the waters of Apsu, as they did at the beginning of *Enuma elish*.[88] Thus, in the cosmological traditions of Mesopotamia, there seems to have existed a distinction between the domain or area of the "sea" and that of the subterranean ocean.

---

84. See below, pp. 58–63.

85. See *SD* A/2 133. Cf. *AHw*, 1353.

86. On the initial section of *Enuma elish*, see H. L. J. Vanstiphout, "Enûma eliš, tablet i:3," *NABU* (1987/4), 52–53. He suggests that "in l. 5 the waters are to be taken as subject of the verb *iḫîqû* . . . 'to be intermixed' " (p. 53). It should be noted here that the verb does not even indirectly suggest the initial state of the primordial oceans as "chaotic." According to Lambert (oral communication), this "intermingling" of these two waters was orderly in itself, that is, "as one" (*ištēniš*). See pp. 72–74 on Ee I 1ff.

87. Lambert and Millard, *AH*, 166.

88. Jacobsen thinks that Enki's "connections with the salt water, the sea (a-ab-ba[k]), are at best peripheral, the sea playing a very small role in the life of Sumerians." Cf. T. Jacobsen, "Sumerian Mythology: A Review Article," *JNES* 5 (1946), 145; S. N. Kramer, "(Review of) H. and H. A. Frankfort, John A. Wilson, Thorkild Jacobsen, William A. Irwin, *The Intellectual Adventure of Ancient Man: An Essay on Speculative Thought in the Ancient Near East*. The University of Chicago Press, Chicago, 1946, VI, 401pp.," *JCS* 2 (1948), 43 n. 6, and 48 n. 16.

However, the use of terms for these waters was not always as precise as modern people expect; for example, the term *tiāmtum, tâmtum* could refer to both salt- and sweet-waters, that is, "sea" and "lake," in Akkadian;[89] and in southern Babylonia, river water is known to be salty. In Sumerian, it seems, there is no evidence that the sweet and the bitter sea were distinguished. For example, at Ebla[90] the Sumerian a-ab is identified once with *tihām(a)tum* "sea" and once with *bù-la-tum* (/buʾratum/ "well, cistern") in Eblaite.[91] In other words, in Sumerian "the sea [= a.ab.ba] was conceived as a single body of water."[92] It may be that the Mesopotamian Tiamat came to be understood as the representative of only the salt-water sea, particularly as the enemy of the storm-god Marduk in *Enuma elish*, in keeping with the "earlier" Canaanite or "northern" tradition[93] of conflict between the storm and the sea (*ym*).[94]

Regarding the earlier meaning of the Akkadian *tiāmtum* or *tâmtum*, Albright suggested that it was "'the subterranean fresh-water sea', Sumerian ab-zu (Acc. *apsû*)," "as shown by Hebrew and Ugaritic."[95] However, it is more reasonable to think that Ugaritic *thm(t)* and Hebrew *tĕhôm(ôt)* experienced a narrowing down of the semantic field of the Proto-Semitic term *tihām-, the meanings and uses of which are reflected in Eblaite *tihām(a)tum* and Akka-

---

89. *AHw*, 1353: "Meer, See." Note that both Akkadian *tiāmtum, tâmtum* and Sumerian a-ab-ba could be used for "lake" as well as for "sea." See *SD* A/2 133; Jacobsen, "Sumerian Mythology: A Review Article," 145 n. 28; Albright, *Yahweh and the Gods of Canaan*, 81 n. 102.

90. *VE* 1343′ = MEE 4, 79:rev.III:8′–9′.

91. Note that Akk. *būrtu* can refer to the "source" of a river as well as to "well, cistern"; cf. *CAD* B 335–38, esp. 338. However, Akk. *būrtu* normally corresponds to Sum. PÚ, never to a.ab.ba. Cf. Krebernik, "Zu Syllabar und Orthographie der lexikalischen Texte aus Ebla, Teil 2 (Glossar)," 43; Fronzaroli, "The Eblaic Lexicon: Problems and Appraisal," 148.

92. M. H. Pope, *El in the Ugaritic Texts* (VTSup 2; Leiden: Brill, 1955), 63; Kramer, "(Review of) H. and H. A. Frankfort . . . The Intellectual Adventure of Ancient Man . . . , 1946 . . . ," 43 n. 6. Cf. Jacobsen, "Sumerian Mythology: A Review Article," 139–40.

93. See above (n. 22, p. 39).

94. However, McCarter's following comment is not convincing: "In contrast to the Mesopotamian situation, the distinction between salt and sweet waters is not important in Northwest Semitic cosmologies. Hence, for example, 'sea' and 'river' may comprise a poetic pair" (P. K. McCarter, "The River Ordeal in Israelite Literature," *HTR* 66 [1973], 405 n. 6). For one thing, even in Mesopotamia the distinction between the salt-water and sweet-water is not always made clear lexically. Moreover, *tâmtu* and *apsû* appear as a word pair also in Akk. literary texts. For example, in Lambert, *BWL*, 136–37, line 172; 128–29, lines 37–38. Cf. J. C. de Moor and P. van der Lugt, "The Spectre of Pan-Ugaritism," *BO* 31 (1974), 15.

95. Albright, *Yahweh and the Gods of Canaan*, 81 n. 102; also idem, "Contributions to Biblical Archaeology and Philology," *JBL* 43 (1924), 369.

dian *ti'āmtum* and its Sumerian counterpart ab-a or a-ab-ba,[96] "sea, ocean," which refers both to the salt-water sea and to the sweet-water ocean. In other words, the Akkadian *tiāmtum, tâmtum* probably has a much wider semantic field than its West Semitic cognate terms, Hebrew *tĕhôm(ôt)* and Ugaritic *thm(t)*, which became hyponymous to *'ereṣ/arṣ*, as noted above. Thus Hebrew *tĕhôm* semantically corresponds more closely to *apsû* than to *tiāmtum*, though it corresponds morphologically to the latter.

In light of the above discussion, one can conclude with B. Alster that "the parallels are not sufficiently specific to warrant the conclusion that *Enūma eliš* was the source of the biblical account."[97]

Excursus:
A "Canaanite" Dragon Myth in Genesis 1:2?

While in *Enuma elish* the motif of the conflict of a storm-god with the sea is integrated into the story of the creation of the cosmos, in Ugaritic the Baal-Yam conflict is not related to the "primordial struggle in connection with the creation" at all. Unfortunately, despite this, the theme of *Chaoskampf* tends to be presupposed in any cosmogonic story in the ancient Near East. For example, J. Day suggested that the term *tĕhôm* in the Genesis story can be traced back to an earlier Canaanite dragon myth that he thinks is related to the creation theme. The term *tĕhôm* is then understood as a depersonification of the original mythological divine name in Canaanite.

However, is there a Canaanite dragon myth in the background of Gen 1:2, as Day assumes?

Tĕhôm: Not "Canaanite"

According to Day, "both *tĕhôm* and Tiamat are derived from a common Semitic root,"[98] and the fact that Ugaritic *thm* (cf. 1.100:1) is "comparable" to Hebrew *tĕhōm* supports "the view that the OT term is Canaanite."[99] However, if the Hebrew term is common Semitic, there is no reason why it should be considered especially "Canaanite," rather than Hebrew.

Also, as noted above, Hebrew *tĕhôm* is a morphologically older form[100] than the probable Ugaritic form, *tahāmu. If the Hebrew term were a loanword from this "Canaanite" divine name and had been depersonified subsequently,

---

96. See *SD* A/2 133–42.
97. Alster, "Tiamat," *DDD*, 1638.
98. Day, *God's Conflict with the Dragon and the Sea*, 50.
99. Ibid., 7.
100. For other words that follow the sound change *qital > qĕtōl, see W. R. Garr, "Pretonic Vowels in Hebrew," *VT* 27 (1987), 140.

one would expect the Hebrew term to be something like *tāhôm*. Therefore it is very unlikely that Hebrew *tĕhôm* derived from a Canaanite divine name.

Tĕhôm: Not Depersonification

Day explains that *tĕhôm* in Gen 1:2 is "not a divine personality hostile to God," and it is used "to denote the impersonal watery mass which covered the world before God brought about the created order." However, he holds that the term did denote "a mythical personality" a long time ago and suggests that the term *tĕhôm* is a depersonification of the original Canaanite divine name.

However, as noted above, since the Hebrew term *tĕhôm* is most likely a common noun in origin, like the Ugaritic, Akkadian, and Eblaite terms, there is no strong reason to take *tĕhôm* as a depersonification of the original divine name.

The Canaanite Sea-Dragon[101] *Is Yam, Not Taham*

In the attested Ugaritic texts, a personified divine *thm(t)* "ocean" appears only twice: once in an incantation text entitled the "Serpent Charm," the term appears as a compound divine name "Heaven-and-Ocean" *šmm-w-thm* (1.100 [607]:1), and once in a multilingual vocabulary list it appears as *Tahāmatu* (= *thmt; Ug.* 5, 137:III:34″), the female counterpart of the god "Heaven" *Ša-mūma* (= *šmm*). Not only is the frequency of the name low, but the types of literature in which the name appears are limited. In particular, the divine name Tahām does not appear at all in the major myth, the Baal Cycle, or in other mythological texts. Nor is the term *šmm* ever found personified in Ugaritic myths.

It is especially noteworthy that the goddess[102] *Thm(t)* never appears in the conflict scenes, where the sea-dragon, the antagonist of Baal, is Yam/Nahar. There is no evidence in the available Ugaritic mythology that *Thm(t)* was a

---

101. Ugaritic scholars are unsettled about whether the sea-god Yam and the serpent/dragon are identified with each other. On an iconographical basis, Williams-Forte argues for the god Mot, rather than Yam, as the serpent in Ugaritic mythology; cf. E. Williams-Forte, "The Snake and the Tree in the Iconography and Texts of Syria during the Bronze Age," in *Ancient Seals and the Bible* (ed. L. Gorelick and E. Williams-Forte; Malibu, Calif.: Undena, 1983), 18–43. However, note the critical remarks by W. G. Lambert, "Trees, Snakes and Gods in Ancient Syria and Anatolia," *BSOAS* 48 (1985), 435–51; D. Collon, "(A Review of) L. Gorelick and E. Williams-Forte (eds.), *Ancient Seals and the Bible.* Malibu, Undena, 1983 (= The International Institute for Mesopotamian Area Studies, Monographic Journals of the Near East: Occasional Papers on the Near East Vol. 2/1)," *AfO* 33 (1986), 99–100.

102. The short form *thm*, without a feminine ending *-t*, in the compound name *šmm-w-thm* is probably feminine. For a divine couple forming a compound name, see *ltpn. w qdš* (1.16:I [125]:11, 21–22).

helper of Yam or that the storm-god Baal ever fought with the ocean-goddess *Thm(t)*. The term does not appear even as a common noun in the context in which the enemies of Baal and Anat are listed (KTU 1.3 ['nt]:III:38ff. [35ff.], 1.5 [67]:I:1ff.). Therefore it is almost certain that, even if there should be an undiscovered myth[103] in which a "creator"-god had to fight a Canaanite sea-dragon, the dragon would not be Tahām.

Baal Is Not a Creator-God

Though Baal is the most active deity in Ugaritic mythology, he is not a creator-god. There is "no suggestion in the Baal Cycle that, for instance, like Marduk . . . he constructed the firmament out of the defeated monster's carcass."[104] As de Moor notes, "Baal is able to repair (*bny*) the broken wings of birds in a miraculous way (1.19:III:12ff. [1Aqht:118ff]), but except for the lightning (1.3:III:26, par.) he does not create anything new."[105] Baal is thus simply a "preserver and savior" of the cosmos.[106]

In Ugaritic mythology the creator-god is the god El.[107] El is the creator of mankind; he is called "Father of mankind" (*ab adm*). He is a progenitor of various gods and goddesses. For example, in 1.23 [52]:30ff. El appears as the father of a divine pair, Šḥr and Šlm, as well as of the "Good Gods" (*ilm n'mm*).[108] Furthermore, if Šnm is a divine name, El's title *ab šnm* "Father of Šnm" suggests that he is also the father of another god.

Another epithet of El, *bny bnwt* "creator of creatures" (KTU 1.6 [49]:III:5, 11; 1.4 [51]:II:11, III:32; 1.17 [2Aqht]:I:24 [25])[109] also suggests that El is the creator-god. De Moor notes similar epithets in Akkadian, *bānu nabnīt* and *bān binûtu*, both meaning "creator of creatures," for the Babylonian god Ea,[110] who is also described as having created "land and sea" in an Akkadian

---

103. Canaanite myths are also attested outside of Ugaritic literature, for example, an Egyptian version of "Astarte and the Tribute of the Sea" (translated by J. A. Wilson, in *ANET*, 17–18) and a story of El-kunirsha in a Hittite version, "El, Ashertu and the Storm-God" (translated by A. Goetze in *ANET*, 1969³, 519; now by G. Beckman in *CS* 1.149); see also H. A. Hoffner, Jr., "The Elkunirsa Myth Reconsidered," *RHA* 23 (1965), 5–16.

104. J. C. L. Gibson, "The Theology of the Ugaritic Baal Cycle," *Or* 53 (1984), 212 n. 16.

105. De Moor, "El, the Creator," 186.

106. M. S. Smith, "Interpreting the Baal Cycle," 320; idem, *The Ugaritic Baal Cycle* (VTSup 55; Leiden: Brill, 1994), 1.83.

107. See Smith, "Interpreting the Baal Cycle," 320 n. 43 for bibliography.

108. Note that the text carefully distinguishes the birth of Šḥr and Šlm from that of the *ilm n'mm*. Cf. my *Ugaritic Drama of the Good Gods* (Ph.D. diss,, Brandeis University, 1973), 22, 56; idem, "Kings and Cults in Ancient Ugarit," in *Priests and Officials in the Ancient Near East* (ed. Kazuko Watanabe; Heidelberg: Carl Winter, 1999), 228–36.

109. Gordon, *UT* 19.483.

110. De Moor, "El, the Creator," 182–83. See below, pp. 132–133.

ritual text (Racc. 46, 30).[111] Therefore, as de Moor says, no other Ugaritic
god besides El, the head of the pantheon,[112] qualifies for the role of creator of
the cosmos.[113]

Thus, "in Ugaritic mythology creation and the subduing of the monsters of
chaos are functions divided among different gods, notably El and Baal."[114] It
should also be noted that even outside of Ugaritic literature El is considered a
Canaanite creator-god: for example, El-kunirsha (= El, *qn ʾrṣ* "creator of the
earth").[115]

Yām Does Not Appear in Genesis 1:2

Finally, if the Genesis account were the demythologization of a Canaanite
dragon myth, one might expect to find in the initial portion of the account the
term *yām* "sea," the counterpart of the Ugaritic sea-god Yam, who corresponds to the god ᵈA.AB.BA (= *Tiʾāmat* or *Ayabbu*?[116]), in the official pantheon list from ancient Ugarit.[117] However, the term *yām* does not appear in
Gen 1 until v. 10, where its plural form, *yammîm*, appears as the antithesis of
"land" (*ʾereṣ*).

In light of the above discussions, it is difficult to assume that, behind Gen
1:2, an earlier Canaanite dragon myth existed—such as a myth in which a
creator-god won victory over a chaos-dragon, for example, Yam, Nahar,
"dragon," or "serpent."[118] As Harland recently confirms, "Whilst such echoes
may be present in both Psalms and Isaiah (e.g., Isa 51:9ff.) it does not necessarily follow that they are also found in Gen. 1."[119] There is no evidence that
the term *tĕhôm* in Gen 1:2 is the depersonification of an original Canaanite
deity, as Day assumes.[120] The Hebrew term *tĕhôm* is simply a reflection of the

---

111. *AHw*, 1353.

112. However, the creator-god need not be head of the pantheon. Enki/Ea was never
that. On the similarity between El and Ea, see below, pp. 130–139.

113. De Moor, "El, the Creator," 186.

114. Korpel and de Moor, "A Review of J. Day, *God's Conflict with the Dragon and
the Sea*, 1985," 244. For a detailed discussion, see ch. 8.

115. *KAI* 2.42–43. Cf. H. Otten, "Ein kanaanäischer Mythus aus Boğazköy," *MIOF* 1
(1953), 125–50; H. A. Hoffner, Jr., "The Elkunirsa Myth Reconsidered," *RHA* 23 (1965),
5–16. See also P. D. Miller, Jr., "El, the Creator of Earth," *BASOR* 239 (1980), 43–46, esp.
43–44.

116. See above, n. 50, on *ayabba* "sea" in Amarna Akk.

117. RS 20.24:29 // KTU 1.47 [UT 17]. Cf. *Ug.* 5, 58.

118. On the conflict theme in the poetic texts of the Old Testament, see chs. 8–11.

119. P. J. Harland, *The Value of Human Life: A Study of the Story of the Flood (Genesis 6–9)* (VTSup 64; Leiden: Brill, 1996), 95.

120. In his review of the first edition of my book, J. Day (*Expository Times* 1990, 211)
contends that my view "savours of special pleading," though the burden of proof is on his

common Semitic term *tihām- "ocean," and there is no relation between the Genesis account and the so-called *Chaoskampf* mythology.

---

shoulders for claiming a Canaanite mythological background for Gen 1:2. Compare his review with the more positive reviews by J. C. L. Gibson, *SOTS Book List*, 1990, 94; G. A. Rendsburg, *JBL* 110 (1990), 136–38; R. W. L. Moberly, *JTS* 42 (1991), 451–52, J. E. Rybolt, *CBQ* 53 (1991), 312–13, D. Mathias, *BZ* 36 (1992), 119–20, etc. See also ch. 8 (below).

3

*The Earth-Waters-*rûaḥ *in Genesis 1*

In the previous chapters, the etymology and meaning of terms such as *tōhû wābōhû* and *tĕhôm* were discussed in order to clarify the initial states of the earth and the waters described in Gen 1:2. However, the semantic investigation of these terms is not complete unless we elucidate the "meaning relationship" between the terms *'ereṣ* and *tĕhôm* in the present context.

In the following sections,[1] I will first discuss some theoretical grounds for investigating the relationship between the meanings of these two terms. Then I will examine the nature of the relationship between the referents of these terms, noting other biblical examples, in order to understand correctly the relationship between the "bare" (*tōhû wābōhû*) earth and the *thm*-waters in Gen 1:2. Last, I will discuss the exegetical problems of *rûaḥ 'ĕlōhîm* and its relationship with the earth and the waters.

The "Hyponymous" Word Pair '*rṣ–thm(t)*

For a semantic discussion of any word pair, it is not enough to analyze the meaning of each word etymologically. The meaning relation between paired words of this kind should be investigated thoroughly and placed adequately in their context.

Traditionally, the meaning relation of paired words has been treated in terms either of synonymy or of antonymy. However, for some word pairs it might be profitable to take note of the meaning relation "hyponymy," which is sometimes explained as "inclusion"[2]—that is, what term "A" refers to *includes* what term "B" refers to. However, the term "hyponymy" is preferred to "inclusion," for it is "a relation of sense which holds between lexical items" rather than a relation of "reference"—that is, "entities which are named by

---

1. An earlier version of this chapter was published as "A 'Hyponymous' Word Pair: *'rṣ* and *thm(t)*, in Hebrew and Ugaritic," *Bib* 69 (1988), 258–69.

2. C. R. Taber, "Semantics," in *IDB Supplement* (Nashville: Abingdon, 1976), 803–4 lists four types of "conceptual relationships between the sense of different forms": (1) synonymy and similarity, (2) inclusion, (3) antonymy, and (4) polar opposition.

lexical items."[3] "Inclusion" thus entails "hyponymy," but "hyponymy" can be used also for a relationship between terms that have no "reference."[4]

Our term *hyponym* therefore means that "sense" [A] of the more general term "A" (e.g., "fruit") completely includes "sense" [B] of the more specific term "B" (e.g., "apple"), and hence what "A" refers to includes what "B" refers to. In other words, when the referent {B} of the term "B" is a part of, or belongs to, referent {A} of the term "A," we can say that "B" is *hyponymous* to "A."[5] Thus, *ymn* "right hand" is hyponymous to *yd* "hand," because what the term *ymn* refers to is normally a part of what the term *yd* refers to.[6]

This approach can guide the interpretation of debated terms. In the case of a word pair such as Hebrew *'ereṣ* – *těhôm(ôt)* and Ugaritic *arṣ* – *thm(t)*, it is not easy to determine the meaning relationships, for the specific meaning of each term is not transparent in some instances, and the referent of *'ereṣ* or *arṣ*, for example, varies from "earth," "land," and "ground" to "underworld," depending on the context.[7] However, by a careful analysis of the nature of collocations, or word associations, within a parallelism, one should be able to determine the meanings of paired terms.

For example, in the Ugaritic text KTU 1.3 [ʿnt]:III:24–25 [21–22]:[8]

tant[9] . *šmm* . *ʿm* . *arṣ*
thmt . *ʿmn* . *kbkbm*

---

3. Cf. J. Lyons, *Introduction to Theoretical Linguistics* (Cambridge: Cambridge University Press, 1968), 453ff.

4. The same meaning relation between paired words has been noted by A. Berlin, "Parallel Word Pairs: A Linguistic Explanation," *UF* 15 (1983), 11; idem, *The Dynamics of Biblical Parallelism* (Bloomington: University of Indiana Press, 1985), ch. 4.

5. This meaning relation should be also noted for parallelism. Berlin's "particularizing" parallelism and Cline's "parallelism of greater precision" are "hyponymous" parallelism in my terminology. Cf. D. J. A. Clines, "The Parallelism of Greater Precision: Notes from Isaiah 40 for a Theory of Hebrew Poetry," in *Directions in Biblical Hebrew Poetry* (ed. E. R. Follis; Sheffield: JSOT Press, 1987), 77–100, esp. 96 n. 2.

6. The analysis of meaning relations in terms of "meaning inclusion" (= hyponym) and "meaning exclusion" (= antonym) would be extremely profitable for the semantic discussions of word pairs, for, set in the context of poetic parallelism, the two terms seem to acquire a closer association to each other than in an ordinary prose context.

7. Note also that "earth" (*erṣetu*) in Akkadian can mean both "earth" in the English sense and "underworld." In the ancient Babylonian cosmology, there are three "earths": (1) the abode of men, (2) the Apsû, and (3) the underworld. Cf. W. G. Lambert, "The Cosmology of Sumer and Babylon," in *Ancient Cosmologies* (ed. C. Blacker and M. Loewe; London: Allen & Unwin, 1975), 59; Lambert and Millard, *AH*, 166.

8. See *CS*, 1.251.

9. For this term, see D. Pardee, "The New Canaanite Myths and Legends," *BO* 37 (1980), 277.

The murmur of the heavens to the earth
Of the deeps to the stars. (Gordon, *PLMU*, 79),

there are six possible word pairs: (1) *šmm – arṣ*, (2) *šmm – thmt*, (3) *šmm – kbkbm*, (4) *arṣ – thmt*, (5) *arṣ – kbkbm,* and (6) *thmt – kbkbm*. Three combinations of these word pairs are possible.

(1) šmm – arṣ and (6) thmt – kbkbm

Grammatically the most natural analysis of the parallel structure would be as follows:

a–b–c–d

b'–c'–d'

The words *šmm* (b) and *arṣ* (d) as well as *thmt* (b') and *kbkbm* (d'), are connected syntagmatically, that is, grammatically, to each other by the preposition *ʿm(n)* "to" (c // c'). Because *šmm* "heaven" (b) and *arṣ* (d) are a universally acknowledged "antonymous" pair,[10] the latter term should mean "earth," which refers to everything under heaven, rather than "land" or anything else. The relationship between *thmt* (b') and *kbkbm* "stars" (d')[11] may also be taken as contrastive, based on this parallelistic structure, though *thmt* and *kbkbm* are not a "parallel" word pair in this context. Both pairs, (1) and (6), are thus "antonymous" (or "exclusive") and the two elements of these pairs refer to two opposite directions—that is, "heaven" ↔ "earth" and "oceans" ↔ "stars."

---

10. Among Semitic languages, Heb. has *šāmayim – ʾereṣ* and *ʾereṣ – šāmayim*; Ug., *šmm – arṣ* and *arṣ-w-šmm* (cf. *RSP* 1, II 71 [p. 126f.], II 208 [p. 190], II 554 [p. 356]); Akk., *šamû – erṣetu* as well as Phoen. *šmm – ʾrṣ* and Aram. *šmyʾ – ʾrqʾ / ʾrʿʾ*. Cf. Y. Avishur, *Stylistic Studies of Word-Pairs in Biblical and Ancient Semitic Literatures* (AOAT 210; Neukirchen-Vluyn: Neukirchener Verlag, 1984), 603. In non-Semitic languages, Sum. has AN – KI; Japanese, following Chinese, *ten – chi*, etc. See pp. 65–68 on *bipartite* cosmology. It is interesting to note that, in a NA mythological explanatory text, the initial state of the world described in Ee, lines 1–2,

> When the heavens above were not (yet) named,
>> the earth (*ammatum*) below had not (yet) been given a name
>> (*CAD* N/1 34),

is explained as "when heaven and earth were not created" (*kī šamê erṣeti lā ibbanûni*). Cf. Livingstone, *MMEW*, 79ff. Note that the term *ammatum* seems to refer to the "earth" in general (cf. *CAD* A/2 75; *AHw*, 44), which is in contrast to "heaven" rather than "underworld" (cf. M. Hutter, "*ammatu*: Unterwelt in Enuma Eliš I 2," *RA* 79 [1985], 187–88). For discussions about the translation "earth," see H. L. J. Vanstiphout, "*Enûma eliš*, tablet i:3," *NABU* (1987/4), 53. R. Labat also translates the term "la Terre" in R. Labat et al., *Les religions du Proche-Orient asiatique* (Paris: Fayard/Denoël, 1970), 38.

11. Note the similar pair *tĕhômôt* "oceans" // *šĕḥāqîm* "clouds" in Prov 3:20.

(2) šmm – thmt and (5) arṣ – kbkbm

In a parallelistic structure such as this, the "vertical" correspondence rather than the "horizontal" adjacency[12] may be the dominant factor that "activates word pairs." Thus, *šmm* (b) may better be understood as closely related paradigmatically to *thmt* (b′) rather than to *arṣ* (d).

This "antonymous" word pair, *šmm* "heaven" and *thmt* "ocean(s)," is certainly a traditional one, similar to *šmm* "heaven" and *ym* "sea"[13] in the ancient Northwest Semitic languages, as is suggested by the divine couple *šamuma* (= *šmm*) "Heaven-god" and *tahāmatum* (= *thmt*)[14] "Ocean-goddess" in Ugarit, which corresponds to the Sumerian AN and his female counterpart ANTUM in a multilingual vocabulary text (*Ug.* 5, 137:III:33″–34″). This divine couple appears also as the compound divine name *šmm w thm* "Heaven-and-Ocean" (KTU 1.100 [607]:1) like the divine name *ltpn. w qdš* (1.16:I [125]: 11, 21–22), though the goddess *thm* here lacks the feminine ending *t*.[15]

Hebrew *tĕhôm* also stands in an "antonymous" relationship to *šāmayim*.[16] For example, in Gen 7:11, where the beginning of the Great Flood is mentioned, "the springs of the great deep" (*maʿyĕnōt tĕhôm rabbâ*) and "the floodgates of the heavens" (NIV) (*ʾărubbōt haššāmayim*) appear as an "exclusive" pair. The same pair with a slight variation also appears in Gen 8:2, where the closing of *maʿyĕnōt tĕhôm* and *ʾărubbōt haššāmāyim* is mentioned. Also in Prov 8:27, *šāmayim* is set in contrast to *tĕhôm* in a parallelism,[17] and in Gen 49:25 and Deut 33:13, the same antonymous pair appears in parallelism. *Šāmayim* and *tĕhômôt*, the plural form of *tĕhôm*, also appear as an antonymous pair in Ps 107:26.

The other two words, *arṣ* (d) and *kbkbm* "stars" (d′), can also be taken paradigmatically as a word pair like Ugaritic *arṣ – ʿrpt* "cloud" in KTU 1.4:V:6ff.[51:V:68ff.]. However, the "earth-and-stars" combination is rather unusual.

---

12. For a grammatical discussion of the problem of adjacency and dependency in poetic parallelism, see my "Literary Insertion, A×B Pattern, in Hebrew and Ugaritic: A Problem of Adjacency and Dependency in Poetic Parallelism," *UF* 18 (1986), 351–61.

13. Cf. *RSP* 1, II 555 (p. 356). For an Akkadian example, see J. C. de Moor and P. van der Lugt, "The Spectre of Pan-Ugaritism," *BO* 31 (1974), 22.

14. For a discussion of the vocalization of this term and its etymology, see the previous chapter, p. 43.

15. Hebrew *tĕhôm*, without the ending -t, appears both as a masculine noun (e.g., Hab 3:10) and as a feminine noun (e.g., Gen 49:25, Deut 33:13). See above (ch. 2).

16. Cf. *RSP* 1, II 560 (pp. 358–59); Avishur, *Stylistic Studies of Word-Pairs*, 407.

17. See ch. 8 on this passage.

(3) šmm – kbkbm and (4) arṣ – thmt

Since the referential directions between "heaven" and "earth" in the first colon and between "oceans" and "stars" in the second colon are opposite, that is,

$$šmm \text{ [above]} \Rightarrow arṣ \text{ [below]}$$
$$thmt \text{ [below]} \Leftarrow kbkbm \text{ [above]},$$

a chiastic structure has been suggested for this parallelism in spite of the for-
mal and grammatical pattern given above.[18]

The parallelistic structure based on this referential correspondence would
be as follows:

$$a–b–c–d$$
$$d'–c'–b'$$

In this structural understanding, *šmm* "heaven" (b) and *kbkbm* "stars" (b') are
considered to be as closely related to each other as a "parallel" word pair. This
word pair often appears both in Ugaritic and Hebrew,[19] and its meaning relation is hyponymous, since what the term *kbkbm* refers to is a part of what the
term *šmm* refers to. Hence, two terms are juxtaposed in a construct chain as
kôkěbê haššāmayim (Gen 22:17, etc.), and their order cannot be reversed.

As for the other pair,[20] Dahood thought that the chiastic arrangement
would "favor the meaning 'netherworld' " for *arṣ*, which is parallel with *thmt*
"depths."[21] The meaning relation of these two words is apparently understood
as synonymous, and the "conditional" meaning, "netherworld," has been sug-

---

18. M. Dahood, "Ugaritic–Hebrew Syntax and Style," *UF* 1 (1969), 25; *RSP* 1.127, followed by W. A. van der Weiden, *Le Livre des Proverbs: Notes philologiques* (Rome: Pontifical Biblical Institute, 1970), 37; M. K. Wakeman, *God's Battle with the Monster*
(Leiden: Brill, 1973), 101; A. R. Ceresko, "The A:B::B:A Word Pattern in Hebrew and
Northwest Semitic with Special Reference to the Book of Job," *UF* 7 (1975), 74; J. S. Kselman, "The Recovery of Poetic Fragments from the Pentateuchal Priestly Source," *JBL* 97
(1978), 163; W. G. E. Watson, "Strophic Chiasmus in Ugaritic Poetry," *UF* 15 (1983), 263:
"Essentially, the chiasmus here is *semantic.*"

19. Cf. *RSP* 1, II 282 (pp. 225–26) and II 556 (p. 357); Avishur, *Stylistic Studies of
Word-Pairs*, 566.

20. See ibid., 353–54.

21. Cf. M. J. Dahood, "Northwest Semitic Philology and Job," in *The Bible in Current
Catholic Thought* (ed. J. L. McKenzie; New York: Herder & Herder, 1962), 58; idem, *Prov-
erbs and Northwest Semitic Philology* (Rome: Pontifical Biblical Institute, 1963), 52; idem,
"Ugaritic–Hebrew Syntax and Style," 25; idem, *Psalms II* (AB 17; Garden City, N.Y.: Dou-
bleday, 1968), 176, followed by van der Weiden, *Le Livre des Proverbs*, 37; J. J. Scullion,
"Some Difficult Texts in Isaiah cc. 56–66 in the Light of Modern Scholarship," *UF* 4 (1972),
122, esp. n. 85; M. H. Pope, *Job* (3rd ed.; AB 15; New York: Doubleday, 1973), 91; Ceresko,
"The A:B::B:A Word Pattern in Hebrew and Northwest Semitic," 74. Note, however, that

gested for *arṣ*. However, since the meaning relation of *kbkbm* (b′) and *šmm* (b) is hyponymous in this parallelistic structure, it seems that the meaning relation of *arṣ* (d) and *thmt* (d′) is also hyponymous. In other words, what the term *thmt* refers to may be taken as a part of what the term *arṣ* refers to.[22] And the term *arṣ,* which is contrasted with *šmm* in the first colon, most likely refers to everything that is under heaven.

This hyponymous relationship may be supported by OT examples. For example, Ps 71:20 has the construct chain *tĕhōmôt hā'āreṣ,* which suggests that the term *tĕhōmôt* is hyponymous to rather than synonymous with *'ereṣ.*[23] In other words, what *tĕhōmôt* refers to is a part of what *'ereṣ* refers to. Kraus takes *'ereṣ* as referring to the "netherworld" and suggests that *tĕhōmôt hā'āreṣ* here refers to "the Chaos-water of the netherworld through which the dead pass to Sheol."[24] It should be noted that, unlike Dahood, Kraus takes the two terms as hyponymous. However, "Chaos-water of the netherworld" would not fit the present context of the Ugaritic text, because *thmt* is contrasted with *kbkbm* "stars."

Therefore, the meaning relation in both pairs, *šmm* ("heaven") – *kbkbm* ("stars") and *arṣ* ("earth") – *thmt* ("deeps"), is hyponymous.

"Heaven" – "Earth" – "Sea":
A Tripartite Division of the World

Now, it is important to note that in the Old Testament *tĕhôm(ôt)* never appears as a term for "sea(s)" in a tripartite description of the world, that is, "heaven–earth–sea,"[25] though *tĕhôm(ôt)* is sometimes closely associated with

---

not everyone who suggests the chiastic structure interprets *arṣ* as "the nether world," as does Dahood. For example, Wakeman and Watson interpret it as "earth"; see above.

22. In the immediately following text, KTU 1.3 ['nt]:III:26–28, where the term *arṣ* is again contrasted with *šmm*, and "men" (*nšm*) is parallel with "folk of the land" (*hmlt arṣ*), the term *arṣ* means "earth/land," not "the netherworld."

23. M. K. Wakeman, "The Biblical Earth Monster in the Cosmogonic Combat Myth," *JBL* 88 (1969), 317 n. 18 holds that, because *'ereṣ* and *tĕhôm* are "synonymous," they "come to form a hendiadys" in Ps 71:20. However, this construct chain is not a hendiadys, though a hendiadys may be broken up to constitute a construct chain. Moreover, her argument for synonymity based on a simple "substitution" in the case of the meaning relation between *hā'āreṣ* and *tĕhōmôt* (Ps 77:17, 19, etc.) or *hārîm* and *tĕhōmōt* (Exod 15:8) is not convincing.

24. H.-J. Kraus, *Psalmen*, vol. 2: *Psalmen 60–150* (5th ed.; Neukirchen-Vluyn: Neukirchener Verlag, 1978), 653: "die unterirdischen Chaosgewässer, durch die der Tote zur שאול eingeht."

25. L. I. J. Stadelmann, *The Hebrew Conception of the World* (AnBib 39; Rome: Pontifical Biblical Institute, 1970), 9–10 lists Ps 135:6 and 148:1–7 as examples of the *šmym* –

yām.[26] The best known passage is Exod 20:11, where "the heaven," "the earth," and "the sea," as well as "all that is in them" are mentioned. The first three of these elements seem to be fixed in a Hebrew expression, since they are virtually the same in several passages, with variants for the fourth, as shown in the following list:

Exod 20:11	*haššāmayim* : *hāʾāreṣ* : *hayyām*	: *kol-ʾăšer-bām*
Ps 146:6	*šāmayim* : *ʾāreṣ* : *hayyām*	: *kol-ʾăšer-bām*
Hag 2:6	*haššāmayim* : *hāʾāreṣ* : *hayyām*	: *heḥorābâ*
Ps 96:11	*haššāmayim* : *hāʾāreṣ* : *hayyām*	: *mĕlōʾô*
Ps 69:35	*šāmayim* : *ʾāreṣ* : *yammîm*	: *kol-rōmēś bām*
Ps 135:6	*baššāmayim* : *bāʾāreṣ* : *bayyammîm*	: *kol-tĕhômôt*
Neh 9:6	*haššāmayim* : *hāʾāreṣ* : *hayyammîm*	

In Ps 146:6, the expression is the same as in Exod 20:11 except for the definite articles. In Hag 2:6 and Ps 96:11, the same pattern, "heaven"–"earth"–"sea," is mentioned before the fourth element, "the dry land" (*heḥorābâ*) or "all that is in it" (*mĕlōʾô*). In Pss 69:35 and 135:6, the third item is a plural form of *yām*, and the fourth element, as in 96:11, consists of additional items that are related only to the "sea(s)"—that is, *kol-rōmēś bām* "all that moves in them" and *kol-tĕhômôt* "all oceans," respectively. While in 96:11 and 69:35 the additional phrases are hyponymous to *yam(mîm)*, in 135:6 *kol-tĕhômôt* is either synonymous or hyponymous to it.[27]

Exodus 20:4 and Deut 5:8 describe these three divisions as *baššāmayim mimmaʿal* "in heaven above," *bāʾāreṣ mittāḥat* "on the earth beneath," and *bammayim mittaḥat lāʾāreṣ* "in the waters below" (lit., "beneath the earth"). The creatures in three divisions—"birds," "animals," and "fish"—are never mentioned in this order but in the following two different orders: (1) "sea"–"heaven"–"earth" (or "field") in Gen 1:26, 28; and Ezek 38:20; (2) "earth" (or

---

ʾrṣ – thwmwt scheme and Prov 8:27–32 and Ps 33:6–8 as examples of the *šmym – tbl – thwm(wt)* scheme. However, in Ps 135:6, *tĕhōmôt* is not the third term but the fourth (see below), and in 148:1–7, *tĕhōmôt* refers to a part of the earth (see below, pp. 66–67). In Prov 8:27–32, *tĕhôm* corresponds to *šāmayim* only in v. 27, and the term *tēbēl* appears only in v. 31. Note that the relationship between the earth and the sea is described in terms of *ʾāreṣ* and *yām* in v. 29. Psalm 33:8, which mentions *hāʾāreṣ* // *yōšĕbê tēbēl*, should be treated separately from vv. 6–7. J. M. Vincent, "Recherches exégétiques sur le Psaume XXXIII," *VT* 28 (1978), 447 recognizes in Ps 33:5–7 a triad, *hāʾāreṣ* (v. 5), *šāmayim* (v. 6), and *mê hayyām* (v. 7), "terre–ciel–mer."

    26. Cf. *RSP* 1, II 236 (pp. 204–5).

    27. Y. Avishur takes (*bā*)*ʾāreṣ* and (*kol-*)*tĕhômôt* in Ps 135:6 as a parallel word pair like those in Ps 148:7; Prov 3:19–20, 8:27–29; and Gen 1:2, as well as in Ps 71:20 and Sir 16:18. Cf. Avishur, *Stylistic Studies of Word-Pairs*, 353.

"field")–"heaven"–"sea" in Gen 9:2, Hos 4:3 (Zeph 1:3), and Ps 8:8–9. However, in none of the passages cited above does the term *těhôm(ôt)* appear.

Thus, in the framework of the tripartite understanding of the world, it is *yām* "sea," not *těhôm* "ocean," that constitutes the third part and thus corresponds, though not exactly, to the Apsû[28] of the Babylonian scheme of "heaven/earth/ Apsû." On the other hand, Hebrew *těhôm(ôt)*, which is hyponymous to Hebrew *'eres*—hence, what *těhôm(ôt)* refers to—is a part of the "earth" (*'eres*), probably corresponding to Apsû in the Babylonian scheme of three levels of "earth," that is, "abode of men/Apsû/underworld."[29]

"Heaven" – "Earth":
A Bipartite Division of the World

Psalm 148

1. Praise the LORD.
   Praise the LORD from the heavens,
   　praise him in the heights above.
2. Praise him, all his angels,
   　praise him, all his heavenly hosts.
3. Praise him, sun and moon,
   　praise him, all you shining stars.
4. Praise him, you highest heavens
   　and you waters above the skies.
5. Let them praise the name of the LORD,
   　for he commanded and they were created.
6. He set them in place forever and ever;
   　he gave a decree that will never pass away.

7. **Praise the LORD from the earth,**
   　you great sea creatures and all ocean depths,
8. lightning and hail, snow and clouds,
   　stormy winds that do his bidding,
9. you mountains and all hills,
   　fruit trees and all cedars,
10. wild animals and all cattle,
    　small creatures and flying birds,
11. kings of the earth and all nations,
    　you princes and all rulers on earth,

---

28. On Apsû as a place where fish live, see *CAD* A/2 194–95. See also below, pp. 135–136.

29. See above, p. 59 n. 7.

12. young men and maidens,
        old men and children.
13. Let them praise the name of the LORD,
        for his name alone is exalted;
        his splendor is above the earth and the heavens.
14. He has raised up for his people a horn,
        the praise of all his saints,
        of Israel, the people close to his heart.
    Praise the LORD. (NIV)

This psalm seems to treat the universe bipartitely, and the relation between
'ereṣ and *tĕhôm(ôt)* here seems to be hyponymous. Let us look at v. 7.

halĕlû 'et-YHWH min-hā'āreṣ
tannînîm wĕkol-tĕhōmôt
        Praise the Lord from the earth,
        you great sea creatures and all ocean depths. (NIV)

In this context, the ocean depths are part of the earth from which the Lord is
to be praised, and hence the term *tĕhōmôt* is hyponymous to the term *hā'āreṣ*.

In this passage, Dahood took the meaning relation of *haššāmayim* (v. 1)
and *hā'āreṣ* (v. 7) as polar opposition and suggested that *'ereṣ* here too should
mean "the netherworld," "the opposite extreme" of heaven.[30] However, it
should be noted that, while vv. 2–4 mention items in the heavens, vv. 7bff.
have no items in the netherworld. On the other hand, Dahood's own comment
points out a problem for his assumption that the psalmist here has a tripartite
understanding of the universe: "What does appear singular is the fact that the
psalmist dedicates only one verse to the subterranean beings, after having
given six verses to celestial bodies, and reserving the next seven for terrestrial
creatures."[31]

As the literary studies of Ps 148 show, the psalm should be divided into
two structural sections, vv. 1–6 and vv. 7–14.[32] While the first section refers
to various items in the heavens, the second mentions those under the heavens.
This literary structure suggests that in the present context the psalmist seems
to use the term *'ereṣ* in the sense of everything under heaven, including the
sea.[33] It is contrasted with "heaven" in the "exclusive" word pair, and both

---

30. M. Dahood, *Psalms III* (AB 17A; Garden City: Doubleday, 1970), 353.

31. Ibid., 353–54.

32. E.g., D. R. Hillers, "A Study of Psalm 148," *CBQ* 40 (1978), 328; P. Auffret, *La sa-
gesse a bâti sa maison* (Orbis biblicus et orientalis 49; Fribourg, 1982), 385–404.

33. Cf. Stadelmann, *The Hebrew Conception of the World*, 3. He includes the sea in the
"second level of the world" in the "three-leveled structure of the world," heaven – earth –

tannînîm and *tĕhōmôt* are treated as belonging to the earth.[34] Thus, in Ps 148, the psalmist's understanding of the world is bipartite, rather than tripartite.

The "logic"[35] that allows the psalmist to include in the second section several meteorological phenomena, such as "storm-wind" (v. 8) and "flying birds" (v. 10) as well as *tannînîm* and *tĕhōmôt* (v. 7), may look strange at first glance. But it is the fact that they are all terrestrial rather than celestial.

The psalmist's logic can be supported by the "logic" of the ancient Semites, as illustrated by *Enuma elish* which, according to Lambert, combines two originally separate cosmologies, one that is bipartite (heaven–earth)[36] and is "obtained in this story by the splitting of Tiamat's body," and another that is tripartite (heaven–earth–Apsu), the three levels represented by Anu, Enlil, and Ea (Enki), respectively.[37]

bipartite	heaven	
	earth	
tripartite	heaven	: Anu
	earth	: Enlil
	Apsû	: Ea (Enki)

The latter cosmology of "a three-decker universe" can also be identified in the *Atra-Ḫasīs* epic (I i 7–18).[38] This tripartite cosmology seems to have been transformed into a bipartite form, because the author of *Enuma elish* seems to locate Enlil in Ešarra (between the heavens and the Apsû), "a lower heaven,"[39] thus appointing Anu and Enlil to the heavens (i.e., "the heaven" and "a lower heaven") and Marduk and Ea to the earth (i.e., "Esagila" and "Apsu").[40]

---

underworld; see his pp. 154ff. However, no discussion of the term *tĕhôm(ôt)* is offered in section C, which deals with the problem of the sea.

34. Note also that in KTU 1.23 [52]:62–63 the "sea" (*ym*) in an ordinary sense is hyponymous to the "earth" (*arṣ*), which is parallel with *šmm*, though Dahood suggested here also the translation of "nether world" for *arṣ* (cf. *RSP* 1, II 64 [p. 122–23]).

35. Hillers, "A Study of Psalm 148," 328: "We must not demand perfect logic of the psalmist's cosmology; we must permit him to list dragons and deeps, fire and storm-wind under the rubric 'earth.'" Note also Auffret's explanation: "the term at the same time is able to include both the deep and the land" ["il s'agit là à la fois de l'abîme et de la terre"] (p. 396) as a criticism of Dahood's position.

36. See above, p. 60, on the word pair "heaven" and "earth" in various languages.

37. Lambert, "The Cosmology of Sumer and Babylon," 58.

38. Cf. Lambert and Millard, *AH*, 166.

39. Lambert, "The Cosmology of Sumer and Babylon," 58.

40. On four divisions of the world, see Livingstone, *MMEW*, 79ff. However, in a text published by R. Borger (*BO* 30 180:72 ii 4), the triad gods, Anu, Enlil, and Ea, are understood as controlling "heaven and earth" (AN *u* KI), i.e., the entire universe; see *CAD* M/1 228; J. Bottéro, *Mythes et Rites de Babylone* (Geneva: Slatkine / Paris: Champion, 1985), 300f.

Enuma elish
heaven	: Anu
Ešarra (= "a lower heaven")	: Enlil
Esagila (= "earth")	: Marduk
Apsû	: Ea

Therefore, it is not surprising to note that in the psalmist's logic the term *hā-ʾāreṣ*, which is in contrast to *haššāmayim*, refers to everything under the heavens, including storm and oceans. In other words, the terms *hāʾāreṣ* and *haššāmayim* are mutually exclusive within the framework of bipartite cosmology. They are not in a polar opposition, such as "heaven" ↔ "underworld," which Dahood assumed for this psalm.

For the meaning of *tĕhōmôt* in Ps 148:7, Kraus suggests either "the Cosmic Flood (Akk. Tiamat), which lies under the earth," or simply "the Sea."[41] However, in Mesopotamian cosmology, the waters under the earth are called Apsu rather than Tiamat. Because *ʾereṣ* in this verse most likely means "earth" rather than "underworld," its hyponym *tĕhōmôt* in the present context would mean "oceans" in an ordinary sense, like Ugaritic *thm*, Akkadian *tiāmtum*, and Eblaite *tihām(a)tum*.

Proverbs 3

19.	*Yhwh bĕḥokmâ yāsad-ʾāreṣ*	(A)
	kônēn šāmayim bitbûnâ	(B)
20.	*bĕdaʿtô tĕhômôt nibqāʿû*	(A′)
	ûš(ĕ)ḥāqîm yirʿăpû-ṭāl	(B′)

19. Yahweh by wisdom founded <u>the earth</u>,
    he established <u>the heavens</u> by understanding;
20. by his knowledge <u>the deeps</u> were divided,
    and <u>the clouds</u> drop down the dew.

Now, in Prov 3:20, the term *tĕhômôt* stands in antonymous parallel relationship to *šĕḥāqîm* "clouds." Similarly, in the preceding verse (v. 19) the term *ʾāreṣ* is put in direct opposition to the term *šāmayim*. Moreover, *šāmayim* and *šĕḥāqîm* often appear as a word pair in Hebrew (cf. Deut 33:26; Isa 45:8; Jer 51:9; Job 35:5; Ps 36:6, 57:11, 108:5), and such correspondences as *šĕḥāqîm* = *niblê šāmayim* (Job 38:37) and *šĕḥāqîm* = *daltê šāmayim* (Ps 78:23) indicate that *šĕḥāqîm* ("clouds") is hyponymous to *šāmayim,* as *kbkbm* "stars" is hyponymous to *šmm* "heaven" in KTU 1.3 [ʿnt]:III:24–25 [21–22] and in bib-

---

41. Kraus, *Psalmen*, 1143: "die Urfluten (akkad. Tiâmat), die unter der Erde ruhen"; "des Meer."

lical passages.[42] Therefore, here also the term *tĕhômôt* should be taken as hyponymous to *ʾāreṣ*; and thus, the deeps are part of the earth.

A Flooding of the Subterranean Waters?

The meaning relationship between *hāʾāreṣ* and *tĕhôm* in Gen 1:2 also seems to be hyponymous. The text reads:

1. *bĕrēʾšît bārāʾ ʾĕlōhîm ʾēt haššāmayim wĕʾēt hāʾāreṣ*
2. *wĕhāʾāreṣ hāyĕtâ tōhû wābōhû*
   wĕhōšek ʿal-pĕnê tĕhôm
   wĕrûaḥ ʾĕlōhîm mĕraḥepet ʿal-pĕnê hammāyim

Here *tĕhôm* "ocean" is a part of *hāʾāreṣ,* because the term *hāʾāreṣ,* which constitutes an antonymous or exclusive word pair together with *haššāmayim* in Gen 1:1,[43] must refer to everything under the heaven.[44] In other words, the cosmology in vv. 1–2 is bipartite, as in Ps 148, rather than tripartite, describing the entire world in terms of "heavens and earth."

It should be noted that in v. 2 the term *tĕhôm*, rather than *yām* "sea," appears. The term *yām* would constitute the third division of the tripartite universe, "heaven/earth/sea." On the other hand, the "ocean" (*tĕhôm*) and its "waters" (*hammāyim*) are never treated as the third division of the tripartite cosmology in the Old Testament, as noted above.

What this hyponymous word pair, *hāʾāreṣ* // *tĕhôm*, refers to is described in this passage by another pair of expressions, *tōhû wābōhû* // *ḥōšek*,[45] "not yet" normal—that is, "not yet productive and inhabitable and without light."[46]

---

42. See above, p. 62.

43. Sometimes even today it is suggested that Gen 1:1 is a later addition (by P) to the older source, which begins with v. 2. However, if this were the case, it would be strange that a Hebrew creation narrative should begin with the present word order of v. 2, *waw* + NP VP, without any temporal description. For a useful summary of various positions on the interpretation of the initial verses, see G. J. Wenham, *Genesis 1–15* (WBC 1; Waco, Tex.: Word, 1987), 11–13.

44. It is not necessary to posit that *hāʾāreṣ* has different meanings in v. 1 and v. 2 (cf. ibid., 15: "Compounded with 'heaven' it designates the whole cosmos, whereas in v. 2 it has its usual meaning 'earth'"). J. Sailhammer, "Exegetical Notes: Genesis 1:1–2:4a," *TJ* 5 (1984), 77, interprets Gen 1:1–2:4a as "an introduction to the author's view of the covenant at Sinai" and understands *ʾereṣ* (v. 2) as "land," that is, the *land* of Israel. However, a shift in focus from the totality of the universe ("heaven and earth") in v. 1 to the "earth" in v. 2 does not necessarily result in a change of meaning for the term *hāʾāreṣ*.

45. Verse 2a and v. 2b constitute a chiastic parallelism; cf. Kselman, "The Recovery of Poetic Fragments," 164 n. 13. See above, p. 29.

46. See above, pp. 33–35.

However, the water (*hammāyim*) of *tĕhôm* seemingly covered all the "earth" like the Deluge, as vv. 6ff. suggest. In other words, the earth = *tĕhôm*-water relationship in v. 2 was an extraordinary one. One might thus explain the initial situation visually as darkness being over the *tĕhôm*-water, which covered the entire earth at that time, as a great flood.

rûaḥ '*ĕlōhîm*[47]

DARKNESS

tĕhôm-water

THE EARTH

It should be noted again that the term *hā*'*āreṣ* here refers to everything under the heavens (cf. v. 1), not the land in opposition to the seas (*yammîm*; see v. 10). In other words, the "earth" is viewed vertically from above, as in Ps 104:6, which refers to God's creation of the earth as follows:

> You covered it with the deep as with a garment; the waters stood above the mountains. (NIV)

On the other hand, Prov 8:29 and Ps 104:9 describe the earth horizontally.

> when he [= God] gave the sea its boundary so the waters would not overstep his command, and when he marked out the foundations of the earth (Prov 8:29)

> You set a boundary they [= the waters] cannot cross; never again will they cover the earth. (Ps 104:9)

In a normal situation the ocean is under control and may not pass its limit (i.e., "its edge"[48] *pîw* in Prov 8:29 or "boundary" *gĕbûl* in Ps 104:9), as is also suggested by an Akkadian expression "the bolt, the bar of the sea" (*šigaru naḫbalu ti*'*āmtim*) in the *Atra-Ḫasīs* epic.[49] As Millard aptly notes, "If

---

47. See below; see also ch. 7 on the relationship between God and the water.

48. Dahood, "Proverbs 8, 22–31: Translation and Commentary," 513.

49. AH I i 15–16 (also cf. S v 1; x rev. i 6, 10; x rev. ii 4, 11, 18, 34). Note that in this context the term *ti*'*āmtim* is not personified but has an ordinary sense. Cf. Lambert and Millard, *AH*, 166. See the previous chapter, p. 45.

A similar flooding situation is mentioned in several Akkadian texts. For example, a Sumerian–Akkadian bilingual hymn to Nergal says:

ta a.ab.ba   ki an e.da.ab.uś
minâ ša tâmtu erṣeta umallakum
With what from the Sea has one filled the earth?

Cf. J. Böllenrücher, "Gebete und Hymnen an Nergal," *LSS* 1/6 (1904), 43, 46 ("womit man das Meer, die Erde für dich gefüllt hat?"); *CAD* M/1 176.

a parallel is to be sought in the biblical narrative it may be found in Genesis 1:9."[50]

A similar but not identical earth–water relation in the context of creation is also described in a bilingual version of the *Creation of the World by Marduk* on a tablet from the Neo-Babylonian period, where the initial state of the world is described both negatively and positively. In lines 1–9 the state of "not yet" is explained in concrete terms:[51]

1. <u>A holy house, a house of the gods</u> in a holy place, <u>had not been made</u>;
2. A reed had not come forth, a tree had not been created;
3. A brick had not been laid, a brick mould had not been built;
4. A house had not been made, a city had not been built;
5. A city had not been made, a living creature had not been placed (therein);
6. Nippur had not been made, Ekur had not been built;
7. Uruk had not been made, Eanna had not been built;
8. The *Apsû* had not been made, Eridu had not been built;
9. <u>A holy house, a house of the gods</u>, its dwelling, <u>had not been made</u>.

Note that line 1 and line 9 constitute an *inclusio*, thus grouping this negative "not yet" description[52] as a unified entity.[53] Then, in lines 10–11, the same initial state of the world is described positively as follows:

---

50. A. R. Millard, "A New Babylonian 'Genesis' Story," *TynBul* 18 (1967), 7. There is no hint of a battle with the sea in this Akkadian expression, though it implies that "the sea is an unruly element in need of control."

51. Translation is by A. Heidel, *The Babylonian Genesis* (2nd ed.; Chicago: University of Chicago Press, 1951), 62. Also cf. L. W. King, *The Seven Tablets of Creation*, Vol. 1: *English Translations, etc.* (London: Luzac, 1902). 130–33; R. W. Rogers, *Cuneiform Parallels to the Old Testament* (2nd ed.; New York: Abingdon, 1912, 1926), 48; Bottéro, *Mythes et Rites de Babylone*, 303.

52. For another myth that describes the initial situation in "not yet" terms, see the so-called "Eridu Genesis," UET VI. 61. lines 1'–17', though this myth as now preserved has no description of a watery beginning like *Enuma elish* and others. Cf. T. Jacobsen, "The Eridu Genesis," *JBL* 100 (1981), 513–29; P. D. Miller, Jr., "Eridu, Dunnu, and Babel: A Study in Comparative Mythology," *HAR* 9 (1985), 233, 237, 244; T. Jacobsen, *The Harps That Once . . . : Sumerian Poetry in Translation* (New Haven: Yale University Press, 1987), 145–50. See also below, pp. 78–80, on Gen 2:5ff.

53. Bottéro notes that the order Ekur (of Enlil) – Eanna (of Anu) – Eridu (of Ea) is the reverse of their antiquity. In other words, the oldest city, Eridu, is mentioned last. See Bottéro, *Mythes et Rites de Babylone*, 305. For the antiquity of Eridu, see also W. W. Hallo, "Antediluvian Cities," *JCS* 23 (1970), 65–66.

10. All the lands were sea;
11. the spring in the middle of the sea was (nothing more than) a gutter.[54]

After this *double* description of the original state, the "creation" of the world is finally mentioned in lines 12ff.:

12. Then Eridu was made, Esagila was built. . . .
14. Babylon was made, Esagila was completed.

Though "the lands" *mātātu* (10) is not a cognate of Hebrew *ʾereṣ* in Gen 1:2, the overall discourse structure between this Neo-Babylonian "creation" story and Genesis 1 is similar:

1. *Setting*: a negative description—the earth/land was "bare" (i.e., unproductive and uninhabited) and was "not yet" the same as it is now;
2. *Setting*: a positive description—the "ocean-water" (*tâmtum // tĕhôm*) was covering the whole earth/land (*mātātu // ʾereṣ*);[55]
3. *Event*: (Then) the earth/land became as it is now.

However, while there are structural similarities between these two stories, there is also a clear distinction in theme and purpose between the two. In the Neo-Babylonian story, particular cities, such as Eridu and Babylon, are treated as the first created things. On the other hand, no particular city names appear as God's creation in the story of Gen 1, because in the Genesis stories, unlike the Mesopotamian stories, "the building of the cities . . . is a purely human enterprise" (cf. Gen 4:17, 10:10–12, 11:1–9).[56]

Excursus:
Structure of *Enuma elish* I 1–9

The discourse structure of the initial section of *Enuma elish*, Ee I 1–9, may be analyzed as follows:[57]

---

54. *napḫar mātātu tâmtuma // īnu ša qereb tâmti rāṭumma.* See *SD* A/2 141. Cf. L. W. King, *The Seven Tablets of Creation*, 1.132. Note also J. Bottéro's translation, "Tous les territoires ensemble n'étaient que Mer! Lors (donc) que le contenu de (cette) Mer (ne) formait (encore qu')un fossé (?)," in *Mythes et Rites de Babylone*, 303.

55. Lines 10 and 11 are sometimes interpreted as "le Chaos originel," like *Enuma elish*; cf. ibid. It is clear from the context that *tâmtum* "sea" is not "the enemy of creation" but simply a term for "a mass of water" that is not personified, as is Tiamat in *Enuma elish*. But, even in *Enuma elish*, the mingling of Apsû and Tiamat was *orderly*; see p. 51 n. 86.

56. Miller, "Eridu, Dunnu, and Babel," 239.

57. The translation (with emphases mine) given here is based on Heidel's 1951 version, but is revised in light of later developments. Cf. Heidel, *The Babylonian Genesis* (2nd ed.), 18. For details, see H. L. J. Vanstiphout, "*Enûma eliš*, tablet i:3," *NABU* (1987/4), 52–53; W. L. Moran, "*Enūma elîš* I 1–8," *NABU* (1988/1), 15–16.

1. When above, the heaven was <u>not</u> named;
2. below the earth was <u>not</u> called by (its) name,
3. But as for[58] Apsû the primeval, their begetter,
4. (and) the craftsman,[59] Ti'āmat, she who gave birth to them all,
5. their waters[60] were being mingled[61] together;
6. But <u>no</u> pasture land had been formed; <u>no</u> reed marsh was seen;[62]
7. When <u>none</u> of the gods had (yet) appeared;
8. they had <u>not</u> been called by (their) names; (their) destinies had <u>not</u> been fixed,
9. (Then) were the gods created within them (*ibbanû-ma ilānū qiribšun*).

Here, as Moran notes, in lines 1–8 predication is through nominals, statives, and the "durative" verb *iḥiqqū*, all of which are "an apt description of event-less flux." Certainly, seven negatives, which may well mark the completeness

---

58. Moran, ibid., 15–16 notes that the *-ma* of *Apsû-ma* "can only mark the grammatical predicate." This "(existential) predicate" *-ma* may be used here for topicalization like the Ugaritic existential particle *w* ("and"). For a similar understanding of its syntax, see King, *The Seven Tablets of Creation*, 1.3.
59. Cf. *CAD* M/2 197. Cf. Heidel, *The Babylonian Genesis* (2nd ed.), 18, who takes Mummu as a separate entity in this line and translates: Mummu (and) Ti'âmat, she who gave birth to them all" (cf. Ee I 30, etc.).
60. As Vanstiphout notes, A.MEŠ-*šunu* "their waters" is to be taken as nominative in light of the variant reading *mu-ú-šu-nu*.
61. Moran suggests that the Akk. verb *i-ḫi-qu-ú* should be taken as *iḫiqqū* with a dura-tive sense, rather than as *iḫīqū*.
62. Cf. *AHw*, 1223. Moran, following Held and Wilcke, suggests the verb *šê'u* "to mat, stuff, lay out" and translates the line as follows: "No solid sward was with thickets matted." However, taking *gipāra* and *ṣuṣâ* as resultatives (objects) of the verbs, line 6 might be bet-ter translated literally as follows:

(But) into a pasture land they (= their waters) had not yet congealed;
nor as a marshland were they recognizable.

Note that the verb *kaṣāru* can be used with a liquid such as "oil" or "blood" (e.g., Ee VI 5 cf. *CAD* E 342) in the sense of "to congeal" or "to coagulate"; the same verb is used with "cloud" in Ee V 49; cf. *AHw*, 456f.; *CAD* K 260, 262; B. Landsberger and J. V. Kinnier Wilson, "The Fifth Tablet of *Enuma Eliš*," *JNES* 20 (1961), 158–59. Cf. also R. Labat, "Les origins et la formation de la terre dans le poème Babylonien de la création," *Studia Biblica et Ori-entalia*, vol. 3: *Oriens Antiquus* (AnBib 12; Rome: Pontifical Biblical Institute, 1959), 214.
Note that the (marsh)land is understood as a product of the waters in this myth; cf. "Water came first, and gave birth to Earth" (W. G. Lambert, "Kosmogonie," *RlA* 6 [1980–83], 218–22); see below, p. 110, on the creation of a marshland in Gen 2:6–7. In an Egyp-tian creation myth, Atum-Re is described as having begun his creation "upon a primeval hillock arising out of the abysmal waters, Nun" (J. A. Wilson, "Another Version of the Cre-ation by Atum," *ANET*, 3–4).

of "absence and negation," in lines 1–2 and 6–8 are used to describe the initial situation of the universe as "not yet," like other "creation" myths, as noted above. In lines 3–5, the same initial situation is described positively, as in lines 10–11 of the Neo-Babylonian version of the *Creation of the World by Marduk*. Then, "only in line 9, with the creation of the gods, do we meet a punctive, and it is fronted. With *ibbanû-ma* we enter time and narrative sequence."[63]

To summarize, the overall structure of *Enuma elish* I 1ff. is as follows:

1. *Setting*: a negative description—lines 1–2, 6–8 (seven times "not yet")
2. *Setting*: a positive description—lines 3–5 ("waters")
3. *Event*: "(Then) were the gods created . . ." (line 9).

Thus, the discourse structure of the initial section of this "creation" epic is similar to that of the Neo-Babylonian "creation" story and Genesis 1. However, there is a difference in theme and purpose. While the latter two stories are concerned with the initial state of the earth or land, the initial section of *Enuma elish* is concerned with the creation of gods and goddesses, and no reference is made to the earth–water relationship, for the primeval waters, Apsu and Tiamat, in *Enuma elish* are understood as having existed without any relationship with the "earth."

In Gen 1, the earth in v. 2 is simply a part of the created cosmos ("heaven and earth" in v. 1) and refers to everything under the heaven, including the subterranean waters. However, the earth was totally covered by waters and the dry land was "not yet" formed (*or* seen) until v. 9, where God said: "Let the waters from under the heaven be gathered to one place and let the dry land appear." Unlike the cosmology in *Enuma elish* and other ancient myths, the land in Gen 1:9–10 was not a product of the primeval water, hence a part of the water; it was a product of divine fiat by which God gathered the waters from under the heaven "to one place," that is, as "seas," which are a part of the earth.

Exegetical Problems of rûaḥ ʾĕlōhîm

Whether one translates *rûaḥ ʾĕlōhîm* "the wind of God" or "the spirit of God" depends on whether one recognizes in v. 2c "a description of precreation chaos" or "a reference to divine creative potency" (W. P. Brown).[64] G. von Rad translates *rûaḥ ʾĕlōhîm* "storm of God" (i.e., "terrible storm"), be-

---

63. Moran, "*Enūma eliš* I 1–8," 15.

64. W. P. Brown, *Structure, Role, and Ideology in the Hebrew and Greek Texts of Genesis 1:1–2:3* (SBLDS 132; Atlanta: Scholars Press, 1993), 75–77.

cause he sees here the description of chaos, "that peculiar intermediate state between nothingness and creation."[65] T. C. Vriezen holds a similar view. According to him, *rûaḥ ʾĕlōhîm* refers to the wind proceeding from God, "the power emanating from God which keeps the waters of the *Tehom* in check."[66]

However, as discussed above, the chaos theory should be rejected for the following reasons:

1. The phrase *tōhû wābōhû* has nothing to do with chaos; it simply refers to the "desolate and empty" state of the earth. It describes the initial state of the earth as "not yet" normal, as we know.
2. Linguistically, the borrowing of *tiʾāmat* into *tĕhôm* is unlikely, for a loss of /h/ when a word is borrowed is the norm, not the other way around. Both Akkadian *tiʾāmat* and Hebrew *tĕhôm* are derived from the common Semitic *tīhām- ("great amount of water"). Their similarity is due to their common origin, not to a mythological borrowing;
3. While Akkadian *tiʾāmat(um)* refers to "sea," the Hebrew word *tĕhôm* normally means "underground water." In Hebrew, the term for "sea" is *yām*, which appears first in Gen 1:10;
4. The motif of a "storm-sea battle" in *Enuma elish* is not Mesopotamian in origin but was probably introduced from the west.

Contextually, *ʾĕlōhîm* of *rûaḥ ʾĕlōhîm* (2c) refers to "God," who created the universe ("the heaven and the earth" as merismus) in v. 1. In v. 2c he is about to get involved positively in the universe as *rûaḥ*. Because God's creative action was performed by his utterance in v. 3, v. 2c seems to describe a situation in which God's words were *not yet* uttered;[67] in other words, God's breath was not articulated as a voice to pronounce his creative word but was ready to get involved in such creative actions. Hence, *rûaḥ ʾĕlōhîm* (v. 2c) is best translated "the breath of God."[68]

---

65. G. von Rad, *Genesis: A Commentary* (rev. ed.; OTL; Philadelphia: Westminster, 1972), 49–50.

66. T. C. Vriezen, "Ruach Yahweh (Elohim) in the Old Testament," in *Biblical Essays 1966* (= *OTWSA* 9), 56.

67. See ch. 1 on the "not yet" pattern in Gen 1:2 and 2:5.

68. Van Wolde explains that "even God is not yet the creator God, but is an indefinable spirit of God moving upon the face of the waters." She sees God in Gen 1:2 "not yet as a speaking, seeing, dividing, creating, generating or name-giving אלהים." See E. van Wolde, "Facing the Earth: Primaeval History in a New Perspective," in *The World of Genesis: Persons, Places, Perspectives* (ed. P. R. Davies and D. J. A. Clines; JSOTSup 257; Sheffield: Sheffield Academic Press, 1998), 25. However, it is more suitable for the immediate context to take God only as "not yet speaking."

Therefore, T. C. Vriezen's view that *rûaḥ ʾĕlōhîm* (1:2) had no creative function, and "this function is taken over completely by the word of God"[69] in 1:3ff. is to be rejected. To the contrary, a close relationship between "God's breath" and his creative action is attested also in Ezek 37:1–14; Ps 104:30, 33:6; as well as in Gen 2:7.

1. Ezek 37:14

    I will put my Spirit (*rûaḥ*) in you and you will live, and I will settle you in your own land. Then you will know that I the LORD have spoken, and I have done it, declares the LORD. (NIV)

2. Ps 104:30

    When you send your Spirit (*rûaḥ*), they are created, and you renew the face of the earth. (NIV)

3. Ps 33:6

    By the word of the LORD were the heavens made, their starry host by the breath (*rûaḥ*) of his mouth. (NIV)

4. Gen 2:7

    the LORD God formed the man from the dust of the ground and breathed into his nostrils the breath of life (*nišmat ḥayyîm*), and the man became a living being. (NIV)

In all of these passages, it was God's *rûaḥ*, or the equivalent word *nĕšāmâ*, who created (Ps 104:30, 33:6) or animated (Ezek 37:14, Gen 2:7) human beings and other creatures. In the same manner, God's *rûaḥ* in Gen 1:2 was ready to become engaged in his creative action. God uttered his word, "Let there be light!" and there was light (v. 3).

---

69. Vriezen, "Ruach Yahweh (Elohim) in the Old Testament," 56.

4

The Earth in Genesis 2

It is clear that the general situation of the earth described in Gen 2:5–6 is that of a "not-yet-productive" earth. Some scholars have interpreted this non-productive earth as a "dry chaos," J's equivalent of P's "watery chaos in 1:2." For example, Schmidt thinks that Gen 2:5 describes *Chaos* before *Schöpfung* in 2:7.[1] However, according to our analysis in the previous chapters, the initial situation of the earth and its relationship with the *tĕhôm*-water in Gen 1:2 has nothing to do with a "watery chaos" or a *chaotic* situation as such; therefore, explaining the dry earth in Gen 2:5–6 as a "dry chaos" appears to be totally misleading. In the following sections, we will deal with the structure of the Hebrew text of Gen 2:5–6 as a whole and discuss the etymological problems of such terms as *ʾēd* and *ʿēden*.

The Earth in a Bare State

Judging from the discourse analysis of the narrative story in Gen 2:4–4:26, 2:4 as a whole is a temporal description ("when"), while 2:5–6 is a SETTING for the first stated EVENT (*wayyîṣer YHWH ʾĕlōhîm* "the LORD God formed") in 2:7, just as 1:1 is a temporal description ("In the beginning") and 1:2 is a SETTING for the first stated EVENT (*wayyōʾmer ʾĕlōhîm* "God said") in 1:3.[2] As in 1:2, the SETTING in 2:5–6 describes the initial state of the earth, which is

1. W. H. Schmidt, *Die Schöpfungsgeschichte der Priesterschrift: Zur Überlieferungsgeschichte von Genesis 1:1–2:4a und 2:4b–3:24* (2nd ed.; Neukirchen-Vluyn: Neukirchener Verlag, 1967), 197.

2. For a brief summary of discourse analysis with bibliographies, see W. R. Bodine, "Linguistics and Philology in the Study of Ancient Near Eastern Languages," in *"Working with No Data": Semitic and Egyptian Studies Presented to Thomas O. Lambdin* (ed. D. M. Golomb; Winona Lake, Ind.: Eisenbrauns, 1987), 51–54; cf. F. I. Andersen, *SBH*, 18–19. On the Genesis stories, see idem, "On Reading Genesis 1–3," in *Backgrounds for the Bible* (ed. M. O'Connor and D. N. Freedman; Winona Lake, Ind.: Eisenbrauns, 1987), 137–50; R. E. Longacre, "The Discourse Structure of the Flood Narrative," in *Society of Biblical Literature 1976 Seminar Papers* (ed. G. MacRae; Missoula, Mont.: Scholars Press, 1976), 235–62; idem, *Joseph: A Story of Divine Providence: A Text Theoretical and Textlinguistic Analysis of Genesis 37, and 39–48* (Winona Lake, Ind.: Eisenbrauns, 1989; 2nd ed., 2003). For recent developments, see ch. 1, pp. 33–34, above.

in a close relationship with the waters. Before we proceed to a discussion of the earth itself, let us analyze the structure of these two verses.

Structure of Genesis 2:5–6

<u>wĕkōl</u> śîăh haśśādeh ṭerem yihyeh bāʾāreṣ
<u>wĕkol</u>-ʿēśeb haśśādeh ṭerem yiṣmāh
    kî lōʾ himṭîr YHWH ʾĕlōhîm ʿal-hāʾāreṣ
<u>wĕʾādām</u> ʾayin laʿăbōd ʾet-hāʾădāmâ
<u>wĕʾēd</u> yaʿăleh min-hāʾāreṣ
    wĕhišqâ ʾet-kol-pĕnê-hāʾădāmâ

No shrub of the field had yet appeared on the <u>earth</u>;
no plant of the field had yet sprung up.
    —The Lord God had not sent rain on the <u>earth</u>—
No man was there to till the <u>land</u>.
ʾĒd-water was coming up[3] from the earth
    and watered the whole surface of the <u>land</u>.

Modern English Bible translations are divided between (1) translations that take wĕʾādām ʾayin laʿăbōd ʾet-hāʾădāmâ "No man was there to till the land" as a part of the kî-clause and (2) those that take it as being outside of the kî-clause.[4] The former position attributes the lack of vegetation not only to the lack of "rain" but also to the absence of "man"; the latter, only to the lack of "rain."

Schmidt, for example, takes position (1) and holds that v. 5b presents "a duplicate foundation" for the lack of śîăh haśśādeh "desert shrubs" (Gen 21:15; Job 30:4, 7) and ʿēśeb haśśādeh "vegetables" (Gen 3:18; Ps 104:14, 106:20; Deut 11:15), that is, "wild and cultivated plants."[5] Westermann goes one step further in discussing the relationship between the lack of vegetation and the double foundation and argues that śîăh refers to wild plants that "need only rain for their growth," while ʿēśeb refers to "cultivated plants which need man's care."[6] Wenham however distinguishes between "shrub" and "plant" in

---

3. Or "used to come up," taking yaʿăleh as having "frequentative force" (cf. S. R. Driver, *A Treatise on the Use of the Tenses in Hebrew* [Oxford: Clarendon, 1892], 128). However, this yqtl-form verb may be taken as an old "preterite" and may describe a state ("was coming up") in the past in this SETTING.

4. While the NIV, JPSV, and NAB take the former position (1), the NEB, REB, NRSV, and JB take the latter (2).

5. Schmidt, *Die Schöpfungsgeschichte der Priesterschrift*, 196; translations mine.

6. C. Westermann, *Genesis*, vol. 1: *Genesis 1–11* (BKAT 1/1; Neukirchen-Vluyn: Neukirchener Verlag, 1974), 272 [ET 199]. Cf. D. Kidner, "Genesis 2:5, 6: Wet or Dry?" *TynBul* 17 (1966), 109 and n. 1.

"whether they may be eaten or not" and takes the latter as referring to both "wild and cultivated plants," based on the other occurrences in 1:29, 30; and 3:18.[7] Thus the vegetation classification in Gen 2:5 has been taken as ⟨wild – cultivated⟩ or as ⟨edible – inedible⟩ by scholars.

Cassuto,[8] who also takes position (1), thinks that *śîaḥ* refers to some type of "thorn," in light of *qôṣ wĕdardar* (3:18),[9] and interprets 2:5 as describing the state of "no thorns" because of no rain, and "no grain" because of no man. He thus seems to classify the vegetation as inedible wild "thorns" and edible cultivated "grain."

However, the explanations based on structural understanding (1) are not without difficulties. For one thing, it is hard to understand why the author described both *śîaḥ* and *ʿēśeb* as "of the field," while he described man's function as tilling the "land." In other words, the primary concern of man in his relationship with the earth is *ʾădāmâ*, not *śādeh*. If the term *śādeh* refers to the wild uncultivated "field" in contrast to the "land" (*ʾădāmâ*), the "shrub" and "plant" of the field should be taken as wild plants that grow without man's efforts, regardless of edibility. In this case, the inclusion of "no man was there to till the land" (*wĕʾādām ʾayin laʿăbōd ʾet-hāʾădāmâ*) in the *kî*-clause would be unnecessary and even contradictory.

Structurally, position (2) seems to be the better supported: the clause *wĕʾādām ʾayin laʿăbōd ʾet-hāʾădāmâ* goes with the sentence *wĕʾēd yaʿăleh min-hāʾāreṣ wĕhišqâ ʾet-kol-pĕnê-hāʾădāmâ*, because both begin and end with the same or similar sounds. On the other hand, both the beginning and the end of the clause *wĕkōl śîaḥ haśśādeh ṭerem yihyeh bāʾāreṣ* correspond to those of *wĕkol-ʿēśeb haśśādeh ṭerem yiṣmāḥ kî lōʾ himṭîr YHWH ʾĕlōhîm ʿal-hāʾāreṣ*. Moreover, the two subject matters in the second section, "man" and "*ʾēd*-water," are deeply involved with the land (*ʾădāmâ*); those in the first, "shrubs" and "plants," are "of the field" (*śādeh*) and are supposed to be "on the earth" (*bāʾāreṣ*).[10]

---

7. G. J. Wenham, *Genesis 1–15* (WBC 1; Waco, Tex.: Word, 1987), 58.

8. U. Cassuto, *From Adam to Noah* [part 1 of *A Commentary on the Book of Genesis*] (Jerusalem: Magnes, 1961 [1944, orig.]), 102.

9. Compare the Akkadian phrase *giṣṣu daddaru* (C. J. Gadd, "Inscribed Prisms of Sargon II from Nimrud," *Iraq* 16 [1954], 192, lines 52–53) in a Neo-Assyrian royal annal, which, Gadd observed (p. 195), is "the almost verbal equivalent of *qoṣ wĕdardar* (Gen. III, 18) in God's curse upon the Garden after the Fall of Man (also Hosea X, 8)." Note that the Akk. form *giṣṣu* developed from *qiṣṣu*, because Akk. words cannot have two of the phonemes /q/, /ṣ/, and /ṭ/ simultaneously (as pointed out to me by Prof. W. G. Lambert).

10. A similar "grammatical" structure has been suggested by G. Castellino, "Les origines de la civilisation selon les textes bibliques et les textes cunéiformes," *Volume du Congrès: Strasbourg, 1956* (VTSup 4; Leiden: Brill, 1957), 125–26; repr. and trans. "The Origins of

Thus, structurally, vv. 5–6 are better divided into two halves: the first is concerned with wild uncultivated plants, that is, "shrub" and "plant," on the earth (*'ereṣ*); the second with man who tills the land (*'ădāmâ*) and the *'ēd*-water that waters the land (*'ădāmâ*). In other words, Gen 2:5–6 presents a twofold description of the earth: the first section (vv. 5a–5c) speaks broadly about the unproductive and bare "earth" (*'ereṣ*) in which *even* the wild plants are not yet growing because of the lack of rain; the second (vv. 5d–6b) describes more specifically the "land" (*'ădāmâ*), which has "no man to till it" and[11] is watered throughout by the *'ēd*-waters.[12] This structure thus provides a clue to the meaning and purpose of the initial part of this creation story.

"Earth," "Field," and "Land"

In the present context the "land" (*'ădāmâ*), which was watered throughout by the *'ēd*-waters from the "earth" (*'ereṣ*), is seemingly contrasted to the wild uncultivated "field" (*śādeh*), which requires rainwater for fertilization.[13] Wenham explains: "Gen 2:5 therefore distinguishes two types of land: open, uncultivated 'plain' or 'field,' the wilderness fit only for animal grazing, and the dusty 'land' where agriculture is possible with irrigation and human effort."[14]

While these terms are semantically contrasted in Gen 2:5–6, structurally, in the SETTING of this narrative, vv. 5–6, the subject matter (i.e., the participant), switches from vegetation (i.e., "shrub" and "plant") to man and the *'ēd*-water, and the location or stage of these participants shifts from the "earth" (*'ereṣ*) to the "land" (*'ădāmâ*) rather than from the wild uncultivated "field" (*śādeh*) to the "land" (*'ădāmâ*).

Civilization according to Biblical and Cuneiform Texts," in *"I Studied Inscriptions from before the Flood": Ancient Near Eastern, Literary, and Linguistic Approaches to Genesis 1–11* (ed. R. S. Hess and D. T. Tsumura; SBTS 4; Winona Lake, Ind.: Eisenbrauns, 1994), 83–84.

11. The conjunction *wĕ* in the beginning of v. 6 is often translated "but" (e.g., Wenham, *Genesis 1–15*, 44, 46), in keeping with a positive clause after three successive negative clauses. See Andersen, *SBH*, 183, who lists Gen 2:6 as an example of "antithesis after negation."

12. Schmidt thinks that v. 6 is in opposition to v. 5 and is set between "Chaos" (v. 5) and "Creation" (v. 7). Cf. Schmidt, *Die Schöpfungsgeschichte der Priesterschrift*, 197. However, the shift of focus from the "earth" to the more specific area, the "land," occurs in v. 5d, not v. 6a.

13. This threefold distinction in words for the earth is possibly parallel to the Akkadian one, that is, "earth" *erṣetu*, "field" *ṣēru*, "land" *mātu*. Cf. Castellino, "Les origines de la civilisation," 121 [repr., 79–80].

14. Wenham, *Genesis 1–15*, 58.

The term *ʾereṣ* appears here right after the merismatic expression "earth and heavens"[15] (v. 4b), just as *hāʾāreṣ* (1:2) follows immediately after the expression "the heavens and the earth" (1:1). Hence, contextually, the term *ʾereṣ* can refer to everything that is under the heavens as in 1:2.[16] Thus, in 2:5–6 "earth" (*ʾereṣ*) has a much wider semantic field than the term *ʾădāmâ*, comprising both the surface of the earth,[17] upon which later "the LORD God sends rain" (2:5) from above, and the underground, from which the subterranean waters "come up" (2:6).[18] In other words, *ʾădāmâ* is part of the *ʾereṣ*—*ʾădāmâ* is thus hyponymous to *ʾereṣ*.[19]

Therefore, the stage of the narrative setting in Gen 2:5–6 moves from the wider area, *ʾereṣ*, to the narrower area, *ʾădāmâ*, from whose "dust" (*ʿāpār*) "man" (*ʾādām*) is going to be formed (cf. v. 7). This focusing (or narrowing down) of the geographical area as the setting for the Eden narrative is certainly the primary purpose of Gen 2:5–6. It should be noted that the four "circumstantial" clauses initiated by *wĕ-* noun phrases are not mentioned in chronological or sequential order as is the *wayqtl* construction,[20] but rather in topical order, that is, "vegetation" – "man" – "*ʾēd*-water," with an emphasis on the *ʾēd* that watered the whole surface of the *ʾădāmâ*. Furthermore, it is in this well-watered land (*ʾădāmâ*),[21] specifically in Eden (*ʿēden*),[22] that God planted a garden (*gan* in 2:8).

---

15. For the Ugaritic expression *arṣ wšmm*, which is in the same word order, and other examples, see above, p. 60.

16. See above, pp. 69–70.

17. Here, the surface of the earth comprises both the "field" (*śādeh*) and the "land" (*ʾădāmâ*).

18. See below, the following chapters.

19. E. J. Young, *Studies in Genesis One* (Philadelphia: Presbyterian and Reformed, 1964), 63 n. 51, also notes that the *ʾădāmâ* is "more restricted in reference" than *ʾereṣ*. See also Wenham, *Genesis 1–15*, 58: "'land' comprises but a part of the earth." Note that the "field" (*śādeh*) is also a part of the earth.

20. See ch. 1, n. 122.

21. It is interesting to note that Sumerian á-dam "settlement" (*CAD* N/1 233) or "lieu habité" (*RlA* 6.632), which constitutes a merismatic pair with uru "town" to denote totality of human settlement, refers to a place "which is fructified with water"; cf. W. W. Hallo, "Antediluvian Cities," *JCS* 23 (1970), 58. The etymology of á-dam is not certain, but Sjöberg suggests that "a₂-dam is a 'Canaanite', West-Semitic loanword in Sumerian," in Å. W. Sjöberg, "Eve and the Chameleon," in *In the Shelter of Elyon: Essays on Ancient Palestinian Life and Literature in Honor of G. W. Ahlström* (JSOTSup 31; Sheffield: JSOT Press, 1984), 223. For a discussion on *ʾādām* as "earth," see R. S. Hess, "'ADAM as 'Skin' and 'Earth': An Examination of Some Proposed Meanings in Biblical Hebrew," *TynBul* 39 (1988), 141–49.

22. In other words, Eden is a part of the *ʾădāmâ*. Cf. Castellino, "Les origines de la civilisation," 122 [repr., 80–81]. For the etymology of Eden as a "well-watered" place, see below, pp. 116–125.

In light of the above, in the initial part of Gen 2 one can identify a threefold focusing or narrowing down of the geographical area: (1) from *’ereṣ* to *’ădāmâ*, (2) from *’ădāmâ* to *ʿēden*, and (3) from *ʿēden* to *gan*. In other words, the garden, the main stage for this Eden narrative, is a part of Eden, which is a part of the land, which is a part of the earth.

No Vegetation

The two terms for vegetation in v. 5, "shrub" (*śîăḥ*) and "plant" (*ʿēśeb*), may be a merismatic word pair, like "plant" (*ʿēśeb*) and "tree" (*ʿēṣ*) in Gen 1:11.[23] In other words, *śîăḥ* and *ʿēśeb* probably signify the totality of vegetation that normally grows in the "field."

The totality of vegetation edible by man, that is, "food," that is produced by the earth is expressed in *Atra-Ḥasīs* S iv 49,[24] which reads:

[*li*]-*bal-kat erṣetu re-em-šá*	Let the earth's womb be out of order,
šam-mu ia ú-ṣa-a šu-ú ia i-im-ru	Let no vegetables shoot up,
	no cereals grow.

In this text, *šammu* "vegetables" and *šuʾu* "cereals"[25] seem to constitute a merismatic word pair and signify the totality of edible vegetation that the earth (*erṣetu*) produces in normal circumstances. Furthermore, in *Enuma elish* VII 2, where the god Marduk is called "creator of barley and flax, who causes the green vegetable to shoot up" (*ba-nu-ú še-am u qé-e mu-še-ṣu-ú ur-qí-t[i]*), the totality of vegetation useful to man seems to be expressed by *šeʾu(m)*, *qû*, and *urqītu*.[26]

Thus, while there is a difference in the nature of vegetation in these examples, it seems that "shrub" and "plant" in Gen 2:5 are also a merismatic word pair that signifies the totality of vegetation in the "field" and hence that the first half of vv. 5–6 describes the unproductive and "bare" state of the

---

23. The Masoretic punctuation suggests that *deše’* (Gen 1:11; cf. 12) is a cognate accusative of the verb *tadše’* and means "vegetation" (cf. NIV). This term is then explained by concrete terms, that is, "plants" and "trees."

24. Lambert and Millard, *AH*, 108–9; also see pp. 110–11; see above, pp. 18–21.

25. Note that the term *šuʾu* could be an Akk. cognate of Heb. *śîăḥ*, though Akk. *šuʾu* "grain" is attested only in later times, LB and NA, and could be an Aram. loanword. Cf. *AHw*, 1294: "eine Getreideart." Also Ug. *šḥt* (KTU 1.100:65) might be related to Heb. *śîăḥ*; cf. M. C. Astour, "Two Ugaritic Serpent Charms," *JNES* 27 (1968), 25; Huehnergard, *UVST*, 96 n. 61.

26. Cf. W. G. Lambert and S. B. Parker, *Enuma Eliš: The Babylonian Epic of Creation—The Cuneiform Text* (Oxford: Clarendon, 1966), 41; *CAD* Q 286 (on *qû*); *AHw*, 1222 (on *šeʾu[m]*), 1432 (on *urqītu*).

earth without any vegetation at all. This state of the "bare" earth is virtually the same as *tōhû wābōhû* earth (Gen 1:2), though in Gen 2:5–6 more concrete terms are used for describing the initial unproductive state of the earth, and the water was covering only a part of the earth, the "land" (*'ădāmâ*).

No Man to "Till" the Land

It is very interesting to note that the "unproductiveness" of the earth is expressed not only in terms of "no vegetation" but also in terms of "no people" in the Old Babylonian version of the *Atra-Ḫasīs* epic:

Atra-Ḫasīs epic II iv 4–6[27]

$^{4)}$*u-ul ul-da er-ṣe-tum re-e*[*m-ša*]
$^{5)}$*ša-am-mu ú-ul ú-ṣi-a* [. .] $^{6)}$*ni-šu ú-ul am-ra-*[*tu₄*]

The womb of earth did not bear,
Vegetation did not sprout [. .]   People were not seen [. .][28]

This "unproductiveness" of the earth has been discussed above in relationship to the term *nabalkutu* in the Assyrian version. In Gen 1 this situation is expressed positively ("still") by *tōhû wābōhû*, which might be indirectly related to *nabalkutu* "to become unproductive." In Gen 2, on the other hand, it is described negatively ("not yet"[29]) in more concrete terms, that is, "no vegetation" and "no man," as in the Old Babylonian version, though the term *'ādām* in the Genesis context bears a more specific meaning than the Akkadian *nišū*.[30]

---

27. Lambert and Millard, *AH*, 78–79. See above, pp. 19–20.

28. Though Lambert and Millard analyze line 6, *ni-šu ú-ul am-ra-*[(*a*)-*ma*], as a monocolon, it seems that line 5 and line 6 constitute the second half of a bicolon, which as a whole corresponds to line 4, because column iv (D) is always composed of bicola, and a monocolon normally appears in a transitional point, for example, II ii 20, in poetry (for monocolons in Pss 18:2, 23:1, 139:1; and in Ug. epics, see my "Problem of Childlessness in the Royal Epic of Ugarit: An Analysis of Krt [KTU 1.14:I]:1–25," in *Monarchies and Socio-Religious Traditions in the Ancient Near East* [ed. T. Mikasa; Wiesbaden: Harrassowitz, 1984], 11–20). Note the following correspondence: AH S iv 58b–59: /*ibbalkat erṣetu rēmša*/ :: /*šammu ul uṣā šū ul i'ru*/ = 8 :: 9 // AH II iv 4–6: /*ul ulda erṣetum rēmša*/ :: /*šammu ul uṣia* [ ] *nišu ul amrāma*/ = 8 :: 11.

29. See above, ch. 1, n. 126.

30. While the Hebrew *'ādām* refers only to the male human in the Gen 2 creation story (cf. v. 15: "to till the garden"), the "man" in the context that describes the initial state of the earth (vv. 5–6) may possibly mean "man" in the generic sense, "mankind." Cf. R. S. Hess, "Splitting the Adam: The Usage of *'ADAM* in Genesis i–v," in J. A. Emerton (ed.), *Studies in the Pentateuch* (VTSup 41; Leiden: Brill, 1990), 1–15.

In conclusion, the initial state of the earth in Gen 2:5–6 is described as unproductive in concrete terms: "no shrub" and "no plant," as well as "no man to till the land." In other words, the earth in Gen 2:5–6 was also the "bare" earth, which had "no vegetation" and "no man," like the earth in Gen 1:2, which is described as *tōhû wābōhû* "desolate and empty," though the earth–water relationship is not the same in the two passages.[31]

---

31. See below, pp. 107–112.

5

The Waters in Genesis 2

Rain and ʾēd

As noted in the previous chapter, in Gen 2:5–6 the unproductive state of the earth, which is described concretely in terms of "no shrub of the field" and "no plant of the field," is explained as being due to the lack of rain. Rain, which of course comes from above (i.e., heaven), is described as water caused by the Lord God (i.e., "The Lord God had not sent rain on the earth"). On the other hand, another form of water, ʾēd, is described as "coming up" (yaʿăleh) from the earth (ʾereṣ), either from the surface of the earth or from underground.[1] Thus, in Gen 2:5–6, ʾēd, the water from below, is clearly distinguished from rainwater, the water from above.[2]

In Gen 2:5–6, however, rainwater does not play a significant role. On the other hand, the ʾēd-"water" is an important factor in the initial state of the earth, which is described negatively as a "not yet" normal (or productive) earth. But, unlike the water in Gen 1:2, the ʾēd-water in 2:6 does not cover the whole earth. The author carefully distinguishes the "land" (ʾădāmâ), which was watered by the ʾēd-water, from the "earth" (ʾereṣ), from which the ʾēd-water was coming up.

The word ʾēd appears in the OT only here and in Job 36:27, where it appears either as a suffixed form ("his ʾēd ") or as the allomorph ʾēdô. Its meaning and etymology have been hotly disputed by scholars and have not yet been settled. Let us examine in detail various suggestions for its etymology and place the term in its proper biblical context.

The term ʾēd has been rendered in various ways since the earliest translations; the LXX, Vulg., Peshitta, and Aquila translate ʾēd "spring" or "fountain" (LXX: πηγή). On the other hand, Aramaic versions render it ʿănānāʾ

---

1. The term ʾereṣ can mean any of the following: (1) the surface of the earth, (2) the underground, or (3) the netherworld. See above, p. 59.

2. It is noteworthy that the Genesis account of the Garden of Eden (2:4–3:24) does not give the rain any role in bringing fertility to the land. In Canaanite religion it is Baal, the god of rain and storm, who brings fertility to the land. See below, p. 117, for various rain-gods who bring abundance to the land.

"(rain-)cloud" or "vapour, mist."[3] For example, the Targumim, both *Onqelos* and *Jonathan*, translate it *ʿănānāʾ* in Job 36:27 as well as in Gen 2:6. The LXX translates it νεφέλην "a mass of clouds" in Job 36:27. As Barr points out, "it is, indeed, precisely this passage that caused traditional sources to understand the Gen 2:6 passage as 'mist' from the beginning."[4]

Modern English versions translate it "mist" (KJV, RSV, NEB note, NIV note), "flood" (RSV note; NEB), "water" (JB), "stream" (NRSV), or "streams" (NIV). These versions reflect the modern trend in etymological discussions of *ʾēd*. While the traditional meaning "mist" is still preserved as an option, the emphasis has shifted from "mist" to "flood" and from "flood" to "streams."

The translation "vapor" or "mist" lacks justification etymologically;[5] moreover, it presents contextual problems. Cassuto, for example, notes that "it is not *from the earth* but from the water that vapour rises," and "vapour waters the ground only through *rain*."[6] Hence he argues that "vapour" is not suitable

---

3. Cf. M. Ellenbogen, *Foreign Words in the Old Testament: Their Origin and Etymology* (London: Luzac, 1962), 13.

4. J. Barr, "Limitations of Etymology as a Lexicographical Instrument in Biblical Hebrew," *Transactions of the Philological Society* (1983), 50.

5. M. Görg suggests *yꜣd.t* as an Eg. etymology for the term *ʾēd* and interprets it as "dew." Cf. M. Görg, "Eine heterogene Überlieferung in Gen 2.6," *BN* 31 (1986), 19–24. However, his view is not convincing either etymologically or contextually. For one thing, Eg. *yꜣd.t* involves two consonants, /y/ and /ʾ/, while Hebrew has only one. If Arab. *ʾiyād* "Dunst" ("vapor"), as cited by him, were indeed a cognate, that would suggest that the second consonant of the Egyptian term was preserved as /y/ throughout the centuries. On the other hand, if Hebrew borrowed the Egyptian word earlier (i.e., before the New Kingdom), it could not have been from Eg. *yꜣd.t*, for the Eg. term would have corresponded to Heb. *yrd or *yld before the New Kingdom. Cf. A. Erman and H. Grapow, *WÄS*, 1.36. Note also that they suggest the meanings "Tau des Himmels" ("dew of heaven") and "Wasser" ("water"), which should be distinguished from *yd.t* "Duft" ("odor"). Moreover, "dew" does not go up from the "earth." Since no rain was yet on the earth, no dew could be expected on the earth; cf. the Ug. expression *bl . ṭl . bl rbb* "no dew, no rain" (KTU 1.19 [1Aqht]:I:44) and the name and epithet of one of Baal's daughters in Ug.: *ṭly bt rb* "Dew-girl, daughter of rain" (KTU 1.4 [51]:I:18 [17], IV:56, etc.; see Gordon, *UT*, 406, 482). Cf. M. Görg, "Noch einmal zu *ʾēd* (Gen 2,6)," *BN* 50 (1989), 9–10; also G. F. Hasel and M. G. Hasel, "The Hebrew Term *ʾed* in Gen 2,6 and Its Connection in Ancient Near Eastern Literature," *ZAW* 112 (2000), 332. If Görg, followed by Hasel and Hasel, takes the "phonetic compatibility" between Heb. *ʾēd* and Eg. *yꜣd.t* "mist" as due to the latter's being "a loanword from a Semitic *ʾiyâd/ʾid/ʾed*" or both being "Hamito-Semitic," he is certainly dealing with the origin ("etymology") of the Hebrew term. What then would be the common or basic Canaanite or West Semitic form behind all four of these forms? For Hasel and Hasel's lack of control of Sumerian-Akkadian material, see below.

6. U. Cassuto, *From Adam to Noah* [part 1 of *A Commentary on the Book of Genesis*] (Jerusalem: Magnes, 1961 [1944, orig.]), 103.

for the initial situation of the earth without "rain," the water from above. On the other hand, Dahood thinks that this "vapour, mist" came up ultimately from the subterranean waters, the water below.[7] But *hāʾāreṣ* does not mean "cosmic reservoir," even though it sometimes does refer to the underworld.

Barr suggests that the vapor might have "damped the surface, but it did not provide enough water for the plants to grow. . . . Perhaps the writer discounted the irrigative value of mist: for him only rain was enough to sustain proper plant life, and especially a garden."[8] But it is hard to hold that the author discounted the "irrigative value" of *ʾēd* when he says that it watered the whole surface of the land."

Etymology of ʾēd

For the etymology of *ʾēd*, three possible sources have been proposed: Semitic, Sumerian via Akkadian, and Sumerian directly.

Semitic Etymology?

No satisfactory Semitic etymology has been suggested for the term *ʾēd*. Brown, Driver, and Briggs simply note that the derivation is dubious, though they cite Arabic *ʾada* "be strong" as a cognate.

Dahood argues for a Semitic etymology of *ʾēd*, which he proposes to translate "rain cloud" in light of the Eblaite month name *i-du*. He translates the verse "so he made a rain cloud come up from the nether ocean, and it watered all the surface of the ground."[9]

According to him, because the terms *ʾēd* and *i-du* are "associated with rain," they should mean "rain cloud," which he thinks "admirably suits" the texts in which he says the terms appear: Gen 2:6, Job 36:27, in the personal name *maṭrēd* (Gen 36:39, 1 Chr 1:50), and in the New Calendar of Ebla. For etymology, he cites Arabic *ʾāda* (ʾwd) "to bend, burden, weigh down" and *ʾawda* "burden, load," which he thinks "can easily be reconciled with the proposed definition of *ʾēd* as "rain cloud" or "mass of clouds," which give the impression of an overhanging burden."[10]

However, his etymological argument for *ēd* on the basis of Arabic *ʾāda* (ʾwd) is not well founded. First, he ignores the Masoretic distinction between the two terms *ʾēd* and *ʾêd*. The latter is always spelled with *yôd* and very

7. According to Dahood, *ʾēd* refers to the rain clouds that "ascend from the cosmic reservoir under the earth"; cf. M. Dahood, "Eblaite *i-du* and Hebrew *ʾēd*, 'Rain Cloud'," *CBQ* 43 (1981), 536.

8. Barr, "Limitations of Etymology as a Lexicographical Instrument," 51.

9. Dahood, "Eblaite *i-du* and Hebrew *ʾēd*, 'Rain Cloud'," 536.

10. Ibid., 538.

likely belongs to a "different word type" from the former. And even for *ʾêd*
(ʾ-y-d) "calamity," an etymology from Arabic *ʾwd is nothing but "a conceivable speculation," as Barr notes.[11]

His major argument, that Eblaite *ì-du* is "associated with rain" and that hence Hebrew *ʾēd* means "rain cloud," is not certain. For one thing, the reading of the Eblaite month name [itu]NI.DU as [itu]*ì-du* has not been established, and a different reading, *ì-túm,* has now been suggested by Pettinato in a new treatment of the calendars of Ebla.[12] Moreover, the correspondence between the month names of the Old Calendar and those of the New Calendar is not simple. The fact that [itu]g a - š ú m "month of rain" in the Old Calendar has a name of a "celestial nature" does not support the contention that *ì-du* in the New Calendar does also.[13]

Furthermore, his translation, "*so* he made a rain cloud come up . . . ," is not syntactically acceptable for Gen 2:6, even though the verb can be taken as *hiphil.*[14] If that were its meaning, one would expect the Hebrew text to be something like *wayyaʿăleh ʾēd.* Also, "the nether ocean" is not an acceptable translation for *ʾereṣ*; one would expect *tĕhôm(ôt).*[15] Moreover, his translation of *lĕʾēdô* (Job 36:27) as "from his rain cloud" is based on his interpretation of Gen 2:6 and hence cannot be accepted.

Finally, if the Masoretic vocalization of the name *maṭrēd* were the assimilated form of *māṭār* + *ʾēd* ("Rain from the Rain Cloud"),[16] one would expect the form *mĕṭārēd* < *mĕṭar-ʾēd* < *māṭār* + *ʾēd.*[17] Moreover, although the LXX transcription Ματραειθ in Gen 36:39 may indeed reflect an older spelling, that would have to be the spelling *maṭrāʾēd,* not *mĕṭarʾēd.*[18] This form, *maṭrāʾēd,*

---

11. Barr, "Limitations of Etymology as a Lexicographical Instrument," 50–51.

12. G. Pettinato, *The Archives of Ebla: An Empire Inscribed in Clay* (Garden City, N.Y.: Doubleday, 1981), 150: itu ì-túm "month of the taxes." See also W. H. Shea, "The Calendars of Ebla, Part I: The Old Calendar," *AUSS* 18 (1980), 127–37; "The Calendars of Ebla, Part II: The New Calendar," *AUSS* 19 (1981), 59–69; "The Calendar of Ebla, Part III: Conclusion," *AUSS* 19 (1981), 115–26; D. Charpin, "Mari et le calendrier d'Ebla," *RA* 76 (1982), 2.

13. Dahood, "Eblaite *ì-du* and Hebrew *ʾēd,* 'Rain Cloud'," 537 n. 13.

14. Dahood thinks that "Yahweh is preferably understood here as the agent." Cf. ibid., 536.

15. See above, p. 50, on this term.

16. Dahood, "Eblaite *ì-du* and Hebrew *ʾēd,* 'Rain Cloud'," 537.

17. There would be loss of /ʾ/ and subsequent shift of accent.

18. Baumgartner, *HAL,* 544 [*HALOT,* 575], citing Meyer. According to Meyer, "מטרד, LXX Ματραειθ. Danach ist Wincklers Deutung מטראד 'Regen der Wolke' (Gesch. Isr. I 193, 1) wohl richtig." Cf. E. Meyer, *Die Israeliten und ihre Nachbarstämme* (Halle: Max Niemeyer, 1906), 375 n. 1.

might change to *maṭrād* (< *maṭrā-ēd* < *maṭrāʾēd*),[19] as reflected in the LXX transcription Ματραδ in 1 Chr 1:50, but not to *maṭrēd*.

Thus, the revived claim for a Semitic etymology of the term *ʾēd* in light of Eblaite and Arabic has no solid foundation. The only other possibility is to seek a non-Semitic etymology for this term.

Sumerian Loanword via Akkadian?

A Sumerian connection has been suggested by many scholars ever since the end of the nineteenth century. Some suggest that the word is a Sumerian loanword into West Semitic via Akkadian, and others, a Sumerian loanword directly into West Semitic. We shall examine the former suggestion first.

The word *edû* "flood," which is a Sumerian loanword from A.DÉ.A, was the first Akkadian candidate for the origin of the Hebrew term *ʾēd*. It was adopted by A. Dillmann (1892),[20] Friedrich Delitzsch (1896),[21] P. Leander (1903),[22] H. Zimmern (1915),[23] H. Gunkel (1917), and Gesenius and Buhl.[24] However, soon after, another term, *id* "river," was suggested by scholars such as P. Dhorme (1907)[25] and E. Sachsse (1921).[26] But this view was not as popular as the derivation from *edû* until W. F. Albright (1939)[27] reinforced it with new information. He was soon followed by scholars such as U. Cassuto (1944).[28] However, E. A. Speiser (1955)[29] supported the *edû* etymology once

---

19. On vowel *sandhi*, here the fusion of *ā* and *ē* after the loss of intervocalic *ʾalep*, see my "Vowel sandhi in Biblical Hebrew," *ZAW* 109 (1997), 575–88.

20. A. Dillmann, *Die Genesis* (Kurzgefasstes exegetisches Handbuch zum Alten Testament 11; Leipzig, 1892), 52 cited by E. A. Speiser, "*ʾed* in the Story of Creation," *BASOR* 140 (1955), 9 n. 2 [= *Oriental and Biblical Studies: Collected Writings of E. A. Speiser* (ed. J. J. Finkelstein and M. Greenberg; Philadelphia: University of Pennsylvania Press, 1967), 19 n. 2]; O. Kaiser, *Die mythische Bedeutung des Meeres in Ägypten, Ugarit und Israel* (BZAW 78; Berlin: Alfred Töpelmann, 1959), 101 n. 71.

21. Cited by Speiser, "*ʾed* in the Story of Creation," 9 n. 2.

22. P. Leander, *Über die sumerischen Lehnwörter in Assyrischen* (Uppsala Universitets Årsskrift; Uppsala: Akademiska, 1903), 19.

23. Zimmern, *AFw*, 44: "akk. *edū* Flut, Hochwasser: > viell. hebr. *ʾēd* Gen. 2,6; Hi. 36,27 (oder gar < sum. *id* Fluss?)."

24. Cited by Kaiser, *Die mythische Bedeutung des Meeres*, 101 n. 71.

25. P. Dhorme, *RB* (1907), 274, cited by Speiser, "*ʾed* in the Story of Creation," 9 n. 2.

26. E. Sachsse, "Der jahwistische Schöpfungsbericht: Ein Erklärungsversuch," *ZAW* 39 (1921), 281–82, who interprets *ʾēd* as "Kanalwasser."

27. W. F. Albright, "The Babylonian Matter in the Predeuteronomic Primeval History (JE) in Gen 1–11," *JBL* 58 (1939), 102–3.

28. Cassuto, *From Adam to Noah*, 104.

29. Speiser, "*ʾed* in the Story of Creation," 9–11.

again. Since then, those supporting an Akkadian etymology of ʾēd have been split into two camps.

While Albright's view (ʾēd = id) is supported by a majority of scholars, such as G. Castellino (1957), P. Reymond (1958), G. Fohrer (1963), E. J. Young, G. von Rad, W. H. Schmidt (1967), M. Sæbø (1970), P. K. McCarter (1973), C. Westermann (1974), P. D. Miller, Jr. (1985), G. J. Wenham (1987), and others,[30] Speiser's view (ʾēd = edû) is followed by O. Kaiser (1959), M. Ellenbogen (1962), W. von Soden (1965), W. Baumgartner (1967), and others.[31]

According to Albright, the Hebrew term ʾēd should be identified with *Id* "the subterranean fresh-water stream" in light of "the name of the chief god of the Middle Euphrates region, . . . the river-god Id, perhaps also pronounced *Edda* by the Semites."[32] Then he says, "The deity Id appears both as masculine and as feminine; it represents the fresh-water river in the underworld, whence all terrestrial rivers flow and whence the fertility of the Mesopotamian plain is derived." After noting "a hymn to the river of creation" and the "cult of the masculine Id" in Mari and in the Euphrates region, Albright concludes: "It is to the Id, the subterranean source of fresh water, that the ʾed of Gen 2:6 must be traced."[33] Thus, he sees a close connection between the divine name *Id* and Hebrew ʾēd, both the source of fertility.[34]

---

30. G. Castellino, "Les origines de la civilisation selon les textes bibliques et les textes cunéiformes," in *Volume du Congrès: Strasbourg, 1956* (VTSup 4; Leiden: Brill, 1957), 121–22 [repr. and trans. "The Origins of Civilization according to Biblical and Cuneiform Texts," in "*I Studied Inscriptions from before the Flood*": *Ancient Near Eastern, Literary, and Linguistic Approaches to Genesis 1–11* (ed. R. S. Hess and D. T. Tsumura; SBTS 4; Winona Lake, Ind.: Eisenbrauns, 1994), 80–81]; P. Reymond, *L'eau, sa vie, et sa signification dans l'ancien testament* (VTSup 6; Leiden: Brill, 1958), 169; Young, *Studies in Genesis One*, 62 n. 50; G. von Rad, *Genesis* (OTL; Philadelphia: Westminster, 1961), 74; W. H. Schmidt, *Die Schöpfungsgeschichte der Priesterschrift: Zur Überlieferungsgeschichte von Genesis 1:1–2:4a und 2:4b–3:24*, vol. 2: *Überarbeitete und erweiterte Auflage* (Neukirchen-Vluyn: Neukirchener Verlag, 1967), 197 n. 1; M. Sæbø, "Die hebräischen Nomina ʾed und ʾēd: Zwei sumerisch-akkadische Fremdwörter?" *ST* 24 (1970) 130–41; P. K. McCarter, "The River Ordeal in Israelite Literature," *HTR* 66 (1973), 403; C. Westermann, *Genesis*, vol. 1: *Genesis 1–11* (BKAT 1/1; Neukirchen-Vluyn: Neukirchener Verlag, 1974), 273; P. D. Miller, Jr., "Eridu, Dunnu, and Babel: A Study in Comparative Mythology," *HAR* 9 (1985), 239; Gordon J. Wenham, *Genesis 1–15* (WBC 1; Waco, Tex.: Word, 1987), 6, etc.

31. Kaiser, *Die mythische Bedeutung des Meeres*, 102–4; Ellenbogen, *Foreign Words in the Old Testament*, 13; von Soden, *AHw* 1.187; Baumgartner, *HAL*, 11, etc.

32. Albright, "The Babylonian Matter," 102.

33. Ibid., 102–3 n. 25.

34. The river-goddess Idu in the Harab Myth has been identified with Hebrew ʾēd by P. D. Miller, Jr., "Eridu, Dunnu, and Babel," 239. He says: "As in Genesis 2, the first thing that is done in the creation is the creation of water, though in Genesis 2 it is sweet water to water the plants (ʾēd) and in Harab it is sea (Tamtu). But in the Harab myth, river, i.e., Idu

Soon after, Cassuto (1944) followed Albright's view, claiming that the term *ʾēd*, like the divine name *Id*, refers to "the waters of the deep generally and to all the springs issuing therefrom." This view, according to Cassuto, accords with the statement in Gen 2:10, where "the garden was watered by a river emanating from a spring, and not by rain." And "this blissful state of affairs prevailing in the garden of Eden and the similar circumstances obtaining in Egypt served as classic examples of a land blessed with fertility . . . (xiii 10)."[35]

In response to Albright's view, Speiser (1955) reiterated the older view that Hebrew *ʾēd* should be compared with Akkadian *edû* (A.DÉ.A) "flood." He argues against Albright's reading of the divine name *Id,* and tries to show that *edû* meant subterranean waters. In his Genesis commentary (1964) he reconfirms his view and says: "The sense would be that of an underground swell, a common motif in Akkadian literary compositions."[36] He translates Gen 2:6 as "instead, *a flow* would well up from the ground and water the whole surface of the soil."[37]

Speiser's view has been supported by two major dictionaries, one Akkadian and the other Hebrew. *AHw* 1.187, mentioning Speiser's article, relates Hebrew *ʾēd* to Akkadian *edû*, which is, however, defined as "(*bedrohliche*) Wasserflut, Wogenschwall" ("[threatening] flood, deluge"). Baumgartner, *HAL* [= *HALOT*] 11, follows Speiser's view more closely and translates *ʾēd* (Gen 2:6) as "d. unterirdische Süsswasserstrom, Grundwasser(?)" ("the subterranean stream of fresh water, groundwater (?)"), while he translates *ʾēdô* (Job 36:27) as "d. himmlische Strom" ("the celestial stream").

However, Sæbø[38] responded to Speiser's view in detail, concluding that the Hebrew term *ʾēd* should be identified with the Sumero-Akkadian *id*. Through him, Albright's equation *ʾēd = id* has been accepted by Westermann and other scholars.[39] Thus, the modern trend appears to favor Albright's view, but let us examine the arguments once more in light of recent scholarly development.

Each view presents problems. The main problem (*ʾēd = id*) is graphemic: was the cuneiform sign really read *id* in the Akkadian passages, as Albright and the others maintain to support their theory? For *edû,* the problem is

---

(= Heb. *ʾēd*), comes in the next generation as daughter of sea (Tamtu)" (pp. 238–89). However, Gen 2 has nothing to do with the "creation of water" as such. See below, pp. 102–105, on Sumerian etymologies of the Hebrew term *ʾēd*.

35. Cassuto, *From Adam to Noah*, 104.

36. Idem, *Genesis* (AB 2; Garden City: Doubleday, 1964), 16.

37. Ibid., 14.

38. Sæbø, "Die hebräischen Nomina *ʾed* und *ʾēd*," 130–41.

39. See Wenham, *Genesis 1–15*, 58; T. Stordalen, "Man, Soil, Garden: Basic Plot in Genesis 2–3 Reconsidered," *JSOT* 53 (1992), 13.

phonological—could *edû* have been borrowed into West Semitic as *'ēd?* For both we must ask, does its meaning fit the context of Genesis 2?

The Graphical or Graphemic Problem

Should the Sumerian ^{d}íD be read in Akkadian as *Id* or as *Nāru?*[40]

Albright (1939) argued that *'ēd* derived from the reading *id* of the Sumerogram íD "river." Normally, in Akkadian, the character is read as *nāru*, but Albright said that when used as a divine name it is read *Id*, and this is the source of the Hebrew word. He supports his view by citing other examples of the name of the river-god *Id*,[41] ^{d}(A-ENGUR) *I-id* as well as the personal name *I-dì-*^{d}*Id*. While he admits that the divine name was probably also read as *Nâru* in Akkadian,[42] he holds that "there is no clear evidence pointing to this alternative."[43] Thus, he thinks that the divine name íD was read as *Id* in Akkadian.

On the other hand, Speiser (1955) points out that the Sumerian sign íD was generally read in Akkadian as *nāru*, not as *id*, and "could not, as such, have led to Heb. *'ēd.*"[44] And "*id*, when so pronounced, had a specific cultic bearing, notably so in the Assyrian Laws."[45] While he admits that there are exceptions to this, he says that "we can be sure of Akkadian *id* as distinct from *nāru* *only* when the term is spelled out syllabically; and such explicit instances are relatively rare."[46]

Sæbø thinks that Speiser's explanation that "the Sumerian Logogram in question was read in Akkadian as *nāru* 'river'" is probably right. However, he questions Speiser's conclusion that it "could not, as such, have led to Heb. *'ēd,*" for Sæbø holds that Sumerian íD was read also as *id* in Akkadian, citing

---

40. This problem is similar to the problem of reading a Chinese character in a Japanese text. There are two major ways, one based on the (usually Han period) Chinese pronunciation ("on-yomi" reading), the other the Japanese word for the concept of the character ("kun-yomi" reading). For example, the Chinese character GOD can be read using the "Chinese" reading *shin* or the Japanese reading *kami*, the ordinary word for "god." Only one reading is correct in any given context, however. (Actually, each type of reading has several variants, so there are not just two readings.) In this monograph, a sequence of capital letters (e.g., A.DÉ.A) or hyphenated noncapital letters (e.g., e₄-dé-a) stands for the Sumerian sign or reading, while italic letters indicate how they were read in Akkadian. For example, the Sumerian sign íD can be read in the Akkadian language either as *id* (Sumerian reading) or as *nāru* (Akkadian reading).

41. CT 12 26, 38128, col. IV–VI, 16; CT 24 16, 23; CT 29 46, 23; Assyrian Law-code, col. III, 93, etc.

42. Albright, "The Babylonian Matter," 102–3 n. 25.

43. Ibid.

44. Speiser, "'ed in the Story of Creation," 9.

45. Ibid.

46. Ibid. 9 n. 7.

AHw 1, *CAD* I–J, and *AHw* 2.[47] However, he cites them uncritically. Let us examine his references.

According to *CAD* I–J, the river-god ^{d}ÍD appears as *Id* in the following Akkadian texts: (1) in contexts referring to the river ordeal—the Code of Hammurabi (OB) and others; (2) the Maqlu-incantation text; (3) Middle Assyrian laws (written as ^{d}ÍD$^{i\text{-}id}$) as well as in some Sumero-Akkadian bilingual lexical texts.[48] *AHw* also cites similar texts under "*id* auch *ittu* III? (sum. Fw.) 'Fluß-(gott).'"[49] However, *AHw* on *nāru(m)* expresses reservations about the reading of ^{d}ÍD in the Code of Hammurabi (OB), citing there the same text, "KH V 39," which earlier had been cited under *id* (*AHw* 1.364). Three texts (CT 24, 16, 23/5; Šurpu S. 52, 23; mA KAV 1 III 93) are cited as examples of texts where ^{d}ÍD is read as the god *Id*. However, "Schöpfungsfluß" (DINGIR.ÍD), which refers to a feminine deity,[50] is read as *nāru* in *AHw*: *attīn. bānât kalâma* (TuL 91, 10 u D).[51] Sæbø seems to misrepresent this explanation in *AHw* by adding his own comment, "(vgl. hierzu Gen 2:6 u. 2:10ff)" after *AHw*'s comment: "im Ordal u als Gott. a) ^{d}ÍD meist wohl ^{d}ID zu lesen . . . b) Schöpfungsfluß."

In 1965, Lambert presented new evidence that the divine name ^{d}ÍD was read *nāru* in Akkadian texts. For example, in a PN *na-ru-um-ìl* ("The-river-is-a-god")[52] from the Old Babylonian period, the divine river is spelled *nārum*.[53] Furthermore, in an Akkadian text from Ugarit, the god of the river ordeal is referred to as *nāru*, not as *Id*: *tá-me-e a-na na-ri* (*BWL*, 116, 3). Furthermore, according to Lambert, "In a *tamītu*-text from the libraries of Ashurbanipal (K 4721 obv. 2, unpublished) there is reference to [*annanna ap*]*il annanna šá ina* ^{d}*na-rum a-mat-*[."[54] Therefore, Albright's view that the Sumerian ^{d}ÍD should be read *Id* in Akkadian and that there is "no clear evidence" pointing to the reading *Nāru* is no longer tenable. Certainly, as Lambert says, "the glosses in the Middle Assyrian laws (*i-id*) do not prove that for every occasion ^{d}íd is to be read *id* not *nārum*."

---

47. Sæbø, "Die hebräischen Nomina ʾed und ʾēd," 132 n. 18.
48. *CAD* I–J 8. Based on the "evidence" in this volume, McCarter also held in 1973 that "this name for the cosmic river was normally pronounced *id* in Akk. as well as Sum." Cf. McCarter, "The River Ordeal in Israelite Literature," 403 and n. 4.
49. *AHw* 1.364.
50. Note, however, that there is a variant text with masculine *at-ta*. Cf. L. W. King, *The Seven Tablets of Creation* (London: Luzac, 1902), 128–29 n. 2 and 200–201.
51. *AHw* 2.748.
52. This name may simply mean "The river is divine," as suggested by R. S. Hess.
53. Cf. *Na-ru-um*-DINGIR (CT 4 50b:8, also TCL 18, 103:3) cited by *CAD* N/1 374.
54. W. G. Lambert, "Nebuchadnezzar King of Justice," *Iraq* 27 (1965), 11.

Hirsch (1968–69) also supports the reading *nāru* for Sumerian ^díD. He cites an Old Assyrian title, *ku-um-ri-im ša na-ri-im* "priest of the god River," which is replaced by AḪ.ME *ša* íD in one text.[55] Although the DINGIR sign is missing before íD, Hirsch thinks that "Fluß-(gott)" is doubtless meant in the context. Thus, the reading *nārum* for the (masculine) divine name íD is confirmed in Old Assyrian. Moreover, while lexical texts like CT, xxiv, 16 cannot be discounted, the reading *Id* seems to be "a post-Old Babylonian, perhaps artificial, conscious distinction," as Hirsch holds.[56] Similarly, J. J. M. Roberts includes the god *Nāru* in his list of the earliest Semitic gods and goddesses. According to him, *Nāru*, "a genuine Semitic name for the river god," was sometimes replaced by a Sumerian loanword, *Id*, "later than the Old Akkadian period."[57]

In 1978, Borger mentioned two possibilities for ^díD: "^díD = Flussgott ^í*Èd* oder *Nāru* (*AHw* 364a, CAD I/J 8 [dazu CAD A/1 150f.], Lambert Iraq 27 11)."[58] As for *CAD*, the ^díD in Maqlu III 62 and 77, which *CAD* 20 years earlier took as masculine and therefore discussed under *id* (*CAD* I–J 8), is now discussed under *nāru* (*CAD* N/1, 374). In other words, *CAD* now accepts that, regardless of its gender, ^díD can be read *nāru*, thus reversing its earlier opinion that the "logogram ^díD, because it is constructed as masc., is to be read *id* rather than *nāru*, which is fem."[59] Other examples of the river-god *Nāru* cited by *CAD* N/1, in addition to those cited by Lambert and Hirsch, are *na-ru-um* (RA 44, 43:5 [Old Babylonian extispicy]) and PN *ša na-ri-im* (ICK 1, 84:9).[60]

In his comprehensive treatment of the river ordeal in ancient Mesopotamia, Bottéro (1981) reads the ^díD in the Code of Hammurabi (e.g., §2) and the Ur-Nammu Code (§132) as *Nārum*.[61] On the other hand, he recognizes the reading *Id* as the name of the river-god in the Middle Assyrian law code (^{íd}*I-id* in §17:II:71, etc.) and the newly published Mari letters (^d*I-id* on p. 1036, line 23; p. 1037, line 29).[62] However, he reads íD.DA in the Mari letters as *Nârum*,[63] the same way as he usually reads íD in the Mari letters.

---

55. In unpublished tablets from Kültepe. See now *CAD* N/1 375.

56. H. Hirsch, "Zur Lesung von ^díD," *AfO* 22 (1968–69), 38: "eine nachaltbabylonische, vielleicht künstliche, bewußte Differenzierung." His suggestion has been supported by scholars such as J. Bottéro, *Mythes et rites de Babylone* (1985), 290.

57. Roberts, *ESP*, 46.

58. Borger, *ABZ*, 200.

59. *CAD* I–J 8.

60. *CAD* N/1 375.

61. J. Bottéro, "L'Ordalie en Mèsopotamie ancienne," *ASN* 3rd series 11/4 (1981), 1021–24.

62. Ibid., 1024, 1036–37.

63. Ibid., 1043, line 33 and 1044, line 33; 1044, lines 35, 44. See also n. 53 (above).

In light of the above, the initial question, "Should the Sumerian ^díD be read in Akkadian as *Id* or as *Nāru*?" can be answered as follows: While the equation ^díD = *id* is possible in special cases, such as Middle Assyrian ^díD^{i-id} with "a specific cultic bearing," the Sumerian ^díD was probably read *Nāru* under normal situations, as in the case of the common noun *nāru* (= íD) "river."[64] The fact that the reading of ^díD was specified as ^{i-id} in some places suggests that that reading was not the normal one for the Sumerian sign. Thus, we must reject the view of Albright and others that *ʾēd* came from Addadian *id*, agreeing with Speiser that "we can be sure of Akkadian *id* as distinct from *nāru* *only* when the term is spelled out syllabically; and such explicit instances are relatively rare. Moreover, the Sumerian logogram in question was read generally in Akkadian as *nāru* 'river' and could not, as such, have led to Heb. *ʾēd.*"

Phonological Problems

Does the *ʾēd–edû* equation have a phonological difficulty? Could the Akkadian *edû* have been borrowed into Hebrew as *ʾēd,* as suggested by Speiser?

According to S. A. Kaufman, "Akkadian nouns ending in a final long vowel usually appear in Aramaic with final *-ê*, which becomes *-yâ* in the emphatic state, [e.g.], *asû, attalû, burû,* . . ."[65] Moreover, Akkadian *edû* was actually borrowed into the Babylonian Talmud as *ʾ(y)dw(w)tʾ* "foam of the sea" with the long vowel *-û* preserved.[66] The two exceptions are, according to him, Assyrian terms,

bārānû	"rebel"	→ Aram. *brywnʾ*
šinepû	"two-thirds"	→ Aram. *snb*[67]

However, it is not certain whether or not the second example had a final long vowel in the Neo-Assyrian period.[68] This evidence about Akkadian loanwords in Aramaic suggests that an Akkadian word with a final long vowel was normally borrowed into Hebrew, or Canaanite, with the final long vowel.

Speiser gives two defenses for his view against the criticism that "*edû* should have resulted in some such form as Heb. **ʾēdê.*" First, he says, the term *ʾēd* in Hebrew is rare, appearing only twice, and Akkadian *edû* is itself a

---

64. Note that in *Ug.* 5, 238, the sign "i" is used for i₇(íD) and is equated with Akk. *na-a-ru* (Text 135 [RS 21.62]: rev.: 9′). Also *CAD* N/1 368; Huehnergard, *UVST,* 66.
65. Kaufman, *AIA,* 149.
66. Ibid., 47; cf. *HAL,* 11.
67. Kaufman, *AIA,* 41, 103. Because the last two are loans from Assyrian, Kaufman conjectures that Heb. *ʾēd,* which is frequently connected with the Akk. *edû,* might be considered "a loan from Assyrian as well" (p. 47 n. 80).
68. See *AHw,* 1242.

Sumerian loanword. Second, "even an established *ʾēdê could have developed an alloform ʾēd." Speiser claims that "Heb. ʾēš 'fire' has a well-attested alloform ʾiššê,"[69] which supports the possibility of this development.

In rebuttal, Sæbø, following Hoftijzer,[70] points out that ʾiššê is not "fire" but a term for offering like Ug. ʾiṭṭ "offering."[71] It is certainly difficult to support Speiser's view that ʾēd is an alloform of *ʾēdê by analogy with ʾēš–ʾiššê, if the term ʾiššê has nothing to do with fire.[72]

However, in fact, a form of *edû* without the loss of the final vowel is preserved in Hebrew in the form ʾēdô (Job 36:27), as suggested by M. H. Pope.[73] Kaufman even suggests that the ʾēd in Gen 2:6 be emended to ʾēdô in the light of the Job passage.[74]

Therefore, phonologically, it is entirely possible that the Akkadian term *edû* is the source of ʾēdô (Job 36:27). It is also possible that ʾēdô subsequently experienced a loss of the final long vowel: /edû/ → /ʾed/ > /ʾēd/, as in the geographical name Akkad (Akk. *akkadû* > Heb. ʾakkad)[75] and developed the alloform ʾēd. Therefore, though Speiser's example, ʾēš "fire"–ʾiššê, for explaining the proposed form *ʾēdê as an alloform of ʾēd should be abandoned, his basic suggestion that ʾēd = *edû* is possible.

The Semantic Problem

Does Akk. *edû* really refer to a rare and catastrophic event? It is often argued that the Akkadian word *edû* refers to a rare and catastrophic event, which does not fit the context of Gen 2:5–6. Hence, many commentators have followed Albright's view. The main issue here is: What kind of event does Akk. *edû* really refer to?

---

69. Speiser, "ʾed in the Story of Creation," 11.

70. J. Hoftijzer, "Das sogenannte Feueropfer," *Hebräische Wortforschung: Festschrift zum 80. Geburtstag von Walter Baumgartner* (VTSup 16; Leiden: Brill, 1967), 133. Cf. also G. R. Driver, "Ugaritic and Hebrew Words," *Ug.* 6 (1969), 181–84. However, the identification of Heb. ʾiššê with *Ug. iṭṭ* has been questioned by M. Dietrich, O. Loretz, and J. Sanmartín, "Ein Brief des Königs an die Königin-Mutter (RS 11.872 = CTA 50): Zur Frage ug. *iṭṭ* = hebr. ʾšh?" *UF* 6 (1974), 460–62.

71. Sæbø, "Die hebräischen Nomina ʾed und ʾēd," *ST* 24, 134.

72. Note that in Ugaritic the term for "fire" *išt* is etymologically different from *iṭṭ*.

73. M. H. Pope, *Job* (3rd ed.; AB 15; New York: Doubleday, 1973), 273; cf. F. I. Andersen, *Job* (TOTC; Leicester: IVP, 1976), 263. See below, p. 105, for a further discussion of this passage.

74. Kaufman, *AIA*, 47.

75. B. Groneberg, *Die Orts- und Gewässernamen der altbabylonischen Zeit* (RGTC 3; Wiesbaden: Reichert, 1980), 7, listing OB spellings *a-ka-dum, ak-ka-du-ú*, etc.

In order to support the equation *'ēd* = *edû*, Speiser first cites the Sumerian-Akkadian bilingual vocabulary in VAT 10270 iv 44ff., which lists the following entries:[76]

(Sum.)	A.GI$_6$.A	= (Akk.)	*e-gu-[u]*
	A.DÉ.A	=	*e-du-u*
	A.SI.GA	=	*e-si-gu*
	A.ZI.GA	=	*me-lu*
	A.MAḪ	=	*bu-tuq-tum*

He explains that "all these are synonyms for certain bodies of water (= A). . . . The character of the group as a whole is indicated by . . . *butuqtum* 'break-through' (of the subterranean water); *mēlu* 'flood, (ground) flow'."[77] Thus Speiser sees here some association of meanings between *edû* and *mīlu* and *butuqtum*.

Second, he recognizes one of the common uses of *mīlu* as "the flow that rises from underground springs" in the *Atra-Ḫasīs* epic and adds the following comment: "Synonymous with it is the term for water that has broken through to the surface (*butuqtum*), and also *edû*." However, here too Speiser uses the term "synonymous" in a very loose and rather impressionistic way.

Third, he makes note of another lexical text where "*edû* is defined as *šaqû ša eqli* 'watering of the field'." Speiser notes that this equation has long been known[78] and that "both with Hebrew *'ēd* and with Akkadian *edû* the same verb (*šqy*) [is] employed to describe the function of the respective nouns." Consequently, Speiser sees the three terms *'ēd*, *ya'lê* and *hišqâ* in Gen 2:6 as corresponding to three Akkadian words, *edû*, *mēlu*, and *šaqû*, and concludes, "Plainly, the Biblical verse might have been lifted verbatim from an Akkadian lexical work."[79]

Speiser's argument is certainly semantically loose. His use of "synonymous" and "synonyms," especially, is not precise enough, and his examples are not strong enough to be evidence that *edû* means "subterranean water." Hence, he is sharply criticized by Sæbø.

Sæbø claims that Speiser's comment, "all . . . [are] synonymous for certain bodies of water," is only conjecture. He says that, though Speiser takes *mīlu*

---

76. Cf. *CAD* E 336.

77. Speiser, "*'ed* in the Story of Creation," 10.

78. Cf. P. A. Deimel, *Šumerisches Lexikon* (Rome: Pontifical Biblical Institute, 1930), 579, 324b; it was cited, for example, by E. Sachsse, "Der jahwistische Schöpfungsbericht: Ein Erklärungsversuch," *ZAW* 39 (1921), 281. (Speiser, "*'ēd* in the Story of Creation," 10 n. 10.)

79. Speiser, ibid., 11.

and *edû* as being synonymous, this contradicts the meanings of the two words because, according to *CAD*, the "phenomenon referred to by *edû* . . . is a rare and catastrophic event . . . as against *mīlu*, the annual high water."[80] Hence, Sæbø concludes that Speiser's attempt to understand *edû* as "unterirdisches, hervorbrechendes (Grund-)Wasser" ("subterranean, erupting [ground]-water") is untenable. Sæbø also claims that, because the Hebrew word "disaster" derives from *edû*, *edû* must refer to a catastrophic event. However, the examples that he cites as evidence for the phonological change *edû* > *ʾêd* "misfortune" ("Unglück") are not convincing.[81]

Barr[82] also follows *CAD*'s comment without reservation. He says: "As *CAD* (E, p. 35f.) makes clear with numerous examples, *edû* means something far more violent and catastrophic than can be related to the Hebrew passage." He cites the following examples: First, "*CAD* gives as its main gloss *onrush of water, high water*: it is something like a huge wave that may sink a ship, or again it is 'the high tide of the sea' which can overwhelm a camp." Second, "used of rivers, *edû* may be its high flooding, but *CAD* emphasizes that this is a rare and catastrophic phenomenon." Third, in "a hymn to Marduk . . . *bēl kuppī naqbī e-di-e u tâmāti* 'lord of sources, springs, high waters and seas', it is the *kuppu* and the *naqbu* . . . that might have fitted the Hebrew passage, while the *edû* is a phenomenon of the high seas."

Thus, Sæbø and Barr depend heavily on *CAD*'s examples and especially on its final remark: "The phenomenon referred to by *edû* (a.dé.a in contrast to [a.si].ga . . .) is a rare and catastrophic event (cf. the correspondence m i r = *edû*) as against *mīlu*, the annual high water."[83]

---

80. *CAD* E 36: "The phenomenon referred to by *edû* (a.dé.a in contrast to [a.si].ga also in ASKT p. 98:34, Akk. col. broken) is a rare and catastrophic event (cf. the correspondence m i r = *edû*) as against *mīlu*, the annual high water. Albright, RA 16 175."

81. He lists the following examples (see Sæbø, "Die hebräischen Nomina ʾed und ʾēd," 140):

akk. *bulû* (mA *bulaʾu*) 'Dürrholz' > hebr. *būl*,
akk. *kutū* > hebr. *kūt* (2 Kg 17,30) bzw. *kūtā* (2 Kg 17,24),
akk. *qutū* bzw. *sutū* > hebr. *qōʿ*

The first example might support the interchange of the noun of III weak pattern (cf. mA *bulāʾu*) with that of II weak (*bwl) in Semitic languages. However, this does not help explain the change *edû* > *ʾēd*, since Akkadian *edû* itself is a loanword from non-Semitic, i.e., Sumerian. The second example is not valid, because it is based on the wrong information on *Kutū* in KB, 429, which *HAL* corrects as *Kūtū*. The /t/ – /ʿ/ correspondence in the third example is rather hard to explain; we would expect a Hebrew form like *qōt* or *qōʾ*.

82. Barr, "Limitations of Etymology," 49.

83. *CAD* E 36.

mir = *edû*

However, a closer look at the evidence shows that the Akkadian term *edû* does not necessarily refer to violent water as such. For one thing, *CAD*'s comment on *edû* as "a rare and catastrophic event" in connection with the "correspondence mir = *edû*" is not well founded. In a bilingual lexical text from the Old Babylonian period, lines 11 and 12 certainly refer to similar phenomena.[84]

| line 11 | mi-ir | // | TÙN-*gunû* | // | *me-ḫu-ú-um* | "storm" |
| line 12 | mi-ir | // | TÙN-*gunû* | // | *e-du-ú-um* | "flood" |

However, other correspondences in the same text show that they are not necessarily synonymous. Note the following "correspondences":

line 7	gi-ém	//	TÙN	//	*ši-iq-lum*	"shekel-weight"
line 8	gi-ém	//	TÙN	//	*pa-a-šum*	"axe"
line 23	ša-a	//	ŠÀ	//	*li-ib-bu-um*	"heart"
line 24	ša-a	//	ŠÀ	//	*ir-ru-um*	"intestines"

Therefore, there is no reason to take *edû* as synonymous with *meḫûm* "storm," hence as referring to a "catastrophic" event.

High Water

Moreover, *edû* (e_4-dé-a) in contrast to *esigu*[85] (e_4-si-ga) "ebb, low water" simply implies that the former means "high water." In fact, the term *edû* refers to "the annual high water" of spring in several of the texts cited by *CAD* itself. For example, in the text that reads *ina mīli* (A.KAL) *kiššati edû pān šatti napališ ušētiq* "I crossed [the Tigris and the Euphrates] as if it were dry land at the height of the flooding, the high water of spring,"[86] the term *edû* appears in apposition to *mīlu* without any implication that it has a destructive power. One other text, which mentions *ina Ajari ūmu adanni edê pān šatti* "in the month of Ajaru, at the season of the high waters of spring [the beginning of the year],"[87] suggests that *edû* sometimes means "the annual high water" like *mīlu*. In another text, irrigation (*šqy*) "with waters as abundant as the huge waves of the (annual) inundation" (*kî gipiš edî mê nuḫši*)[88] is mentioned.

---

84. B. Landsberger, *Die Serie Ur-e-a = nâqu* (MSL 2; Rome: Pontifical Biblical Institute, 1951), 149: 11–12.

85. *CAD* E 336.

86. H. Winckler, *Die Keilschrifttexte Sargons* (Leipzig: Pfeiffer, 1889), 44 D 36, cited by *CAD* E 36, b; M/2 70.

87. OIP 2 104 v 70 (Senn.), cited by *CAD* E 36, b.

88. Lyon Sar. p. 6:37, cited by *CAD* E 36, b.

It is interesting to note that in the last-cited example, *gipiš*, the attributive of *edû*, is used also with *mīlu* in a positive sense, as in *mīlu gapšum illakam* "an abundant [beneficial] flood will come."[89] On the other hand, *edû* certainly can appear in negative contexts, as in the following texts:

> *edû dannu ina tâmtim liṭabbīšina*
> may a huge wave [in parallelism with *šamru agû*] sink them [your ships]
>   in the sea[90]

> *edû tâmati gapši[š iš]šamma qirib zarātija ērumma*
> the high tide of the sea rushed on in great mass and entered my tents[91]

> *edû gapšu ša la iššannanu* MURUB₄-*šu*
> the strong tide whose onslaught cannot be rivaled[92]

However, it is important to note that the violence has nothing to do with the term *edû* itself. It is its adjectives, such as *dannu* (// *šamru*) and *gapšu* (also *ezzu* and *kaššu* in the following example), that add a "catastrophic" nature to the term *edû*. Even *mīlu* can be destructive, as in the following examples, where it is followed by the adjective *kaššu*:

> *Araḫti nār* (ÍD) *ḫegalli agû ezzi edû šamru* [var. [*a*]*gû šamru edû ezzu*]
> *mīlu kaššu tamšil abûbu ibbablamma āla . . . mê ušbiʾ*

> the Arahtu, river of fertility, (now) an angry wave, a raging tide, a huge flood, a very Deluge, overflowed and inundated the city [of Babylon].[93]

It is not just *agû* and *edû* that refer to catastrophic water in this text; even the usually "beneficial" flood (*mīlu*) is also used for describing the destructive nature of the river Araḫtu. Therefore, *CAD*'s comment, the "phenomenon referred to by *edû* is a rare and catastrophic event as against *mīlu*, the annual high water," is not supported by this text either.[94]

While Barr argues for the catastrophic nature of *edû* on the basis of a hymn to Marduk[95] that mentions *bēl kuppī naqbī edê u tâmāti* "lord of sources,

---

89. YOS 10 25:58 (OB omen), cited by *CAD* M/2 71. Note also *mīlu ṭaḫdum illakam* (*RA* 44 pl. 3 p. 40:22 [OB omen]), cited by *CAD* M/2 71.

90. Borger Esarh. 109 iv 12 (treaty), cited by *CAD* E 35.

91. OIP 2 74:74 (Senn.), cited by *CAD* E 35.

92. AKA 223:15 (Ashurnasirpal), cited by *CAD* Q 13.

93. Borger Esarh. 14 Ep. 7:39, cited by *CAD* E 35; N/1 372. See also Nabopolassar and Nebuchadnezzar, cited by *CAD* M/2 72.

94. See also *mê mīli rašubbat* ÍD "water of the high flood, overwhelming power of the river" (Maqlu VII 179), cited by *CAD* N/1 372.

95. BA 5 393 i 34 (SB hymn to Marduk). On Marduk and his relation with water, see pp. 130–131.

springs, high waters and seas," this title simply describes Marduk as the "lord of high waters," and it has nothing to do with *edû* as a negative entity, though Barr interprets it as "the high seas." This text simply puts *edû* "high waters" and *tâmātu* "seas" in close contact, without specifying whether the former is the "high waters" of a river or of the sea.

High Tide?

The term *edû* sometimes refers to a "high tide" of the sea in texts such as the *edû dannu ina tâmtim* cited above and seems to have a close association with the sea just as *mīlu* has a connection with the river.[96] However, the ancient Semites seemingly understood the *edû*-water to have come out of Apsu, the subterranean ocean. In *Gilgamesh* epic XI:297–98, Gilgamesh bewails his loss of the plant of life and says to his companion (in von Soden's translation):[97]

(297) Jetzt steigt zwanzig Doppelstunden weit die Flut (= *edû*)
(298) Und ich liess, als den Schacht ich grub, das Werkzeug fallen!
(299) Welches könnte ich finden, das an meine *Seite ich legte*?
(300) Wäre ich doch zurückgewichen und hätte das Schiff am Ufer
    gelassen!

Albright took this passage as "primarily an aetiological myth explaining the origin of the tides."[98] However, no scholar now reads *tâmta* "sea" in line 299,[99] and hence there is no evidence that *edû* here refers to the tide of the sea. Because the *edû* is understood as having risen as a result of the hero's

---

96. *AHw*, 187: *edû ša tâmti* (Sn 74, 72); *AHw*, 1353: *tiāmtu*: j). On the other hand, *mīlu* is a "seasonal flooding of the rivers—association with the rivers, rain, and the depth (*nagbu*)"; cf. *AHw*, 652–53; *CAD* M/2 70–71.

97. A. Schott and W. von Soden, *Das Gilgamesch-Epos* (Stuttgart: Reclam, 1958, 1982), 105.

98. W. F. Albright, "Notes on Assyrian Lexicography and Etymology," *RA* 16 (1919), 175. See also Speiser's translation in *ANET* (1950) 96:

And now the tide will bear (it) twenty leagues away!
When I opened the *water-pipe* and spilled the gear.

Following Albright, Speiser explains that "the opening of the *rātu* (normally 'pipe, tube'), apparently took place in connection with Gilgamesh's dive (cf. also l. 271)." Speiser also notes that the same term is used, referring "perhaps to a pipe connecting with a source of sweet waters which would nourish the miraculous plant" in the *Eridu Creation Story* (n. 232).

99. Cf. R. C. Thompson's reading in *The Epic of Gilgamish: Text, Transliteration, and Notes* (Oxford: Clarendon, 1930); A. Heidel, *The Gilgamesh Epic and Old Testament Parallels* (2nd ed.; Chicago: University of Chicago Press, 1949), 92; Speiser, *ANET*, 97; von Soden's translation; R. Labat et al., *Les religions du Proche-Orient asiatique* (Paris: Fayard/Denoël, 1970), 221: "le flot."

forgetting to replace "the cover of *rāṭu* which communicated with the *apsû*,"[100] it here refers to the flooding of the subterranean ocean.

Subterranean Water

If, as Albright and the others claim, Hebrew *ʾēd* referred to the "river," one would have to ask why the writer of Genesis would borrow the Akkadian "divine" name *Id* when there was a common Akkadian noun, *nāru*, for river. In fact, the writer uses *nāhār*, the cognate of Akkadian *nāru*, just a few verses later in 2:10. This makes it even more difficult to suppose that *ʾēd* is an Akkadian (< Sumerian) loanword with the meaning "river."

On the other hand, *edû*, defined as "water flooding out of the subterranean ocean," seems a better candidate, without philological difficulties. Moreover, this interpretation is basically supported by the ancient versions (LXX, Aquila, Vulgate, and Peshitta), which translate the term *ʾēd* "spring, fountain" (cf. Num 21:17),[101] and fits the Genesis context well.[102]

However, before we discuss the relationship of *ʾēd*-water with the earth in its context,[103] let us review another possibility for the origin of the term.

Direct Sumerian Loanword?

We discussed whether *ʾēd* could have come from Akkadian *id* or *edû*; now we shall discuss whether it could have come directly from the Sumerian behind either of those two words.

From Sumerian íd?

Already in 1915, Zimmern commented, as an alternative to the *ʾēd* = *edû* equation, that the term *ʾēd* might be a direct Sumerian loanword: "oder gar < sum. *id* Fluss?"[104] (Some scholars misinterpret Albright's view as claiming that Hebrew *ʾēd* is a direct loanword from Sumerian. For example, Castellino says, "W. F. Albright took a stand for the Sumerian id, but more recently E. A. Speiser entered into the debate in favor of the Akkadian *edû*. But perhaps the arguments in favor of a Sumerian derivation have not been entirely exhausted."[105]) Castellino suggests that phonetically *ʾēd* corresponds better to

---

100. Albright, "Notes on Assyrian Lexicography and Etymology," 176.

101. According to Cassuto, "it is hard to imagine that Scripture refers to only *one* spring, since it says: *and watered the* WHOLE FACE OF THE GROUND"; cf. Cassuto, *From Adam to Noah*, 104. However, if the term *ʾēd* refers to an unusually huge "fountain," there should be no problem in rendering it thus.

102. For the usage in Job 36:27, see below, p. 105.

103. See below, p. 111.

104. Zimmern, *AFw*, 44.

105. Castellino, "Les origines de la civilisation," 121–22 (repr. and trans. as "The Origins of Civilization according to Biblical and Cuneiform Texts," in *"I Studied Inscriptions*

Sumerian[106] íd than to Akkadian *edû*.

Barr suggested as one possibility that "'*ēd* is indeed derived from the Mesopotamian culture but represents not the Akkadian *edû* . . . but the Sumerian *id* from which it is said to be derived and which commonly means 'river', being translated into Akkadian as *nāru* with this meaning. The Hebrew would then be derived directly from the Sumerian." And he admits that this Sumerian derivation is "quite possible purely linguistically."[107]

However, it is not positive that Sumerian íd (A.ENGUR) would have been borrowed as *'*id* > '*ēd* into Hebrew (or rather Canaanite), because there are suggestions that the Sumerian íd was actually pronounced /ḫid/. For one thing, the place-name ᵘʳᵘíd may refer to the modern Ḫīt on the Euphrates,[108] which suggests that Sumerian íd was actually pronounced /ḫid/. It is possible that the place-name Ḫīt does not reflect íd but means "place where pitch comes" (< Iṭṭû "pitch"), while íᴅ by itself was pronounced /i/.[109]

Even more suggestive are the correspondences for the name of the Tigris River, idig(i)na (Sum.) // *idigra-um* (Ebla.) // *idiqlat* (Akk.) ↔ Hebrew *ḥiddéqel* (< *ḥid + iqlu). A possible explanation is that the Hebrew form preserves a pre-Sumerian name.[110] However, because the name makes good sense in Sumerian, "flowing river" (íd + gina),[111] this is an unlikely

---

from before the Flood": Ancient Near Eastern and Literary Approaches to Genesis 1–11 [ed. R. S. Hess and D. Tsumura; SBTS 4; Winona Lake, Ind.: Eisenbrauns, 1994]), 80–81.

106. Note that Sæbø, "Die hebräischen Nomina '*ed* und '*ēd*," 135, cites Castellino's "Sum. id" as the Akk. (or "sum-akk.") *id*.

107. Barr, "Limitations of Etymology," 64 n. 10.

108. Cf. S. Parpola, *Neo-Assyrian Toponyms* (AOAT 6; Neukirchen-Vluyn: Neukirchener Verlag, 1970), 172; J. N. Postgate, "(A Review of) Khaled Nashef, *Die Orts- und Gewässernamen . . . 1982,*" *AfO* 32 (1985), 97; A. Poebel, "Sumerische Untersuchungen IV," *ZA* 39 (1930), 145. Cf. also I. J. Gelb, *Old Akkadian Writing and Grammar* (2nd ed.; MAD 2; Chicago: University of Chicago Press, 1961), 26.

109. Suggested by W. G. Lambert, private communication.

110. That is, an "Ubaidan" or "Proto-Euphratean" (see *DANE*, 1975). If the Heb. term were a Sum. loanword via Akk., a form like *'iddiqlāh (note the doubling of /d/ for preserving the short /i/ in the initial syllable) or *'ědiqlāh, with the fem. ending /-āh/ (or /-at/), rather than *ḥiddéqel* should be expected. As far as the ending is concerned, a masculine form in Eblaite *i-di-gi-ra-um* /'idigla-um/ (VE 1423') is closer to the Hebrew form. However, its initial sign ⟨i⟩ probably stands for the simple vowel /i/ (see M. Krebernik, "Zu Syllabar und Orthographie der lexikalischen Texte aus Ebla, Teil 1," *ZA* 72 [1982], 219; M. Civil, "Bilingualism in Logographically Written Languages: Sumerian in Ebla," in *BaE*, 80) and the term is masculine as against the feminine form in Akkadian: (Sum.) /idig(i)na/—(Ebla.) /idigra-um/—(Akk.) /idiqla-t/. Note that the Eblaite form with the ending /-um/ is a "Semitized" form. See below, p. 114, on the discussion of Eblaite sign list B.

111. See below, pp. 125–126, on its etymology.

hypothesis. The other possibility is that Hebrew /ḥid-/ reflects Sumerian íd (or its first element i-)[112] or the first element of Sumerian i₇-digna.[113]

The Akkadian form *idiqlat* on the other hand may derive either from the loss of the word-initial consonant /ḫ/ of an early Sumerian name for "Tigris" or simply reflect the first vowel of the later Sumerian /idigna/. Thus, Hebrew *ḥiddéqel* could be a reflection of a direct (or indirect, i.e., via a non-Akkadian language) borrowing of an early Sumerian name into Canaanite, which would suggest that the Sumerian íd could possibly have been borrowed as /ḥid/. Therefore, though we cannot say that it could not have been borrowed directly from the Sumerian íd, there remains some uncertainty from the phonological standpoint.

From Sumerian e₄-dé?

However, I should like to suggest the possibility that Hebrew *ʾēd* is a direct loan from Sumerian e₄-dé (A.DÉ),[114] the source of the Akkadian *edû*, similarly to the situation where the Sumerian a-kà-dè entered Hebrew as *ʾakkad* "Akkad" and Akkadian as *Akkadû*.[115] Phonologically as well as semantically the term e₄-dé "high water"[116] is a better candidate for the etymology of the Hebrew *ʾēd* than Sumerian íd if we propose a "direct" borrowing of a Sumerian original.

As noted above, it is possible that *ʾēd* is a shortened form of *ʾēdô* as the result of the loss of the final vowel when or after Akkadian *edû* was borrowed into ancient Canaanite. However, since the Sumerian original of Akkadian *edû* is A.DÉ (= e₄-dé) or its alternate A.DÉ.A (= e₄-dé-a),[117] I would like to suggest that:

---

112. Cf. Leander, *Über die Sumerischen Lehnwörter in Assyrischen*, 61: "i(d) A.íD *nâru*."

113. Poebel, "Sumerische Untersuchungen IV," 145.

114. The Sumerogram A can be read either as a or e₄.

115. See above, p. 96.

116. The newest Sumerian dictionary, *SD* A/1 60 gives the meanings "(yearly) inundation"; "onrush of water." My rendering "high water" is thus not "an actually rare meaning" (G. F. Hasel and M. G. Hasel, "The Hebrew Term *ʾed* in Gen 2,6, and Its Connection in Ancient Near Eastern Literature," *ZAW* 112 [2000], 325); see below.

117. *SD* A/1 60 lists both a-dé-a and a-dé as variant forms. Hasel and Hasel seem to lack adequate control of recent Sumerian-Akkadian information. Before they criticized my approach as "dubious," they should have checked recent materials such as the *SD* and the *CAD* Š/2 26–28. Regrettably, despite the fact that they wrote in an article published in 2000, "the best lexical sources" available to them were only those of 1903, 1958, and 1977; see "The Hebrew Term *ʾed* in Gen 2,6," 325. Cf. Lieberman, *SLOBA*, 215–16 n. 161; A. R. Millard, "The Etymology of Eden," *VT* 34 (1984), 104. However, *CAD* E 35 and *AHw*, 187 list only a-dé-a for the Sum. original.

1. the short Hebrew form *ʾēd* (Gen 2:6) is a "direct" loan from Sumerian e₄-dé;
2. the long form *ʾēdô* (Job 36:27) is a Sumerian loanword via Akkadian *edû* (< Sum. /edea/).

Both *ʾēd* and its allomorph *ʾēdô* mean "high water" and refer to the water flooding out of the subterranean ocean.

A final judgment on the meaning and etymology of any term, however, cannot be made until the term is set in its context adequately. Especially "in the case of rare words," as Barr rightly notes, "literary questions are relevant and one cannot proceed purely linguistically."[118]

What is the connection between the *ʾēd*-water in Gen 2:6 and the *nāhār*-water in v. 10?[119] While the *ʾēd*-water springs from the ground and waters the entire surface of the "land" (*ʾădāmâ*),[120] the river water originates in Eden, the well-watered place, which is in the eastern part of the "land."[121] Thus, apparently the *ʾēd*-water eventually gathers together and forms a river in Eden that waters the garden.

As for *ʾēdô* in Job 36:27, Andersen, who takes *ʾēd* to mean "upswell (of groundwaters)," remarks that "the usage in Job 36:27 can be clarified by comparison with other meteorological passages, notably Proverbs 3:19–20; 8:22–31, as well as Genesis 6–8."[122] After stating that more than one "ocean" is mentioned in these passages, he suggests that, "just as the *ʾēd* (!) comes up from the ground in Genesis 2, so water from God's *ʾēd* (!) comes down to the ground in Job 36."[123] However, it is not certain that the "his *ʾēd* (!)" (*ʾēdô*) in Job refers to "the river of God." For one thing, Andersen has left undecided whether *ʾēd* is a borrowing from Sumerian i d or from Akkadian *edû*. Moreover, *tĕhômôt* in Prov 3:20 is better taken as referring to the subterranean waters, as noted above (ch. 2). In Job 36:27, as in Gen 2:5–6, both the "rain" (*māṭār*), which is the water from above, and the *ʾēd*-water, *ʾēdô*, are mentioned. Therefore, it is most likely that the *ʾēd*-water refers to the water from below in both passages. The two waters in Job 36:27 might be compared with the meteorological phenomenon described by the Ugaritic expression *šrʿ thmtm* "surging of the two *thmt*-waters" (KTU 1.19 [1Aqht]:I:45).[124]

---

118. Barr, "Limitations of Etymology," 51.

119. Personal communication with Thomas Finley.

120. See ch. 4 (above).

121. See ch. 6 (below).

122. F. I. Andersen, "On Reading Genesis 1–3," in *Backgrounds for the Bible* (ed. M. P. O'Connor and D. N. Freedman; Winona Lake, Ind.: Eisenbrauns, 1987), 139.

123. Andersen, ibid., 139–40, taking *-ô* as 3rd masc. sing.

124. See below, p. 122.

Summary and Conclusions

The term *'ēd* in Gen 2:6 is of uncertain etymology and has been interpreted in a variety of ways throughout the ages, as "spring," "cloud," "mist," "flood," "streams," and so on.

No good case has been made for a West Semitic etymology, and scholars have usually supported an Akkadian or Sumerian etymology.

The two Akkadian candidates are:

1. *edû* "flood," a Sumerian loanword from e_4-dé-a (A.DÉ.A)
2. *id* "river," written with ÍD.

The problem with (b) is that the Sumerogram ÍD was probably read *nāru*, the ordinary word for river, in most circumstances in Akkadian. Furthermore, why would the writer of Genesis borrow the Akkadian "divine" name *Id* when there was a common Akkadian noun, *nāru*, for river and he uses its cognate, *nāhār*, a few verses later in v. 10? This makes it even harder to believe that *'ēd* is from an Akkadian *id* meaning "river."

Looking at (a), there is no phonological difficulty in equating Akkadian *edû* and Hebrew *'ēdô* (Job 36:27). Therefore, if one considers *'ēd* a shorter form of *'ēdô*, which is possible, (a) is possible. However, a solution that does not require the dropping of a long vowel (ô) would be preferable.

We also looked at the possibility of borrowing directly from the Sumerian originals of *id* or *edû*, that is, íd or e_4-dé(-a).

A derivation from íd (A-ENGUR) presents some difficulties, including the question of the actual pronunciation of íd (ÍD). A more promising suggestion is that *'ēd* is a loanword, borrowed from the Sumerian e_4-dé(-a).

Therefore, I have made the following suggestions:

1. *'ēd* (Gen 2:6) is a loanword borrowed directly from Sumerian e_4-dé;
2. *'ēdô* (Job 36:27) is a loanword from Sumerian e_4-dé-a via Akkadian *edû*.

The question then is what does e_4-dé(-a) mean? It is often said that its Akkadian derivative *edû* refers to unusually violent water, but this view does not hold up under examination. One use seems to be "water flooding out of the subterranean ocean." This fits the context of Gen 2:6 very well.

6

The Earth-Waters Relationship in Genesis 2

In an earlier chapter, we discussed the nature of the relationship between the earth and the waters described in the initial part of Gen 1 and concluded that the těhôm-water in Gen 1:2 covered the whole earth, though the těhôm-water in the biblical cosmology is a part of the earth ('ereṣ) in normal contexts. In this chapter, we will discuss the nature of the relationship between the earth and the waters described in the initial part of Gen 2. This involves a further discussion of the term 'ēd (2:6) in its proper context and an etymological treatment of the term 'ēden.

A Flooding of the Subterranean Waters

In light of the etymological discussions in the previous chapter, it is likely that the term 'ēd refers to the subterranean water that came up *to* the surface of the earth rather than referring to mist or vapor that came up *from* the surface of the earth. However, we should ask how this water from under ground was related to the earth after "coming up" from the earth in Gen 2. Did it form a stream, like the water of the Sumerian íd (= Akkadian nāru) "river," or was it flooding water like that referred to by the Sumerian e₄-dé(-a) (= Akkadian edû) "high water"?

"River"?

Both the 'ēd-water in Gen 2:6 and the river in v. 10 are subjects of a verbal form of šqh "to water." Therefore, Sæbø thinks that Gen 2:6 and 2:10ff. are exegetically closely connected and that the waters in both these verses are "a river."[1] However, in Joel 4:18, the subject of this verb is "a spring" (ma'yān); hence, šqh can have any watery entity as its subject. Therefore, the similarity of the verbal forms in Gen 2:6 and 2:10 does not necessarily imply that the subjects have identical meanings or that 'ēd also means "river."

---

1. M. Sæbø, "Die hebräischen Nomina 'ed und 'ēd: Zwei sumerisch-akkadische Fremdwörter?" *ST* 24 (1970), 132–33.

Moreover, if ʾēd means "a river," why is the river presented in two forms in Gen 2, ʾēd and nāhār? To this, Castellino, who takes ʾēd to be "a river" (Sum. id), has answered, "The nāhār is not a useless repetition of the ʾēd of 2:6. The ʾēd corresponds to the ʾădāmâ, and the nāhār is for the gan ['garden'], reflecting two distinct entities."[2]

However, probably more significant than their common verb and different objects, ʾădāmâ and gan, is the difference in the verbs that describe their origin: yaʿăleh (2:6) and yōṣēʾ (2:10). It seems that the author of Genesis purposely makes a clear distinction between the ʾēd-water that "comes up from the earth" and the "river" that "comes out of Eden." The ʾēd-water is that which comes up from underground and waters the whole surface of the land (ʾădāmâ). On the other hand, in v. 10 the waters "come out of" one place and "water" a different place, forming a stream or streams, like the "spring" (maʿyān) of Joel 4:18.[3]

Irrigation of the Land

Again, if the ʾēd-water is a river, why did it not irrigate the soil?[4] The initial state in Gen 2:5–6 is described as without rain but with the ʾēd-water coming up from underground to water the whole surface of the land. Barr thinks that it "is not easy to make good sense of this in the context" but, instead of assuming plural documentary sources as some critics do, he wonders whether ʾēd is not "after all a mist?"[5] However, as already noted in the previous chapter, ʾēd as meaning "vapor, mist" has no etymological support, though it is true that etymology does not determine meaning.

The situation in 2:5–6 as a whole was simply this: because of the lack of rain, there were no plants in the fields, while the ʾēd-water was flooding out of the earth to water, that is, inundate,[6] the entire surface of the "land" (ʾădāmâ), which was only a part of the "earth" (ʾereṣ). Because this ʾēd-water refers to

---

2. G. Castellino, "Les origines de la civilisation selon les textes bibliques et les textes cunéiformes," *Volume du Congrès: Strasbourg 1956* (VTSup 4; Leiden: Brill, 1957), 123 [repr. and trans. "The Origins of Civilization according to Biblical and Cuneiform Texts," in *"I Studied Inscriptions from before the Flood": Ancient Near Eastern, Literary, and Linguistic Approaches to Genesis 1–11* (ed. R. S. Hess and D. T. Tsumura; SBTS 4; Winona Lake, Ind.: Eisenbrauns, 1994), 82].

3. In Joel 4:18 the verbal form yēṣēʾ is used with the place that the "spring" originates, prefixed by the preposition min.

4. The question was raised by J. Barr, "Limitations of Etymology as a Lexicographical Instrument in Biblical Hebrew," *Transactions of the Philological Society* (1983), 64 n. 10.

5. Ibid., 51.

6. For the possible Sumerian etymology of e₄-dé with the meanings of "(yearly) inundation," "onrush of water," see above (ch. 5).

the water flooding out of the earth, without man's irrigating and tilling activities the land (*'ădāmâ*) was not suitable for plants to grow. The problem here was not the lack of water but the lack of adequate control of water by man for tilling purposes.[7] This well-watered situation is certainly in keeping with Eden, the "well-watered place" where God planted a garden (2:8).[8] To the discussion of the etymology of "Eden" we shall turn shortly.

Excursus: Time and Place of Man's Creation

If the *'ēd*-water refers to water flooding out of the earth to water the entire surface of the land (*'ădāmâ*), how could God "form" the man out of the soil of the land (*'āpār min-hā'ădāmâ*)? And when and where did it happen? Barr, who takes *'ēd* as "vapour," says, "[The vapour] only damped the surface, perhaps thus making the earth pliable for God to fashion man out of the soil."[9] But if, as I think, *'ēd* "high water" was covering the entire land (*'ădāmâ*), it is difficult to understand how the soil (*'āpār*) of the land (*'ădāmâ*) was used for making the man.

According to my discourse analysis of Gen 2,[10] vv. 7–8 should be analyzed thus:

[UNIT 1]: *wayyîṣer* (action 1) *YHWH 'ĕlōhîm . . . wayyippaḥ* (action 2)
[UNIT 2]: *wayyiṭṭa'* (action 3) *YHWH 'ĕlōhîm . . . wayyāśem* (action 4)

Here, the actual "chronological" order of events could not have been anything but (action 1) – (action 2) – (action 4): the LORD God "formed" and

---

7. For a description of the beginning of irrigation and agriculture in Sumerian society, see J. van Dijk, *LUGAL UD ME-LÁM-bi NIR-GÁL: Le récit épique et didactique des Travaux de Ninurta, du Déluge et de la Nouvelle Création*, vol. 1: *Introduction, Texte Composite. Traduction* (Leiden: Brill, 1983), 94–97 (lines 344–66); also J. van Dijk, "Lugal-e," *RlA* 7.134–36.

8. For a brief summary of various theories on the location of Eden, see G. J. Wenham, *Genesis 1–15* (WBC 1; Waco, Tex.: Word, 1987), 66–67.

9. Barr, "Limitations of Etymology," 51; cf. H. Gunkel, *Genesis* (Göttingen: Vandenhoeck & Ruprecht, 1902), 5, cited by D. Kidner, "Genesis 2:5, 6: Wet or Dry?" *TynBul* 17 (1966), 113.

10. To summarize my basic assumptions,

1. A new subparagraph (discourse unit) is begun by every new *wayqtl* with a stated subject; *waw* here is "initial."
2. *Wayqtl* without a stated subject indicates that this action or event is in a sequence with the previous action or event; *waw* here is "sequential."
3. *Wayhî* should be treated as one level away from the main line of narrative discourse.

See above, p. 77 n. 2, for bibliography of Longacre's works.

"breathed" and "put." But we do not know when the "planting" (3) of the garden happened. [UNIT 2] simply explains that (3) happened before the LORD
God "put" (4), and the actual "chronological" order of events can be (1)–(2)–
(3)–(4) or (1)–(3)–(2)–(4) or (3)–(1)–(2)–(4). Of course, it is also possible
that "planting" (3) could happen together with (1) or (2).[11]

It may be conjectured that, when God planted a garden "in Eden in the
east" (*bĕʿēden miqqedem*),[12] the *ʾēd*-water that had been covering the whole
surface of the land had receded in Eden, and the land there was dry enough
for God to make a garden. But, how dry did the land have to be for God to
form a man and make a garden?

A. R. Millard has suggested (private communication) that, "if *ʾēd* covered
the land surface by issuing from below and produced a situation unsuitable
for tilling, it was presumably creating a marsh of some sort." This situation
accords with that in the initial section of *Enuma elish* I 6, which mentions that
the waters had "not yet" produced the marshland.[13] Therefore, it is reasonable
to think that, at the time when God formed the man from the soil of the land,
the *ʾēd*-water had probably created a marshy situation in Eden and, if this was
so, lumps of soil could be scooped up for God to form a man.[14] Moreover,
when God made the garden in Eden, he must have drained the *ʾēd*-water by
the rivers to make the land dry enough to plant trees.[15] The garden in Eden,
"the well-watered place,"[16] then was naturally drained of the water by rivers,
thus producing arable land.[17]

---

11. As E. J. Young, *Studies in Genesis One* (Philadelphia: Presbyterian and Reformed,
1964), 74, notes, "a chronological order is not intended here."

12. Note the Ug. phrase "the city of the East" (*ʿr. d qdm*) in KTU 1.100:62; cf. J. C. de
Moor, "East of Eden," *ZAW* 100 (1988), 105ff. Note that the spatial relationship among
various locations in Gen 2:5ff. would be suggested in the following scale, from the widest
area to the narrowest:

earth (*ʾereṣ*) > land (*ʾădāmâ*) > Eden (*ʿēden*) > garden (*gan*).

13. See above, pp. 72–74.

14. Note that, when Ea created man, he pinched off a lump of clay (*ikruṣa ṭidda*) in the
apsû, his abode in the subterranean ocean, in a text cited in *CAD* A/2 195. See below,
pp. 130–139, on a "creator"-god and his relationship with the waters.

15. A bilingual version of the *Creation of the World by Marduk* (Heidel, *BG*, 63, line
32) mentions that Marduk made a swamp into dry land by piling up a dam at the edge of
the sea (cf. line 31). See A. R. Millard, "A New Babylonian 'Genesis' Story," *TynBul* 18
(1967), 8.

16. For this meaning, see below, pp. 116–125.

17. See the similar situation described in Lugal-e, lines 356–59; cf. van Dijk, *LUGAL
UD ME-LÁM-bi NIR-GÁL*, 96.

ʾĒd as Hyponymous to ʾEreṣ

In Gen 2:6, the relationship between the "earth" (*ʾereṣ*) and the *ʾēd*-water is described with two verbal forms, *yaʿăleh* and *wĕhišqâ*. The first verb suggests the nature of the water in this passage. While the "river" in v. 10 "comes out of Eden," the *ʾēd* in v. 6 "comes up from the earth."[18] In other words, the "water" referred to by *ʾēd* in 2:6 is different from the water that "comes out of" one place and forms a stream or streams like the "river" (*nāhār*) of Gen 2:10 and the "spring" (*maʿyān*) of Joel 4:18, as noted above. And the phrase *min-hāʾāreṣ* itself indicates the *ʾēd*-water originated underground and hence was a part of the "earth." Thus in Gen 2:5–6 the term *ʾēd* is hyponymous[19] to *ʾereṣ*, the "earth."

As for the second verb, *wĕhišqâ*, Ellenbogen holds that it refers to "a thorough soaking or drenching."[20] It certainly suggests that *ʾēd* refers to abundant water, because it covered all the surface of the land (*ʾădāmâ*). However, the verb *šqh* (*hiphil*)[21] is never used in the sense of "destructive" flooding such as the Great Deluge (cf. Akk. *abūbu*) but usually in a positive sense.[22]

Since the *ʾēd*-water flooded out of the subterranean water in Gen 2:6, in this regard it is related to the *tĕhôm(ôt)*-water, the water of the subterranean ocean. However, the verb *šqh* (*hiphil*) never appears with *tĕhôm(ôt)* and in Gen 2:6 has the specific meaning "to inundate (the land)." Unlike the situation in Gen 1:2 where the *tĕhôm*-water seemingly covered the entire "earth" (*ʾereṣ*), the *ʾēd*-water was inundating only a part of the "earth," the "land" (*ʾădāmâ*), in Gen 2:6.[23]

Two "Waters"

It is significant to note that in Gen 2:5–6 both the water from above (i.e., rain) and the water from below (the *ʾēd*-water) are mentioned in the description of the initial state of the earth, though the former is treated negatively, as

---

18. Cf. Num 21:17. Thus, Aquila's ἐπιβλυσμός "gushing forth" → "gushing water" (or "overflowing water" < ἐπιβλύω "flow over") and LXX's πηγή "fountain, source" (also Vulgate; Peshiṭṭa), can be supported rather than the Targums' Aramaic translation "cloud."

19. For this term, see above, pp. 58–63.

20. M. Ellenbogen, *Foreign Words in the Old Testament: Their Origin and Etymology* (London: Luzac, 1962), 13.

21. Cf. Gen 2:6, 10; Ezek 17:7, 32:6; Joel 4:18; Ps 104:11; Eccl 2:6.

22. In Ezek 32:6, which NIV translates "I will drench the land (*ʾereṣ*) with your flowing blood," it is "blood" that adds a negative sense to the text.

23. Kidner thinks that "the whole earth was inundated by water"; cf. Kidner, "Genesis 2:5, 6: Wet or Dry?" 109–14. See the previous chapter on the relationship among "earth" (*ʾereṣ*), "field" (*śādeh*), and "ground" (*ʾădāmâ*).

"not yet," and the latter positively, as "already."[24] This may suggest that the separation between the upper water and the lower water that is described in Gen 1:6–7 had already occurred in Gen 2:5–6.

These two waters might be compared with the two *thmt*-waters in Ugaritic. For example, as discussed below, the expression *šrˤ thmtm* "surging of the two *thmt*-waters" (KTU 1.19 [1Aqht]:I:45) is mentioned in a meteorological context and seems to refer to the waters above in heaven and the waters below the earth, as in Gen 7:11 and 8:2. Since this upper *thmt*-water is probably the same as the rainwater in the heavens, the lower *thmt*-water may correspond to the *ʾēd*-water of the "earth" in the context of Gen 2:5–6.[25]

Etymology of Eden

We noted in the previous section that, according to the biblical description, Eden (*ˤēden*), where God planted a garden (cf. Gen 2:8), was located in a part of the land (*ʾădāmâ*) that was once watered by the *ʾēd*-water, the flooding of the subterranean water. Thus Eden was good land suitable for planting a garden. What then is the etymology of "Eden"?

Until two decades ago, scholars commonly accepted that the Hebrew term *ˤēden* was a Mesopotamian loanword that ultimately derived from Sumerian e d i n.[26] For example, Speiser explains that "this word [*edinu*] is rare in Akk. but exceedingly common in Sum., thus certifying the ultimate source as very ancient indeed. The traditions involved must go back, therefore, to the oldest cultural stratum of Mesopotamia."[27] However, since the publication of the Aramaic–Akkadian bilingual text from Tell Fekheriyeh in 1982, several scholars have revived a Semitic etymology.[28]

---

24. Note that in the Sumerian myth of *Enki and the World Order*, "a rain of prosperity" and "a high flood" are mentioned in connection with Enki's activities; see S. N. Kramer, *The Sumerians: Their History, Culture, and Character* (Chicago: University of Chicago Press, 1963), 175.

25. See below, pp. 122–123, on the relationship between "rain" and *ˤdn* in the Ugaritic text and pp. 136–139 on El's watery abode "in the midst of the streams of the two *thmt*-waters."

26. For a brief summary of the Mesopotamian connection, see A. R. Millard, "The Etymology of Eden," *VT* 34 (1984), 103–4; C. Westermann, *Genesis*, vol. 1: *Genesis 1–11* (BKAT 1/1; Neukirchen-Vluyn: Neukirchener Verlag, 1974), 286–87 [ET 210].

27. E. A. Speiser, *Genesis* (AB 1; Garden City: Doubleday, 1964), 19.

28. A. Abou-Assaf, P. Bordreuil, and A. R. Millard, *La statue de Tell Fekherye et son inscription bilingue assyro-araméenne* (Paris: Recherche sur les civilisations, 1982). See Millard, "The Etymology of Eden," 103–6; A. Lemaire, "Le pays d'Eden et le Bît-Adini aux origines d'un mythe," *Syria* 58 (1981), 313–30; J. C. Greenfield, "A Touch of Eden," in *Orientalia J. Duchesne-Guillemin Emerito Oblata* (Hommages et Opera Minora 9; Leiden:

Theoretically there are three possible explanations for the etymology of the Hebrew term *ʿēden*, though scholars often do not distinguish between the first two:[29] (1) the term *ʿēden* is a Sumerian loanword that entered West Semitic via Akkadian; (2) the term is a Sumerian word borrowed directly into West Semitic; and (3) the term is a West Semitic word.

Sumerian Loanword via Akkadian?

Scholars[30] who suggest a Sumerian origin for this term usually base their argument on the following Sumerian–Akkadian vocabulary items in Vocabulary S[b], lines 90–91:[31]

90. e-di-in : edin : *e-di-nu*
91. e-di-in : edin : *ṣe-e-ru* "plain, steppe"[32]

In this list, the "phonetic" reading of the ideographic sign EDIN ("plain, steppe") is listed in the first column, and its Akkadian equivalent, or meaning, is listed in the third column. Scholars have taken line 90 as evidence for the existence of Akkadian *edinu* and for the Sumerian connection of Hebrew *ʿēden* via Akkadian *edinu*.

However, because the term *edinu* is a very rare word and is not attested in Akkadian except in this lexical list, Millard suggests that it is "simply a learned scribal transcription of the Sumerian word-sign in the Syllabary."[33] In fact, the third column of some copies of this syllabary has *e-din*, the same reading as the first column, for line 90.[34] Some might ask where the final *-u* of the variant form *edinu* would have come from in this case. For this, it may be profitable to note that in the Eblaite sign list, Sumerian sign names are seemingly Semitized with the Semitic nominative case ending *-um*.[35] For example, the B-list (TM.75.G. 1907 + 12680) has the following entries:

Brill, 1984), 219–24. Also H. N. Wallace, *The Eden Narrative* (HSM 32; Atlanta: Scholars Press, 1985), 84.

29. Westermann, *Genesis*, 286–87 [ET 210], for example, does not discuss the possibility of direct borrowing from Sumerian e d i n.

30. A short historical survey is given by Millard, "The Etymology of Eden," 103. For a bibliography, see also Lemaire, "Le pays d'Eden et le Bît-Adini," 315 n. 1.

31. B. Landsberger, *MSL* 3 (Rome: Pontifical Biblical Institute, 1955), 104 (5 copies preserve line 90; 3 copies, line 91).

32. The Sumerian e d i n is identified in *VE*, no. 1247′ with the Eblaite term *ṣa-lum*, a cognate of Akk. *ṣēru(m)* "Steppe."

33. Millard, "The Etymology of Eden," 104.

34. Landsberger, *MSL* 3, 104, copies A and S₁.

35. A. Archi, "The 'Sign-List' from Ebla," *Eblaitica* 1 (1987), 91.

edin   : ì-dì-núm   /edin-um/
ezen   : ì-zi-núm   /ezen-um/
idigna : ì-dì-gi-ra-um   /idigra-um/[36]

Hence, the form *edinu* in Vocabulary S[b] may well be a Semitized name (with
a nominative case ending /-u/) for the Sumerian sign EDIN rather than an
Akkadian term for "plain, steppe."[37]

Even if *edinu* should turn out to be a normal Akkadian word[38] that modern
scholars happen not to know except from Vocabulary S[b], it is still phonologically difficult to regard the Hebrew term *ʿēden* as a loanword from *edinu*,
since the initial syllable of this Akkadian term has no phoneme /ʿ/. In other
words, if the Hebrew term were a Sumerian loanword in West Semitic via
Akkadian *edinu*, the expected form in Hebrew would be *ʾēden* like (Sum.)
é-kur → (Akk.) *ekurru* → (Aram.) *ʾgwr* [39] and (Sum.) e₄-dé-a → (Akk.)
edû → (Heb.) *ʾēdô*.[40]

Therefore, I conclude that Hebrew *ʿēden* cannot be a loanword from or via
Akkadian *edinu*. However, the possibility remains that it is a direct (or not by
way of Akkadian) borrowing from a Sumerian word.

---

36. Cf. ibid., 101–2; also K. Butz, "Bilinguismus als Katalysator," in *BaE*, 127 on *VE*
1423′: idigna?-mušen = *ì-dì-gi-ra-um*.

37. Note that *edin(u)* and *ṣēru* are similar to the Japanese "on-yomi" readings (based on
the Chinese pronunciation) and "kun-yomi" readings (translation of the meaning of the
character into Japanese), respectively. See ch. 5 n. 40 (p. 92) above.

38. However, Lieberman, *SLOBA*, does not cite *edin* in his list of Sum. loanwords in
OB Akk.

39. Cf. *AHw*, 196. Note that the origin of Heb. *hêkāl*, Ug. *hkl* as well as Arab. *haikal* is
not a Sum. loanword via Akk. (cf. Kaufman, *AIA*, 27), because Akk. *ekallu* does not have
/h/ as an initial consonant. In light of the developments in Eblaite studies, it is probable that
these West Semitic terms came from an earlier Semitic form, /haikal/, from Sum. ḫa-gal
(É.GAL). On É (ʾà) for /ḫa/, see I. J. Gelb, "Ebla and the Kish Civilization," in *LdE*, 20;
M. Krebernik, "Zu Syllabar und Orthographie der lexikalischen Texte aus Ebla, Teil 1," *ZA*
72 (1982), 219–20; idem, *Die Personennamen der Ebla-Texte: Eine Zwischenbilanz* (BBVO
7; Berlin: Reimer, 1988), 74; also see above, pp. 46–47, on Eblaite *ti-ʾà-ma-tum* /tihām(a)-
tum/. This confirms Falkenstein's explanation (cf. A. Falkenstein, *Das Sumerische* [Hand-
buch der Orientalistik I/II/1/2/i; Leiden: Brill, 1959], 24 [§7Ce]) that a phoneme /h/ is possible for the old Sumerian from the old loanword into Canaanite *haikal < *hai-kal. Cf.
É. Lipiński, "Emprunts suméro-akkadiens en hébreu biblique," *ZAH* 1 (1988), 65. See also
Gelb, "Ebla and the Kish Civilization," 23–24 for the controversy about whether the diph-
thong /ai/ was preserved in Eblaite or monothongized to /ā/. According to Lambert (personal communication, 15 July 1987), a Hittite-Hurrian bilingual text (to be published by
E. Neu) has a Hurrian term *haikal*. Thus, the West Semitic term might be a Sum. loanword
via Hurrian.

40. See above, p. 96.

Direct Sumerian Loanword?

Some might think that the Sumerian e d i n "plain, steppe" could have been borrowed directly into Canaanite as *ʿēden* or the like. However, here too there is a phonological difficulty. Namely, it is difficult to associate the initial sound /e/ of Sumerian e d i n, written syllabically as ⟨e⟩ (E) in Vocabulary Sᵇ and as ⟨ì⟩ (NI) in the Eblaite "sign-list" B, with the Canaanite syllable /ʿe/ of Hebrew *ʿēden*, because Sumerian presumably has no phoneme /ʿ/.[41] In fact Sumerian words such as e z e n and i d i g n a, both written syllabically with the initial sign ⟨ì⟩ in the Eblaite "sign-list" B, were borrowed into Akkadian as *isinnu* or *idiqlat*, showing no hint of an initial phoneme /ʿ/ in their Sumerian originals.[42] Therefore, it is not likely that Sumerian e d i n was borrowed directly into Canaanite as *ʿēden* or the like.

An objection has also been raised against this Sumerian connection from a semantic point of view. For example, the meaning "plain, steppe," that is, uncultivated land, for Hebrew *ʿēden* does not fit the context of Genesis well, because the term *ʿēden* in its context refers to a place that is part of a well-watered land (*ʾădāmâ*) rather than part of a field (*śādeh*), uncultivated land.[43]

---

41. Cf. M.-L. Thomsen, *The Sumerian Language: An Introduction to Its History and Grammatical Structure* (Mesopotamia 10; Copenhagen: Akademisk, 1984), 41; Millard, "The Etymology of Eden," 104; Wallace, *The Eden Narrative*, 84, 98. In Vocabulary of Ebla, *VE*, the Sumerian sign NI (= *bu* ₓ, *ì*, *ʾa* ₓ, *ʾu* ₓ[?], *ni* and *lí* [?]) stands for /ʾi/ or /ʿi/ in Eblaite (e.g., *i-sa-du* /ʾišātu/ and *ì-rí-sa-tum* /ʿirištum/). Cf. Krebernik, "Zu Syllabar und Orthographie der lexikalischen Texte aus Ebla, Teil 1," 198–99. But there is no evidence that /ʿ/ was established as an independent phoneme in Sumerian. Hence, the equation *ʿîrād* (Gen 4:18) = Eridu (e - r i - d u), suggested by W. W. Hallo, "Antediluvian Cities," *JCS* 23 (1970), 64, 67, is not without phonological difficulty.

42. Normally, in Akkadian the Semitic phoneme */ʿ/ is realized as /e/ in the initial position. See below, pp. 125–126 (excursus), for the Hebrew *ḥiddéqel* "Tigris."

43. Wallace, *The Eden Narrative*, 84; U. Cassuto, *From Adam to Noah* [part 1 of *A Commentary on the Book of Genesis*] (Jerusalem: Magnes, 1961 [1944, orig.]), 107. It is interesting to note that at Ebla, in Text no. 79 (g): /2/ (*MEE* 4, 98), the Sumerian term e d i n is explained in Eblaite as follows:

e d [i n] = g[u?]-lu[m] sà-[du]m wa da-bí-tum wa gu-zu: zu: um wa ga-za-um.

Sumerian e d i n is thus "paraphrased" as, in Butz's highly speculative translation, "die 'Grünzone der Ebenen', der 'Berg', der 'Wald', die 'abgeernteten Felder' und die 'Ödstellen mit kniehohem Gras' " ("the 'green region of the plains', the 'mountain', the 'forest', the 'harvested fields', and the 'wastelands with knee-high grass' "; Butz, "Bilinguismus als Katalysator," 130–31. Note Jacobsen's view that e d i n is an ancient word for "the sheep country, the broad grassy steppe"; cf. T. Jacobsen, "Formative Tendencies in Sumerian Religion," in *The Bible and the Ancient Near East: Essays in Honor of William Foxwell Albright* (ed. G. E. Wright; Anchor Books; Garden City: Doubleday, 1961), 360; also G. Castellino, "Les origines de la civilisation selon les textes bibliques et les textes cunéiformes," *Volume du Congrès: Strasbourg 1956* (VTSup 4; Leiden: Brill, 1957), 122, citing

Though it is conceivable that Hebrew *ʿēden* reflects a direct borrowing into ancient Canaanite from a Sumerian *ʿedin*, *if* Sumerian possessed the phoneme /ʿ/ at an earlier stage, the evidence for this is very thin. Meanwhile, a more immediate West Semitic origin should be seriously considered.

Common West Semitic?

While a Sumerian–Akkadian connection remains popular, some scholars have suggested a Semitic etymology for *ʿēden* in light of Ugaritic *ʿdn* as well as the Hebrew plural noun **ʿădānîm* "delights" (Jer 51:34, 2 Sam 1:24, Ps 36:8). For example, G. R. Driver connected Hebrew *ʿēden* "luxury" with Arabic *ġadanu* "delicacy" and Ugaritic *ʿdn* "abundance, delight."[44] Cassuto also accepted this correspondence but explained *ʿēden* in light of the Ugaritic *ʿdn*, which he translated "moisture" in KTU 1.4:V:6–7 [51:V:68–69]:

> *wn ap ʿdn mṭrh bʿl yʿdn ʿdn*
> and now also the moisture of his rain / Baal shall surely make moist.

Thus, he interpreted the term *ʿēden* "in connection with the watering of the ground" and explained "Eden" in Gen 2:8 as the place "where there was an exceedingly rich water-supply."[45]

However, though Cassuto's interpretation is contextually attractive, there is a difficulty in claiming a phonological correspondence between Heb. /ʿ/, Arab. /ġ/, and Ug. /ʿ/. Hence, most Ugaritic scholars (Gordon;[46] Gibson; de Moor; Pope; et al.)[47] have sought a different etymology and translated the Ugaritic term *ʿdn* in 1.4:V:6–7 [51:V:68–69] as "time" or "season," from the root **yʿd* "to appoint (time)."[48] On the other hand, the question why both the verbal form *yʿdn* and the nominal form *ʿdn* end in /n/ has been left unanswered, though both are possible forms, from a purely morphological point of view.

Aramaic: The Fekheriyeh Inscription

In 1982, an important Aramaic–Akkadian bilingual inscription from Tell Fekheriyeh was published.[49] In this text Hadad, the god of life-giving water,

---

Jacobsen's explanation (in *Archaeology* 7 [1954], 54). However, this meaning does not fit the context of Gen 2.

44. Driver, *CML*, 141 and n. 8.

45. Cassuto, *From Adam to Noah*, 107. Westermann follows Cassuto and says that "Ugaritic has a word which corresponds exactly to the Hebrew and has a similar meaning, 'delight'" (Westermann, *Genesis*, 286 [ET 210]).

46. *UT* 19.1823, *ʿdn* I "season": *ʿdn mṭrh* (1.4 [51]:V:6 [68]) "his season of rain," *yʿdn . ʿdn* (:7[69]) "he appoints a season."

47. See below, pp. 118–119, for the sources.

48. De Moor, *SPUMB*, 149, following Hoftijzer.

49. A. Abou-Assaf, P. Bordreuil, and A. R. Millard, *La statue de Tell Fekherye et son inscription bilingue assyro-araméenne* (Paris: Recherche sur les civilisations, 1982).

is called the "water-controller of all rivers" (*gwgl nhr klm*) in Aramaic and immediately after is described, both in Aramaic and in Akkadian, as *m^{c}dn mt kln // muṭaḫḫidu kibrāti*. This bilingual phrase is translated "who makes all lands abound" (Millard[50]); "qui fait prospérer tous les pays" (Abou-Assaf, Bordreuil, and Millard); "he who makes all the lands luxuriant" (Kaufman; also Greenfield[51]).

Thus, scholars have recognized here "'*dn* in a verbal form" and, in light of the parallel Assyrian verb that means "to enrich, make abundant," have suggested a similar sense for the Aramaic verb, "although the two texts are not absolutely identical in every phrase."[52] Millard cautiously concludes that "clearly Old Aramaic gave a sense to '*dn* which was very similar to its value in Biblical Hebrew . . . this new example . . . reinforces the earlier interpretation," which links Eden with "words with '*dn* as their base and the common idea of 'pleasure, luxury.'"[53]

However, Akkadian *ṭaḫdu* "überreichlich" and *ṭuḫdu* "überreichliche Fülle," whose denominative verb in the participial form is *muṭaḫḫidu*,[54] often appears in descriptions of the abundance of "rain" and "high water" (*mīlu*) from Old Babylonian onward.[55] For example, in the *Hymn to Marduk*, line 27, the god Marduk is called *bēl ṭuḫ-di ḫeng[alli? (. . .) m]u-šá-az-nin nuḫši* "Lord of Abundance and Plen[ty], who sends copious rain."[56] In another text, the rain-god Adad is described as follows: ^{d}*Adad ú-šá-az-na-an eli nišī šamût ṭuḫdi* "Adad lets it rain copiously for the people."[57] As Lambert notes, "*nuḫšu, ṭuḫdu* and *ḫegallu* . . . refer to abundance of water and profusion of plant life . . . [and] are often found in association with Adad."[58]

Thus, the Aramaic verbal form *m^{c}dn*, the counterpart of the Akkadian *muṭaḫḫidu* in the present context, probably has the literal meaning "to make

50. Millard, "The Etymology of Eden," 105.

51. S. A. Kaufman, "Reflections on the Assyrian–Aramaic Bilingual from Tell Fakhariyeh," *MAARAV* 3 (1982), 161; Greenfield, "A Touch of Eden," 221: "who makes the whole world luxuriant."

52. Millard, "The Etymology of Eden," 105.

53. Ibid., 104, 105.

54. Note that the Aramaic counterpart, *m^{c}dn*, is also the D-stem in a "factitive" sense.

55. *AHw*, 1378, 1393.

56. See W. von Soden, "Zur Wiederherstellung der Marduk-Gebete BMS 11 und 12," *Iraq* 31 (1969), 85–86 ("Herr von Häufung und Über[fluss, der da] Fülle regnen lässt"). For *nuḫšu* "abundance, plenty, prosperity," which refers to water, "the flood of fertility," not simply to "abundance in general," see W. F. Albright, "Notes on Assyrian Lexicography and Etymology," *RA* 16 (1919), 185; *CAD* N/2 320. For *ḫegallu*, see *CAD* Ḫ 167–68.

57. SEM 117 iii 15, cited by *CAD* Z 43. See also *šamû ṭaḫittum iznunma* "it rained hard" (ARM 2, 140:9; also cf. KAR 153 rev.(!) 10 [SB]), cited by *CAD* Z 42.

58. W. G. Lambert, "Trees, Snakes and Gods in Ancient Syria and Anatolia," *BSOAS* 48 (1985), 436.

abundant in water-supply," though it may mean secondarily "to enrich, prosper, make luxuriant." The Aramaic phrase *mᶜdn mt kln* "one who makes the whole land abundant in water-supply" as an epithet of the rain-god Hadad certainly fits the context of this bilingual inscription very well.

This new evidence has led scholars to rethink the possibility of finding a cognate of *ᶜēden*. Greenfield and others have already reinterpreted the meaning of *ᶜdn* in the Ugaritic text KTU 1.4:V:6–7 [51:V:68–69] in light of the Aramaic evidence.

Ugaritic

KTU 1.4:V:6–7 [51:V:68–69]

wn ap . ᶜdn . mṭrh ⁶⁹⁾*bᶜl . yᶜdn .*
ᶜdn . ṭkt . b glṭ

The poetic structure of this text is usually understood as an unbalanced bicolon with word count 5:3 and has been translated in various ways: for example,

Now moreover Baal will abundantly give abundance of rain,
abundance of moisture with snow. (Driver, *CML*, 97)

Lo Baal sets the season of his rain
The season of the ship on the ocean. (Gordon, *PLMU*, 95)

Moreover, Baᶜlu should appoint the time of his rain,
the time of the *ṭkt*-ship with snow. (de Moor, *SPUMB*, 148)

(*Écoute*) *encore ceci:*
Baᶜal va fixer l'heure de sa pluie,
l'heure du *jaillissement* des flots. (Caquot and Sznycer, *TO*, 207)

Now at last Baal may appoint a time[59] for his rain,
a time for (his) barque (to appear) in the snow. (Gibson, *CML²*, 60)

And moreover Baal will provide his luxuriant rain,
a luxuriant . . . with overflow." (Greenfield[60])

And now Baal will fertilize with the luxuriance of his rain,
the luxuriance of watering in turbulence (flow?). (Smith)[61]

---

59. Note that it is the god Šamaš in Babylonia who usually appoints a time and provides an omen; cf. *CAD* A/1 100; A. R. Millard, "The Sign of the Flood," *Iraq* 49 (1987), 63, line 86: *adanna* ᵈ*šamaš iškunamma* (Gilg. XI:86).

60. Greenfield, "A Touch of Eden," 221.

61. M. S. Smith, "Interpreting the Baal Cycle," *UF* 18 (1986), 314 and n. 5. Cf. idem, "Baal's Cosmic Secret," *UF* 16 (1984), 297, where he translates *ᶜdn* as "season."

De Moor holds that, "regardless whether one connects *bᶜl yᶜdn* with l. 68 or with the rest of l. 69, the resulting verse is rather long. This is, however, not without parallels in Ug. poetry."[62] In his treatment of this text, de Moor, with Korpel, suggests a 3:5 structure and takes the first line as an independent clause, translating:

wn ap . ᶜdn . mṭrh	Also it is the prime time for his rains,
bᶜl . yᶜdn . ᶜdn . ṯkt . b glṯ	Baᶜlu should appoint the time of the barque with snow.[63]

On the other hand, Olmo Lete divides the lines differently, which results in a more balanced structure (4:4):

wn ap . ᶜdn . mṭrh bᶜl .	Ya que así podrá almacenar su lluvia *Baᶜlu*,
yᶜdn . ᶜdn . ṯkt . b glṯ	hacer acopio de abundancia de nieve.

(MLC, 202)

Margalit, who holds that "the prevalent stichometric arrangement of this text [5:3], found or presupposed in (e.g.,) *ANET, CML,* and *TO,* is mistaken,"[64] has a still different analysis for its structure:

wnap . ᶜdn . mṭrh . bᶜl	
yᶜdn . ᶜdn . ṯk(?)t .	
bglṯ . k!t!tn[65] *. qlh .*	From the turbulence (?) he lowered his voice
bᶜrpt . šrh .	From the clouds (he lowered) his flash
larṣ . brqm	(He lowered his flash) to earth as lightning.[66]

However, I would like to suggest a versification of 3:2:3 with AXB pattern,[67] in which an A-line and a B-line have an organic unity despite their inserted modifier, X-line:

---

62. De Moor, *SPUMB*, 148.

63. M. C. A. Korpel and J. C. de Moor, "Fundamentals of Ugaritic and Hebrew Poetry," *UF* 18 (1986), 180.

64. B. Margalit, *A Matter of "Life" and "Death": A Study of the Baal-Mot Epic (CTA 4–5–6)* (Neukirchen-Vluyn: Neukirchener Verlag, 1980), 214 n. 2.

65. This should be read *wtn* /wutina/ (G passive). See my *"verba primae waw*, WLD, in Ugaritic," *UF* 11 (1979), 781 n. 21; del Olmo Lete, *MLC*, 202.

66. Margalit, *A Matter of "Life" and "Death,"* 216.

67. Cf. my "Literary Insertion (AXB Pattern) in Biblical Hebrew," *VT* 33 (1983), 468–82; "Literary Insertion, AXB Pattern, in Hebrew and Ugaritic: A Problem of Adjacency and Dependency in Poetic Parallelism," *UF* 18 (1986), 351–61; "Coordination Interrupted, or Literary Insertion AX&B Pattern, in the Books of Samuel," in *Literary Structure and Rhetorical Strategies in the Hebrew Bible* (ed. L. J. de Regt, J. de Waard, and J. P. Fokkelman; Assen: Van Gorcum / Winona Lake, Ind.: Eisenbrauns, 1996), 117–32.

wn ap[68]. *ʿdn . mṭrh*	Now indeed abundance of his rain
bʿl . yʿdn .	Baal will supply;
ʿdn . ṭrt . b glṭ	abundance of (subterranean) *water from flooding.*

In this structure, *mṭrh* would be interpreted as being parallel with *ṭrt* or with the phrase *ṭrt . b glṭ* as a whole (which stands as a "ballast variant"[69] to *mṭrh*) rather than with *glṭ*.

ṭkt

Two possible readings have been suggested for *ṭkt*, because the second sign can be read either as ⟨k⟩ or as ⟨r⟩:

1. *ṭrt* "moisture" (Driver) in light of Arabic *ṭarra* "gave plentiful water" or *ṭariya* "was well-watered."[70]
2. *ṭkt* "a kind of 'ship'" = New Eg. *śk.ty*" (Gordon);[71] "*ṭkt*-ship" (de Moor);[72] "bateaux" (pl.; Lipiński);[73] *ṭakka* "voyager" (Caquot).[74]

The second reading seems to have a phonological difficulty, for Egyptian *ś* probably corresponds to Hebrew ⟨s⟩ /s/, not to Ugaritic /ṭ/ (compare the way in which Heb. *Pineḥas* corresponds to Egyptian *p(ỉ)nḥśi*).[75] Furthermore, this view does not fit the context well. Pope and Tigay[76] suggest that Herdner's copy, with a shaded *k*, could be "only the partial remains of *r* (in fact the following single horizontal wedge could be the tail-end of the *r*, rather than a *t*)." And they recommend accepting "the reading *ṭrt* advocated by Driver, or *ṭr*." They then conclude that "the word could refer to the subterranean sources of moisture or to the irrigated earth itself." Pope elsewhere translates the term *ṭrt* as "watering."[77] In light of the parallelism, 3:2:3 and AXB, I also would like

68. On the comparison of the Eblaite word AB with Northwest Semitic *ap*, see G. Pettinato, "Il termine AB in eblaita: Congiunzione AP oppure locuzione avverbiale JEŠ?" *Or* 53 (1984), 318–32.

69. Cf. Gordon, *UT*, 135–37.

70. Driver, *CML*, 151, following Gaster, and n. 22.

71. Gordon, *UT* 19.2680. This is a well-attested term for "boat" in the New Kingdom period; cf. A. Erman and H. Grapow, *WÄS*, IV, 315. See Y. Muchiki, *Egyptian Proper Names and Loanwords in North-West Semitic* (SBLDS 173; Atlanta: Society of Biblical Literature, 1999), 255–56 and 283.

72. De Moor, *SPUMB*, 149.

73. E. Lipiński, "Épiphanie de Baal-Haddu: RS 24.245," *UF* 3 (1971), 86f.

74. Caquot and Sznycer, *TO*, 207 note *t*.

75. Pointed out K. A. Kitchen (private communication).

76. Pope and Tigay, "A Description of Baal," 129.

77. Cf. M. H. Pope, *Song of Songs* (AB 7c; Garden City: Doubleday, 1977), 459; also M. S. Smith, "Baal's Cosmic Secret," *UF* 16 (1984), 297; idem, "Interpreting the Baal Cycle," *UF* 18 (1986), 314.

to suggest the reading *ṯrṯ* and a meaning such as "water," whether from above or from below.

glṯ

Many scholars (e.g., Dussaud, Driver, Ginsberg, Gray, Rainey, Herrmann, Aartun, de Moor, Pope and Tigay, Dietrich-Loretz-Sanmartín, del Olmo Lete, and others) take *glṯ* as a metathesis of the first and the third consonants of a hypothetical Ugaritic word *ṯlg*, which they think is a cognate of Hebrew *šeleg* and Akkadian *šalgu* "snow."[78] However, the pairing of "rain" and "snow" does not seem to fit the context, which mentions an abundance of water supply from the storm-god Baal, accompanied by his thunder, lightning, and clouds. In fact, the Mesopotamian rain-god Adad is associated with storm, wind, lightning, clouds, and rain in his epithets—but not with snow.[79]

In 1965, Greenfield[80] discussed the term *glṯ* in light of MH *glš* and translated *wtglṯ thmt* (KTU 1.92 [2001]:5) "and the abyss was roiled." Gordon has suggested a similar view: "move" or "movement," and translated *tglṯ thmt* "she moves the Deep."[81] In 1971, Lipiński explained at greater length that "the word *glṯ* evokes the bounding waves of a tempest. The image is the same as that found in Ps 107:25–27," and translated *wtglṯ thmt* "et l'océan rebondissait" ("and the wave-tossed ocean"; or "et elle [Astarté] fait rebondir l'océan" = "and she [Astarte] has made the ocean bound"). He said that "it also appears that *glṯ* > *glš* refers to the apparent oscillation or heaving of waves when the water is agitated or effervescent."[82] Similarly, Caquot[83] and Pope argue that the term *glṯ* "manifestly designates a motion applicable to water."[84] Greenfield

---

78. Cf. Driver, *CML*, 146; J. C. de Moor, "Studies in the New Alphabetic Texts from Ras Shamra I," *UF* 1 (1969) 180–81; idem, *SPUMB*, 149; M. H. Pope and J. H. Tigay, "A Description of Baal," *UF* 3 (1971), 129; M. Dietrich, O. Loretz, and J. Sanmartín, "Stichometrische Probleme in RS 24.245 = UG. 5, s. 556–559, Nr. 3 v.," *UF* 7 (1975), 534; M. Dahood, *RSP* 2.21; del Olmo Lete, *MLC*, 202. Again, K. Aartun, "Zur Erklärung des Ugaritischen Ausdrucks *inr*," *UF* 15 (1983), 4, discussed similar examples of metathesis.

79. Cf. Tallqvist, *AG*, 246ff.

80. J. C. Greenfield, "Amurrite, Ugaritic and Canaanite," in *Proceedings of the International Conference on Semitic Studies Held in Jerusalem, 19–23 July 1965* (Jerusalem: Israel Academy of Sciences and Humanities, 1969), 99 n. 36.

81. See *UT* 19.584 and *UTS*, 551.

82. Lipiński, "Épiphanie de Baal-Haddu: RS 24.245," 86–87: "le mot *glṯ* doit évoquer le rebondissement des flots dans la tempête. L'image serait alors semblable à celle que l'on trouve au Ps 107, 25–27"; "Il apparaît ainsi que *glṯ* > *glš* qualifie un mouvement oscillatoire pareil au soulèvement de l'eau agitée ou effervescente."

83. *TO*, 208 note *u*: "bouillonner."

84. Pope, *Song of Songs*, 459–60.

later confirmed the view he had expressed earlier and suggested the meaning "overflow" for *glṭ* in our text.[85]

On the other hand, some scholars have suggested translating the term "turbulence(?)" (Margalit; also Smith)[86] or "storm tempest" (Weinfeld),[87] in keeping with the nature of the storm-god. However, it seems better to take the term *glṭ* as referring to some kind of water movement caused by the storm-god rather than as a reference to the storm itself, very much like similar contexts in Akkadian texts: *amat Marduk asurrakku idallaḫ* "the word of Marduk roils the subterranean waters" (4R 26 no. 4:51–52); *ana utazzumišu iddallaḫu apsû* "the depths are stirred up at his (Adad's) groaning" (STC 1 205:9 [SB lit.]).[88] While Pope and Tigay suggest that "in the context *glṭ* probably refers to a meteorological phenomenon like *mṭr* in the parallel clause,"[89] it is more likely that *ṭkt* or *ṭrt* is directly parallel with *mṭr*, as noted above.

Now, it is important to note that abundant water for agriculture is provided either by rain (the celestial water) or by the flooding of the subterranean waters (like Akk. *mīlu, edû*, etc.), and these two waters, both celestial and subterranean, are sometimes understood as being brought about by a rain- or storm-god such as Adad, Baal, or Teshub. For example, as Lambert notes, "the Anatolian storm god controlled springs and fountains" and also "is concerned with thunder, rain and wind." In order to maintain his northern status, "Adad is given 'control of subterranean water (properly Ea's domain).' "[90] Thus, "the storm god would have been involved somehow with terrestrial water."[91] This is certainly in keeping with Hadad's title, "water-controller of all rivers," in the Fekheriyeh Inscription, as noted above.

Furthermore, the Ugaritic text KTU 1.19 [1Aqht]:I:45 mentions the storm- and rain-god Baal along with meteorological phenomena related to him, "dew" (*ṭl*) // "rain" (*rbb*) and "thunder (lit., Baal's voice)" (*ql . bᶜl*) and "surging of the two *thmt*-waters" (*šrᶜ thmtm*). The text reads:

bl . ṭl . bl rbb	Let there be no dew / let there be no rain
bl . šrᶜ thmtm .	Let there be no surging of the two oceans
bl ṭbn . ql . bᶜl	Let there be no goodness of Baal's voice!

(cf. Gordon, PLMU, 22)

---

85. Greenfield, "A Touch of Eden," 221.

86. Margalit, *A Matter of "Life" and "Death,"* 216 and 215 n. 1; also Smith, "Interpreting the Baal Cycle," 314.

87. M. Weinfeld, " 'Rider of the Clouds' and 'Gatherer of the Clouds'," *JANES* 5 (The Gaster Festschrift; 1973), 426 n. 43.

88. Cf. *CAD* D 43, 45.

89. Cf. Pope and Tigay, "A Description of Baal," 129.

90. Lambert, "Trees, Snakes and Gods in Ancient Syria and Anatolia," 437 n. 15: cf. *bēl nag-bi ù zu-un-ni* "lord of abyss and rain" (*BBSt.*, no. 6 ii 41).

91. Lambert, "Trees, Snakes and Gods in Ancient Syria and Anatolia," 449.

Margalit thinks that shifting to "the subterranean deep (*thmt*), the source of uprising spring water" in line 45, after speaking of "heavenly precipitation (*ṭl*, *rbb*)" in line 44 and then returning to "the heavenly arena in the third and final allusion to aquatic phenomena," *ql . bˁl*, is "poetically . . . anti-climactic; contextually, it is redundant."[92] However, since *thmtm* is dual and these "oceans" seem to refer to both the upper and the lower ocean, as in Gen 7:11, 8:2, and so on, there is actually no "shifting" in description from heavenly waters to the subterranean water.[93]

In light of the above, it may be suggested that the immediate context (lines 70–71) of our text, KTU 1.4:V:6–7 [51:V:68–69], which mentions "thunder" (*ytn qlh*) and "lightning" (*šrh*), supports the combination "rain" (*mṭr*) and "(subterranean) *water*" (*ṯrt*) rather than "rain" and "snow," because the meteorological phenomena referred to in lines 68ff. are those of the storm-god Baal, who is less likely to be associated with snow. Hence, the term *glṯ* probably refers to Baal's involvement with the subterranean water; hence "overflow" (Greenfield) or "flooding" may be suggested for the translation of *glṯ*.

ˁdn

The Ugaritic verb *ˁdn* can be explained as meaning "to make abundant in water-supply" in light of its Aramaic cognate in the Tell Fekheriyeh Inscription as well as from the context. Here in KTU 1.4:V:6–7 [51:V:68–69], the literal sense seems to fit the context better than the more abstract sense, because the context refers to the meteorological functions of the storm-god Baal.

Old South Arabic

The root **ˁdn* appears in the text MTBNṬYN hˁdn as one of the titles of the Old South Arabic god MTBNṬYN. Biella suggests that the meaning of **ˁdn* is "to bestow well-being" in light of Hebrew *ˁdn* "to enjoy luxuries" and Arabic *ǵadan* "dainties."[94] However, there is a phonological difficulty in connecting Hebrew /ˁ/ and the Arabic /ǵ/ with Old South Arabic /ˁ/.

---

92. B. Margalit, "Lexicographical Notes on the Aqht Epic (Part II: KTU 1.19)," *UF* 16 (1984), 131.

93. It may be conjectured that the ancient Canaanites considered the "surging" of the two oceans as taking place at or near El's abode; see below, pp. 136–137, on *thmtm* "two *thmt*-waters" at El's abode. Note that Aartun suggested the meaning "Öffnung/Auftun (des Gewässers) der (beiden) Fluten" ("opening/releasing [of the waters] of [both] floods") for *šrˁ thmtm* and the etymology from Semitic **šrˁ*, instead of the conventional *šrˁ*; cf. K. Aartun, "Neue Beiträge zum Ugaritischen Lexikon (II)," *UF* 17 (1985), 36–37.

94. J. C. Biella, *Dictionary of Old South Arabic: Sabaean Dialect* (HSS 25; Chico, Calif.: Scholars Press, 1982), 354. However, there is no entry for *ˁdn* in A. F. L. Beeston et al., *Sabaic Dictionary (English-French-Arabic)* (Louvain-la-Neuve: Peeters, 1982).

If the divine name MTBNṬYN, /môtab-naṭiyân/[95] or /mutîb-natyân/, is related to the Syriac root *nṭ᾽ "to be humid" (Fell)[96] and means "that which assures the fecundity of the land thanks to water," as Ryckmans suggests,[97] the epithet *hʿdn* should probably be translated as one "who supplies abundant water" rather than "([the god] M. who) bestows well-being," in light of Ugaritic *ʿdn*, "to make abundant in water-supply," as well as Aramaic *mʿdn mt kln* "one who makes the whole land abundant in water-supply," a title of the god Hadad in the Fekheriyeh Inscription.

Arabic

The Arabic term *ġadanu* "delicacy" was first suggested as a cognate of Ugaritic *ʿdn* but, since Ugaritic has a phoneme /ġ/ besides /ʿ/, the Arabic term does not correspond to the Ugaritic one phonologically. It is possible to take *ġadanu* as a secondary development in the Arabic language from the root *ʿdn, like Arabic *nġm* "to sing," which corresponds to Ugaritic *nʿm*. However, one should search in Arabic for a term based on *ʿdn as a possible cognate of Ugaritic *ʿdn*, Aramaic *ʿdn*, Hebrew *ʿdn*, and Old South Arabic *ʿdn*.

In fact, there is an Arabic verb *ʿadana* "to dwell, abide"[98] from *ʿdn, and this verb may be related to Ugaritic *ʿdn* and other West Semitic cognate terms. Lane suggests the translation "gardens of abode, or gardens of perpetual abode" for the phrase *jannātu ʿadnin*,[99] which may preserve an ancient tradition about Eden. The sense "(perpetual) abode" in Arabic is perhaps the result of semantic development such as "a well-watered place" > "oasis" > "perpetual abode," like Akkadian *edurû* (loanword from Sum. é-durus "manor or farm on wet ground" or "moistened ground"[100]), which seems to refer etymologically to "a small rural settlement with a permanent water supply."[101]

In light of the above, we may suggest that *ʿēden* means "a place where there is abundant water-supply" (cf. Gen 13:10);[102] its verbal root *ʿdn means

---

95. F. Hommel, *Ethnologie und Geographie des alten Orients* (Munich: Beck, 1926), 143.

96. Cf. A. Jamme, "Le Panthéon Sud-arabe préislamique d'après les sources épigraphiques," *Le Muséon* 60 (1947), 97 n. 345: "celui qui garantit l'humidité?"

97. G. Ryckmans, *Les Noms Propres Sud-sémitiques*, vol. 1: *Répertoire Analytique* (Bibliothèque du Muséon 2; Louvain: Bureaux du Muséon, 1934), 20: "qui assure la fécondité de la terre grâce à l'eau."

98. Del Olmo Lete (*MLC*, 598) notes van Zijl's suggestion to connect Ugaritic *ʿdn* with Arabic cognate *ʿadana*, though with a different meaning, "fecundidad."

99. Lane, *AEL*, 1.1976.

100. W. W. Hallo, "Antediluvian Cities," *JCS* 23 (1970), 58 and n. 16.

101. *CAD* E 39.

102. This etymology is supported by Gen 13:10, which reads: "that it was well watered everywhere like the garden of the Lord." See Cassuto, *From Adam to Noah*, 108.

primarily "to make abundant in water-supply"[103] and secondarily "to enrich, prosper, make luxuriant." The term *ᶜeden (pl. *ʿădānîm* in Ps 36:9),[104] which means "pleasure, luxury," has the same etymology as "Eden" with this secondary meaning, though the MT seems carefully to distinguish *ʿēden* from *ᶜeden.[105] This root may also be reflected in the personal names *ḥmyᶜdn* and *mᶜdnh*, which appear on ancient Hebrew seals.[106]

Excursus:
Etymology of Tigris and Euphrates

Tigris

The Sumerian name for the Tigris, idig(i)na, is attested from the pre-Sargonic period onward.[107] Because it is generally true that geographical names preserve much older traditions than personal names, the initial consonant of the Hebrew *ḥiddēqel* "Tigris," /ḫ/, may preserve a pre-Sumerian or early Sumerian pronunciation.[108] Judging from the correspondence between idig(i)na (Sum.) // *idigra-um* (Ebla.) // *idiqlat* (Akk.) ↔ Heb. *ḥiddēqel* (< *ḫid + iqlu), the Hebrew form is probably an early borrowing of the original via a non-Akkadian language.[109]

Delitzsch (1914) proposed the etymology of Sumerian idigna as being from *idigina, meaning "running river," which was accepted by Albright

---

103. Note that no "rain" had yet affected Eden in Gen 2:8; only "the *ʾēd*-water" was irrigating the whole land.

104. Cassuto translates Ps 36:9 "and Thou givest them to drink from the river of Thy watering" and suggests rabbinic examples: *B. Ketubbot* 10b, "rain waters, saturates, fertilizes and *refreshes* (*mĕᶜaddēn*); "Just as the showers come down / upon the herbs and *refresh* [*mĕᶜaddĕnîm*] them," etc. (*Sifre Deut* 32:2). Cf. Cassuto, *From Adam to Noah*, 107–8.

105. Lemaire interprets both *ʿēden* in the Genesis story and *ᶜeden* in the geographical name *bêt ᶜeden* (= Bit-Adini) in Amos 1:5 as referring to a specific location, "les hautes vallées du Ḫabur, du Baliḫ et de l'Euphrate" ("the high valleys of the Ḫabur, the Baliḫ, and the Euphrate rivers"), which he thinks is the most irrigated and prosperous region of the ancient Near East and corresponds well to the description of Eden in the Genesis story; cf. A. Lemaire, "Le pays d'Eden et le Bît-adini aux origines d'un mythe," *Syria* 58 (1981), 313–30, esp. 327–28. His interesting hypothesis needs to be scrutinized, however, on the basis of other available evidence, such as river names, the stone name *šōham* (2:12), and others. Note also the brief account of the Sumerian "paradise" myth and its proposed connection with Genesis story in Kramer, *The Sumerians*, 147–49.

106. F. Israel, "Quelques précisions sur l'onomastique hébraïque féminine dans l'épigraphie," *SEL* 4 (1987), 80, 86 n. 15.

107. See D. O. Edzard, G. Farber, and E. Sollberger, *Die Orts- und Gewässernamen der präsargonischen und sargonischen Zeit* (RGTC 1; Wiesbaden: Reichert, 1977), 216.

108. See p. 114 n. 39 on the earlier pronunciation of É as /ha/ or /ḫa/ in Eblaite Sumerian.

109. See above, p. 103.

and Lambdin.[110] Lambert similarly explains i d i g i n a as "flowing river" (i d + g i n a), which is a good Sumerian name. Though the Tigris is sometimes explained as "Swift River," the Sumerian term g i n a does not mean "swift."[111] Heimpel gives an entirely new explanation: id "river" ("Fluß") + i g n a "Lazuli,"[112] but this is highly speculative. On the other hand, Baldacci attempts to connect Tigris with the divine name ^{d}NI.DA.KUL, which he reads ì-ta-qul (= Heb. *ḥiddéqel*). But the reading of this divine name is not certain, and his argument needs more positive support,[113] because in Eblaite the river Tigris is spelled *ì-dì-gi-ra-um*. However, a name for the deified river Tigris appears as ^{d}I-d i g l a t or $^{d.íd}$i d i g i n a.[114]

Euphrates

The Sumerian name for the Euphrates, b u r a n u n (> Akk. *purattu* or *purantu*, Heb. *pĕrat*) has been explained as "mighty water source" (Delitzsch[115]) or "lordly river" (Lambert[116]). The Euphrates appears in Eblaite as *bù-la-na-tim*/p u r a n (a) t i m/ (genitive) in ARET 5, 3:IV:3.[117] In Mari texts, the name Euphrates appears both with and without the assimilation of /n/: for example, *pu-ra-tim* (ARM 24 11 et al.) and *pu-ra-an-tim* (ARM 2, 22:21; 2,

110. W. F. Albright and T. O. Lambdin, "The Evidence of Language," in *The Cambridge Ancient History* 1/1: *Prolegomena and Prehistory* (3rd ed.; Cambridge: Cambridge University Press, 1970), 148. Cf. M. C. Astour, "Semites and Hurrians in Northern Transtigris," in *Studies on the Civilization and Culture of Nuzi and the Hurrians*, vol. 2: *General Studies and Excavations at Nuzi 9/1* (ed. D. I. Owen and M. A. Morrison; Winona Lake, Ind.: Eisenbrauns, 1987), 19 n. 109. Prof. Lambert suggested this meaning (personal communication, 15 July 1987).

111. Note Edzard's comment in his review article, D. O. Edzard, "(Review of) A. Kammenhuber: Die Arier im Vorderen Orient. Heidelberg: Carl Winter Universitätsverlag, 1968," *ZDMG* 120 (1970), 313. Cf. Wolfgang Heimpel, "The Natural History of the Tigris according to the Sumerian Literary Composition LUGAL," *JNES* 46 (1987), 312.

112. W. Heimpel, "Das Untere Meer," *ZA* 77 (1987), 51 n. 92.

113. M. Baldacci, "Note semitico-occidentali sulla geografia religiosa ad Ebla," *Biblia e Oriente* 24 (1982), 223 and n. 15; P. Xella, "'Le Grand Froid': Le dieu *Baradu madu* à Ebla," *UF* 18 (1986), 440 n. 14.

114. See W. G. Lambert, "Idigina/Idiglat," *RlA* 5.31–32. Note also that the Hurrian name for the Tigris appears in an Ugaritic alphabetic text as *aršḫ* (KTU 1.100:63, 64); cf. J. C. de Moor, "East of Eden," *ZAW* 100 (1988), 110. On Hurrian names for the Tigris, that is, *Aranzaḫi* and *Araššiḫ*, see G. F. del Monte and J. Tischler, *Die Orts- und Gewässernamen der hethitischen Texte* (RGTC 6; Wiesbaden: Reichert, 1978), 524.

115. Cf. Astour, "Semites and Hurrians in Northern Transtigris," 19 n. 110.

116. Private communication, 15 July 1987.

117. Cf. D. O. Edzard, *Hymnen, Beschwörungen und Verwandtes* (ARET 5; Rome: Pontifical Biblical Institute, 1984), 23.

25:4, 13).[118] The unassimilated forms also appear as *pu-ra-na-ta* (AH S i 7) and *pu-ra-na-ti* (KAR 360.7).[119] Its etymology is still unknown.

Summary

In Gen 2:5–6, unlike in 1:2, both the water from above, rain, and the water from below, the *ʾēd*-water, are mentioned in the description of the initial state of the earth, though the former is treated negatively, as "not yet" and the latter positively, as "already."

Here, the rainwater does not play a significant role. On the other hand, the *ʾēd*-"water," which is a flooding water from underground, is actively involved in the initial state of the earth. But, unlike the *tĕhôm*-water in Gen 1:2, the *ʾēd*-water in 2:6 is covering the "land" (*ʾădāmâ*), only a part of the "earth."

It should be noted that a careful distinction is made between the *ʾēd*-water that "comes up from the earth" and the "river" that "comes out of Eden." The *ʾēd*-water comes up from underground and waters the whole surface of the land (*ʾădāmâ*). On the other hand, the river waters (2:10) "come out of" one place and "water" a different place, forming a stream or streams.

The situation in 2:5–6 as a whole is simply this: Because of the lack of rain, there was no plant life on the earth, while the *ʾēd*-water was flooding out of the earth to water, that is, inundate, the entire surface of the land, which was only a part of the earth. The problem here was not the lack of water but the lack of adequate control of water by man for the purpose of agriculture. This well-watered situation is certainly in keeping with Eden, the "well-watered place" where God planted a garden (2:8).

The two waters in Gen 2:5–6, "rain" and "flooding water," may be compared with the two *thmt*-waters in an Ugaritic expression that seems to refer to the waters above, in heaven, and the waters below, under the earth, as in Gen 7:11 and 8:2. This upper *thmt*-water is probably associated or identified with the god "Heaven," while the lower *thmt*-water may well correspond to the goddess "Ocean" in Ugaritic religion.

---

118. Cf. B. Groneberg, *Die Orts- und Gewässernamen der altbabylonischen Zeit* (RGTC 3; Wiesbaden: Reichert, 1980), 303.

119. Cf. Lambert and Millard, *AH*, 149. For other examples of the unassimilated forms, see G. F. del Monte and J. Tischler, *Die Orts- und Gewässernamen der hethitischen Texte* (RGTC 6; Wiesbaden: Reichert, 1978), 543–44; I. M. Diakonoff and S. M. Kashkai, *Geographical Names according to Urartian Texts* (RGTC 9; Wiesbaden: Reichert, 1981), 111.

7

God and the Waters

In the previous chapters, we noted that in both Gen 1:2 and Gen 2:5–6 the terms (*tĕhôm* and *'ēd*) that are normally used for the subterranean waters appear to describe the initial state of the earth. In Gen 1, the *tĕhôm*-water seems to have covered the whole earth (*'ereṣ*); in Gen 2, the *'ēd*-water is covering only a part of the earth, the "land" (*'ǎdāmâ*). In Gen 1, however, the water from above, from which rain comes, was not separated from the water from below, that is, the subterranean waters, until the creation of *rāqîă'*,[1] a division in the water, in vv. 6ff. But, in Gen 2, the rain has already been referred to, albeit negatively: "The Lord God had not yet caused it to rain."

In this chapter, I will discuss the nature of the relationship between God and the waters in the first two chapters of Genesis in comparison with extrabiblical materials.

God as a Rain-Giver

The rain-giving god, who is one of the most active deities in many parts of the world, is known not only from written texts such as myths and legends but also from iconographies, for example, in various cylinder seal impressions from the ancient Near East.[2] He is known as Hadda in Eblaite,[3] as Adad or Addu in Akkadian,[4] as Baal, Hadad, or Haddu in Ugaritic, and as Teshub in Hurrian and Hittite.

---

1. For a useful discussion of this term, see P. Collini, "Studi sul lessico della metallurgia nell'ebraico biblico e nelle lingue Siro-Palestinesi del II e I millennio A.C.," *SEL* 4 (1987), 19–20, 33–34 nn. 93–98.

2. He is represented in nos. 725–26, 779–80, 782, and 787–92 of D. Collon's list, and his consort is pictured as a nude goddess with rainfall in no. 780; cf. D. Collon, *First Impressions: Cylinder Seals in the Ancient Near East* (London: British Museum, 1987), 170.

3. In Eblaite, "one of the most frequently occurring gods is Adda, probably pronounced Hadda, biblical Baal or Hadad, the storm god"; cf. W. G. Lambert, "Old Testament Mythology in Its Ancient Near Eastern Context," *Congress Volume: Jerusalem 1986* (VTSup 40; Leiden: Brill, 1988), 130.

4. Cf. Roberts, *ESP*, 13–14, for the early attestation of Adad or Addu in old Semitic PNs. Also Tallqvist, *AG*, 246–49.

This deity is often called "a giver of abundant water-supply." In the Akkadian text cited above,[5] the rain-god Adad is described as the god who "lets it rain copiously for the people" (*ušaznan eli nišīšamût ṭuḫdi*). The Tell Fekheriyeh text also mentions Hadad, the god of life-giving water, as *mᶜdn mt kln // muṭaḫḫidu kibrāti* "one who makes the whole land abundant in water-supply." Immediately prior, he is called the "water-controller of all rivers" (*gwgl nhr klm*). Thus, he is sometimes understood not simply as a rain-giving god but also as a controller of the subterranean waters, just as Ea, the god of Apsû, controlled the subterranean ocean.

Similarly, Yahweh-Elohim of Gen 2 is understood as a rain-giver, as well as the controller of the subterranean waters. While he has not yet sent rain to the earth (v. 5), he supposedly drained the *ʾēd*-water into the rivers so that he could make a garden and plant trees in it (vv. 8–9). Though the narrator simply reports, as background information,[6] that a river was coming out of Eden (v. 10), Yahweh-Elohim, the single dramatis persona in this section of the story, must have controlled the course of the river water from the well-watered place of Eden when he planted the garden. Thus, he was the controller of both rain and subterranean water, like Hadad.[7] However, Yahweh-Elohim is more than a water-controller who gives abundant water-supply. He is the maker of the whole universe, "earth and heaven" (*ʾ ereṣ wĕšāmāyim*),[8] as expressed in the beginning of this story (2:4).

Watery Beginning

Because God is deeply involved with the *tĕhôm*-water through his *rûăḥ* and his word in Gen 1:2, how shall we interpret the nature of the relationship between God and the *tĕhôm*-water in comparison with other Near Eastern mythologies that deal with a watery beginning?

According to Kramer, "the Sumerian thinkers assumed that before the universe came into being there existed nothing but water, that is, they postulated

---

5. See above, p. 117.

6. Gen 2:10–14, in which not a single *wayqtl* appears, is off the main story-line, thus constituting an embedded discourse; see above, p. 77, for sources.

7. For a detailed discussion of the Yahweh-Baal relationship, see ch. 8. Note the recent treatment of Ps 29 by C. Kloos, who argues that Yahweh is presented as an Israelite Baal in this psalm; cf. C. Kloos, *Yhwh's Combat with the Sea: A Canaanite Tradition in the Religion of Ancient Israel* (Leiden: Brill, 1986); and J. Day's review of this book in "(A Review of) *Yhwh's Combat with the Sea: A Canaanite Tradition in the Religion of Ancient Israel.* By Carola Kloos. Pp. 243. Leiden: Brill, 1986," *JTS* 39 (1988), 151–54. For a reappraisal of the alleged connection between God, who is depicted as a warrior king in Hab 3, and Baal, the victor over Yam, see ch. 10.

8. For this idiomatic pair, see above, p. 60 n. 10.

the existence of a primeval sea."[9] It is significant however to note, with Lambert, that the motif of a "watery beginning" (*der wässeriger Anfang*) was by no means only a Mesopotamian notion. "The ancient Egyptians quite generally acknowledged the god of the primaeval waters Nu (Nun)[10] as the source of all things. In early Greece . . . Ocean is described as the father (γένεσις) of the gods in Homer, and water is the prime element in the cosmologies of Thales and Anaximander. Thus the watery beginning of Genesis is in itself no evidence of Mesopotamian influence."[11]

The "watery beginning" of Gen 1:2 could well be a reflection of the universal understanding of water as a basic element of the cosmos. Certainly the relationship between the earth and the waters is a primary concern of mankind: on the one hand, water is the source of life in a normal physical life and, on the other hand, flooding is a major threat to life on the earth. Therefore, it is no surprise that many ancient traditions are concerned with the initial state of the earth in relation to water.[12]

However, while there is a similarity between these ancient traditions and the Genesis story in terms of a watery beginning, there are also differences in the nature of the relationship between the water and the creator-god as well as in the details of the description. In the following section, we shall deal specifically with such creator-gods as Marduk, El, and Ea, who correspond in some way to Elohim in the Genesis story.

A "Creator"-God and the Water

Marduk, Ea, and El

While scholars have noted similarities between the Marduk of *Enuma elish* and the Baal of the Ugaritic myths in that both are "storm" gods, have fights with sea-dragons, and become the king of the gods, and so on, there is a major difference between these two deities: Marduk "created" or rather

9. S. N. Kramer, "(Review of) H. and H. A. Frankfort, John A. Wilson, Thorkild Jacobsen, William A. Irwin. *The Intellectual Adventure of Ancient Man: An Essay on Speculative Thought in the Ancient Near East*. The University of Chicago Press, Chicago, 1946, VI, 401 pp.," *JCS* 2 (1948), 43; idem, *The Sumerians: Their History, Culture, and Character* (Chicago: University of Chicago Press, 1963), 113.

10. For this term, see A. Erman and H. Grapow, *WÄS*, 2.214: *nnw/nw.w?/nwnw?* Cf. Gk. Νουν and Coptic *Nūn*. Also see F. Stolz, "Sea," in *DDD*, 1391–92.

11. W. G. Lambert, "A New Look at the Babylonian Background of Genesis," *JTS* 16 (1965), 293; idem, "Babylonien und Israel," *TRE* 5.71; idem, "Kosmogonie," *RlA* 6.218–22, esp. 220; idem, "Old Testament Mythology in Its Ancient Near Eastern Context," 126. For Egyptian parallels, see J. K. Hoffmeier, "Some Thoughts on Genesis 1 and 2 and Egyptian Cosmology," *JANES* 15 (1983), 39–49.

12. See now my "Water," in *NDBT*, 840–41.

formed the cosmos, but Baal did not.[13] As noted above, as far as the creation of the cosmos is concerned, in Ugaritic mythology it is the god El, not Baal, that apparently corresponds to the "creator"-god Marduk. Therefore, it is suggested by some that El's relationship with *thm(t)* should be compared to Marduk's relationship with Tiamat and that both should be compared to Elohim's relationship with "the water of *těhôm*" in Genesis.

De Moor interprets the "two *thmt*-waters" near El's abode as the "Upper and Lower Flood" because, he thinks, "the Ugaritians were acquainted with the idea of a celestial and a subterranean *thmt*."[14] Then he compares the two "floods" with the two parts of Tiamat divided by Marduk and the upper and lower waters separated by Yнwн. He explains that, like Marduk (Ee IV 135ff.) and Yнwн (Gen 1:6; Prov 3:19–20; cf. 2 Sam 22:16), "the Ugaritic god El was held responsible for the separation of the cosmic waters."[15]

However, it should be noted that what Marduk created by splitting the body of Tiamat were "heaven" (Ee IV 137–38) and "earth" (Ee V 62), neither of which includes the subterranean water, for Ea had already established his abode on Apsû (Ee I 73ff.) when Marduk defeated Tiamat (Ee IV 101–4).[16] Moreover, Marduk's abode is never associated with waters, while the god El in Ugaritic myths is described as dwelling "at the sources of the two rivers," that is, "in the midst of the streams of the two *thmt*-waters."

In *Enuma elish*, it is the god Ea who resides at the watery location, Apsû. On the other hand, Marduk's palace Esagila is located on the earth, between Ešarra (= "lower heaven"), Enlil's domain, and Apsû, Ea's domain.[17] Therefore, Ea is more similar to El than to Marduk in terms of the relationship between creator-gods and their abodes near or in the water.

C. H. Gordon summarizes a number of common features that Ea, who is the Sumerian Enki,[18] shares with El in Ugaritic mythology. In the following,

---

13. See above, pp. 55–56.

14. J. C. de Moor, "Studies in the New Alphabetic Texts from Ras Shamra I," *UF* 1 (1969), 182 n. 108. See also his explanation of *qrb.apq.thmtm* "in the bedding of the Two Floods," that is, in the stream-bed of the Upper and Lower Flood (J. C. de Moor, "El, the Creator," in *The Bible World: Essays in Honor of Cyrus H. Gordon* [ed. G. Rendsburg et al.; New York: KTAV, 1980], 183); *bʿdt thmtm* "at the confluence of two Floods." See below, pp. 137–139.

15. "Although these acts of creation ended the state of chaos, the Floods had to be kept under tight control . . . El dwelt at this remote point of the cosmos . . . to maintain the order" (de Moor, "El, the Creator," 183).

16. In fact, Marduk was born "within the *Apsû*." Cf. Ee I 81–82.

17. See above, pp. 67–68.

18. En-ki ("Lord of Earth") is called É-*a* in Akkadian texts, but because the term supposedly has no Semitic etymology, Kramer suggests that "Ea" may be of "Ubaidian" origin

we will note in detail the similarity between Ea and El as "creator"-gods and their living in a watery abode.[19]

Similarity between Ea and El

<u>Creator of Creatures</u>

Ea has the title *bānû nabnīt* "creator of creatures," similar to El's epithet *bny bnwt* "creator of creatures,"[20] in a text that reads:

> *Ea . . . bānû nabnīt pātiq kullat mimma šumšu*
> Ea, who creates creatures, who forms everything.
>> (Borger Esarh. 79:4)[21]

This title is used only with the god Ea in Akkadian. Another title of Ea, *bān binûtu*, which is the exact counterpart of Ugaritic *bny bnwt*,[22] appears in the expression [^{d}*Ni*]*nšiku mummu bān binûtu* (PSBA 20 158:14).[23] Ea is also

---

(S. N. Kramer, *In the World of Sumer: An Autobiography* [Detroit: Wayne State University Press, 1986], 202). However, Gordon proposes a Semitic etymology in light of a Sumerian-Eblaite bilingual vocabulary,

EN.KI : É-*um* /ḫay(y)um/ "The Living One,"

and compares the god Ḫay(y)a with the Ugaritic god Baal, whose epithet is also "Prince, Lord of Earth" (*zbl bʕl arṣ* in KTU 1.6 [49]:I:42–43 [14–15], etc.) and who is "a dying and rising god, mourned when dead (*mt*) and joyously hailed when again alive (*ḥy*)." É-*a* = Ḫay(y)a is thus the living "Lord of Earth"; cf. C. H. Gordon, "Eblaitica," *Eblaitica* 1 (1987), 20; "(A Review of) S. N. Kramer, *In the World of Sumer: An Autobiography*. Detroit: Wayne State University Press, 1986," *JCS* 39 (1987), 249. W. G. Lambert (*JCS* 41 [1989], 3) also accepts that ^{d}en.ki was "probably pronounced Haya." See also Roberts, *ESP*, 20, where he suggests **ḥyy* "to live" as a possible etymology of É-*a*.

19. Other aspects that Gordon discusses are as follows:

1. *wisdom*: "Enki's wisdom matches El's sagacity" (Gordon, "[A Review of] S. N. Kramer, *In the World of Sumer*, 1986," 249).
2. *god of magic*: "The spell of Enki recalls El's exorcism in the Epic of Kret (1.16 [126]: V:25)" (Gordon, "[A Review of] S. N. Kramer, *In the World of Sumer*, 1986," 249). Note that "as god of ablution magic he was usually called En-uru: 'Lord Reed Bundle', after the reed bundles out of which was constructed the reed hut in which the rites were performed" (Jacobsen, *TIT*, 22).
3. *drunken god*: "The tipsy Enki is to be compared with the drunken El" (Gordon, "[A Review of] S. N. Kramer, *In the World of Sumer*, 1986," 249). See Kramer, *The Sumerians*, 161.

20. See above, pp. 55–56, for the fact that El, not Baal, is the creator-god in Ugaritic myths.

21. *CAD* N/1 28; cf. Tallqvist, *AG*, 69.

22. Cf. de Moor, "El, the Creator," 182–83.

23. Ninšiku was an epithet of Ea; see Lambert and Millard, *AH*, 148–49 note to line 16.

called "creator of everything" (*bān kala*) with the title *mummu*, which is usually used with him (and Marduk).[24] Anu and Enlil, the other two gods of the triad of the great gods, were also called *bānû kalāma* "creator of everything,"[25] but neither these great gods nor Marduk,[26] the "creator"-god, were called *bān binûtu* or *bānû nabnît*.

Creator of the Cosmos

Ea, like El, is also the creator of the cosmos. Ea created "land and sea" (*šadî u tâmāti*)[27] and is called *mummu bān šamê u erṣeti* "the *mummu*, creator of heaven and earth" (LKA 77 i 29–30).[28] A similar title, "creatress of heaven and earth" (*bānât šamê u erṣeti*), is used with Nammu, the mother of Enki,[29] in whose chamber Ea (Enki) dwells. Ea is also called *pātiq šamê u erṣeti* "creator of heaven and earth" and *bān kullati* "creator of everything,"[30] and as a creator god his name was Nudimmud.[31] Ea is called *zārū māti* "progenitor (or father) of the land."[32] Thus, as the water god,[33] Ea was the creator of cosmos par excellence, though Marduk and Šamaš were also called "creator" (*bān[û]*) of "heaven and earth" (*šamê u erṣeti*).[34]

Father of the Gods

Just as El is the "father" of Baal and other deities (*bn ilm*), Ea, the father of Marduk who is "the first born of Enki," is called *abu ilāni* "father of the gods."[35]

---

24. Iraq 15 123:19; etc.; cf. *CAD* M/2 197; *CAD* B 87–88.

25. Tallqvist, *AG*, 254, 300. Note the similar title of a river-god, *bānât kalāma*. See above, p. 93.

26. Tallqvist, *AG*, 366.

27. Racc. 46, 30, cited by *AHw*, 1353.

28. *CAD* M/2 197. See the Sumerian myth "Enki and the World Order: The Organization of the Earth and Its Cultural Processes" (Kramer, *The Sumerians*, 122, 171–83, 294), for a detailed account of Enki's creative activities.

29. Tallqvist, *AG*, 71; Stolz, "Sea," in *DDD*, 1392.

30. Tallqvist, *AG*, 289.

31. Ee I 16; cf. Jacobsen, *TIT*, 22.

32. Tallqvist, *AG*, 289; cf. Kramer, *The Sumerians*, 175.

33. Tiāmat is also described by the title *mummu* in Ee I 4 (see above, p. 73), but she was never a supreme deity in Mesopotamia. Note that the river-goddess appears as a creator in the *Harab Myth* (see above, pp. 90–91 n. 34) as well as in a myth of "Schöpfungsfluß": *Nāru bānât kalâma* (see above, n. 24).

34. Tallqvist, *AG*, 69.

35. Ibid., 289; Livingstone, *MMEW*, 75. Cf. also *CAD* A/2 195.

Father of Mankind

Like El, the "father of man" (*ab adm*), Ea is called *bānû nišē* "creator of
people."[36] Ea as a "creator" fashioned man from the blood of Kingu: *ina
damēšu ibnâ amēlūtu* (Ee VI 33).[37] Ea also created man in *Atra-Ḫasīs*, or at
least it was Ea's idea; he was also the creator of man in the Old Babylonian
Agušaya hymn, as well as in the Sumerian myth of *Enki and Ninhursag*.[38]
The *Eridu Genesis* mentions that Anu, Enlil, Enki, and Ninhursag fashioned
the dark-headed (people).[39]

When de Moor concluded his discussion on "El, the creator," by saying
"Like Sumerian Enlil,[40] Babylonian Marduk[41] and YHWH, El, the supreme
god of the Canaanites, was thought to be the 'creator of both the cosmos and
man,' "[42] he seems to have ignored two other supreme gods in ancient Mesopotamia, Anu and Ea, who were also recognized as creator-gods and were
both "father of the gods" (*abu ilāni*). In Mesopotamian mythology, Marduk[43]
was a latecomer, and the triad of deities, Anu, Enlil, and Ea (Enki), was already established in the Old Babylonian and Kassite periods[44] before Marduk
was exalted among the gods.

---

36. Tallqvist, *AG*, 69, 289. Note the different title, *bānû ṣalmāt qaqqadi*, for Marduk
and Nabû; cf. *CAD* N/1 28; B 87; Tallqvist, *AG*, 69.

37. Cf. Jacobsen, *The Treasures of Darkness*, 181.

38. See Kramer, *The Sumerians*, 149–50. For the most recent treatment of "Enki and
Ninhursag," see P. Attinger, "Enki et Ninḫursaǧa," *ZA* 74 (1984), 1–52. For the goddess
Ninḫursaǧa, see T. Jacobsen, "The Eridu Genesis," *JBL* 100 (1981), 514 n. 5; W. G. Lam-
bert, "Kosmogonie," *RlA* 6.219.

39. Jacobsen, "The Eridu Genesis," 515. For these four gods, see Kramer, *The Sumerians*, 118–22.

40. Ibid., 118–19. Note also Lambert's study on the structure of the Hurrian pantheon,
which, according to him, "could well have been modelled on an archaic Sumerian pantheon
from the first half of the Third Millennium with Enlil alone at its head." See W. G. Lambert,
"The Mesopotamian Background of the Hurrian Pantheon," *RHA* 36 (1978), 134.

41. For detailed studies of Marduk, see W. Sommerfeld, *Der Aufstieg Marduks: Die
Stellung Marduks in der babylonischen Religion des zweiten Jahrtausends v. Chr.* (AOAT
213; Neukirchen-Vluyn: Neukirchener Verlag, 1982); T. Oshima, *Hymns and Prayers to
Marduk and the Descriptions of His Divine Aspects in the Texts* (Ph.D. diss.; Jerusalem:
Hebrew University, 2003), especially 338–68.

42. De Moor, "El, the Creator," 186.

43. Note that Marduk is described as holding "the Anuship, the Enlilship, and Eaship"
(cf. Jacobsen, *The Treasure of Darkness*, 234). Cf. P. D. Miller, Jr., "The Absence of the
Goddess in Israelite Religion," *HAR* 10 (1986), 242.

44. Livingstone, *MMEW*, 76. See above, p. 67, on tripartite cosmology. Also cf. A. Cavigneaux, H. G. Güterbock, and M. T. Roth (eds.), *The Series Erim-ḫuš = anantu and Anta-gál = šaqû* (MSL 17; Rome: Pontifical Biblical Institute, 1985), 91, where Anu, Enlil,
and Ea correspond to ᵈen-za, ᵈmaḫ-za, and ᵈki-za-za, respectively. Most recently, see
Oshima, *Hymns and Prayers to Marduk*, 348–55.

In a similar way, the Ugaritic senior deity El had already established his status as head of the pantheon before Baal became a king among the gods. Baal, however, was never called a "creator," and El remained active as the creator-god and was "not demoted to less than an honorable position."[45]

Watery Abode

Ea and El are similar not only in being the *senior* creator-god and the father of mankind and gods, but also in living near or in the waters. On the other hand, Enlil and Marduk as well as Baal are never associated with a watery abode. Gordon notes that "Enki's inhabiting a watery shrine in the Deep corresponds to El's abode at the sources of the two cosmic Rivers or Deeps."[46] However, the nature and location of El's abode is highly disputed by Ugaritic scholars. Before we deal with this problem, let us summarize the nature and location of Ea's abode.

Ea's Watery Abode

Ea's (Enki's) titles that suggest the nature and location of his abode are Lugal-id(ak) "owner of the river," Lugal-abzu(ak)[47] = *šar apsî* "the king of the Apsû," and *bēl naqbi* "the lord of the source."[48] They present him as the specific power in rivers or the subterranean waters. In a section in one late text, Ea is associated with water: *ul-la-nu:* ^{d}*ea* (40): *mu-ú* "Primeval : Ea : water."[49] Here the "water" refers to the primeval Apsû.

Ea's abode is in Apsû, the underground sweet waters.[50] Ea (Enki) lies in the "chamber of Nammu" (*mayālu ša* ^{d}*Nammu*), the goddess of the water-bearing strata; these chambers are down in the earth, just above the "surface of the underworld" (*ašar erṣetimma*).[51] This accords with the description of his abode in the "middle earth," which is between the abode of men and the underworld.[52] Ea (Enki)'s watery chamber with two gateposts is probably

---

45. M. S. Smith, "Interpreting the Baal Cycle," *UF* 18 (1986), 338 n. 129.
46. Gordon, "(A Review of) S. N. Kramer, *In the World of Sumer*, 1986," 249.
47. Jacobsen, *The Treasures of Darkness*, 111.
48. Livingstone, *MMEW*, 30–31.
49. *RA* 62 52 17–18, cited by Livingstone, *MMEW*, 74.
50. See *CAD* A/2 194–97; also *SD* A/2 184–202, esp. p. 202, for the relationship between a b z u and e n g u r "deep waters."
51. T. Jacobsen, "Sumerian Mythology: A Review Article," *JNES* 5 (1946), 145 n. 28. He also notes that e n g u r is distinguished from a-ab-ba "sea," on p. 140 n. 21. This is supported by the Eblaite vocabulary, *VE*, which lists:

1343': ab-a   *ti-ʾà-ma-tum* (79:rev.III:8'–9')
1344': ^{d}nammu (ENGUR)   *ší-nu ḫa-mi-um* (63–64:v.III:20–21)

52. See above, p. 65.

depicted in seal no. 760 in the cylinder seal impressions republished in D. Collon's book.[53]

Ea is usually pictured with two streams,[54] which Jacobsen thinks are the Euphrates and the Tigris,[55] flowing out of his shoulders or from a vase he holds. On the other hand, in Ee V 55, the Euphrates and the Tigris are described as the two eyes of Tiamat,[56] rather than being related to Ea's abode in Apsû. However, in seal impressions such as Collon no. 761, fish are pictured in these two "waters." These waters are probably subterranean waters, because fish are usually described as being in the Apsû in Akkadian texts and the waters of the Euphrates and the Tigris presumably originated in Apsû.[57]

El's Watery Abode

El's abode[58] is near or in the waters (*mbk nhrm* "at the sources of the two[59] rivers" // *qrb apq thmtm* "in the midst of the streams of the two *thmt*-waters" or *b'dt thmtm* "in the assembly of the two *thmt*-waters"), and this watery nature of El's abode is probably pictured on an object from Ugarit, the "drinking mug with painted scene."[60]

There have been two opposing views about the location of El's abode. M. H. Pope suggests that "the nature of El's abode is . . . similar to that of the Sumero-Akkadian Enki-Ea, who dwells in the *apsû*,"[61] and he takes El's

---

53. Cf. Collon, *First Impressions*, 165; also Kramer, *The Sumerians*, plate following p. 160.

54. Collon, *First Impressions*, 165 and nos. 760–62, 673.

55. Jacobsen, *The Treasures of Darkness*, 111.

56. Cf. B. Landsberger and J. V. Kinnier Wilson, "The Fifth Tablet of *Enuma Eliš*," *JNES* 20 (1961), 160–61. Also note: "The Tigris: her right eye. The Euphrates: her left eye," in Livingstone, *MMEW*, 82–83; cf. Landsberger and Kinnier Wilson, "The Fifth Tablet of *Enuma Eliš*," 175; and "eyes of Tiāmat" in Livingstone, *MMEW*, 163. On the origin of the Tigris River in the Ninurta-Asakku myth, see W. Heimpel, "The Natural History of the Tigris according to the Sumerian Literary Composition LUGAL," *JNES* 46 (1987), 309–17.

57. *CAD* A/2 194–95 and see above, p. 65.

58. For other sources on this subject, see Smith, "Interpreting the Baal Cycle," 328 n. 83.

59. N. Wyatt, "The Hollow Crown: Ambivalent Elements in West Semitic Royal Ideology," *UF* 18 (1986), 426 n. 32 suggests that *nhrm* perhaps signifies "four rivers" in accordance with common iconographic and biblical (Gen 2:10–14) traditions. However, the dual form *thmtm* in the parallel expressions *qrb apq thmtm* and *b'dt thmtm* suggests, rather, that the number of rivers is two.

60. AfO 20 [1963], 211: fig. 30, as discussed by M. H. Pope, "The Scene on the Drinking Mug from Ugarit," in *Near Eastern Studies in Honor of William Foxwell Albright* (ed. Hans Goedicke; Baltimore: Johns Hopkins University Press, 1971), 400.

61. M. H. Pope, *El in the Ugaritic Texts* (VTSup 2; Leiden: Brill, 1955), 71.

abode to be in the underworld, as was Ea's abode. The same view has been taken by O. Kaiser.[62]

On the other hand, Clifford[63] takes El's abode to be in the mountain (*ḫršn*), on the basis of internal textual evidence.[64] He is followed by Mullen, who compares El's abode at the "sources of the rivers" with "the garden of God" // "the mountain of God" (Ezek 28:13, 16).[65] He explains that "the mount of ʾEl was the *ḫuršānu*, the place of entrance to both the Underworld and Heaven . . . at the sources of the life-giving rivers."[66] A. S. Kapelrud also explaines in detail that "(El) is still living on his mountain."[67]

El's living at or near the source of rivers can be compared with Elkunirša's abode, that is, "tent," at "the source of the Mala-river (i.e., the Euphrates)" in a Canaanite myth from Boğazkoy.[68] However, in the Ugaritic texts, no specific name is given for these rivers.

These two *thmt*-waters[69] may be compared with various Mesopotamian traditions in which heaven and *apsû* are paired and possibly refer to "a celestial and a subterranean *thmt*" as de Moor suggests, though his proposal to compare the two "floods" with the two parts of Tiamat is not acceptable, as noted above.[70] It is interesting to note here that the expressions "the upper sea" (a.ab.ba an.ta = *tāmtu elītu*) and "the lower sea" (a.ab.ba ki.ta =

---

62. O. Kaiser, *Die mythische Bedeutung des Meeres in Ägypten, Ugarit und Israel* (BZAW 78; Berlin: Alfred Töpelmann, 1959), 54–55.

63. R. J. Clifford, *The Cosmic Mountain in Canaan and the Old Testament* (HSM 4; Cambridge: Harvard University Press, 1972), 35–57.

64. These two opposing views are summarized by H. N. Wallace, *The Eden Narrative* (HSM 32; Atlanta: Scholars Press, 1985), 94 and 98 n. 88.

65. E. T. Mullen, Jr., *The Divine Council in Canaanite and Early Hebrew Literature* (HSM 24; Chico, Calif.: Scholars Press, 1980), 153. Note that the mountain waters come out of Apsu, the subterranean sweet waters. Cf. J. van Dijk, *LUGAL UD ME-LÁM-bi NIR-GÁL: Le récit épique et didactique des Travaux de Ninurta, du Déluge et de la Nouvelle Création*, vol. 1: *Introduction, Texte Composite: Traduction* (Leiden: Brill, 1983).

66. Mullen, *The Divine Council in Canaanite and Early Hebrew Literature*, 162.

67. A. S. Kapelrud, "The Relationship between El and Baal in the Ras Shamra Texts," in *The Bible World: Essays in Honor of Cyrus H. Gordon* (ed. G. Rendsburg et al.; New York: KTAV, 1980), 82.

68. H. A. Hoffner, Jr., "The Elkunirsa Myth Reconsidered," *RHA* 23 (1965), 8, 14; *CS*, 1.149.

69. Cf. *ti'āmat tu'amtu*, "à deux faces, homme et femme," in van Dijk, *LUGAL UD ME-LÁM-bi NIR-GÁL*, 26. Also see n. 100: "W. von Soden in AHw s. *tu'amtu*[!] = «la double (Ti'āmat)?»."

70. De Moor, "Studies in the New Alphabetic Texts," 182 n. 108; de Moor, "El, the Creator," 183.

tāmtu šaplītu), appear in a MA tablet[71] of mystical explanatory works: while "the upper sea" is connected with Šamaš, "the lower sea of the rising sun" is described as serving Ea, the god of the subterranean ocean.

It is also interesting to note that the two bodies of water were seemingly once personified as a divine couple, *Šamūma* "Heaven(-water)" and *Tahāmatu* "Ocean(-water)," or a composite divine being, *Šmm-w-Thm*, in Ugaritic religion. This divine pair, "Heaven"-god *Šamūma* (= *šmm*) and "Ocean"-goddess *Tahāmatu* (= *thmt*), corresponds to Sumerian AN and ANTU, respectively, in *Ug.* 5, 137:III:33″–34″. Therefore, it seems that these preserve an ancient tradition about the separation of heaven-water[72] and ocean-water that is reflected in the Genesis Creation story, not in 1:2 but in 1:6ff.,[73] as well as in the Flood story (Gen 7:11, 8:2). As de Moor pointed out, in the Ugaritic incantation text KTU 1.100, an older mythological tradition in which the sun-goddess (*špš*) was "the mother of Heaven (male) and Flood (female)" seems to be presupposed.[74] In a mythological explanatory work from the Neo-Assyrian period,[75] a similar cosmological tradition may have influenced preserving two primeval gods, Anšar ("totality of the upper world")[76] and his "Antu" Tiamat,[77] who are equated with Aššur and Ištar.

A similar tradition may be recognized in a Neo-Babylonian ritual text that describes the initial creation of the universe as follows: "Anu created 'heaven' (*šamê*) // ᵈNudimmud (= Ea) created Apsû."[78] In *Enuma elish* IV 141–42, it is Marduk who shaped the "heavens" to match the Apsû.[79] The same pair of

---

71. *RA* 60 73 8–9, cited by Livingstone, *MMEW*, 77.

72. Note the artificial etymology of "heaven" (*šamê*) as "of water" (*ša mê*) in a Babylonian mystical explanatory work; cf. Livingstone, *MMEW*, 32–33, line 6. Note the same view held by H. Bauer and P. Leander, *Historische Grammatik der hebräischen Sprache des Alten Testaments* (Hildesheim: Olmes, 1922 [1962]), 621. In the Genesis story, however, what God called "heaven" was *rāqîă'* (v. 8), not the water above it (as Stieglitz suggests). Cf. R. R. Stieglitz, "Ugaritic Sky-Gods and Biblical Heavens," *NUS* 35 (April, 1986), 13.

73. See Stieglitz, ibid. This tradition is therefore Canaanite and not "a piece of learning which was picked up in Babylon by the Jewish religious leaders" (C. Kloos, *Yhwh's Combat with the Sea*, 85). On the biblical "heavens," see my "שמים: Heaven, Sky, Firmament, Air," *NIDOTTE* 4.160–66.

74. J. C. de Moor, "East of Eden," *ZAW* 100 (1988), 106 n. 3.

75. Livingstone, *MMEW*, 233–34.

76. Cf. Borger, *ABZ*, 160: šár = *kiššatu* "Gesamtheit, Welt."

77. In an inscription of Sennacherib, Anšar is depicted "setting out in battle against Tiāmat, followed by a retinue of gods." See Livingstone, *MMEW*, 232.

78. F. Thureau-Dangin, *Rituels accadiens* (Paris: Leroux, 1921), 46; also see *CAD* A/2 195.

79. Marduk made the heavens (*šamê*) "a likeness of the Apsû, the abode of Nudimmud (Ea)" (*mi-iḫ-rit ap-si-i šu-bat* ᵈ*nu-dím-mud*). Cf. Livingstone, *MMEW*, 80.

"heaven" and *apsû*, "cosmic subterranean water," appears quite often[80] and can be compared with the Hebrew pair *šāmayim* and *tĕhôm(ôt)* in Gen 7:11, 8:2, 49:25; Deut 33:13; Ps 107:26.

In light of the above, El's abode was probably located at the farthest horizon, where "heaven" and "ocean" meet together. The biggest difference between El and Ea is this: while El's abode seems to be related to the "two *thmt*-waters," possibly "heaven" and "ocean," Ea's abode is related only to the subterranean ocean. While El is the supreme god in Ugarit, Ea was one of three traditional supreme deities during the 2nd millennium B.C. in southern Mesopotamia, and he controls only one of the three areas of universe, that is, Apsû. According to Lambert, in the third-millennium Sumerian pantheon as well as in the second-millennium Hurrian pantheon, which reflects the northern Mesopotamian tradition, Enki-Ea was a second-rank deity. In this aspect, the Ugaritic god El as a creator is more similar to Elohim of Genesis than to Ea.

Thus, the two creator-gods, Ea and El, who have close associations with the waters, have similar characteristics and functions. In Ugaritic, the "two *thmt*-waters" (*thmtm*) and the "sea" (*ym*) are distinguished and are connected with two different gods, El and Baal, just as in the Akkadian *Enuma elish*, in which Ea's abode is the subterranean ocean Apsû, while Marduk's enemy is Tiamat, the sea-goddess. However, El's abode "at the sources of the two rivers," that is, "in the midst of the streams of the two *thmt*-waters," seems to preserve older traditions about the watery abode of a creator-god in the ancient Near Eastern cosmologies.

Conclusion

The biblical Elohim is also deeply involved with the water of the *tĕhôm* through his "spirit"[81] (Gen 1:2) and "word" (1:6ff.), but furthermore, the author of the passage ascribes to Elohim the creation of the total cosmos, "heavens and earth," which includes the subterranean water of *tĕhôm*. Hence the relationship between Elohim and *tĕhôm* is that of the creator and the creature.

The Genesis account has similarities with the Ugaritic mythological traditions in the sense that both deities, Elohim and El, are the supreme gods of creation, who had a close relationship with the waters. The Babylonian Ea, though similar to El in characteristics and functions, is not supreme god.

---

80. *CAD* A/2 194–96, esp. b, 1′: "parallel to *šamû*."

81. The current emphasis on *rûaḥ* as "wind" (e.g., R. Luyster, "Wind and Water: Cosmogonic Symbolism in the Old Testament," *ZAW* 93 [1981], 1–10; Day, *God's Conflict with the Dragon and the Sea*, 39, 107) appears to be based on the supposition that there is a Canaanite dragon myth behind Gen 1:2. See ch. 3 above.

Because the extant Ugaritic myths seem to presuppose the earlier (pre-historic?)[82] traditions about the creation of the cosmos, probably by El rather than by Baal, it may well be that both Genesis and the Ugaritic myths reflect much earlier "common" traditions. However, because the linguistic form of Hebrew /tĕhôm/ is older than Ugaritic /tahāmu/ as noted above,[83] it is un-likely that the Hebrew term is a depersonification of the earlier Canaanite di-vine name Tahām and therefore unlikely that Genesis is dependent upon the Ugaritic mythology.

It is true that in the Mesopotamian and Canaanite pantheons certain deities such as Marduk, Ea, and El[84] were called "the creator (or the lord) of heaven and earth," but in the Old Testament theology, when Yahweh-Elohim is repre-sented as the creator of heaven and earth (e.g., Gen 1:1; 14:22), the author is saying not only that he is incomparable in relation to other gods but also that, as the actual creator, he is the only god who can truly be called a god; that is, he is God.[85]

---

82. Cf. Lambert, "Old Testament Mythology in Its Ancient Near Eastern Context," 128: "The creative period of myth lies in prehistory. That was the time of genuine mythic cre-ativity, so that the basic material was spread everywhere from the Aegean to India before our written evidence begins. When the earliest myths and allusions known to us were writ-ten down, the basic concern of myth had already lost some of its force." Cf. de Moor's view that "KTU 1.100 and 1.107 . . . presuppose a Canaanite tradition about the Garden of Eden," in "East of Eden," 106.

83. See above, p. 53.

84. Cf. P. D. Miller, Jr., "El, the Creator of Earth," *BASOR* 239 (1980), 43–46.

85. Cf. C. J. Labuschagne, *The Incomparability of Yahweh in the Old Testament* (Pre-toria Oriental Series 5; Leiden: Brill, 1966).

PART 2

The Chaoskampf *Motif in Poetic Texts*

8

Canaanite Myths and Hebrew Poetry

The "Chaoskampf Myth"

As we have already argued, the background of the Genesis creation story
has nothing to do with the so-called *Chaoskampf* myth of the Mesopotamian
type, as preserved in the Babylonian "creation" myth *Enuma elish*. In Gen 1,
there is no hint of struggle or battle between God and this *tĕhôm*-water. The
creation motif, without *Chaoskampf*, is attested also in Prov 8:27, where the
term *tĕhôm* appears together with *šāmayim*, as it does in Ugaritic:[1]

> When he established the heavens (*šāmayim*), I was there,
> when he drew a circle on the face of the deep (*tĕhôm*)." (NRSV)

The creation psalm, Ps 104, which is "just . . . expounding Israelite cosmology concerning the depths,"[2] also has no *Chaoskampf*-motif. With regard to
the term *tĕhôm* in Gen 7:11, Harland has recently concluded: "there is no allusion to the myth in the story of the flood."[3]

Hebrew *tĕhôm* is certainly etymologically related to the Akkadian divine
name Tiamat; both terms refer to a huge amount of water, as in the Ugaritic
thm(t) and Eblaite *tihāmatum*. All these terms derive from the common Semitic term *tihām-*.[4] In Gen 1:2, the *tĕhôm*-water is simply a part of the
earth,[5] created by God; it covered the entire surface of the earth like a flood,
as in Ps 104:6:

> You cover it with the deep (*tĕhôm*) as with a garment;
> the waters stood above the mountains. (NRSV)

What, then, is the relationship between Hebrew creation stories and the
Ugaritic *Chaoskampf* myth? In this Canaanite version of the *Chaoskampf*

---

1. On the word pair *šmm* and *thmt* in Ugaritic, see p. 61.
2. P. J. Harland, *The Value of Human Life: A Study of the Story of the Flood (Genesis
6–9)* (VTSup 64; Leiden: Brill, 1996), 95.
3. Ibid., 96.
4. See ch. 2 (above).
5. See ch. 3 (above).

myth, the storm-god[6] Baal fights with the sea-god Yam and his associates, such as the dragon and serpent. Since Gunkel, it has been claimed that expressions in the poetic texts of the Bible such as "mighty waters" (e.g., Hab 3:15), Leviathan (Pss 74:14, 104:26; Isa 27:1), Rahab (Ps 89:10, Isa 51:9, etc.) and "monster" (Ps 74:13) refer to Baal's adversaries.

There are some similarities between the Babylonian myth *Enuma elish* and the Ugaritic myths of the Baal cycle, because both deal with the combat between the storm-god and the sea-god and his associates. But there are also significant differences between them: the Ugaritic sea-god Yam (masc.) is etymologically related to Heb. *yām*, not to Akk. Tiamat (fem.). And, most significantly, Baal never created anything. Thus, the Canaanite *Chaoskampf* myth has nothing to do with the creation of the universe or even of a part of it.[7]

Though J. Day sees "evidence that the Canaanites may have associated the creation with the conflict with the dragon"[8] in some Ugaritic texts (e.g., KTU 1.3 III:37–IV:3; 1.5 I:1–3), which mention Baal's defeat of his enemies, Yam and his associates such as the dragon *tnn* and the serpent *Ltn*, his argument is highly speculative and circular. For one thing, he bases his view on "the fact that the Old Testament so frequently uses the imagery of the divine conflict with the dragon and the sea in association with creation." However, this biblical "fact" is in fact based on Gunkel's assumption that those biblical texts have a Canaanite mythological background. One cannot but see the gap in Day's logic when he asserts that Baal's victory over the dragon and the sea was "associated" with the creation of the world, though he holds that Baal himself was "not" the creator.[9]

Furthermore, one might note that in the Ugaritic texts cited by Day, Baal's victory over the enemy Yam and his associates is treated as a then-already-ancient event but has nothing to do with cosmic origins. A recent article by M. Dietrich and O. Loretz[10] is extremely cautious with the question of the

6. On the storm-god in Canaan, see W. Herrmann, "Baal" in *DDD*, 250–63; D. E. Fleming, "'The Storm God of Canaan' at Emar," *UF* 26 (1994), 127–30. Most recently, see A. R. W. Green, *The Storm-God in the Ancient Near East* (Biblical and Judaic Studies from the University of California, San Diego, 8; Winona Lake, Ind.: Eisenbrauns, 2003).

7. See ch. 2, excursus (above, pp. 53–57).

8. J. Day, *God's Conflict with the Dragon and the Sea: Echoes of a Canaanite Myth in the Old Testament* (Cambridge: Cambridge University Press, 1985), 17.

9. Ibid., 17–18. On the issue of terminology such as "creation" and "cosmogony," see M. S. Smith, *The Ugaritic Baal Cycle*, vol. 1: *Introduction with Text, Translation and Commentary of KTU 1.1–1.2* (VTSup 55; Leiden: Brill, 1994), 81–83.

10. M. Dietrich and O. Loretz, "Baal, Leviathan und der siebenköpfige Drache *Šlyṭ* in der Rede des Todesgottes Môt (KTU 1.5 I 1–8 // 27a–31)," *Aula Orientalis* 17–18 (1999–2000), 55–80.

interrelation between the biblical passages and KTU 1.5 I 1–8 and other Mesopotamian traditions.

While it is generally agreed that El, not Baal, was the "creator"-god par excellence in Ugaritic mythology, scholars such as Fisher have nevertheless called the Baal-Yam myth a "creation" myth of "the Baal type," in contrast with the usual creation of the world, which Fisher designates one of "the El type."[11] In the former, the establishment of kingship or "order" as the result of the victory over "chaos" has been interpreted as "creation," while in the latter, the cosmic origins are dealt with. Significantly enough, in *Enuma elish* both types coexist. Marduk created the universe (i.e., heaven and earth) out of the corpse of the dead Tiamat, while he established the kingly rule ("order") as the result of his victory over the chaotic enemy, Tiamat. Thus, both the theme of cosmic origins and that of the *Chaoskampf*—that is, "order out of chaos"— are intricately integrated into the grand epic of creation as *Enuma elish*.

However, it is significant to note that in the Baal cycle only the theme of *Chaoskampf* appears, and it is the god El, not Baal, who has to do with cosmic origins. As Smith puts it, "The Baal Cycle does not describe primordial events such as the creation of the cosmos, but rather its maintenance through the power of the storm-god. . . . (It) does not assert that Baal 'creates' or even 'arranges' the cosmos."[12]

Accordingly, it is probably wise to limit the meaning of "creation" to El's activities in ancient Ugarit and to distinguish *Chaoskampf* myths with a creation motif, such as *Enuma elish*, from *Chaoskampf* myths without a creation motif, such as the Baal cycle.[13] In fact, even in Mesopotamia, there are myths of divine combat that have no essential connection with creation. Conversely, as H. W. F. Saggs puts it, "in Mesopotamian thought cosmic creation did not of necessity involve a divine combat."[14]

As for the *Chaoskampf*-motif in the poetic texts of the Old Testament, Podella has recently argued that Pss 93 and 46 deal with the "Triumph des Königsgottes" as the result of *Chaoskampf*, while others deal with the "battle" (*Kampf*) itself.[15] It is certainly important to distinguish between the two

---

11. L. R. Fisher, "Creation at Ugarit and in the Old Testament," *VT* 15 (1965), 314–15.

12. Smith, *The Ugaritic Baal Cycle*, 1.82–83. See also ch. 2 (above).

13. See C. Kloos, *Yhwh's Combat with the Sea: A Canaanite Tradition in the Religion of Ancient Israel* (Leiden: Brill, 1986), 67–74.

14. H. W. F. Saggs, *The Encounter with the Divine in Mesopotamia and Israel* (London: Athlone, 1978), 59. For more detail, see ch. 11 (below).

15. T. Podella, "Der 'Chaoskampfmythos' im Alten Testament: Eine Problemanzeige," in *Mesopotamica – Ugaritica – Biblica: Festschrift für Kurt Bergerhof zur Vollendung seines 70. Lebensjahres am 7. Mai 1992* (ed. M. Dietrich and O. Loretz; AOAT 232; Neukirchen-

groups. Nevertheless, the idea of "triumph" itself presupposes a "battle," and these biblical texts should be carefully examined in detail in their own contexts to determine whether the *Chaoskampf* itself was involved.[16]

Before getting into individual poetic passages, we will examine some methodological questions affecting comparative study of extrabiblical myths and Old Testament poetic texts.

Methodological Principles

A major methodological problem confronts anyone wishing to relate ancient Near Eastern texts to the Old Testament. Control needs to be established over matters such as genre and purpose. Unfortunately, there is evidence that scholars have tended to "biblicize ancient Near Eastern documents before they are compared with OT materials."[17] At the same time, the biblical documents are often interpreted mythologically.

J. M. Sasson has suggested that "it is imperative that the literature of each culture be appreciated on its own merits" before it is compared with the biblical material.[18] Whenever we discuss the "relationship," "connection," "association," "correspondence," "parallelism," "similarity," and so on between them, as Kitchen notes, "it is necessary to deal individually and on its own merits with each possible or alleged case of relationship or borrowing by making a detailed comparison of the full available data from both the Old Testament and the Ancient Orient and by noting the results."[19]

When we come to the matter of the relationship between Ugaritic literature and the Old Testament, the comparison is basically between different genres of literature. As P. C. Craigie notes,

> Ugaritic has provided no prophetic poetry. It has left us no unambiguous examples of psalmody, with the exception of those passages which might be identified as originally hymnic, but have survived only through integration within different and larger literary forms (myth or legend), and it has no extensive examples of literary narrative prose. This observation is important,

Vluyn: Neukirchener Verlag, 1993), 313–18. Cf. M. Görg, " 'Chaos' und 'Chaosmächte' im Alten Testament," *BN* 70 (1993), 48–61.

16. See ch. 9 (below).

17. J. M. Sasson, "On Relating 'Religious' Texts to the Old Testament," *MAARAV* 3/2 (1982), 223.

18. Sasson, "On Relating 'Religious' Texts," 224.

19. K. A. Kitchen, *Ancient Orient and Old Testament* (Chicago: InterVarsity Press, 1966), 87–88.

for it means that virtually all Hebrew-Ugaritic comparative studies involve the comparison of *different* literary forms.[20]

Now, 20 years later, the situation has not changed much. Let us examine several issues that appear in comparative studies.

It has become almost customary in modern scholarship to hold, for example, that Hab 3 was *influenced* by Canaanite poetry.[21] It may be questioned, however, whether this argument pays due attention to the difference between the two literary genres.

Gunkel's line of argument regarding the Mesopotamian Marduk-Tiamat myth was developed by W. A. Irwin,[22] but a majority of recent scholars see *Canaanite-Ugaritic* influence on Hab 3. For example, Cassuto suggests that Hab 3 contains reminiscences of the *Chaoskampf* myth involving conflict between Yahweh and the primordial dragon Sea or River.[23] He says, "despite the successive changes of thought, the literary tradition is preserved in all its details."[24] Thus, he even thinks that the word *'ōmer* at the end of a problematic verse, Hab 3:9, is an allusion to the club *aymr*, with which Baal defeated Yam in KTU 1.2. Wakeman holds the view that "only Hab iii 8 reflects the myth *directly*,"[25] although she admits that *ym* and *nhr* appear frequently as a poetic cliché. Hiebert, who also takes the *-m* of *nhrm* as an enclitic *mem*, following Albright, also sees in v. 8 "an enduring reflection of the ancient name of the dragon of chaos."[26]

J. Day also argues that Hab 3 contains a number of mythological allusions that have their background in Baal mythology. For example, according to

20. P. C. Craigie, "Ugarit and the Bible: Progress and Regress in 50 Years of Literary Study," in *Ugarit in Retrospect: Fifty Years of Ugarit and Ugaritic* (ed. G. D. Young; Winona Lake, Ind.: Eisenbrauns, 1981), 107.

21. The history of research on the so-called *Chaoskampf*-motif in Hab 3 has been thoroughly surveyed by Jöcken. See P. Jöcken, *Das Buch Habakuk: Darstellung der Geschichte seiner kritischen Erforschung mit einer eigenen Beurteilung* (Cologne, 1977), 290–313. See also F. I. Andersen, *Habakkuk: A New Translation with Introduction and Commentary* (AB 25; New York: Doubleday, 2001), 350–55.

22. W. A. Irwin, "The Psalm of Habakkuk," *JNES* 1 (1942), 10–40.

23. U. Cassuto, "Chapter III of Habakkuk and the Ras Shamra Texts," *Biblical and Oriental Studies*, vol. 2: *Bible and Ancient Oriental Texts* (Jerusalem, 1975), 3–15. Cf. W. F. Albright, "The Psalm of Habakkuk," in *Studies in Old Testament Prophecy* (ed. H. H. Rowley; Edinburgh: T. & T. Clark, 1950), 2–3.

24. Cassuto, "Chapter III of Habakkuk," 13.

25. M. K. Wakeman, *God's Battle with the Monster: A Study in Biblical Imagery* (Leiden: Brill, 1973), 93 (italics mine). See ch. 10 (below) for Albright's view.

26. T. Hiebert, *God of My Victory: The Ancient Hymn in Habakkuk 3* (HSM 38; Atlanta: Scholars Press, 1986), 23.

him, Hab 3:9 makes an "allusion/reference to Yahweh's seven arrows,"[27] and thus Yahweh's seven thunders and lightnings are attested there, like Baal's seven lightnings in KTU 1.101 [UT 603]:3b–4 (RS 24.245 lines 3b–4).[28] He also claims that "the allusion to Resheph's participation in the conflict with chaos has its ultimate background in the Ugaritic text KTU 1.82:1–3."[29]

It is important to note here that Day uses terms such as "allusion" and "reference" not only with respect to literary expressions but for the phenomena that he claims lie behind the expressions. Thus, he uses the term "reference" for a natural phenomenon in a phrase, such as, "reference to Yahweh's seven shafts or arrows of lightning, comparable to his seven thunders depicted in Ps. 29."[30]

It may be helpful to note the fact that scholars have seen a reflection of two or three different versions of the Baal myth in Hab 3. For example, Hab 3:8–10 and 15 has been said to reflect one version of the Baal myth, the "Baal-Yam myth," while Hab 3:5 has been taken as reflecting another version, the "Baal-Tnn myth," which is preserved only on a rather broken tablet. And those who accept Albright's emendation of the text in v. 13 consider a third version, the "Baal-Mot myth," to be the background of Hab 3.[31] Therefore, what scholars have actually practiced when comparing Ugaritic texts and Hab 3 is not really a comparison of two literary wholes from different cultures but an ad hoc comparison of several fragments of Ugaritic myths and a part of the Old Testament prophetic literature.[32]

In studies comparing Ugaritic mythology and Old Testament literature in general, too much emphasis has been put on similarity or the "fact" of sameness[33] in form, and insufficient distinction has been made between the syn-

---

27. Day, *God's Conflict with the Dragon and the Sea*, 146.

28. Ibid., 106–7.

29. J. Day, "New Light on the Mythological Background of the Allusion to Resheph in Habakkuk III 5," *VT* 29 (1979), 353–55.

30. Day, *God's Conflict with the Dragon and the Sea*, 106–7.

31. Thus Wakeman says, "Should this [Albright's] reading be accepted, it [Hab 3:13] would be the only *direct* reference to a conflict between Yahweh and Mot" (italics mine). See Wakeman, *God's Battle with the Monster*, 108; but cf. Hiebert, *God of My Victory*, 37.

32. A similar approach has been taken by P. C. Craigie in his treatment of Ps 18; see pp. 149–151 (below).

33. Whenever we talk about the sameness of two items in a certain language, we must ask the question: in what sense and why? For, in many cases the "sameness" is only superficial or even "fictional." It is meaningful to talk about the sameness between *X* and *Y* only when their differences are clearly identifiable. In this respect, the degree of sameness or dissimilarity (difference) is more important than the fact that sameness exists. This is all the more true when we try to identify the same expressions in two languages, for there is no reason why the same form should always have the same meaning even in two cognate languages. Cf. A. Gibson, *Biblical Semantic Logic* (Oxford: Blackwell, 1981), 140 and 24.

chronic approach and the comparative-diachronic approach. For example, G. E. Wright says,

> The vocabulary of the nature myths of Canaan was used extensively but it was set in a historical context.[34]

> [In Ps 74:12–14] the old Canaanite myth of creation has been transferred to Yahweh. . . . the myth was historicized and used metaphorically to describe Yahweh's great victories in history.[35]

However, there is no evidence that the entire myth of ancient Canaan was transferred to the Bible by means of so-called historicization. It is virtually only in the poetic texts that the "similar" materials appear, and they usually constitute just a group of words or phrases, never sentences or discourses.

Psalm 18 // 2 Samuel 22—Adaptation?

Let us take Ps 18 as an example of this methodological question in comparative studies of Hebrew and Ugaritic literary texts.[36] In this psalm, especially in vv. 8–20, "God's intervention in the form of a theophany" is said to be depicted in language that has "many similarities to Canaanite mythology."[37] These similarities are often explained as being caused by the fact that the language was borrowed or even adapted from the Canaanite myths of Baal. However, one needs to scrutinize this widely accepted theory using both biblical and Ugaritic evidence, for a given expression does not necessarily mean or refer to the same fact when used in different religious documents.

Craigie thinks that such similarities are not simply "borrowing" but "adaptation."[38] In other words, "the dominant motifs of the Baal traditions in Canaanite mythology have been adapted to give cosmic dimension to the psalmist's difficulties and divine deliverance."[39]

Craigie claims a number of similarities between this psalm and Ugaritic myths (see chart, p. 150). However, his argument is somewhat speculative. In Ugaritic mythology, the Baal-Yam myth (KTU 1.2) and the Baal-Mot myth (KTU 1.5) are clearly distinguished: they appear in entirely separate tablets, and nowhere do Mot and Yam appear in the same context; the former story is

---

34. G. E. Wright, *God Who Acts* (London: SCM, 1952), 48.

35. Idem, *The Old Testament against Its Environment* (London: SCM, 1957), 27.

36. This section is based on D. T. Tsumura, "Some Problems Regarding Psalm 18," *Exegetica* 3 (1992), 57–64 [in Japanese with English summary; see *OTA* 16 (1993), 523, no. 1926].

37. M. Dahood, *Psalms I: 1–50* (AB 16; Garden City: Doubleday, 1966), 104.

38. Also, see P. C. Craigie, *Ugarit and the Old Testament* (Grand Rapids: Eerdmans, 1983), 88.

39. Idem, *Psalms 1–50* (WBC 19; Waco, Tex.: Word, 1983), 174.

Psalm 18	*Canaanite Myth*
(1) The psalmist is caught in the *cords of death* (*môt*) and torments of Belial (viz. Yam), vv. 5–6.	Mot and Yam, gods of death and chaos, are ascendant (e.g., KTU 1.2 iii and 1.5 i).
(2) The Lord comes to deliver him in the theophany characterized by storm and earthquake: vv. 7–15.	Baal demonstrates his character as the god of storm (KTU 1.4 vii).
(3) The Lord rebukes *ocean* (*Yam*) and *earth* (viz. the underworld, realm of Mot) and thus delivers his servant: vv. 16–20.	Baal conquers Yam and Mot and establishes order (KTU 1.2 iv and 1.6 vi).

a battle between Baal, the storm-god, and Yam, the sea-god, while the latter is between Baal, the god of life, and Mot, the god of death. The battle with the god of death supposedly occurred after the battle with the sea-god and the building of Baal's palace.[40]

Moreover, Craigie notes that KTU 1.4 vii describes Baal as follows:

Baʿlu (himself) opens up the rift in the clouds,
  Baʿlu emits his holy voice,
    Baʿlu makes the thunder roll over and over again.[41]

This sort of description is what one would expect for a storm-god. However, there is no battle between Baal and Yam in this context. On the other hand, in the context in which the battle against Yam is depicted (i.e., KTU 1.2 iv), Baal does not exhibit any storm-god characteristics except for his epithet "the rider of clouds" (*rkb ʿrpt*). Rather, we find references to falconry and to one-on-one combat, without any "storm" images or any mention of "lightning (= spear)" or "thunder," which one would expect as Baal's weapons.[42]

The reason that Yahweh's theophany is "characterized by storm and earthquake" in vv. 7–15 of this psalm is not due to the fact that Yahweh is here compared with the storm-god Baal but to the fact that Yahweh's theophany was indeed a magnificient event that shook up the whole of nature. Such an extraordinary event is often described metaphorically[43] in terms such as "storm and earthquake."

---

40. See now D. Pardee, in *CS* 1.241–74.
41. Ibid., 1.262.
42. Ibid., 1.248–49. See my "Ugaritic Poetry and Habakkuk 3," *TynBul* 40 (1988), 32.
43. See ch. 11 (below).

Furthermore, though Craigie thinks that "Baal's conquest of Yam marks one of the steps in the process of creation—order is established and chaos is subdued"[44]—there is no "creation" motif in Baal's conquest of Yam, the god of "chaos," as noted above.[45] The nature of the conquest of the "chaotic" sea deity in the Ugaritic myth is very different from the Babylonian creation myth *Enuma elish*. Baal establishes his kingship among gods but has nothing to do with creation or procreation, or even "metamorphosis." Furthermore, the idea of "creation" as the result of victory over the chaos dragon was not a norm, even in Mesopotamia. Instead, in Mesopotamia, creation often took the form of birth; the divine pair "Sky" (An) and "Earth" (Ki) itself engendered other creatures.[46]

Because the idea of creation as establishing "order out of chaos" cannot be demonstrated as a general feature even in extrabiblical materials, we should be extremely careful not to impose foreign ideas on any biblical text without first placing the text in its immediate literary context and considering the possibility of metaphorical devices.

In the case of Ps 18, expressions such as "mighty waters" (*mayim rabbîm*) in v. 16[17] do not refer to a *Chaoskampf* that established order as the result of victory over "chaos" but to the psalmist's situation. The emphasis is on God's sovereign power, which brought about deliverance from the enemy (v. 17). The metaphors in Ps 18 do in fact use storm language, but the very fact that they are metaphors shows that Yahweh himself is not thought of as being a storm-god. Descriptions of storms using war language and of wars using storm language were common in the ancient Near East, as will be seen in detail below (ch. 11).

Craigie's view, that Ps 18 is an adaptation of Canaanite myths, is too simplistic. This becomes clear when we note the epithets for Yahweh in v. 2[3], "my rock, my fortress, and my deliverer, my God, my rock in whom I take refuge, my shield, and the horn of my salvation, my stronghold." In Ugaritic myths, Baal is never described as a "rock," "fortress," or the like. The Ugaritic counterpart (ǵr "mountain")[47] for "rock" (ṣûr) never appears as an epithet of Baal,[48] though it is used to refer to his residence.[49]

---

44. Craigie, *Ugarit and the Old Testament*, 88.
45. See ch. 3, excursus (pp. 72–74).
46. See W. Heimpel, "Mythologie A. I: In Mesopotamien," *RlA* 8.546–47, 558–60 (fig. 6) on "creation" myths in Mesopotamia.
47. In the Ugaritic "pantheon" list (KTU 1.118:18), ǵrm w[ʿmqt] "mountains and valleys" is one of the divine names.
48. Cf. Dahood, *Psalms I: 1–50*, 105.
49. See M. C. A. Korpel, "Rock" in *DDD*, 1338–40.

Psalm 29: A Canaanite Hymn?

Psalm 29 is another psalm in which scholars have seen direct "Canaanite" connections since the discovery of Ugaritic documents in 1929. Earlier scholars such as Ginsberg and Gaster took this psalm to be originally a Canaanite hymn, which was subsequently "Yahwized."[50] Cross also asserted that it was a "Canaanite hymn preserved in the Psalter."[51] Following generations simply have accepted this scholary consensus and have focused their attention on why such an originally pagan hymn to the storm-god Baal was included among the biblical psalms.[52] It has even been explained that the psalm was adapted for a missionary or apologetic effort.

Craigie takes this to be "deliberate imitation for religious purposes"[53] for, according to him, "language normally employed to worship Baal for the awesome might of the thunderstorm did not rightfully belong to him who was no true god. Such language belonged to the God of Israel alone. And so in Psalm 29, imitating so closely the language of the Canaanites, we receive an insight vital to the religion of the Hebrews."[54] However, before trying to decide why the biblical poet used this "Canaanite" hymn, we must clarify whether there is indeed a literary connection between Ps 29 and the Canaanite-Ugaritic myths.

One of the main reasons why earlier biblical scholars have identified a Canaanite connection is v. 10: [55]

> The Lord sits enthroned over the flood (*lammabbûl*);
>> the Lord sits enthroned as king forever. (NRSV)

Craigie thinks that here are "words reminiscent of the formula employed in the praise of Baal," which he thinks are "words known from the Ugaritic mythological texts."[56]

---

50. On the "mythicizing and historicizing" problems, see Kloos, *Yhwh's Combat with the Sea*, 158–90.

51. F. M. Cross, *Canaanite Myth and Hebrew Epic*, 151–56 n. 53.

52. For the history of interpretation, see O. Loretz, *Psalm 29: Kanaanäische El- und Baaltraditionen in jüdischer Sicht* (UBL 2; Soest: CIS, 1984), 11–22; Day, *God's Conflict with the Dragon and the Sea*, 57–61.

53. Craigie, *Ugarit and the Old Testament*, 70.

54. Ibid., 71.

55. Loretz has given a thorough treatment of the Ugaritic connection with v. 10 as a response to the suggestions by J. Day, C. Kloos, and J. Jeremias. See O. Loretz, "KTU 1.101: 1–3a und 1.2 IV 10 als Parallelen zu Ps 29,10," *ZAW* 99 (1987), 415–21; also *Psalm 29*, 49–51 and ch. 9.

56. Craigie, *Ugarit and the Old Testament*, 70.

The verse can be analyzed with a somewhat unbalanced structure as follows:

	words	syllables	letters
YHWH lammabbûl yāšāb	3	(7)	12
wayyēšeb YHWH melek lĕʿôlām	4	(10)	16

Though there have been several attempts to emend the term *mabbûl*, the term is best taken as it stands and interpreted as referring to "the flood or ocean," as Malamat suggests.[57] He calls to scholars' attention a Sumerian term, A-KUL "much, mighty water,"[58] which is identified with Eblaite *ma-ba-lum*,[59] the cognate of Hebrew *mabbûl*.[60]

Traditionally the phrase *lammabbûl* has been interpreted in a locative sense, as reflected in the KJV:

The LORD sitteth upon the flood;
yea, the LORD sitteth King for ever.

In recent years, scholars have advanced this locative interpretation in connection with the Ugaritic Baal myths. For example, according to P. C. Craigie, the phrase *lammabbûl* "over the flood" symbolizes the subjugation of chaotic forces. "The Canaanite tradition may be seen in the depiction of the enthronement of Baal over the conquered 'flood' (Ugaritic *mdb*; see RS 24.245. 1–2), and there has already been allusion to this incident in Ps 29:3."[61] F. M. Cross goes so far as to translate both Hebrew *mabbûl* in Ps 29:10 and Ugaritic *mdb* in KTU 1.101[= RS 24.245]:1–2 as "the Flood dragon."[62] In support of the locative interpretation, he notes the fact that "the idiom *yšb / ytb l-*, 'to sit enthroned,' is typical of Canaanite diction where normally Hebrew prefers *yšb ʿl* (Albright)."[63] Thus, these scholars see here the motif of a warrior-god's being enthroned over the conquered "flood."

---

57. See A. Malamat, "The Amorite Background of Psalm 29," *ZAW* 100 Supplement (1988), 159 n. 16.

58. See above on Ps 18:16. Also, Sumerian a-kur "abundant water"; post-OB (*SD* A/1 98). In a lexical text (Antagal C 105 [MSL 17, 197]) this term, a-kur, is equated with the Akkadian phrase *mi-lu₄ ma-ʾ-du*. Note that "water" (an) refers to *mīlu* "high water"; see on *ʾēd* in ch. 5 (pp. 99–100 above).

59. *MEE* 4 (1982), 272; see C. H. Gordon, "Eblaitica," *Eblaitica* 1 (1987), 28.

60. See Loretz, *Psalm 29*, ch. 9 (pp. 93–96).

61. Craigie, *Psalms 1–50*, 248–49. See Loretz, *Psalm 29*, ch. 12, esp. pp. 119–20.

62. Cross, *Canaanite Myth and Hebrew Epic*, 147 n. 4, 155.

63. Ibid., 155 n. 43. Note also his comment that "the idiom *yšb l (ksʾ*, etc.) of enthronement, is frequent only in early Hebrew poetry (Ps. 132:12; Judg. 5:17; Ps. 29:10) and archaizing contexts (Ps. 9:5, Isa. 47:1 [?])" (*Canaanite Myth and Hebrew Epic*, 97 n. 24).

However, the Ugaritic term *mdb* "flood, ocean" (*k mdb* "like flood" // *k ym* "like sea" in KTU 1.23 [52]:34, 35; cf. *mdbm* 1.82 [1001]:27)[64] is never used to describe Yam/Nahar, the enemy of Baal. Even in KTU 1.101[= RS 24.245]:2 it appears in a metaphor (i.e., *k mdb* "like a flood")[65] for a mighty power; similarly in KTU 1.23:34–35 it is El's (sexual) power (lit., "hand" *yd*) that is referred to.[66] Thus there is no evidence supporting the theory that *mdb* refers to a conquered enemy in Ugaritic mythology.

In the same manner, Hebrew *mabbûl* simply means "a flood," because elsewhere it always refers to the "Deluge."[67] Like the Ugaritic *mdb*, it is never used for describing an enemy of Yahweh; it signifies simply a mighty power by which Yahweh brought about the total destruction of this world. In other words, as far as the biblical evidence goes, Yahweh never fought against the "Deluge" (*mabbûl*). In the Flood story, it was his instrument to destroy mankind. Therefore, it is not likely that the "Deluge" (*mabbûl*) in Ps 29:10 is a conquered enemy on which Yahweh sat enthroned.

It should be noted also that Marduk never sat enthroned over his defeated enemy, the sea-dragon *Ti'āmat*; nor did Baal, his Ugaritic counterpart, sit enthroned over the sea-dragon Yam after his victory. Even if one should recognize in Ps 29:10 the motif of a divine enthronement over a conquered enemy, the motif ought to be compared instead with Ea's establishment of his abode over the conqured enemy Apsû: *ukīnma eli Apsâ šubassu* "Ea established his dwelling on Apsû" (*Enuma elish* I 71). In this case, however, Ea's enemy is not a "flood" but the subterranean water, and the Canaanite god who corresponds to the Mesopotamian Ea, a "creator" who resides at the watery abode, is El, rather than Baal.[68]

While the Hebrew *mabbûl* corresponds neither to Tiamat, Marduk's enemy, nor to Apsû, Ea's enemy, it is certainly similar to the Akkadian *abūbu* "the Deluge"-weapon[69] by which Marduk attacked his enemy Tiamat in *Enuma elish* IV 49 (cf. VI 125). Not only do both Hebrew *mabbûl* and Akkadian *abūbu* refer to that Great Deluge, but they are the divine instruments by

---

64. Gordon, *UT*, 19.1425 (p. 430).

65. Cf. Heb. *zwb* "to flow." See ch. 11 (below). Note that Loretz analyzes the phrase in a totally different way: *km db* "wie ein Bär"; see Loretz, "KTU 1.101:1–3a und 1.2 IV 10 als Parallelen zu Ps 29,10," 417.

66. On this Ugaritic text, see my "Kings and Cults in Ancient Ugarit," in *Priests and Officials in the Ancient Near East* (ed. Kazuko Watanabe; Heidelberg: Carl Winter, 1999), 215–38.

67. It appears 12 times in Gen 6–11; elsewhere only in Ps 29.

68. On the similarity and difference between biblical Elohim, Ugaritic El, and Mesopotamian Ea, see ch. 7.

69. See D. O. Edzard, "Meer. A," *RlA* 8.3. See on Hab 3:9 in ch. 10 (below).

which the deity brought about total destruction. They themselves are not the enemy of the deity. Deities such as Adad, Nergal, Asshur, and Marduk are described as the "holder of the lightning, lord of the Deluge" (*nāšu birqi* EN *abūbi*);[70] the term *abūbu* appears in titles of warrior-gods such as Nabû, Ninurta, Ištar, and Aššur.[71]

In a similar but not identical way, it may be suggested that in Ps 29 Yahweh is depicted metaphorically as the "holder of the lightning, lord of the Deluge." In fact, Yahweh's voice (*qôl YHWH*) is depicted in the images of lightning seven times in vv. 3–9, and he is explained as being enthroned as the eternal king *lammabbûl* in v. 10. Therefore, the term *mabbûl* should not be interpreted in association with the so-called *Chaoskampf*-motif in which a *chaotic* water such as Tiamat or Yam is treated as an enemy of a warrior-god such as Marduk or Baal. Rather, it should be compared with the Deluge (*abūbu*) in the Mesopotamian tradition. In its immediate context (v. 10), the phrase *lammabbûl* seems to be temporal rather than locative and to have the idiomatic meaning "before the Deluge," that is, "from time immemorial," as in the Akkadian idiom *lam abūbi*, which is contrasted with *arki abūbi* "after the Deluge."[72]

It may be concluded that Ps 29's "Canaanite" connection has been somewhat overstated[73] and that v. 10 has nothing to do with Ugaritic mythology directly. The psalm should be appreciated as a purely Hebrew hymn of praise to Yahweh, using "storm" language in metaphorical expressions.

The use of the "storm" motif in Pss 18 and 29 does not support the idea that these psalms are "Canaanite." Hence, one should avoid stating, as Craigie does, that Ps 18 is an "adaptation" of the Canaanite hymn. In fact, in his most recent article, A. Wagner doubts that Ps 29 was an adaptation of a Baal hymn.[74] Such metaphorical expressions are a universal feature of poetic language; they do not necessarily result from "borrowing" or "adaptation."[75]

---

70. BMS 21 rev. 80, cited in *CAD* A/1 80.

71. Cf. *AHw*, 8.

72. See *CAD* A/1 78; *AHw*, 8. For this possibility, see my " 'Deluge' (*mabbûl*) in Psalm 29:10," *UF* 20 (1988), 351–55.

73. Malamat would see in Ps 29 an Amorite or an early Mesopotamian background; see Malamat, "The Amorite Background of Psalm 29," 156–60.

74. A. Wagner, "Ist Ps 29 die Bearbeitung eines Baal-Hymnus?" *Bib* 77 (1996), 538–39.

75. See ch. 11 on metaphor in poetry.

9

A Creation Motif in Psalm 46?

Ever since the influential work of H. Gunkel,[1] the first part of Ps 46 has been interpreted as using a "creation" motif, because vv. 2–3 speak of a "chaotic" sea and hence, it is assumed, its waters are those that existed before "creation," when order was not yet brought into this world. For example, Mowinckel sees here a reference to victory over the primeval sea.[2] Weiser and others[3] see a "creation motif" on the basis of expressions supposedly "borrowed from the primeval myth . . . of the combat against the dragon." However, the "creation motif" does not always coexist with the "combat motif" in the ancient Near Eastern mythologies, as noted above (ch. 8).[4] J. Day, though he does not necessarily relate the text to creation, sees here "a historicization" of a mythological divine conflict with the waters.[5]

Let us examine the text of Ps 46 in detail.[6]

The Relationship between Verses 2–3 and Verse 6

2b.	*bĕhāmîr ʾāreṣ*	though the **earth** should change,[7]
c.	*ûbmôṭ hārîm*	the mountains *shake*
d.	*bĕlēb yammîm*	into the heart of the sea;

---

1. H. Gunkel, *Schöpfung und Chaos in Urzeit und Endzeit* (Göttingen, 1895), 100. See ch. 2 (above).

2. S. Mowinckel, *The Psalms in Israel's Worship* (New York: Abingdon, 1962), 1.87.

3. A. Weiser, *The Psalms: A Commentary* (Philadelphia: Westminster, 1962 [orig. 1959]), 368. For a useful summary of the alleged traditions behind this psalm, see L. Neve, "The Common Use of Traditions by the Author of Psalm 46 and Isaiah," *ExTim* 86 (1974–75), 243–46.

4. See also H. W. F. Saggs, *The Encounter with the Divine in Mesopotamia and Israel* (London: Athlone, 1978), 56–63. He notes: "The theme of divine combat . . . had no essential connection with creation." Also see D. J. McCarthy, " 'Creation' Motifs in Ancient Hebrew Poetry," *CBQ* 29 (1967), 393–406.

5. J. Day, *God's Conflict with the Dragon and the Sea: Echoes of a Canaanite Myth in the Old Testament* (Cambridge: Cambridge University Press, 1985), 127. For "historicization," see ch. 8 (above) on Ps 29.

6. See my "Literary Structure of Psalm 46, 2–8," *AJBI* 6 (1980), 29–55.

3a. *yĕhĕmû yeḥmĕrû mêmâw*   its waters *rage* and foam,
b. *yirʿăšû-hārîm bĕgaʾăwātô*   the mountains tremble with its
                                 swellings.

The second half of v. 2 (2c–2d) and v. 3 are different both in metric structure and in verb forms. Nevertheless, the two are closely bound in content and form. That is, as Weiss has pointed out,[8] there is a chiasmus (ABB′A′) between "mountains" (A)—"sea" (B) of v. 2 and "its waters" (B′)—"mountains" (A′) in v. 3. Verses 2b–3b as a whole are, in turn, chiastically parallel to v. 6: "earth" – "shake" – "rage" // "rage" – "shake" – "earth."[9]

6a. *hāmû gôyim*   (2)   The nations *rage*,
b. *māṭû mamlākôt*   (2)   the kingdoms *shake*;
c. *nātan bĕqôlô*   (2)   He utters his voice;[10]
d. *tāmûg ʾāreṣ*   (2)   the **earth** melts.[11]

In this literary structure, it is reasonable to assume that v. 6c is closely related to v. 6a–6b.

---

7. I would like to call attention to a possible Akkadian parallel to *hāmîr* < **mur*, whose root meaning may be preserved in its byform **mrr* "to break" or "to split," as seen in the following example: (*šumma erṣetu eli mi)-na -ti-šá um-tar-ri-ir* "if the earth is split(?) more than usual (preceded by earthquake omens)" (ACh Adad 20:56). Compare *CAD* M/1 268, which lists three meanings for *marāru*: 1. "to break a field for cultivation," 2.II/2 "to be split(?)," 3.IV "to be broken."

8. M. Weiss, "Wege der neuen Dichtungswissenschaft in ihrer Anwendung auf die Psalmenforschung: (Methodologische Bemerkungen, dargelegt am Beispiel von Psalm XLVI)," *Bib* 42 (1961), 278, also no. 1.

9. Ibid., 289. E. W. Hengstenberg, *Commentary on the Psalms* (Cherry Hill, N.J.: Mack, n.d.), 2.151: "The *whole* verse (7) is rather parallel to verse (3) and (4)." For the chiastic arrangement of two pairs of identical roots (A:B::B:A), see A. R. Ceresko, "The A:B::B:A Word Pattern in Hebrew and Northwest Semitic with Special Reference to the Book of Job," *UF* 7 (1975), 73–88.

10. This phrase clearly corresponds linguistically to the Ugaritic expression *ytn qlh* "(Baal) utters his voice" (KTU 1.4:V:8 [UT 51:V:70], VII:29, 31).

11. It is possible to analyze v. 6 as either two lines or four lines; see G. B. Gray, *The Forms of Hebrew Poetry* (New York: Ktav, 1915, 1972), 163–64. Nevertheless, taking v. 6 as four lines is more suitable to the poetic structure as a whole. First, the complete parallelism between 6a and 6b is better explained. Second, though the verbs of 6a,b,c, are perfect, 6d uses the imperfect form. Third, not only is 6d parallel in content to 2b; the key word "earth" appears only in these two places in the first half (vv. 1–7) of this psalm (also vv. 8, 9, 10). Accordingly, 2c–3b can be considered to correspond to 6a–6b. The four short lines (2–2–2–2) in v. 6 seem to be used for dramatic effect: tension directly before the conclusion of this first section (vv. 1–7). For a similar stylistic feature in the Song of Deborah, see P. C. Craigie, "The Song of Deborah and the Epic of Tukulti-Ninurta," *JBL* 88 (1969), 263.

Here I would like to call attention to an Akkadian inscription relating to the Babylonian storm-god Adad.

šá ina pīšu   at whose voice[12]
ḫuršāni inûšu   the mountains rock
isabuʾu tamâte   the seas[13] swell.

(The Kurbaʾil Statue of Shalmaneser 111, 1.6)[14]

If one compares this Babylonian inscription and Ps 46, the following points are clear: First, the expressions "the mountains rock" and "the seas swell" are similar to expressions in Ps 46:2–3, "the mountains shake" and "(the sea's) waters rage." Next, we find similar words in the inscription and v. 6 but in opposite order: "voice," "rock," and "swell" in the inscription and "rage," "shake," and "voice" in Ps 46:6. This similarity hardly points to a dependent relation between the texts. In fact, a similar description appears in the case of the storm-god Ishkur:

> Ishkur . . . great storm, . . . who masses the clouds, at his rushing in the storm wind he causes the earth to tremble. In broad heaven he is a mighty wind which roars, whose [rum]ble is abundance. At his roar the land and the great mountains are afraid. . . . At his thundering (over) the sea (and) covering the land with ra⟨diance⟩, great (hail)stones rain.
>
> (Sin-Iddinam)[15]

Instead of a dependent relationship, these similar expressions reflect the same natural phenomena such as storm and flooding, which were commonly experienced in the ancient Near East. Neither Adad nor Ishkur has anything to do with creation or a *Chaoskampf*.

The point shown by the above example is that, just as Adad's voice makes "the mountains rock, the seas swell," so the "nations rage, the kingdoms shake" in Ps 46 (6a,b) as a result of God's uttering his voice (6c). Hengstenberg was certainly right when he commented that "it is the Lord that is the ultimate cause of the roaring of the peoples, as of the shaking of the king-

---

12. The voice of Adad, that is, thunder, is expressed in another Akkadian phrase: *ša iddin rīgmašu ina šame kima addi* "who utters his voice in heaven like Adad" (EA 147:13–14). See W. L. Moran, *Les Lettres d'El-Amarna: Correspondance diplomatique du pharaon* (Paris: Cerf, 1987), 378. See also A. Schoors, "Literary Phrases," in *RSP* 1.23–24.

13. Like the Hebrew *yammîm* (e.g., Gen 1:10), the Akkadian word *tamâte* is plural, expressing the huge volume of waters rather than the plurality of the sea.

14. J. V. Kinnier Wilson, "The Kurbaʾil Statue of Shalmaneser III," *Iraq* 24 (1962), 93, 95.

15. *CS* 2.250.

doms."[16] Because v. 6c is contextually associated with v. 6d, it is possible to show that 6c continues both forward and backward. From the above, it is appropriate to conclude that just as Adad causes a tumult, Ps 46:6d ("the earth melts") records the result of Yahweh's destructive action.

The correspondence between Ps 46:6a–6c and vv. 2c–3b in the same psalm has already been noted but, structurally, v. 6 parallels v. 3 very closely. To repeat:

3a. *yehĕmû yehmĕrû mêmâw*   (3)   Ab[17]   Its waters *rage and foam,*
 b. *yir'ăšû-hārîm bĕga'ăwātô*   (3)   a'b'c'   the mountains *tremble* with its swelling

6a. *hāmû gôyim*   (2)   a b   The nations *rage,*
 b. *mātû mamlākôt*   (2)   a'b'   the kingdoms *shake;*
 c. *nātan bĕqôlô*   (2)   C   He utters his voice.

Verse 3 is composed of the following parallelism:

A   (*yehĕmû yehmĕrû*)   a'   (*yir'ăšû*)
b   (*mêmâw*)   b'   (*hārîm*)
   c'   (*bĕga'ăwātô*)[18]

In v. 3a the two verbs in A are linked by asyndeton; they correspond to verb a' in v. 3b. Because the element that corresponds to c' is elided, a' is expanded to A by a "ballast variant."[19] On the other hand, v. 6a–6c can be analyzed according to this structure:

a   (*hāmû*)   a'   (*mātû*)
b   (*gôyim*)   b'   (*mamlākôt*)
   C   (*nātan bĕqôlô*)

The two verbs a and a' in v. 6 correspond to A and a' in v. 3, respectively.[20] *Mwt* and *r'š* are a synonymous word pair[21]—they both have "mountains" as a

16. Hengstenberg, *Commentary on the Psalms*, 2.151.

17. Capital letters A and C are the "ballast variants" to a' and c', respectively. For a ballast variant, see p. 120.

18. This pattern (Ab//a'b'c') can also be recognized in Ps 2:4.

19. For the term "ballast variant," see C. H. Gordon, *UT*, §13.116; W. G. E. Watson, *Classical Hebrew Poetry* (Sheffield: JSOT Press, 1984), 343–48.

20. Note that all three verbs in v. 3 are imperfect, while the two in v. 6 are perfect.

21. For the so-called parallel word pair, see A. Berlin, *The Dynamics of Biblical Parallelism* (Bloomington: Indiana University Press, 1985), ch. 4; M. Dahood in *RSP* 1 (1972) and 2 (1975). Also my "'Hyponymous' Word Pair, *'rṣ* and *thm(t)*, in Hebrew and Ugaritic," *Bib* 69 (1988), 258–69; idem, "The 'Word Pair' **qšt* and **mṭ* in Habakkuk 3:9 in the Light of Ugaritic and Akkadian," in *"Go to the Land I Will Show You": Studies in Honor of Dwight W. Young* (ed. J. Coleson and V. Matthews; Winona Lake, Ind.: Eisenbrauns, 1996), 357–65.

subject in vv. 2c–3b (in Ps 60:4 the order is reversed). Thus, we see that the two pairs of verbs in v. 3 and v. 6 describe the same two actions in the same order: "to rage (and foam)" and "tremble" // "shake."

At first glance, c′ (*běga'ăwātô*) in v. 3 and C (*nātan běqôlô*) in v. 6 appear completely unrelated, but in their context (parallelism) it can be said that they fulfill analogous roles. While in the case of the first it is stated that "by the swelling of its water" (c′) the mountains tremble, in the case of the second God's uttering his voice (C) is the ultimate case of the nations' raging and the kingdoms' shaking, as was noted above. In other words it is the destructive action of Yahweh as judge of history that is being compared to the destructive action of the waters of the sea. In v. 6 we do see the political situation expressed metaphorically by words describing natural phenomena, but the metaphors of v. 6c and v. 3b, though they are closely related, are significantly different. Verse 3b is related to the action of the sea; v. 6c uses an expression used normally of the storm-god, as we saw above. We must note well that in this psalm there is absolutely nothing about a fight between the god of the sea and the god of the storm, as in the Ugaritic myth of Baal and Yam, the so-called *Chaoskampf*-motif, despite the fact that scholars have kept asserting so ever since Gunkel.

The point stressed in this psalm is the tension between the sea and the mountains or earth in vv. 2–3 and the opposition between Yahweh and the nations or the earth in v. 6. The sea of v. 3 and "he (= God)" of v. 6 can both be understood as types of destructive forces. In other words, in Ps 46 we do not find a description of a battle between two powers, God and the sea. Rather, what is depicted as the central motif is the destructive, not "creative," acts of two destructive forces, the sea and God, who is the judge and punisher.[22]

The Relationship between Verses 2c–3 and Verse 4

2c.	*ûbmôṭ hārîm*	(2)	(though) the *mountains* shake
d.	*běléb yammîm*	(2)	into the heart of the *sea*;
3a.	*yehĕmû yehmĕrû mêmâw*	(3)	its *waters* rage and foam,
b.	*yir'ăšû-hārîm běga'ăwātô*	(3)	the *mountains* tremble with its swellings.
4a.	*nāhār pĕlāgâw yĕśammĕḥû*	(3)	As for the *river*, its (two) *streams* gladden

22. Note that in a Ugaritic mythology the "Sea" (*ym*) has the epithet "Judge River" (*ṭpṭ nhr*). Cf. KTU 1.2:IV [UT 68]:15, 16–17, 22, 25. For the "river-ordeal" in Babylonian custom, see G. R. Driver and J. C. Miles, *The Babylonian Laws* (Oxford: Clarendon, 1952), 1.63–64.

b. *ʿîr-ʾĕlōhîm*   (2)   the *city* of God,

c. *qĕdōš miškĕnê ʿelyôn*   (3)   the holiest *habitation* of the Most
                                                High.

It is noteworthy that not just v. 3 but 2c–3b as a whole corresponds structurally to v. 4. When we look at the key words in both, we observe a chiasmus in vv. 2c–3b: "mountains" – "sea" – "its waters" – "mountains" (ABB'A'); while on the other hand, in v. 4 we have this order: "river" – "its streams" – "the city of God" – "the holiest[23] habitation" (AA'BB'). Accordingly, "sea" – "its water" of the former correspond to "river" – "its streams" of the latter.

In Ugaritic mythology the word pair "sea" (*ym*) and "river" (*nhr*) expresses a single god named "Prince Sea" (*zbl ym*) and "Judge River" (*ṭpṭ nhr*), who always opposes the fertility-god Baal.[24] In the Babylonian Flood story, the *Atra-Ḫasīs* epic III iv 5–6, the "sea" (*tiâmta*) and the "river" (*nāram*) appear in parallelism, both describing the destructive flood.[25] In the Old Testament "sea" and "river" are also used as synonymous words indicating the cosmic ocean, as for example, in Jonah 2:4 (*yammîm wĕnāhār*) and in Hab 3:8 (*yām // nĕhārîm*).[26] Thus "sea" and "river" form a "parallel word pair"[27] common to Ugaritic and Hebrew as well as to Akkadian, which in almost all cases is used in synonymous contexts. However, it is noteworthy that the author of Ps 46 deliberately opposes this formulaic word pair by use of the poetic technique of contrast.[28]

To go a bit further, the opposition between vv. 3 and 4 is shown by the contrast in their actions, by the raging and foaming of the waters of the sea and the gladdening caused by the streams of the river. I wonder whether we might imagine a twofold image of "wine" as a common background for this pair of actions. That is, it may be possible that in the background of v. 3a is the image of fermenting grape juice raging and foaming and in the background of v. 4a is an image of wine, which gladdens the hearts of men.[29]

---

23. This adjective, *qĕdōš* in construct form, is to be taken as superlative. Cf. D. Michel, *Grundlegung einer hebräischen Syntax* (Neukirchen-Vluyn: Neukirchener Verlag, 1977), 1.47.

24. KTU 1.2:IV [UT 68]:14–15, 16–17, 22, 24–25.

25. W. G. Lambert and A. R. Millard, *Atra-Ḫasīs: The Babylonian Story of the Flood* (Oxford: Clarendon, 1969), 96–97. [Repr. Winona Lake, Ind.: Eisenbrauns, 1999.]

26. See below (ch. 10).

27. Fisher (ed.), *RSP* 1; 2.233. See also ch. 10 (below) on Hab 3:8.

28. Weiser, *The Psalms: A Commentary*, 369: "the waters which generate blessing are probably deliberately contrasted with the waters which generate desolation."

29. For a detailed study, see my "Twofold Image of Wine in Psalm 46:4–5," *JQR* 71 (1981), 167–75.

Now, the root *ḥmr* ("foam") originally had the basic meaning of "ferment-ing" or "foaming" of wine.[30] The Ugaritic word *ḥmr* is always used to refer to "wine."[31] In Deut 32:14 *ḥāmer* should be translated "wine," synonymous with *dam-ʿēnāb*.[32] The verb in Ps 75:8 depicts wine "foaming up" like cham-pagne. *Ḥōmer mayim rabbîm* in Hab 3:15 parallels "sea" (*yām*), and the sea is described by the words "the foaming up of the many waters" or "the bowl of many waters."[33] From these examples, we see clearly that the root *ḥmr* origi-nally was related to "wine," and the "foaming" of the sea is sometimes ex-pressed metaphorically with a word that describes the "foaming" of wine.[34]

Another root, *hmy*, is often used to depict the raging or roaring of the "sea, water, waves" (Isa 17:12, 51:15; Jer 5:22, 6:23, 31:35, 50:42, 51:55) and the "nations, enemies, and so on" (Ps 8:2; 1 Kgs 1:41; Isa 22:2; etc.).[35] It is also worth noting that it is used to describe wine in places other than Ps 46. In Prov 20:1 it seems to be describing the *effect* of wine, but this may well stem from the fermentation process, when the wine foams up and "rages." Zech 9:15 could also be translated, based on the Hebrew text, "rages like wine."[36]

Based on the above points, I would like to propose that Ps 46:4 vividly de-scribes the destructive action of the sea by poetically using the image of "raging and foaming" wine. Then, in v. 4, the image of wine that "gladdens" the hearts of men is used metaphorically to describe the positive action of the "river."

Now, the river in v. 4 has often been explained as relating to the river of Paradise in Gen 2:10,[37] the stream of Shiloam,[38] or the Euphrates River,[39] or

---

30. In Arabic, *ḥamr* means "wine" (= fermented beverage).

31. See C. H. Gordon, *UT*, §19.972; Tsumura, "Literary Structure of Psalm 46, 2–8," 52 n. 52.

32. In Deut 32:14, the synonynous word pair *dam-ʿēnāb* "the blood of the grape" (A) and *ḥāmer* "wine" (B) is interrupted by a verbal phrase, *tišteh* "you will drink" (X), thus consti-tuting an AXB pattern or "literary insertion," and is translated: "You will drink the blood of the grape, namely wine." See my "Twofold Image of Wine in Psalm 46:4–5," 168; also idem, "Literary Insertion (AXB Pattern) in Biblical Hebrew," *VT* 33 (1983), 468–82; idem, "Coor-dination Interrupted, or Literary Insertion AX&B Pattern, in the Books of Samuel," in *Liter-ary Structure and Rhetorical Strategies in the Hebrew Bible* (ed. L. J. de Regt, J. de Waard, and J. P. Fokkelman; Assen: Van Gorcum / Winona Lake, Ind.: Eisenbrauns, 1996), 117–32.

33. This may be a wordplay on the polysemous word *ḥōmer*, which has the following meanings: I "foaming," II "heap, homer," III "clay." Note that a similar association of the "sea" (*yām*) with a "pot" (*merqāḥâ*) appears in Job 41:23.

34. For the description of the sea as "wine-colour," see C. H. Gordon, "The Wine-Dark Sea," *JNES* 37 (1978), 51–52.

35. Cf. *TDOT* 3.416; *HALOT*, 250.

36. See my "Twofold Image of Wine in Psalm 46:4–5," 171–72.

37. Weiser, Kraus, Delitzsch, Hengstenberg, Anderson, and others.

38. Briggs, Kirkpatrick, Neve, and others.

39. Junker. Cf. J. H. Hayes, "The Tradition of Zion's Inviolability," *JBL* 82 (1963), 423, no. 21. For detailed discussion on this river, see J. B. Bauer, "Zions Flüsse: Ps 45 (46),

others. Certainly these rivers do display the positive work of the river in v. 4, but none of these rivers is described anywhere as something that "gladdens" (the hearts of men). In the Old Testament the word "river" or "water" does not appear as a subject of the verb "to gladden" outside of Ps 46. On the other hand, the root *śmḥ* is used in connection with "wine" (*yayin* or *tîrôš*) at least five times (Judg 9:13, Ps 104:15, Eccl 10:19—the previous all in *piel* form— Zech 10:7, Song 1:4). From these observations, we can infer that behind the expression in Ps 46:4 is the image of wine that "gladdens" men.[40]

In this way, the opposition in content between vv. 3 and 4 has been expressed by the psalmist's deliberately contrasting the words of the formulaic word pair "sea" and "river" by association with two images related to wine. For this poetic device of contrast, "river" is topicalized[41] or "focused"[42] at the beginning of v. 4; thus the word order "river + its streams" is not an impossible construction.[43] A literal translation would be: "as for the river, its streams (or its two streams[44])...."

In light of the above, one can hardly justify the view that Ps 46 deals with the creation motif because of the imagery of "chaotic" seas; the formulaic paired words "seas" and "river" are deliberately contrasted in vv. 2–4. The description of the "raging" seas, and so on, is a metaphorical usage of these terms rather than an adaptation or demythologization of the so-called *Chaoskampf* myths. The waters in vv. 2–3 are a destruction motif[45] rather than a creation motif, as in Ps 29 and others. We shall look in detail at this destruction motif in Hab 3 in the following chapter.

5," in *Memoria Jerusalem: Freundesgabe Franz Sauer* (ed. J. B. Bauer and J. Marböck; Graz, 1977), 59–91.

40. For a detailed discussion, see my "Twofold Image of Wine in Psalm 46:4–5," 173–74.

41. That is, as casus pendens. Cf. P. L. Krinetzki, "Der anthologische Stil des 46. Psalms und seine Bedeutung für die Datierungsfrage," *MTZ* 12 (1961), 54, etc.

42. For the focus theory, see K. Shimasaki, *Focus Structure in Biblical Hebrew: A Study of Word Order and Information Structure* (Bethesda, Md.: CDL, 2002).

43. Weiser, *The Psalms: A Commentary*, 284, no. 1.

44. *Pĕlāgâw* could be a dual with a suffix, as C. H. Gordon pointed out to me (private communication), "its two streams," like Ugaritic *nhrm* "two rivers"// *thmtm* "two deeps" (KTU 1.6:I:33–34 et al.), at the source of which El's abode exists. See ch. 7. According to another text (KTU 1.23[UT 52]:30), El's house (*bt*) is located on the shore of the "sea" (*ym*) // "deep" (*thm*), which can be a variant expression of "two rivers" or "two deeps." This duality of a "cosmic river" can possibly be recognized in the archaic poetry of Hab 3:8, where *nĕhārîm* is parallel with a singular *yam*, while in Hab 3:9 *nĕhārôt* (fem. pl.) is used to describe a plurality of ordinary rivers. See ch. 8 (above) and ch. 10 (below).

45. P. J. Harland, *The Value of Human Life: A Study of the Story of the Flood (Genesis 6–9)* (VTSup 64; Leiden: Brill, 1996) deals with this theme as the theme of "uncreation."

10

A Destruction Motif in Habakkuk 3

Yahweh versus the Sea (Verses 8 and 15)

Verse 8

hăbinhārîm ḥārâ Yhwh	Was your wrath against the rivers, O Lord?
ʾim bannĕhārîm ʾappekā	Or your anger against the rivers,
ʾim-bayyām ʿebrātekā	or your rage against the sea,
kî tirkab ʿal-sûseykā	when you drove your horses,
markĕbōteykā yĕšûʿâ	your chariots to victory? (NRSV)

As noted above,[1] it has long been suggested by many scholars that Hab 3:8 reflects the Hebrew counterpart to the Canaanite *Chaoskampf*-motif in the Ugaritic Baal-Yam myth. For example, U. Cassuto finds in this verse "an echo of the ancient Canaanite concepts, although indirect." He says, "'River' and 'sea' remind us of 'the Prince of the Sea' and of 'the Judge of the River' against whom Baal fought."[2] W. F. Albright, in order to find here a personified "River," emends MT *nhrym* (pl.) "rivers" to *nhr-m* (*nāhārem*), which he thinks "stands for older *nah(a)ri-mi*."[3] Thus, he finds here the direct Hebrew counterpart to the Ugaritic myth of Baal versus *nhr* (River) and *ym* (Sea).

J. H. Eaton seems to claim that this is a description of the actual beginning of a storm. Thus he says,

> The storm has broken, and it is as though the heavenly power with cloud and rain and thunder-bolts fights against rivers and seas which for their part leap and rage against their ancient adversary. As often in Hebrew poetry, the angry waters here represent all opposition to God while the unleashing of heaven's tempest signals God's power and will to subdue such opposition that there may be salvation, the victory of life.[4]

---

1. See ch. 8.

2. U. Cassuto, "Chapter III of Habakkuk and the Ras Shamra Texts," *Biblical and Oriental Studies*, vol. 2: *Bible and Ancient Oriental Texts* (Jerusalem: Magnes, 1975), 11.

3. W. F. Albright, "The Psalm of Habakkuk," in *Studies in Old Testament Prophecy* (ed. H. H. Rowley; Edinburgh: T. & T. Clark, 1950), 11, 15, note y.

4. J. H. Eaton, *Obadiah, Nahum, Habakkuk and Zephaniah* (London, 1961), 113.

Eaton simply assumes an actual storm and personifies the natural phenomena of the storm and the waters (rivers and seas), describing them as opposing powers that fight against each other. But his assumption has no support from the text itself: there is no storm imagery. Moreover, he uses metaphors, such as "angry waters" and "heaven's tempest," to refer to the supernatural powers. However, unlike Ps 46,[5] in Hab 3 it is Yahweh who gets angry, not the waters. Furthermore, this passage, vv. 8–10, seems to represent not just "God's power and will to subdue" but the actual and once-for-all subjection.

Let us examine the Hebrew text itself.

Něhārîm // Yām

The "sea" (*ym*) and the "river" (*nhr*) together form a well-known word pair common to Hebrew and Ugarit, which M. Dahood discusses in *Ras Shamra Parallels* 1.[6] It is significant to note, however, that out of 18 biblical references cited by Dahood, only Hab 3:8 (*něhārîm // yām*) and Isa 50:2 (*yām // něhārôt*) have a motif of victory or destruction. Moreover, only Hab 3:8 has *něhārîm* (masc. pl.); the others are either singular (*nāhār*) or feminine plural (*něhārôt*).[7] As for the Ugaritic pair *ym //nhr*, all but one of the examples cited refer to Baal's enemy, the god Sea and River (sing.). However, the lone pair *ym // nhrm* (KTU 1.3 [ʿnt]:VI:5–6 [broken text]; KTU 1.4 [UT 51]:II:6–7 [on Asherah]), which is the exact counterpart in form of the pair in Hab 3:8 though in reverse order, does *not* appear in the conflict scene.

Hence if Hab 3:8 were based on a Ugaritic conflict scene, one would have expected *yām // nāhār*. The fact that Habakkuk has the rather unusual pair *něhārîm // yām*, which corresponds to the Ugaritic word pair *ym // nhrm* of the non-conflict scene, may suggest that the author used it on purpose for describing an entirely different reality from the Baal-Yam mythology. It is also possible that Habakkuk borrowed not from the Ugarit thought-world but from a south Canaanite center unknown to us, and the words may have been used

---

5. See ch. 9 (above).

6. M. Dahood, "Ugaritic-Hebrew Parallel Pairs," *RSP* 1.203. See ch. 9 (above) on Ps 46:3–4.

7. Out of 18 references, 5 are used for geographical features, such as the Euphrates. The other 13 references are as follows:

(1)	*ym // nhr*	*ymym // nhrwt* (Ps 24:2, Ezek 32:2)
		ym // nhrwt (Ps 89:26, Isa 50:2, Ps 98:7–8)
		ymym // nhr (Jonah 2:4)—cf. Ps 46:3–5
		ym // nhr (Ps 66:6, 72:8, 80:12; Isa 11:15, 19:5)
(2)	*nhr // ym*	*nhr // gly hym* (Isa 48:18)
		nhrym // ym (Hab 3:8)

there in the way that is assumed.[8] Or, perhaps most likely, "sea" and "river" were a traditional pair in ancient Semitic languages,[9] and Habakkuk simply used this word pair metaphorically to describe the "enemy" of Yahweh and his people, without any direct association with the *Chaoskampf*-motif.

Markĕbōt "Chariots"

Day[10] finds "a further mythological allusion" in Hab 3:8 and 15, where he reads of "Yahweh's horses drawing his (cloud-)chariot in connection with his victory over the sea." He says, "since it is probably . . . Baal mythology which underlies the mythological allusions in Hab 3, it is interesting to note the evidence that Baal too had horses drawing his (cloud-) chariot." Then Day refers to Apollodorus (*The Library* I.6.3), who records a battle between Zeus and the serpent or dragon Typhon in which "Zeus . . . suddenly appeared in the sky on a chariot drawn by winged horses." Because part of the battle takes place on Mt. Casius (i.e., Mt. Zaphon), he thinks that "we here have to do with traditions going back ultimately to Baal," and he conjectures that "Baal, like Zeus in the Typhon conflict, had winged horses drawing his cloud-chariot."

However, his evidence is rather thin. For one thing, a Greek myth is rather indirect proof that there were winged horses in Ugarit, and the Song of Ullikummis,[11] which Day says lies behind the Greek myth,[12] has no reference to wings on the horses. His "evidence" is not drawn from the Baal-Yam myth itself, which does not mention Baal's chariot explicitly, but only refers to his epithet *rkb ʿrpt* "Rider of Clouds."[13] Furthermore, there is no description of Baal riding his chariots or horses in the extant Ugaritic corpus.[14]

---

8. A. R. Millard (private communication).

9. Note the Akkadian equivalent of this pair, *ti-a-am-ta* "sea" // *na-ra-am* "river" (*Atra-Ḫasīs* III iv 5–6) in W. G. Lambert and A. R. Millard, *Atra-Ḫasīs: The Babylonian Story of the Flood* (Oxford: Clarendon, 1969), 96–97 [repr. Winona Lake, Ind.: Eisenbrauns, 1999]. See the Ugaritic pantheon lists, where the Ugaritic god *ym* corresponds to the Akkadian *tâmtum* ([d]A.AB.BA).

10. J. Day, *God's Conflict with the Dragon and the Sea: Echoes of a Canaanite Myth in the Old Testament* (Cambridge: Cambridge University Press, 1985), 107.

11. *ANET*, 121–25.

12. Day, *God's Conflict with the Dragon and the Sea*, 33 n. 92.

13. Cf. A. Cooper, "Divine Names and Epithets in the Ugaritic Texts," *RSP* 3.458–60.

14. *Mdlk* (KTU 1.5 [UT 67]:V:6), which J. Day translates "your chariot team" (see "Echoes of Baal's Seven Thunders and Lightnings in Psalm XXIX and Habakkuk III 9 and the Identity of the Seraphim in Isaiah VI," *VT* 29 [1979], 147 and n. 18), should be a term for some "meteorological phenomena," because it appears between *rḥk* "your wind" and *mṭrk* "your rain." See "thy *storm*" (Gordon, *PLMU*, 107) and "your watering devices" (Pardee, *CS*, 1.267). Compare the recent discussion of this term by W. G. E. Watson, "Unravelling Ugaritic *MDL*," *SEL* 3 (1986), 73–78, esp. n. 5 on p. 75.

Day goes on to say:

> The reference to the winged horses is particularly interesting as a parallel to Hab. 3:8, 15. Since the horses draw the cloud-chariot, it is probable that they symbolize the winds. It is therefore extremely interesting that Ps. 18:11 (ET 10) and 104:3 speak of Yahweh's riding on the *wings* of the wind in the context of his conflict with the sea (cf. Gen. 1:2).

However, his assumption that Hab 3:8 and 15 picture Yahweh riding a cloud-chariot drawn by winged horses has no contextual support, because there is no actual reference either to the wings of the horses or to clouds in Hab 3:8 or 15. There is no proof that Baal's hypothetical horses had wings, let alone that Yahweh's had.

It is certainly true that "the concept that the god rides in a chariot was prevalent" in the ancient Near East and has its roots in Sumerian hymns from the 20th century B.C., as has been discussed in detail by Weinfeld.[15] Storm-gods such as Ninurta, Enlil, and Adad rode in chariots, and thunder was taken to be the sound of the wheels of the storm-god's. Therefore, it would not be surprising if Baal, the storm-god of Ugaritic mythology, rode a chariot and the sound of his wheels symbolized thunder. There is nothing in the present texts to suggest that this was the case, however.

In the Baal-Yam myth (KTU 1.2:IV [UT 68]), where the divine battle between Baal and Sea–River is described, no reference is made to Baal's thunder, the sound of his wheels, or to lightning's[16] assisting him in the battle. It is by his two clubs, "Expeller"[17] and "Driver," that he defeats his enemy. These clubs are described as being "like an eagle" that will swoop from his hands. The battle here is thus described in terms of falconry and one-to-one combat between the leaders of two groups.

In Hab 3:8, Yahweh is described metaphorically as a "rider of horses and chariots," neither as a "rider of clouds," as in Ps 68:5 (*rōkēb bāʿărābôt*), nor as one "who rides on the heavens // on the clouds," as in Deut 33:26 (*rōkēb šāmayim // šĕḥāqîm*).[18] In the Habakkuk passage, there seems to be a

---

15. Cf. M. Weinfeld and H. Tadmor (eds.), *History, Historiography and Interpretation: Studies in Biblical and Cuneiform Literatures* (Jerusalem: Magnes, 1983), 142–43 and n. 119.

16. The famous stone relief of Baal pictures him with a spear in his left hand, which symbolizes his flashes of lightning, and with his club or staff in his uplifted right hand, which is a sign of his authority as a king of gods. Cf. *ANEP*, no. 490 [= *Ugaritica* 2 (1949), pl. 24].

17. See below for Cassuto's view. He reads *aymr* in Hab 3:9, a reading that is no longer accepted.

18. Also Ps 104:3. In Hab 3:15, Yahweh's horses are mentioned without reference to his chariots. Even if one accepts that the "horses" here are metonymy for horse-drawn chariots,

metaphorization[19] of the normal military activities of a human king in the ancient Near East. Because Yahweh is not a storm-god, his chariot and the sound of his wheels do not automatically represent or *refer to* clouds or thunder, though his divine action may described as "thunder-like" in a metaphor.

Yahweh's Bow and Mace (Verse 9)

ʿeryâ tēʿôr qaštekā šĕbūʿôt maṭṭôt ʾōmer

This is one of the most difficult passages in the entire Old Testament, "a riddle which all the ingenuity of scholars has not been able to solve."[20] The syntactic structure of v. 9a, which I have discussed in detail elsewhere,[21] can be analyzed as follows:

Internal Object (*ʿeryâ*) + Niphal Verb (*tēʿôr*) + Subject (*qaštekā*),

which is a *niphal* (passive) transformation of the supposed deep structure:

[Polel Verb (*tʿrr*) + Object (*ʿeryâ*)] + Object (*qaštekā*)

which would mean "you uncover the nakedness *of* your bow" (lit., "[you uncover the nakedness] your bow"). In light of the above, the following translation is proposed for the first half of the verse:

Your bow is unsheathed.

Mythological Allusions?

In the second part of v. 9, Day sees another mythological allusion.[22] Altering the term *šĕbūʿôt* to *šibʿat* "seven," he argues that there is here "a reference to Yahweh's seven shafts or arrows of lightning." He then compares them to Yahweh's seven thunders, which he thinks are depicted in Ps 29,[23] though in

---

it seems that the horses, rather than the chariot, are referred to in this verse, because the verb *drk* "to trample" is never used with chariots.

19. Metaphorization often results in the idiomatization of the normal expression. In other words, a normal expression becomes fossilized to an idiomatic expression, or an idiomatic expression de-fossilized:

1. fossilization: [normal → metaphorical → idiomatic]
2. de-fossilization: [normal ← metaphorical ← idiomatic]

Cf. A. Gibson, *Biblical Semantic Logic* (Oxford: Blackwell, 1981), 28.

20. Davidson, cited by G. A. Smith, *The Book of the Twelve Prophets* (London, 1898), 154.

21. D. T. Tsumura, "Niphal with an Internal Object in Hab 3, 9a," *JSS* 31 (1986), 11–16.

22. Day, *God's Conflict with the Dragon and the Sea*, 106–7.

23. Cf. idem, "Echoes of Baal's Seven Thunders and Lightnings," 146–47; *God's Conflict with the Dragon and the Sea*, 106–7.

the latter only the phrase "the voice of Yahweh" is repeated seven times, without explicit mention of "thunder." Then he suggests that "Yahweh's seven thunders and lightnings, attested in Ps 29 and Hab 3:9, have their background in Baal mythology," in light of KTU 1.101.3b–4, which he reads of Baal:

3b.	*šbʿt. brqm.* x[ ]	Seven lightnings . . .
4.	*ṭmnt. ʾiṣr rʿt. ʿṣ. brq.* y[ ]	Eight storehouses of thunder.
		The shaft of lightning . . .

However, the number parallelism "seven" // "eight" is common in both Ugaritic and Hebrew, and the number "seven" appears especially often in literary idioms. So, even if the Habakkuk passage did refer to "seven arrows," it would not necessarily be a reflection of the Baal myth. Moreover, not only is the "seven" an emendation, the term *maṭṭôt* in Hab 3:9 does not mean "arrows," as will be shown below.

Cassuto, who also assumes a Ugaritic background to this chapter, finds an allusion to Baal's club *aymr* in the word *ʾōmer* in v. 9b.[24] However, it is very difficult to accept a phonological change such as */ʾayy-/ > /ʾō-/. Furthermore, he compares *maṭṭôt* with an etymologically unrelated term, *ṣmdm* "(Baal's) two clubs/rods," without justification. As for the problematic term *šĕbūʿôt*, he emends it to a verbal form with the meaning "you brandish," "you grasp," "you lower," or the like. Both Cassuto and Day base their assumptions of a Ugaritic background on textual emendations.

Various Emendations

Many other scholars try to explain the text by emendations based on different etymologies. The following are various suggestions and conjectural translations seemingly based on emended texts:

1. *šibʿat* "seven": "seven arrows with a word" (Day);
2. *šibbaʿtā* "thou hast sated with shafts thy quiver (*ʾšptk*)" (Nowack); "and charge thy quiver with shafts" (NEB);[25] "thy bow was satiated with shafts"(Marti); cf. BHS: LXX[Barb] ἐχόρτασας; Syr., *wnsbʿwn*;
3. "and put the arrows to the string" (RSV).

However, alteration of data should be avoided unless it is absolutely necessary.

There have been at least four different views of the syntax based on the unaltered MT text, taking *šĕbūʿôt* either as the fem. pl. form of *šbʿh* [*šĕbūʿâ*] "oath" or "heptad," or as a *qal* passive participle, fem. pl., of **šbʿ* "sworn." They are as follows:

---

24. Cassuto, "Chapter III of Habakkuk and the Ras Shamra Texts," 11.
25. Cf. L. H. Brockington, *The Hebrew Text of the Old Testament* (Oxford, 1973), 261.

1. NP(*x* of *y*) + NP(*z*): "*according* to the oaths of the tribes, *even thy* word" (KJV); cf. "heptads of spears" (Ewald; cf. BDB);
2. NP(*x*) + NP(*y* of *z*): "oaths, rods of the word" (Hitzig, Steiner; cf. BDB); cf. "powerful shafts," i.e., "shafts of power" (Dahood);[26]
3. VP + NP(*y* of *z*): "sworn were the rods (= chastisements) of (thy) word" (Gesenius; Hitzig; RV margin; cf. BDB); "Sworn are the rods of the word" (JPSV);
4. VP + NP(*y*) + NP(*z*): "the shafts are adjured[27] . . . by the powerful divine utterance" (Eaton).[28]

However, views 3 and 4 may have a difficulty in gender agreement between *maṭṭôt*, which is masc. pl.,[29] and *šĕbū⁽ôt*, which is fem. pl. Therefore, it appears that the nominal interpretation of *šĕbū⁽ôt* provides a better solution to this *crux*.

Unlike the other two terms in v. 9b, *maṭṭôt* is usually not emended and is translated "tribes," "rods," "shafts," "arrows," or "spears." Modern scholars, as seen above, tend to take it as "arrows" or the like, because the term seems to be parallel with *qešet* "bow" in v. 9a. However, it should be noted that in Hab 3 the words for "arrow" and "spear" appear as *ḥiṣṣêkā* "your arrows" and *ḥănîtekā* "your spear" in v. 11. It may be better to understand *qšt* in this verse as including "arrows" in itself, following the principle of *pars pro toto*.

Bow and Mace

It is very interesting to note the word pair *mṭ – qšt* in a certain Ugaritic mythological text; KTU 1.3 [⁽nt]:II:15–16 reads:

mṭm . tgrš / šbm .	With a stick she drives out *foes*
bksl . qšth . mdnt	Her bow *attacking* in the back
	(i.e., of her fleeing foes). (Gordon)[30]

Dahood has taken note of this word pair, "staff"//"bow," common to Ugaritic and Hebrew, and comments: "Though the line remains obscure any advance in its [Hab 3:9] understanding must take this parallelism into account."[31] J. Gibson also quotes Hab 3:9 and 14 for explanation of this Ugaritic pair.[32]

---

26. M. Dahood, *Psalms III* (AB 17A; Garden City: Doubleday, 1970), 21: *mrr > ᵓmr* (*ᵓemār* = Aleph-preformative noun from *mrr*). Cf. D. Pardee, "The Semitic Root *mrr* and the Etymology of Ugaritic *mr(r) // brk*," *UF* 10 (1978), 261–62 n. 78.

27. "Or commissioned to their task."

28. J. H. Eaton, "The Origin and Meaning of Habakkuk 3," *ZAW* 76 (1964), 152.

29. Note that this masculine word appears in this chapter in both masc. and fem. pl. forms: *mṭyw* (v. 14) and *mṭwt*. Compare masc. pl. forms *nhrym* (v. 8) and *nhrwt* (v. 9).

30. Gordon, *PLMU*, 77.

31. Dahood, *RSP* 1.258.

The Akkadian cognate *miṭṭu* appears as a weapon in a god's hand with the sense "mace," the Sumerian counterpart of which is GIŠ.TUKUL.DINGIR ("a weapon of gods").[33] It is clearly distinguished from "arrow" or "shaft." Moreover, in Akkadian texts, the god's majestic weapon is sometimes referred to as "a fifty-headed mace."[34] Therefore, the plural Hebrew term *maṭṭôt* may refer to a majestic divine "mace" or "staff" in the present context, not to many "staves," as Dahood renders.

Now, "mace" and "bow" appear also in Akkadian texts as a word pair. For example, in the following text,

> 35. *šibba ša ana amēli iṭeḫḫû qaštu* [*abūbija*]
>   (I hold) the serpent which attacks man, the bow of my *abūbu* weapon
> 37. *abūb tāḫazi* [GIŠ.TUKUL.SAG.NINNU]
>   (I hold) abūbu-of-Battle, the mace with the fifty heads
>   (Angim III 35–37),[35]

"bow" (*qaštu*) and "the mace with the fifty heads"[36] are not only paired but also are identified with the "Deluge" (*abūbu*)-weapon,[37] thus symbolizing the destructive power of a deity.

This pair of weapons is mentioned as being granted to a human king, Tiglathpileser I, from the storm-gods in the following text:

> Ninurta u Nergal GIŠ.TUKUL.MEŠ-*šu-nu ezzūte u* GIŠ.BAN-*su-nu ṣīrta ana idi bēlūtija išruku*
> Ninurta and Nergal granted me their fierce weapons and their sublime bow to be worn at my lordly side. (AKA 84 vi 59)[38]

---

32. Gibson, *CML*², 47. Note that he translates them as "shaft(s)" and "bow," though the Ugaritic term *mṭ* normally means "staff," as in Hebrew *mṭh ʾlhym* "the staff of God" (Exod 4:20). Cf. C. H. Gordon, *UT*, §19.1642.

33. "The divine weapon" (*CAD* M/2 148; also *CAD* K 398). Cf. J. van Dijk, *LUGAL UD ME-LÁM-bi NIR-ǦÁL: Le récit épique et didactique des Travaux de Ninurta, du Déluge et de la Nouvelle Création* (Leiden: Brill, 1983), 52, line 5, which reads *be-lu šá ina qa-ti-šú el-le-tum me-eṭ-ṭa na-šu-ú* "le Seigneur dont le bras puissant fut prédestiné à (porter) l'arme meurtrière."

34. Cf. *CAD* M/2 148. Note that an actual gold mace-head with twelve mushroom-shaped knobs (heads) from the Early Bronze Age has been excavated in Alaçahöyük in central Anatolia. Cf. *Land of Civilizations, Turkey* (Tokyo, 1985), pl. 56.

35. Cf. *CAD* A/1 79 and Q 147. Also note the phrase [*mi*]-*iṭ-ṭu-uk-ka abū*[*bu*] "your mace, *abūbu* weapon" in a hymn to Marduk (KAR 337:14), cited in *CAD* M/2 148. On "the Deluge" (*mabbûl*) in Ps 29:10, see above (ch. 9).

36. See also *CS*, 2.247.

37. Note also: "Nergal *šar tamḫāri bēl abāri u dunni bēl a-bu-bi* king of the battle, lord of strength and might, lord of the Deluge (weapon)" (Streck Asb. 178:2). Cf. *CAD* A/1 80. See on Ps 29:10 in ch. 8 (above).

38. Cf. *CAD* K 54.

Here, the term "their weapons" (GIŠ.TUKUL.MEŠ-šunu) most likely refers to "maces," because Akkadian *miṭṭu* "mace" is often explained as GIŠ.TUKUL. DINGIR ("a weapon of gods") in Sumerian, as noted above. The same pair, "bow" and "mace," is also mentioned in a context in which actual preparation for battle is commanded. Thus,

> *anantam kiṣṣar q[á-aš-tăm i-ši šar-[da]-pa tu-ru-[uṣ] kak[ka] tumu[ḫ]*
> get ready for battle, take up the bow, pull taut the reins, grasp the mace.
>
> (2N-T343 rev. 6)[39]

Furthermore, the image of YHWH in Hab 3 may be compared with the image of Assur, "raising his bow, riding in his chariot *a-bu-bu [ṣa]-an-du* girt with the Deluge," as described in the text of the Annals of Sennacherib.[40] Habakkuk also, in depicting his God, uses a metaphor based on the normal practice of a human king in wartime.[41] In light of the above discussion, I conclude that the term *maṭṭôt* probably means YHWH's "majestic mace," which is paired with his "bow."[42]

Regarding the word *šĕbū'ôt*, the most natural translation would be "oaths." Although *qaštekā* ("your bow") is parallel to *maṭṭôt* ("a majestic mace") in the bicolon of v. 9, as noted above, it is also closely associated with *šĕbū'ôt* ("oaths"), not only in terms of word order, but also semantically. In other words, it seems that *qaštekā*, which also may mean "your rainbow," may imply God's "oaths" to his people, because the rainbow was a sign of "eternal covenant" with Noah and his family after the Deluge.[43] Thus the word *qšt* here seems to be polysemic, having a double function, corresponding both to *maṭṭôt* and to *šĕbū'ôt* in poetic parallelism in v. 9.[44]

---

39. *CAD* Q 147–48 and K 51.

40. OIP 2 140:7 (Senn.). Cf. *CAD* A/1 80; Q 150.

41. The scene of a king riding in his horse-drawn chariot with a bow in his hand is very common in the ancient Near East, both in Mesopotamia and in Egypt. See, for example, *Ugaritica* 2 (1949), 10 and pl. 6 as well as many reliefs from Assyria and Egypt; cf. A. H. Layard, *Nineveh and Its Palaces* (London, 1853), 224–28 and 233 for figs. 107–11 and 120. For King Shalmaneser III's escort holding a mace and a bow, one in each hand, see M. E. L. Mallowan, *Nimrud and Its Remains* (London, 1966), 2.446–48; and *ANEP*, pl. 821.

42. For a more-detailed discussion of this section, see my " 'Word Pair' *qšt* and *mṭ* in Habakkuk 3:9 in the Light of Ugaritic and Akkadian," in *Go to the Land I Will Show You: Studies in Honor of Dwight W. Young* (ed. J. Coleson and V. H. Matthews; Winona Lake, Ind.: Eisenbrauns, 1996), 357–65.

43. Cf. *qšt* = *'wt bryt* (Gen 9:13); *lzkr bryt 'wlm* (Gen 9:16). Note that *bryt* is parallel with *šbw'h* in Ps 105:8–9 = 1 Chr 16:15–16.

44. For the most recent discussion of polysemy, see D. Grossberg, "Pivotal Polysemy in Jeremiah xxv 10–11a," *VT* 36 (1986), 481–85. Cf. also my "Twofold Image of Wine in Psalm 46:4–5," *JQR* 71 (1981), 169 n. 13, where I discussed briefly the *polyseme* in Hab

The syntax of v. 9b, however, still poses a problem according to normal grammar. While it may be taken as in #2 (above),[45] it can also be understood as an another example of the AXB pattern in poetic parallelism, in which a composite unit (AB) retains its grammatical dependency within itself even if X is inserted between A and B, thus violating the normal grammatical rule of adjacency, and X holds a grammatical relationship with [A . . . B] as a whole. Habakkuk 3:9b should possibly be analyzed according to this poetical pattern:

5. NP(*y*) + NP(*x* of *z*): "mace" *maṭṭôt* + "the oaths of (your) word" *šĕbū'ôt.* . . . *'ōmer.*

It should be noted that a noun phrase such as *šĕbū'ôt 'ōmer* "the oaths of (your) word" is neither peculiar nor improbable. Because *'mr* (masc. sing.) is an archaic term that appears only in poetic texts[46] or in an exalted style (Josh 24:27), the phrase *šĕbū'ôt 'ōmer* might well be compared with the following expressions:

- *šĕbū'at 'issār* "binding oath" (lit., oath of bond) in Num 30:14 (// ndr): "vows" // "pledges binding on (her)" (NIV)
- *šĕbū'at šeqer* "false oath" (lit., oath of falsehood) in Zech 8:17
- *šĕbū'at hā'ālâ* "curse of the oath" (lit., oath of the oath) in Num 5:21 (NIV)

This syntactical analysis is not only possible but also probable, especially when *qašteka* is recognized as polysemous, as noted above. Thus the structure of the parallelism in v. 9 as a whole would be as follows:

qašteka (1) "your bow" // "mace" *maṭṭôt*
           [destruction] : negative side
      (2) "your rainbow" // "the oaths of (your) word" *šĕbū'ôt.* . . .
          'ōmer
          [salvation] : positive side[47]

3:15; and M. Dahood, "The Minor Prophets and Ebla," in *The Word of the Lord Shall Go Forth: Essays in Honor of David Noel Freedman in Celebration of His Sixtieth Birthday* (ed. C. L. Meyers and M. O'Connor; Winona Lake, Ind.: Eisenbrauns, 1983), 61.

45. *Maṭṭôt 'ōmer*: "mace of word." For a similar association of "word" with weapon, see "a king's word" // "a double-edged dagger" (*Ahiqar* vii 95ff.) in J. M. Lindenberger, *The Aramaic Proverbs of Ahiqar* (Baltimore: Johns Hopkins University Press, 1983), 80.

46. Psalm 19:3, 4; 68:12; 77:9; Job 20:29.

47. Note that Yahweh's word, *'mr,* is contrasted with "dumb idols" (Hab 2:18) and "a dumb stone" (2:19). Cf. R. Vuilleumier and C.-A. Keller, *Michée, Nahoum, Habacuc, Sophonie* (Neuchâtel, 1971), 166.

The proposed translation would be as follows:

Your bow is unsheathed,
(your) mace is the oaths of (your) word.[48]

Yahweh's Destruction of the Evil One (Verse 13b)

māḥaṣtā rōʾš mibbêt rāšāʿ
ʿārôt yĕsôd ʿad-ṣawwāʾr

This passage also presents great difficulty in interpretation. Hence, various translations have been suggested; for example,

- Thou didst crush the head of the wicked,[a]
  laying him bare from thigh to neck[b]
    ([a]Cn: Heb head from the house of the wicked; [b]Heb obscure). (RSV)

- You crushed the head of the wicked house,
  laying it bare from foundation to roof. (NRSV)

- You crushed the leader of the land of wickedness,
  you stripped him from head to foot. (NIV)

- You shatter the house of the wicked,
  laying bare its foundations to the bedrock. (REB)

- Thou dost crush the chief of the tribe of the wicked,
  Destroying from head to tail. (Eaton)[49]

- you smote the top off the house of the wicked,
  laying bare the foundation as far as the *rock*. (Day)[50]

Ugaritic Myth?

Cassuto was the first to see a literary relationship with the Ugaritic Baal-Yam myth in v. 13. He states that, "despite the successive changes of thought, the literary tradition is preserved in all its details." Thus he sees in Hab 3:13–14 two blows on the evil one by Yahweh: one on the head and one on the neck, just as Baal smites his enemies Yam and Nahar, "with his rods, two blows, one on the head and one between the shoulders and on the neck. With the rod *aymr,* the blow is . . . on the back of the neck (*qdqd*) and on the fore-

---

48. Another possible translation of the second half would be: "the seven-headed mace *is* (your) word," taking *šbʿwt* as "heptad, sevenfold." See above for the fifty-headed mace and the "gold mace-head with twelve mushroom-shaped knobs (heads)" (see n. 34, p. 171).
49. Eaton, *Obadiah, Nahum, Habakkuk and Zephaniah,* 115.
50. *Ṣūr* for MT *ṣawwāʾr.* Cf. Day, *God's Conflict with the Dragon and the Sea,* 108.

head (*bn ʿnm*). With the stick *ygrš* the blow is . . . on the shoulder (*ktp*) and on the front portion of the neck (*bn ydm*)."[51]

Albright emends MT *mbyt* to *mwt* on the basis of LXX θάνατον and takes the verse as referring to Yahweh's destruction of Death. Wakeman thinks that Hab 3:13 "would be the only *direct* reference to a conflict between Yahweh and Mot," should Albright's emendation be accepted. Thus, Cassuto and Albright see here two different Baal myths; the former identifies it as the Baal-Yam myth, and the latter as the Baal-Mot myth.

In Hab 3:13, Yahweh is certainly described as having crushed (**mḥṣ*) the evil one (*rāšāʿ*). In Ugaritic texts, this verb is also employed to describe the slaying of Baal's enemies.[52] However, this similarity does not prove that this biblical text has a literary connection with Ugaritic conflict myths. The verb **mḥṣ* appears with "head" as the object frequently in the poetic texts of the Old Testament, such as Ps 68:22. In fact, the expression "to smite the head of the enemy" appears also in Akkadian monumental inscriptions.[53] Moreover, the expression "strike/smite the head of somebody" seems to appear in a context other than the *Chaoskampf*-myth even in Ugaritic. Thus, the goddess Anat threatens her father-god El with bodily violence, saying:

[*amḫsk lẓr qdq*] *dk* (KTU 1.18:I [3Aqht]:10–11)
I will strike you on your skull.[54]

It seems that the expression "strike/smite the head of somebody" was already a literary cliché in the Ugaritic literature. Habakkuk simply used this ancient literary idiom for describing Yahweh's destruction of his enemy.

Retaining the MT as it is, Freedman[55] identifies this as an example of the so-called "broken construct chain," our "AXB pattern," and translates:

māḥastā rōʾš mibbêt *rāšāʿ*
You crushed the head of the wicked one *inwards*
(// You ripped him open from fundament to neck)

This translation, however, seems to be influenced by his basic interpretation of this passage as a reflection of a dragon myth. Moreover, the most natural way to understand MT *mibbêt* is as simply "from a house."

---

51. Cassuto, "Chapter III of Habakkuk," 13 and n. 21.

52. Cf. *RSP* 3.238.

53. See, for example, Warad-Sin, in *CS*, 2.251.

54. Cf. KTU 1.3:V:23–24: a*m*x[   ] / qdqd ; *mḥṣ* + *qdqd* (Num 24:17). See M. Dijkstra and J. C. de Moor, "Problematical Passages in the Legend of Aqhâtu," *UF* 7 (1975), 193.

55. D. N. Freedman, "The Broken Construct Chain," *Bib* 53 (1972), 535.

"Inserted Bicolon"

I would like to present a new interpretation of this verse, while retaining the MT as it stands. It has been customary to analyze v. 13b as a two-line parallelism as follows:

| *māḥaṣtā rōʾš mibbêt rāšāʿ* | 4 |
| *ʿārôt yĕsôd ʿad-ṣawwāʾr* | 4/3 |

However, there seems to be enough justification to take it as a four-line parallelism.

māḥaṣtā rōʾš	2
mibbêt rāšāʿ	2
ʿārôt yĕsôd	2
ʿad-ṣawwāʾr	2/1

First, there seems to be alliteration between the first and the second lines: *m - r - m - r*; and another between the third and the fourth: *ʿ - ʿ -*. Second, when we take *mibbêt* as having the plain meaning "from a house," the second line has a direct relationship with the third, which contains the term *yĕsôd* "foundation." Thus, the second and the third lines constitute a parallelism:

mibbêt rāšāʿ
ʿārôt yĕsôd

Third, terms for a part of body appear in both the first and the fourth lines: *rʾš* "head" and *ṣwʾr* "neck." Hence, these two lines are related closely in a distant parallelism:

māḥaṣtā rōʾš
ʿad-ṣawwāʾr

Finally, a four-line parallelism with the meter 2:2:2:2/1 here serves as a kind of climax, as in Ps 46:7; 9:6, 7, especially after the bicolon that announces Yahweh's act of salvation for his people and his anointed.[56]

If the above analysis of the parallel structure is correct, it is to be taken as an example of an "inserted bicolon" (AXYB Pattern). Here, a bicolon X // Y

mibbêt rāšāʿ
ʿārôt yĕsôd

---

56. Note that the term "to save" (*yšʿ*) and its related forms are the key words and appear five times (1:2; 3:8b, 13 [2×], 18) in the entire book. Habakkuk's appeal to Yahweh at the beginning of the book is thus contrasted with confidence in God's saving act for his people and his anointed in the final chapter. Note that after 1:2 the root *yšʿ* does not appear until the third chapter.

is inserted between the A-line and the B-line, which still hold their "grammatical" dependency and hence should be taken as a composite unit.[57] The idiom *ʿārôt yĕsôd* "to lay foundations bare,"[58] though it can mean "to destroy"[59] metaphorically, is used in a literal sense in connection with the word "house" in the preceding line.

Thus the meaning of this "inserted bicolon" would be: "From the house of the evil one (You) laid the foundation bare." Note that total destruction of the city and its houses is sometimes described by the phrase "from its foundations to its parapets" (Sennacherib).[60]

Lines AB would also give an adequate solution for *ʿad-ṣawwāʾr* as it stands.

māḥaṣtā rōʾš
ʿad-ṣawwāʾr

The most natural translation for this parallelism would be: "You crushed the head // *to* the neck." This would mean that Yahweh crushed the head of the evil one *down to* the neck. However, *ʿad-ṣawwāʾr* in two other passages as well as a similar expression in Ugaritic (KTU 1.3 [UT ʿnt]:II:14 *ḥlqm*)[61] means "*up to* the neck" (Isa 8:8, 30:28), never "*down to* the neck," as a description of the height of water. Of course, Hab 3:13b could be the only exception, thus meaning "You crushed the head *down to* the neck." However, the phrase *ʿad-ṣawwāʾr* "to the neck" might well be a result clause/phrase that means "to be 'up to the neck,'" that is, "to become in the state of *up-to-the-neck*-ness"[62] → "to be headless." If this interpretation is correct, the proposed translation would be as follows:

māḥaṣtā rōʾš	You crushed the head to be headless;
mibbêt rāšāʿ	from the house of the evil one
ʿārôt yĕsôd	(You) laid bare the foundation
ʿad-ṣawwāʾr	—

---

57. See my " 'Inserted Bicolon,' the AXYB Pattern, in Amos i 5 and Psalm ix 7," *VT* 38 (1988), 234–36.

58. Also Ps 137:7: *ʿārû ʿārû ʿad haysôd bâ* "Tear it down, . . . tear it down to its foundations!" (NIV).

59. Note that the Akkadian counterpart, *nasāḫu išdu* "to remove the foundation (of a house)," means "to uproot or destroy." Cf. *CAD* N/2 4; I/J 236.

60. *CS*, 2.305.

61. "Up to the neck" (Gordon, *PLMU*, 77).

62. See Gordon, *UT*, 58 n. 1 for the nominalization of the prepositional phrase in Hebrew. T. Matsumoto suggested the possibility of taking *ʿad-ṣawwāʾr* as "up to the neck" (personal communication).

Two-Line Parallelism

Another possible way to interpret the verse without any emendation is to take it as a two-line parallelism in the usual manner:

māḥaṣtā rō'š mibbêt rāšāʿ
ʿārôt yĕsôd ʿad-ṣawwā'r

and to identify three terms related to a (stone) statue: *rō'š* "head," *ṣawwā'r* "neck," and *yĕsôd* "base." The last term can be compared with its Akkadian cognate, *išdu* "bottom (of the exterior of an object)."[63] In this interpretation, the second line would mean that Yahweh destroyed the statue (of the evil one) from its base to its neck.

As for the first line, the key is the interpretation of *mibbêt*. It is noteworthy that the preposition *min*, especially in poetry with a solitary noun, can express a privative idea, "the non-existence of a thing not named in the principal clause,"[64] as in Isa 23:1,

   kî-šuddad mibbayit   *so that there is no* house,

or Ps 49:15,

   mizzĕbūl-lô   *so that it has no* dwelling,

or Ps 52:7,

   yissāḥăkā mē'ōhel   pluck thee up *tentless.*

In light of the above, I suggest another possible interpretation as follows:

māḥaṣtā rō'š mibbêt rāšāʿ   You crushed the head of the evil one[65]
                       so that there might be no house;
ʿārôt yĕsôd ʿad-ṣawwā'r   (You) laid bare the base *up to* the neck.

With either interpretation, it is impossible to assume that there is a "literary" connection between Hab 3:13 and the so-called *Chaoskampf*-myth of Ugarit. Habakkuk seems to use the imagery of destroying a statue of the enemy king in an actual war to describe Yahweh's destructive action against *rāšāʿ*.

"Evil One"

As for the "evil one" (*rāšāʿ*) in Hab 3:13, Eaton thinks that it is the great dragon, "personification of the rebellious waters and representing for the poet the sum of chaos and death."[66]

---

63. Cf. *CAD* I/J 238–39. Also note the Ugaritic counterpart *išd* (UT 19.394) "leg."
64. BDB, 583.
65. Here, I follow Freedman's interpretation, taking *rō'š . . . rāšāʿ* as a "broken construct chain." See n. 77.
66. Eaton, *Obadiah, Nahum, Habakkuk and Zephaniah*, 115.

However, in Hab 3 no "dragon" is mentioned explicitly, and the "rivers" and "sea" in v. 8 are not described as dragons. *Rāšāʿ* appears three times in the book of Habakkuk, and it is used in direct opposition to the "righteous," Yahweh's "people" // "His anointed":

1:4   *rāšāʿ* ↔ *haṣṣaddîq*
1:13 *rāšāʿ* ↔ *ṣaddîq*
cf.   *(napš)-ô* ↔ *ṣaddîq* (2:4)
3:13 *rāšāʿ* ↔ *ʿammekā* // *mĕšîḥekā*

Though Habakkuk could have used fossilized terms such as Leviathan, Rahab, or Taninim (a "dragon"),[67] as in other poetic passages of the Old Testament, to describe the evil power metaphorically (i.e., the enemy of Yahweh and his people), he used an image completely different from the so-called *Chaoskampf.* The description of a god's destroying the "evil one" might better be compared with the description of the goddess Anunitu: "the lady of warfare, who carries the bow and the quiver, who fulfills the command of Enlil her father, who annihilates the enemy, who destroys the evil one" (*CS,* 2.313).

Yahweh and Resheph (Verse 5)

lĕpānâw yēlek dāber	Before him went pestilence,
wĕyēṣēʾ rešep lĕraglâw	and plague followed close behind. (RSV)

According to Day,[68] Hab 3:5 contains a mythological allusion "not so explicitly expressed elsewhere." He says, "Plague and Pestilence are here clearly personified and behind the latter there certainly lies the Canaanite plague-god Resheph." Furthermore, he assumes here an "allusion to Resheph's participation in the conflict with chaos," which he thinks has its ultimate background in Ugaritic text KTU 1.82 [UT1001]:1–3.[69]

1. Baal smote . . . the dragon and rejoiced and poured out . . .
2. . . . on the earth . . . support . . . I have no support
3. . . . the archer Resheph (*bʿl ḥẓ ršp*), son of *Km,* shot his kidneys and his heart.

Even if he is able to argue, based on this "largely fragmentary and obscure" text, that in Ugaritic myth "the god Resheph is represented alongside Baal in his conflict with the dragon,"[70] the conclusion that in the Habakkuk passage

---

67. For these terms, see ch. 11.
68. Day, *God's Conflict with the Dragon and the Sea,* 105–6.
69. Idem, "New Light on the Mythological Background," 353–55. Compare discussion of this text by W. J. Fulco, *The Canaanite God Rešep* (New Haven: American Oriental Society, 1976), 49–51.
70. Day, "New Light on the Mythological Background," 354.

"Resheph belongs with the *Chaoskampf*" does not automatically follow.[71]

First, he assumes that the background of the *entire* section of Hab 3:3–15 is "the Canaanite myth of Baal's conflict with the sea or dragon." As discussed above, however, his argument for the suggested mythological allusions in v. 8 and v. 9—especially the latter—is not so convincing. Moreover, there is no actual description of Resheph's participating, say as an archer, in the "conflict" described in vv. 8–11, where Yahweh's "bow" (v. 9) and "arrows" (v. 11) are mentioned. The only mention of *rešep* ("plague") in the Habakkuk passage is about its marching after Yahweh (v. 5b).

Certainly the god Resheph served as a warrior and also as the god of plagues, as did Apollo in the Greek world and Nergal[72] in the Mesopotamian world. They are all connected with heavenly bodies, mainly with falling stars (meteors), which shoot like arrows.[73] Therefore, it is no surprise if Resheph as a warrior-god participates in the divine conflict as described in the Ugaritic myth cited above. However, in Hab 3, *rešep*, like *deber*, which does not appear as a god at Ugarit, appears as a symbol of Yahweh's destructive power rather than an archer.

Assuming the existence of a specific Ugaritic myth parallel to Hab 3:5, Day thinks that in Hab 3:5 "the god Resheph has been demoted to a kind of demon in Yahweh's entourage."[74] Weinfeld, however, puts the present text in a much wider context of the ancient mythologies and explains as follows: "if the source of the motif of the smiting star and arrow is rooted in the mythology of Resheph, Nergal and Apollo, ... Resheph, Deber, Qeteb etc. in other biblical passages ceased to be independent divine forces. These are not considered divine entities, but rather heavenly bodies which serve as God's emissaries and servants."[75]

---

71. Day thinks that "Albright is wrong in separating Hab 3:3–7 (where Resheph occurs, v. 5) and 3:8–15 (where the *Chaoskampf* is described) as originally two separate poems." See Day, *God's Conflict with the Dragon and the Sea*, 106.

72. In Mesopotamia, Nergal is called "king of the battle, lord of strength and might, lord of the Deluge (weapon)" (*šar tamḫāri bēl abāri u dunni bēl a-bu-bi*), Streck Asb. 178:2—cf. *CAD* A/1 80—and he is "carrying bow, arrow and quiver" (*nāš qašti uṣu u išpat*), Böhl, *BO* 6 p. 166:4 (hymn to Nergal)—cf. *CAD* I/J 257. Cf. Weinfeld and Tadmor (eds.), *History, Historiography and Interpretation*, 136.

73. Ibid., 128 nn. 34–37.

74. Day, *God's Conflict with the Dragon and the Sea*, 106. Fulco also calls Resheph "a lesser divinity in Habakkuk" and takes him as "a quasi-demon accompanying Yahweh in a theophany," but Fulco does not assume any literary connection with Ugaritic myths. Cf. Fulco, *The Canaanite God Rešep*, 61, 70.

75. Weinfeld and Tadmor (eds.), *History, Historiography and Interpretation*, 130. Weinfeld takes Pestilence and Resheph in Hab 3:5 as "the pair of destroying angels . . . who accompany the god on his going out to battles" (p. 135).

Thus, it has sometimes been claimed that Resheph is an example of the ossification[76] of reference by means of demythologization in theological polemics. However, these scholars have not shown that a "Canaanite" mythology stands behind the Habakkuk passage. Day simply assumes such a mythological background by suggesting that Hab 3:5 contains a mythological allusion "not so explicitly expressed elsewhere." But his argument seems to be circular when he says that "the allusion to Resheph's participation in the conflict with chaos has its ultimate background in the Ugaritic text KTU 1.82:1–3." However, the phrase *wyṣʾ ršp* as a whole probably should be taken as a simple metaphorical expression, similar to the English "famine stalks the land."[77]

The often suggested connection between Hab 3 and Ugaritic mythology does not seem to be well founded. The mention of the traditional word pair "rivers" and the "sea" in v. 8 does not automatically justify presupposing that the background is the Canaanite *Chaoskampf*-motif of the Ugaritic Baal-Yam myth. The "chariots" (v. 8) and the "bow" and "mace" (v. 9) are to be compared with the ancient Near Eastern examples of victorious human kings riding a chariot with a bow and a mace in their hands. Habakkuk 3:13b also seems to be imagery reflecting a human battle situation rather than a particular Canaanite myth. As for *rešep*, there is no reason to think it has anything to do with a Ugaritic myth. Metaphorization of an ordinary word should be carefully distinguished from demythologization of a divine name.

---

76. Note that idiomatization does "kill off" or ossify the purported reference in the first-level discourse. Cf. Gibson, *Biblical Semantic Logic*, 28.

77. The text of Hab 3:5 might be more profitably compared with the expression: "(Marduk) caused Nergal, the strongest among the gods, to march at my side; he slew my foes, felled my enemies" in the Autobiography of Nabopolassar (*CS*, 2.307).

11

Metaphor in Poetry

In this final chapter, I would like to summarize the metaphorical features of poetic language, especially with regard to the imagery of war and storm in the Psalms and other poetic texts of the Old Testament.

In the comparative study of the biblical creation stories and ancient Near Eastern myths, until recently, the issue was whether there was a direct literary dependence of Gen 1:2 on *Enuma elish*, because our knowledge of "creation" myths from the ancient Near East was very limited. However, at present, more information from the ancient Near East is available about the *Chaoskampf* myths[1] as well as about the *creation* myths[2] for comparison with biblical literature than there was in Gunkel's time, a hundred years ago. Hence, scholars should be careful about making hasty generalizations about the dependence or influence of biblical narratives on or from extrabiblical traditions.[3] Instead, we should observe the rich literary traditions in the biblical world and especially take note of the use of metaphor.

The term *metaphor* can refer to various literary expressions. A distinction between "simile" and "metaphor" is useful. The former is an overt, *explicit* comparison, while the latter is a covert, *implicit* comparison.[4] However, we may also define "metaphor" in a much broader sense from the perspectives of logics and semantics. According to A. Gibson, "Metaphor is (roughly) the transference of an expression from one semantic domain to another, which involves the preservation of words but a change in their value(s)."[5] In this monograph, I am using the term in the broader sense.

---

1. For example, the myth of Baal versus the sea-god Yam and his associates from Ugarit, that of Adad of Aleppo versus the sea-goddess Têmtum from Mari, and that of Marduk versus the goddess Tiamat in *Enuma elish* from Babylon. See ch. 2 (above).

2. See W. Heimpel, "Mythologie, A. I: In Mesopotamien," *RlA* 8.546–47, 558–60 (fig. 6); G. Beckman, "Mythologie, A. II: Bei den Hethitern," *RlA* 8.570–71; also the section on Egyptian cosmologies in *CS*, 1.5–31. See ch. 8 (above).

3. In fact, new discoveries at sites such as the Hurrian Urkesh and Tell Hamoukar in Syria will probably lead us to rewrite the early history of Syria around 2000 B.C.

4. See W. G. E. Watson, *Classical Hebrew Poetry: A Guide to Its Techniques* (JSOT-Sup 26; Sheffield: JSOT Press, 1984), 254–55.

5. A. Gibson, *Biblical Semantic Logic* (Oxford: Blackwell, 1981), 27.

In these days when "intertextuality" is the fashion among postmodern literary critics,[6] we should be rather careful when comparing similar literary features by means of association among various literary traditions in the ancient Near East. Nevertheless, to appreciate the poetic texts and their skillful techniques, we must observe all details of literary expression in the original language and understand them both linguistically and stylistically.

For example, as discussed above,[7] we might detect the twofold image of "wine" in Ps 46 behind the contrast between the raging and foaming of the waters of the sea (v. 3) and the gladdening of the streams of the river (v. 4). In other words, though no word "wine" appears in the context, we might find in the background of v. 3 the image of fermenting grape juice, raging and foaming, and in the background of v. 4 the image of wine that gladdens the hearts of men.[8] For this interpretation, we need not only observe the word pair "sea" (*ym*) – "river" (*nhr*), common to Hebrew and Ugaritic, in vv. 3–4 but also discover the contrasting use of the "wine" imageries by noticing their attached verbal expressions—"raging and foaming" and "gladdening"—both of which are suitable for describing the activities of wine.[9]

Literary phenomena such as "war" and "storm" metaphors in the ancient Near East must also be clarified before we discuss whether there was any literary "influence" from, "dependence" on, or "allusion"[10] to the *Chaoskampf* myths, such as those from Ugarit, in the biblical poetic texts.

So, let us observe how war imagery and storm imagery are intertwined in literary expressions in ancient Near Eastern literature.

---

6. Derrida, the "founder" of postmodernism, emphasizes the "intertextual" associations among the elements of the text and the literary traditions in the society where it was produced, in connection with the postmodern claims for relativity, multivalency, and indeterminacy. See T. J. Keegan, "Biblical Criticism and the Challenge of Postmodernism," *BibInt* 3 (1995) 1–14, esp. 3; C. G. Bartholomew, "Babel and Derrida: Postmodernism, Language and Biblical Interpretation," *TynBul* 49 (1998), 305–28. "Intertextuality" should be distinguished from diachronic approaches that draw on typology and allusions. The former is fully synchronic, having no intention of discussing the text's author or origin. See B. D. Sommer, "Exegesis, Allusion and Intertextuality in the Hebrew Bible: A Response to Lyle Eslinger," *VT* 46 (1996) 479–89; D. T. Tsumura, "(Review of) Larry L. Lyke, *King David with the Wise Woman of Tekoa: The Resonance of Tradition in Parabolic Narrative* (JSOTSup 255). Sheffield: Sheffield Academic Press, 1997," *Themelios* 24/3 (1999), 48–49.

7. See above, ch. 9.

8. For a detailed study, see my "Twofold Image of Wine in Psalm 46:4–5," *JQR* 71 (1981), 167–75.

9. See above (ch. 9).

10. See above (ch. 8).

War and Storm Imageries

Often, "storm" and "battle" are closely associated, both referring to actual destructive power, as in the following expression: "fire, fire, the fire of the storm (*meḫû*), the fire of the battle (*qabli*) (came out from the depth of the forest)" (AfO 23 40:6, 41:19).[11]

War Described as Storm and Flood

Descriptions of war using storm or flood imagery often appear in Mesopotamian literatures.[12]

Storm Imagery

In the "Lamentation over the Destruction of Sumer and Ur," the enemy attack that resulted in the destruction of the city is depicted as a "storm."

> On that day, when that storm (Sumerian u_4) had pounded again and again, when in the presence of the lady her city was destroyed. . . .
>
> (lines 137–38)

The aftermath of the destructive "storm" was a desolate city surrounded by the bodies of the slain:

> Its men who were slain with the axe,
> (their) heads were not covered with a cloth. . . .
> Its men whom the spear had struck down
> were not bound with bandages. . . .
> Its men who were brought to end by the battle-mace,
> were not bandaged with new (?) cloth. . . .
> He who stood up to the weapon,
> was crushed by the weapon. (lines 219–25)[13]

Thus, the term "storm" is here used metaphorically to describe an attack by foreign enemies.[14]

---

11. *CAD* Q 13; also M/2 5.

12. P. C. Craigie observes the use of the language of storm and flood in the description of battle both in the Song of Deborah, Judg 5:20–21, and in the *Tukulti-Ninurta* epic V:41–43; see Craigie, "The Song of Deborah and the Epic of Tukulti-Ninurta," *JBL* 88 (1969), 262. However, neither "storm" nor "flood" is explicitly mentioned in Judg 5:20–21. Unfortunately, he did not develop this theme much further, except to repeat his view without any further examples in his article on Ps 29; see his "Psalm xxix in the Hebrew Poetic Tradition," *VT* 22 (1972), 148.

13. *CS*, 1.536–37.

14. J. Klein comments: "It is assumed that 'storm' is here a poetic-theological metaphor for the onslaught of the enemy and the destruction of the city" (*CS*, 1.536 n. 16).

Similar "storm" imagery appears in many Mesopotamian literatures, especially in the royal inscriptions. For example, an Old Babylonian inscription about the activity of Ibbi-Sin (ca. 2028–2004 B.C.), the fifth and last king of the Ur III dynasty, states:

> he roared like a storm against Susa.[15]

In the annals of Neo-Assyrian kings, the expression *kīma tīb meḫê* ("like the onset of a storm") appears in contexts describing the destruction of enemies. For example, the expression "like a raging *m.*-storm, I tore up their roots" (Borger Esarh. 58 v 16) appears in Esarhaddon's annal, while in Sennacherib's annal (V:59, 77), the expression "like the onset of a storm (*kīma tīb meḫê*) I swept" (OIP 2, 83:44; also 45:77) describes Sennacherib's quick march against Babylon.[16] The expression also appears in the annals of Ashurbanipal and Sargon.[17] A military march is described in a Ugaritic epic, the story of Keret, thus:

> They will go by thousands like storm-clouds,
> by myriads like rain. (KTU 1.14:II:39–40; IV:17–18)[18]

Flood Imagery

In the annals of the successive Assyrian kings of the late 2nd millennium B.C. onward, the destruction of enemies is described as the result of a "flood." For example, the annal of Sargon records his military destruction of the enemy town as follows:

> I made his towns look as though a flood had passed through them (*kima ša abūbu uabbitu qirbisa*) and heaped up the inhabited villages into ruins. (TCL 3, 31)[19]

The same destructive actions are expressed differently in an earlier Assyrian annal:

> The entire land of the Qutu [I made (look) like] *til abūbi* ruin hills (created by) the deluge (and) I surrounded their army with a circle of sand-storms. (Tukulti-Ninurta 1 ii 14–20)[20]

---

15. *CS*, 2.391.

16. *CS*, 2.305.

17. See *CAD* M/2 6.

18. See *CS*, 2.334, 336.

19. *CAD* K 218; also see A/1 43 for TCL 3, 17.

20. A. K. Grayson, *Assyrian Rulers of the Third and Second Millennia BC (to 1115 BC)* (Royal Inscriptions of Mesopotamia, Assyrian Periods 1; Toronto: University of Toronto Press, 1987), 234.

This expression, *kima til abūbi* ("like ruin hills of the Deluge"), was a well-known literary cliché in Akkadian from OB times,[21] as seen in the following examples:

- I overwhe[lmed] like ruin hills of the Deluge [the cities. . . .
                                    (Shalmaneser III, Kurkh monolith)[22]
- I destroyed 591 cities . . . ruin hills of the Deluge. (Tiglath-pileser III)[23]
- Ukku, together with all of its towns, I destroyed ruin hills of the Deluge.
                                    (Sennacherib, OIP 2, 77)[24]

Additionally, the metaphorical expression "like the Deluge" (*abūbāniš, abūbiš*)[25] often appears in the context of the military activities of the Assyrian kings:

- I devastated like a flood from the land of . . . to the land of. . . .
  (Annals of Shalmaneser III)[26]
- I raged like a lion; I stormed like the flood. (Annals of Sennacherib)[27]

The latter text describes Sennacherib's mighty attack against Merodach-baladan. Elsewhere, Sennacherib records his complete destruction of Babylon as follows:

I made its destruction more complete than that by a flood (*abūbu*).
                                                            (OIP 2, 84)

Thus, military attacks and the resultant destruction are described metaphorically as powerful storms and/or floods in the Mesopotamian literatures.
In the Bible, Nah 1:8,

But with an overflowing flood
he will completely destroy its place / his foes[28]
and will pursue his enemies into darkness,

---

21. See *CAD* A/1 78 for other examples.
22. Cf. *CS*, 2.262.
23. Cf. *CS*, 2.286. See also *CAD* A/1 43; OIP 2, 72:47.
24. Also in OIP 2, 86:17.
25. *CAD* A/1 77. Such similes are not limited to military contexts; they are also attested in Ugaritic literature to describe the strength of El's sexual power (lit., "hand"): "El's hand is strong" *k ym* "like a sea" // *k mdb* "like a flood" (KTU 1.23 [UT 52]:33–35), or the power of Baal's glorious mountain: *kmdb* "like a flood" in KTU 1.101:2.
26. *CS*, 2.265.
27. *CS*, 2.301 for OIP 2, 85:7. Also Nabonid nr. 8, col. II in VAB 4, 273, 275; ANET, 1950, 309.
28. See my "Janus Parallelism in Nah 1:8," *JBL* 102 (1983), 109–11. Here *mĕqômah* (MT) "its place" refers to Nineveh, while the similarly sounding phrase **bĕqāmâw* "in his foes" would be parallel with *'oyĕbâw* "his enemies" in the third line.

the Hebrew term *šeṭep* "a flood" is also used metaphorically for the mighty power by which Yahweh brings about the *kālâ* "complete destruction" of Nineveh.

Storm Described as War

On the other hand, in the flood stories from Mesopotamia, a literal flood and storm are described using war imagery. For example,

- [the flood's (*abūbu*'s)] might came upon the peoples [like an assault] [*kīma qabl*]*i eli nišī ibā' kašūšu.* (Atra-Ḥasis III iii 12; *AH*, U rev. 19; also see III viii 12)[29]
- How could I have . . . spoken up for an assault (*qabla*) to the death against my people?
  ana ḫulluq nišīja qabla aqbīma. (Gilgamesh XI 121)
- When the seventh day arrived, the windstorm (*meḫû*) and deluge (*abūbu*) left off their assault (*qabla*),
  Which they had launched, like a fight to the death (*kima ḫayālti*).
  The sea grew calm, the tempest grew still, the deluge (*abūbu*) ceased.
  (Gilgamesh XI 129–31)[30]

Thus, in many literary contexts neither storm imagery nor war imagery has anything to do with the *Chaoskampf* theme or the *creation* theme; they are simply metaphors describing an actual war or storm. References to the storms, floods, or seas in poetic texts of the Bible such as Ps 46[31] and Hab 3[32] also have no relationship with either the *creation* theme or the *Chaoskampf* theme. Rather, they refer to the destructive features of storm and war; hence, the motif in such biblical texts is destruction, not creation.

Destruction Motif

Devastation Caused by the Flood

It is important to distinguish between destructive actions, such as enemy attacks, and the state of destruction as the result of these actions. The images of sea and flood are sometimes used to describe the devastation caused by war, rather than the war itself. For example, in the Assyrian royal annals, Shalmaneser III refers to his action:

---

29. Lambert and Millard, *AH*, 94, 104, 124. See *CS*, 1.452; *CAD* Q 13.
30. *CS*, 1.459.
31. See ch. 9 (above).
32. See ch. 10 (above).

Like Adad, I rained down upon them a devastating flood (*riḫiṣtu*).

(Kurkh monolith)[33]

Sennacherib also claimed to have destroyed Babylon by making "its devastation greater than that of 'the Flood.'" Here, Sennacherib compares the devastation to Babylon caused by his attack with that brought by the great destructive Deluge. He thus "completely destroyed (Babylon) with water and annihilated it like inundated territory."[34]

In biblical poetic texts, expressions such as *šeṭep mayim rabbîm* "flood of mighty waters"[35] (Ps 32:6) are used to describe the psalmist's calamity:

> Therefore let everyone who is godly pray to you in a time when you may
> be found; surely in a flood of mighty waters they shall not reach him.

The image of a raging flood or sea is also a metaphor for destructive power in many poetic texts.[36]

The Deluge as God's Agent for Destruction

In Mesopotamian literature, the "Deluge" (*abūbu*) was often personified as Deluge, "the ultimate of wrath, aggressiveness, and destructiveness."[37] Hence we find references to the Deluge-weapon, a divine agent for destruction. For example, this is reflected in the phrase,

> destructive weapon of the gods, Deluge in battle (*kašūš* DINGIR.MEŠ
> *abūb tamḫāri*). (Tukulti-Ninurta I, 24 9)[38]

The warrior-god Ninurta is said to have held "the serpent which attacks man, the bow of my *abūbu* weapon" (Angim III 35).[39] Also, in a hymn to Marduk, the expression [*mi*]*ṭṭukka abū*[*bu*] (KAR 337:14)[40] "your mace, *abūbu* weapon" appears. Another warrior-god, Assur, is described as "raising his

---

33. See *CAD* R 334–35; *CS*, 2.262; see also S. Yamada, *The Construction of the Assyrian Empire: A Historical Study of the Inscriptions of Shalmaneser III (859–824 BC) relating to His Campaigns to the West* (Culture and History of the Ancient Near East 3; Leiden: Brill, 2000), 162, 372–79.

34. *CS*, 2.305.

35. *HALOT*, 1475 translates this phrase as "a great flood of water."

36. See below.

37. *CAD* A/1 78. See on Hab 3:9 in ch. 10 (above).

38. Grayson, *Assyrian Rulers of the Third and Second Millennia BC*, 275. See also my "'Word Pair' *qst* and *mṭ* in Habakkuk 3:9 in the Light of Ugaritic and Akkadian," in *Go to the Land I Will Show You: Studies in Honor of Dwight W. Young* (ed. J. E. Coleson and V. H. Matthews; Winona Lake, Ind.: Eisenbrauns, 1996), 357–65.

39. Cf. *CAD* A/1 79; Q 147.

40. Cited in *CAD* M/2 148.

bow, riding in his chariot and girt with the Deluge (*abūbu* [*ṣ*]*andu*)," as described in the text of the Annals of Sennacherib.[41]

Hebrew *mabbūl* "Deluge" also signifies the mighty power by which Yahweh brought about the total destruction of this world. In Genesis, the Deluge (Gen 6–7) brought about the destruction of almost all earth-dwelling creatures. It was thus God's instrument to fulfill his holy decree against human *ḥāmās* "injustice" (6:11). The Deluge (Heb. *mabbūl*; Akk. *abūbu*) was clearly distinguished from the annual flooding "high waters" (cf. Heb. *'ēd*; Akk. *milu*).[42] The expression "all the springs of the great deep burst forth, and the floodgates of the heavens were opened" (Gen 7:11b) in the biblical Flood story describes well the devastation caused by Yahweh; it has nothing to do with the return of the earth to precreation chaos. As P. J. Harland concludes, "there is no allusion to the myth [i.e., *Enuma elish*] in the story of the flood where *thwm* (7:11) means 'deep.' "[43]

We might compare Yahweh, "who sat *before* the Deluge (*lammabbūl yā-šāb*)," in Ps 29:10 with Ninurta, "who rides upon the Deluge" (*rākib abūbi*) in 1R 29 i 10 (Šamši-Adad V).[44] However, Yahweh's sitting here denotes his enthronement as a king (hence "sits enthroned"), while Ninurta's riding "upon the Deluge" signifies his attack against his enemy using this mighty *Deluge*-weapon. The Hebrew expression *lammabbūl* seems to have an idiomatic meaning, as discussed above.[45]

The Sea as God's Enemy to Be Destroyed

In Sumerian, the most frequent attributes of the sea are "fright" and "terror." For example,

- Nergal, terrifying sea (aba-ḫu-luḫ), invested with awesome terror, no one knows how to confront him.[46]
- (the god) is terrifying like a flood-wave, furious like the wind, furious like the sea. (TCL 16, 77:4–7)[47]

These expressions describe the awesomeness and terribleness of gods.

At the same time, the sea deity is the enemy of the storm-gods, such as Baal, Marduk, and Adad. In the *Chaoskampf* myths, it is the sea deity and

41. OIP 2 140:7; cf. *CAD* A/1 80; Q 150.
42. See ch. 5 (above).
43. P. J. Harland, *The Value of Human Life: A Study of the Story of the Flood (Genesis 6–9)* (VTSup 64; Leiden: Brill, 1996), 96.
44. Cited by *CAD* A/1 80; *AHw*, 8.
45. See ch. 8, pp. 152–155.
46. Sjöberg, ZA 63, 2 no. 1:14.
47. See *SD* A/2 135.

his/her associates who are destined to be destroyed. In the same manner, the "sea" is used to represent the object of Yahweh's destruction in the Bible. For example, the "sea" and the "mighty waters" of vv. 8 and 15 in Hab 3 stand for Yahweh's enemies, who are destined to be destroyed. In other words, Yahweh is described as a king[48] fighting with enemies symbolized by destructive waters such as the "sea" and "mighty waters" (Hab 3:15), which are often *personified* and symbolized as Rahab (Ps 89:10, Isa 51:9), Leviathan (Ps 74:14, Isa 27:1), or dragons (Ps 74:13), and so on. These enemies of God are treated as those who are to be destroyed by the God Yahweh. Because no cosmic dualism is allowed in biblical theology, Yahweh's enemies have no chance of victory over him.

Many scholars, following H. Gunkel, have combined the *Chaoskampf* theme and the *creation* theme and have seen this compound theme in many ancient Near Eastern myths as well as in Gen 1:2.[49] Hence, they have identified the enemies with the uncreated "chaos" water, the enemy of the creator in primordial time, such as Tiamat in the Babylonian "creation" story of *Enuma elish*. But such a combination of these two themes appears only in *Enuma elish* out of all the ancient Near Eastern literature discovered thus far. The Ugaritic Baal myth is a *Chaoskampf* myth, but there is no creation involved. On the other hand, Gen 1 gives no hint of battle in its description of the creation of the universe.

The images of "destructive" waters in the biblical poetic passages should be explained as the *conflict without creation* type, in which enemies are destined to be destroyed by Yahweh, the God of history, who is "enthroned in the heavens" (Pss 2:4, 29:10, etc.), whether they refer to the historical enemies of Israel (e.g., Exod 15:6, 9) or to spiritual ones (e.g., Isa 27). Often it is difficult to distinguish whether the enemies are historical or spiritual.

---

48. In a survey of the topic of the kingship of Yahweh, J. C. L. Gibson ("The Kingship of Yahweh against Its Canaanite Background," in *Ugarit and the Bible: Proceedings of the International Symposium on Ugarit and the Bible, Manchester, September 1992* [ed. G. J. Brooke, A. H. W. Curtis, and J. F. Healey; Münster: Ugarit-Verlag, 1994], 101–12) says that Yahweh's royal image in Hab 3 comes from the language of the storm-god Baal, while I argue that it comes "from the metaphorization of a normal usage of military activities of a human king in the Ancient Near East" ("Ugaritic Poetry and Habakkuk 3," *TynBul* 40 [1989], 33; also ch. 10 [above]).

49. As noted above (ch. 8), see, for example, J. Day, *God's Conflict with the Dragon and the Sea: Echoes of a Canaanite Myth in the Old Testament* (Cambridge: Cambridge University Press, 1985).

Personification and Metaphor

As seen above, in the Mesopotamian traditions not only was the sea personified and deified, as the goddess *Tiamat*, but the deluge (*abūbu*) was also personified as the gods' weapon "Deluge." In the biblical traditions, though the deluge (*mabbûl*) is never personified, destructive waters such as those of the sea are sometimes personified as God's enemies, as in the cases of Rahab (Ps 89:10; Isa 51:9; Job 9:13, 26:12) and Leviathan (Ps 74:14, Isa 27:1).

Rahab [50]

For example, Ps 89:9–10 reads:

9. You rule the raging of the sea;
   when its waves rise, you still them.
10. You crushed Rahab like a carcass;
    you scattered your enemies with your mighty arm.

(NRSV)

Here the two verses constitute two, two-line parallelisms that express God's mighty rule over his enemies, symbolized by the sea and Rahab. The expression "the raging of the sea" (*gē'ût hayyām*) in the first line of v. 9 is balanced by "when its waves rise" (*běśô' gallâw*) in the second line. In v. 10, it is clear from the parallelistic structure that Yahweh's "enemies" are personified as Rahab. [51]

The expression "you crushed Rahab" (*dk' + *Rāhab*) is restated as "you scattered your enemies" (*pzr + *'ôyěbêkā*) in the second line of parallelism. Similar parallel expressions, "to cut Rahab in pieces (*ḥṣb + *rahab*)" // "to pierce the dragon (*ḥll + *tannîn*)," and "to still the Sea (*rg' + *hayyām*)" // "to strike down Rahab (*mḥṣ + *rāhab*)" also appear in Isa 51:9 and in Job 26:12, respectively. These destructive actions of Yahweh are understood as having happened in the ancient times, as the former text says,

Awake, awake, put on strength,
   O arm of the LORD!
Awake, as in days of old,
   the generations of long ago!
Was it not you who cut Rahab in pieces (*ḥṣb + *rahab*),
   who pierced the dragon (*ḥll + *tannîn*)?

(Isa 51:9, NRSV)

---

50. See *HALOT*, 1193; K. Spronk, "Rahab," in *DDD*, 1292–95.
51. Rahab even became a proper geographical name, like Babylon and others, in Ps 87:4.

These biblical texts may refer to a mythological scene where a dragon was destroyed, similar to the Ugaritic mythological texts KTU 1.3 III 37–IV 3 and 1.5 I 1–3, which mention Baal's defeat of his enemy Yam and his associates, such as the dragon *Tnn* and the serpent *Ltn*.[52] These events, like those in Isa 51:9, are taken as having already happened in very ancient time even from the perspective of Late Bronze Age Ugarit, but, as noted above (ch. 8), they have nothing to do with cosmic origins.

Similarly, in these biblical passages there is no allusion to the "creation" of the heaven and the earth as in the case of *Enuma elish*. The name Rahab (*Rāhab*), still unattested in any extrabiblical text,[53] is another indication of the diversity of the dragon myths in Canaan. The biblical authors of the Iron Age could use these already-antiquated expressions to describe metaphorically Yahweh's destructive actions toward his enemies. Furthermore, these metaphorical expressions seem to have already become idiomatic or nearly idiomatic when the authors used them, as the following text seems to suggest:

> For Egypt's help is worthless and empty,
> therefore I have called her,
> > "Rahab who sits still (*rahab hēm šābet*)." (Isa 30:7, NRSV)

Leviathan

As with the case of Rahab, the term "Leviathan"[54] is simply a personification in texts such as Job 3:8,

> Let those curse it who curse the Sea,
> those who are skilled to rouse up Leviathan (NRSV),

and the word pair "Sea" – "Leviathan" had become almost a literary cliché in the Hebrew language.

Expressions similar to "to crush Rahab" // "to scatter the enemies" are used also for the destruction of Leviathan, the personification of the sea dragon. However, the expression "crushed the heads of Leviathan" (**rṣṣ + ra'sê liwyātān*) in Ps 74:14 is slightly distinct from those used for Rahab, "to cut Rahab in pieces (**ḥṣb*)" // "to pierce (**ḥll*) the dragon," and "to still (**rgʿ*)

---

52. Interestingly enough, in no known Ugaritic myth does the name "Rahab" appear, though the sea dragon Yam and its associates are indirectly referred to in Job 9:13 which reads:

> God will not turn back his anger;
> the helpers of Rahab (*ʿozĕrê rāhab*) bowed beneath him. (NRSV)

53. The phrase *brḥbn* (KTU 9.432:18) has nothing to do with "Rahab" (*rahab*), because the consonant involved is /ḥ/, not /h/.

54. See C. Uehlinger, "Leviathan," in *DDD*, 956–64.

the Sea" // "to strike (*mḫṣ) down Rahab," as cited above. Only with the cases of Leviathan are the "heads" (pl.) mentioned.

For example, Ps 74:13–14 reads:

13. You made the sea flee[55] (*prr + *yām*) by your might;
    you smashed the heads of the dragons (*šbr + *rāʾšê tannînîm*)
    in the waters.
14. You crushed the heads of Leviathan (*rṣṣ + *rāʾšê liwyātān*);
    you gave him as food for the creatures of the wilderness.

In this context, Yahweh's saving act (see v. 12: "salvations" *yĕšûʿ ôt*) of destroying his enemies, the sea and its associates, is described with highly metaphorical expressions. While the sea is forced to flee, the sea dragons and their representative, Leviathan, are smashed/crushed (*šbr/*rṣṣ*) on their heads. Greenfield takes the fleeing and being smashed as contrastive: thus, "The Sea is subdued and forced to flee, but his henchmen Tannin and Liwyatan are destroyed."[56] However, both expressions are probably metaphors for the same action, that is, the calming down of "the roaring of the sea" (*šĕʾ ôn yammîm*, as in Ps 65:8), for the withdrawal of the sea is brought about as a result of the destruction of the sea dragon's heads, that is, the cessation of surges.

The heads of the dragons/Leviathan are to be compared with the seven-headed serpent/dragon[57] in ancient Near Eastern mythology, such as in Ugaritic myths. KTU 1.5:I:1–3 reads:

K tmḫṣ . ltn . bṯn . brḥ
tkly . bṯn . ʿqltn .
šlyṭ . d . šbʿt . rašm

When you smite Lôtan,[58] the fleeing serpent,
finish off the twisting serpent,
the close-coiling one with seven heads.

(D. Pardee in CS, 1.265)

---

55. Following J. C. Greenfield, "*ʾattā pōrartā bĕ ʿozkā yam* (Psalm 74:13a)," in *Language, Theology, and the Bible: Essays in Honour of James Barr* (ed. S. E. Balentine and J. Barton; Oxford: Clarendon, 1994), 113–19.

56. Ibid., 118.

57. See E. Unger, "Drachen und Drachenkampf," *RlA* 2.231–35; D. Collon, *First Impressions: Cylinder Seals in the Ancient Near East* (London: British Museum, 1987), 179 (no. 839–40); also M. Dietrich and O. Loretz, "Baal, Leviathan und der siebenköpfige Drache *Šlyṭ* in der Rede des Todesgottes Môt (KTU 1.5 I 1–8 // 27a–31)," *AuOr* 17–18 (1999–2000), 75.

58. Ugaritic *ltn* corresponds to Hebrew *liwyātān* "Leviathan"; see J. A. Emerton, "Leviathan and *ltn*: The Vocalization of the Ugaritic Word for the Dragon," *VT* 32 (1982), 327–31; *HALOT*, 524. See most recently Dietrich and Loretz, "Baal, Leviathan und der siebenköpfige Drache *Šlyṭ*," 59.

Another text, Isa 27:1, is in the same literary tradition, though the author uses
the metaphor in an eschatological context:

> On that day the LORD with his cruel and great and strong sword will
> punish Leviathan the fleeing serpent, Leviathan the twisting serpent, and
> he will kill the dragon that is in the sea. (Isa 27:1, NRSV)

Such stories of fights with dragons were well known from the prehistoric era
both in Mesopotamia and in Syria–Palestine.

While the extrabiblical evidence for such dragon stories is still unavailable
in southern Canaan due to the perishable nature of the writing materials (e.g.,
papyrus), northern Syria and Anatolia provide evidence of them. The evidence that the Canaanite *Chaoskampf* traditions were known in Anatolia is
available from two mythological fragments that may belong to the Baal cycle.
One text, KUB 33, 108, even alludes to the victory of the storm-god over the
Sea.[59] These are certainly indications that the *Chaoskampf* traditions were
widespread *before* the Late Bronze Age in eastern Mediterranean lands, because myths were presumably well known orally before they were written
down—that is, during the prehistoric era.

Therefore, it is reasonable to assume that many people knew about the
Chaoskampf myths and understood what the expressions "to smash the heads
of the dragons" and "to crush the heads of Leviathan" meant and to what they
referred, even if they knew only fragments of myths or had different versions.[60] Just as the Ugaritic Baal cycle had nothing to do with the *creation*
theme,[61] the psalmist had no intention of bringing this theme into his poem.
The idea here is Yahweh's complete destruction of his enemies, both historical and spiritual, symbolized by the "sea" and the "waters." By such destructive action against his enemies, Yahweh accomplished his salvation; passages
such as Ps 74:13–14 have nothing to do with the creation motif, despite
J. Day's assumption.[62] It is a totally distinct motif from *Enuma elish*, in
which the dead corpse of Tiamat is divided by Marduk to "create" the heaven
and the earth.

---

59. See Beckman, "Mythologie, A. II: Bei den Hethitern," *RlA* 8.569.
60. The biblical authors used these expressions as metaphor rather than as polemic, as
J. Day and others advocate; see Day, *God's Conflict with the Dragon and the Sea*, 27–28.
61. See above (ch. 8).
62. J. Day, *God's Conflict with the Dragon and the Sea*, 39; idem, "Ugarit and the
Bible: Do They Presuppose the Same Canaanite Mythology and Religion?" in *Ugarit and
the Bible: Proceedings of the International Symposium on Ugarit and the Bible, Manchester, September 1992* (ed. G. J. Brooke, A. H. W. Curtis, and J. F. Healey; Münster: Ugarit-
Verlag, 1994), 43.

In Ps 104:26 and Job 41:1, the term "Leviathan" is simply a poetic metaphor for huge sea creatures.

There go the ships,
and Leviathan that you formed to sport in it.
(Ps 104:26, NRSV)

Can you draw out Leviathan with a fishhook,
or press down its tongue with a cord?
(Job 41:1[40:25], NRSV)

The fact is that the ancient Israelites were well aware that they were dealing with metaphors. As noted by D. Pardee, the Ugaritians also clearly distinguished between a window of Baal's palace and a rift in the clouds and yet used the former term metaphorically for the latter in KTU 1.4 vii 25–37.[63]

Thus, storm, flood, or sea imagery is used in various ways in the ancient Near Eastern literature, including the Old Testament. It can be used metaphorically to describe a devastating force, as that of a human army or a divine being. The "Deluge" appears in Akkadian as one of the weapons in the divine arsenal. In the Bible, the deluge is described only in natural terms as rain and water, but it is clearly Yahweh's weapon.

Sea waters also appear as the enemy of a god, usually the storm-god, in the *Chaoskampf* myths of the ancient Near East. In the Bible, there are references to fights with monsters such as Rahab and the sea dragon Leviathan, but they are used as metaphors. Most of these contexts could be paraphrased "just as you crushed your enemies of old, crush them now," similar to contexts that refer to historical events. There is no connection, though, between these sea-storm images and the creation motif, either in the ancient Near Eastern literatures (except *Enuma elish*) or in the Bible.

---

63. See Pardee in *CS*, 1.262 n. 184. See also ch. 9 (above).

Conclusions

The original purpose of this monograph was to examine the validity of Gunkel's thesis that the biblical creation stories, especially Gen 1, were greatly influenced by the Babylonian "creation" story, *Enuma elish*, and that the term *tĕhôm* in Gen 1:2 was simply borrowed from the Akkadian divine name Tiamat, the goddess of the sea, and subsequently was transformed into the setting of the Hebrew creation story.

An overview of the current research clarified some of the long-standing misunderstandings and confusions by appealing to a linguistic investigation of several key terms, such as *tōhû wābōhû*, *tĕhôm*, *'ēd*, and *'ēden*; and appealing to a literary approach to some poetic texts of the Bible.

The major conclusions are summarized here:

1. The phrase *tōhû wābōhû* has nothing to do with the idea of a chaotic state of the earth. It simply refers to a desolate and empty earth. Genesis 1:2 provides the SETTING information before the actual creation ACTION is narrated.

2. The term *tĕhôm* in Gen 1:2 is a Hebrew form derived from the Proto-Semitic *tihām- "ocean," and it usually refers to the underground water, which, however, was overflowing and covering the entire surface of the earth in the initial state of creation. It has nothing directly to do with the Akkadian goddess Tiamat.

3. The earth-water relationship in Gen 2:5–6 is different from that in Gen 1:2. In Gen 1:2, the earth was totally under the water; in Gen 2:5–6, only a part of the earth, namely the land (*'ădāmâ*), was watered by the *'ēd*-water, which was overflowing from an underground source. The Garden of Eden was made in this well-watered part of the earth, as the etymology of *'ēden* suggests. Hence, there is no contradiction in cosmology between the two chapters of the Genesis creation story. The situation in Gen 2:5–6 simply reflects a stage later than that in Gen 1:2.

4. The biblical poetic texts that are claimed to have been influenced by the *Chaoskampf*-motif of the ancient Near East (e.g., Pss 18, 29, 46; Hab 3) in fact use the language of storms and floods metaphorically and have nothing to do with primordial combat. Some of these poetic texts have the theme of destruction rather than of creation. Each biblical text

should be carefully interpreted in its own context before it is compared with other Near Eastern literatures. Gunkel and those who have relied on his work have often neglected to distinguish various types of "creation" myths. In particular, we need to distinguish between myths having a divine combat motif without creation, such as the Baal myth, and myths having a creation motif without combat. Among the latter, the Genesis stories are unique in that no goddess is involved in producing the earth and humankind.

Indexes

Index of Authors

Aartun, K.   121, 123
Abou-Assaf, A.   112, 116–117
Aistleitner, J.   11
Albright, W. F.   10–14, 44–45, 52, 89–
   93, 95–96, 98, 101–102, 117, 125–
   126, 147–148, 153, 164, 175, 180
Alster, B.   36, 39, 47–48, 53
Andersen, F. I.   33, 77, 80, 96, 105, 147
Anderson, B. W.   2–3, 34, 36, 49, 162
Apollodorus   166
Aquila   9, 85, 102, 111
Archi, A.   113
Astour, M. C.   82, 126
Attinger, P.   134
Auffret, P.   66–67
Avishur, Y.   60–62, 64

Baldacci, M.   126
Barr, J.   86–88, 98, 100–101, 103, 105,
   108–109
Barth, K.   2
Bartholomew, C. G.   183
Bauer, H.   138
Bauer, J. B.   162
Baumgartner, W.   88, 90–91
Beckman, G.   55, 182, 194
Beeston, A. F. L.   123
Berlin, A.   59, 159
Biella, J. C.   123
Bodine, W. R.   77
Böllenrücher, J.   70
Bordreuil, P.   112, 116–117
Borger, R.   67, 94, 100, 132, 138, 185
Bottéro, J.   40, 67, 71–72, 94
Briggs, C. A.   87, 162
Bright, J.   28, 31
Brockington, L. H.   169

Brown, W. P.   74, 87
Buhl   89
Butz, K.   114–115

Caquot, A.   10, 118, 120–121
Carroll, R. P.   28, 31
Cassuto, U.   10, 12–14, 79, 86, 89, 91,
   102, 115–116, 124–125, 147, 164,
   167, 169, 174–175
Castellino, G.   79–81, 90, 102–103,
   108, 115
Ceresko, A. R.   62, 157
Charpin, D.   88
Childs, B. S.   2–3, 28, 36
Civil, M.   103
Clifford, R. J.   11, 137
Clines, D. J. A.   59
Collini, P.   128
Collon, D.   54, 128, 136, 193
Cooper, A.   12, 41, 166
Cotterell, P.   33
Craigie, P. C.   146–153, 155, 157, 184
Cross, F. M.   12, 152–153

Dahood, M. J.   47, 62–63, 66–68, 70,
   87–88, 121, 149, 151, 159, 165,
   170–171, 173
Davidson, A. B.   168
Dawson, D. A.   33
Day, J.   37, 41–42, 53–54, 56, 129, 139,
   144, 147–148, 152, 156, 166–169,
   174, 179–181, 190, 194
Deimel, P. A.   97
Delitzsch, F.   89, 125–126, 162
Derrida, J.   183
Dhorme, E.   27
Dhorme, P.   89

199

Diakonoff, I. M.   127
Dietrich, M.   11, 17, 96, 121, 144, 193
Dijk, J. van   109–110, 137, 171
Dijkstra, M.   26, 175
Dillmann, A.   89
Driver, G. R.   11, 96, 116, 118, 120–121, 160
Driver, S. R.   3, 27, 78, 87
Durand, J.-M.   39
Dussaud, R.   10, 121

Eaton, J. H.   164–165, 170, 174, 178
Ebach, J.   14
Ebeling, E.   14
Edzard, D. O.   44–46, 48, 125–126, 154
Ellenbogen, M.   86, 90, 111
Emerton, J. A.   193
Endo, Y.   33
Erman, A.   86, 120, 130

Falkenstein, A.   114
Farber, G.   125
Fishbane, M.   28–29, 31
Fisher, L. R.   145
Fleming, D. E.   144
Fohrer, G.   90
Freedman, D. N.   175, 178
Fretheim, T. E.   2–3
Fronzaroli, P.   47, 52
Fulco, W. J.   179–180

Gardiner, A.   49
Garr, W. R.   53
Gaster, T. H.   11, 120, 152
Gelb, I. J.   43, 103, 114
Gesenius, F. H. W.   89, 170
Gibson, A.   148, 168, 181–182
Gibson, J. C. L.   4, 10, 33, 42, 55, 57, 116, 118, 170–171, 190
Ginsberg, H. L.   10, 121, 152
Görg, M.   14–15, 86, 146
Gordis, R.   27
Gordon, C. H.   10, 17, 45, 55, 60, 86, 116, 118, 120–122, 131–132, 135, 153–154, 159, 162–163, 166, 170–171, 177

Grapow, H.   86, 120, 130
Gray, G. B.   27, 157
Gray, J.   11, 121
Grayson, A. K.   185, 188
Green, A. R. W.   144
Greenfield, J. C.   112, 117–118, 121–123, 193
Greenstein, E. L.   10–11
Grønbæk, J. H.   41
Groneberg, B.   96, 127
Grossberg, D.   172
Gunkel, H.   2–3, 36, 89, 109, 144, 147, 156, 160, 182, 190, 196–197
Gunton, C. E.   9

Hallo, W. W.   71, 81, 115, 124
Harland, P. J.   56, 143, 163, 189
Hartley, J. E.   27
Hasel, G. F.   86, 104
Hasel, M. G.   86, 104
Hayes, J. H.   162
Hecker, K.   17
Heidel, A.   37, 40, 43, 71–73, 101, 110
Heimpel, W.   40, 126, 136, 151, 182
Held, M.   74
Hengstenberg, E. W.   157–159, 162
Herdner, A.   10, 120
Herrmann, W.   121, 144
Hess, R. S.   44, 80–81, 83, 93
Hiebert, T.   147–148
Hillers, D. R.   66–67
Hirsch, H.   46, 94
Hoffmeier, J. K.   130
Hoffner, H. A.   55–56, 137
Hoftijzer, J.   96, 116
Holladay, W. L.   29–31
Hommel, F.   124
Horst, P. W. van der   13
Huddlestun, J. R.   1
Huehnergard, J.   12, 17–18, 21–22, 42–44, 82, 95
Hutter, M.   60

Irwin, W. A.   147
Irwin, W. H.   24
Israel, F.   125

Jacobsen, T.   38–39, 41–42, 47, 51–52, 71, 115–116, 132–136
Jamme, A.   124
Jeremias, J.   152
Jirku, A.   11
Jöcken, P.   147
Johnstone, W.   11
Junker, H.   162

Kaiser, O.   32, 35, 37, 49, 89–90, 137
Kapelrud, A. S.   137
Kashkai, S. M.   127
Kaufman, S. A.   37, 95–96, 114, 117
Keegan, T. J.   183
Keller, C.-A.   173
Kidner, D.   78, 109, 111
Kienast, B.   17
Kikawada, I. M.   34
King, L. W.   71–73, 93
Kirkpatrick, A. F.   162
Kitchen, K. A.   120, 146
Klein, J.   184
Kloos, C.   41, 129, 138, 145, 152
Knudtzon, J. A.   44
Korpel, M. C. A.   41–42, 56, 119, 151
Kramer, S. N.   51–52, 112, 125, 129–134, 136
Kraus, H.-J.   63, 68, 162
Krebernik, M.   17, 43, 47, 52, 103, 114–115
Krecher, J.   43, 47
Krinetzki, P. L.   163
Kselman, J. S.   29, 62, 69
Kupper, J.-R.   46

Labat, R.   60, 74, 101
Labuschagne, C. J.   140
Lambdin, T. O.   126
Lambert, W. G.   15, 17–19, 21–22, 31, 38–42, 46, 49–52, 54, 59, 67, 70, 74, 79, 82–83, 93–94, 103, 114, 117, 122, 126–128, 130, 132, 134, 139–140, 161, 166, 187
Landsberger, B.   74, 99, 113, 136
Lane, E. W.   10, 13, 124
Laroche, E.   15–16

Layard, A. H.   172
Leander, P.   89, 104, 138
Lemaire, A.   112–113, 125
Lieberman, S. J.   104, 114
Lindenberger, J. M.   173
Lipiński, E.   114, 120–121
Livingstone, A.   12, 50, 60, 67, 133–136, 138
Longacre, R. E.   29, 77, 109
Loretz, O.   11, 96, 121, 144, 152–154, 193
Lugt, P. van der   52, 61
Luyster, R.   139
Lyons, J.   59

Malamat, A.   44, 46, 48, 153, 155
Mallowan, M. E. L.   172
Margalit, B.   11, 119, 122–123
Marti, K.   169
Mathias, D.   57
Matsumoto, T.   177
Mayer, W.   17
McCarter, P. K.   52, 90, 93
McCarthy, D. J.   156
McKane, W.   28–29, 31
Meyer, E.   88
Meyer, J.-W.   19
Michel, D.   161
Miles, J. C.   160
Millard, A. R.   14, 18–19, 31, 46, 50–51, 59, 67, 70–71, 82–83, 104, 110, 112–113, 115–118, 127, 132, 161, 166, 187
Miller, P. D.   56, 71–72, 90, 134, 140
Mitchell, T. C.   40
Moberly, R. W. L.   57
Monte, G. F. del   127
Moor, J. C. de   11, 16, 18, 41–42, 52, 55–56, 61, 110, 116, 118–121, 126, 131–132, 134, 137–138, 140, 175
Moran, W. L.   44, 72–74, 158
Mowinckel, S.   156
Muchiki, Y.   120
Mullen, E. T.   137

Neu, E.   114

Neve, L.   156, 162
Nougayrol, J.   15–16, 18, 43
Nowack, W.   169

O'Connor, M.   49
Oden, R. A.   14
Olmo Lete, G. del   11–12, 119, 121, 124
Oshima, T.   134
Otten, H.   56
Otzen, B.   2–3, 34, 37

Pardee, D.   12, 59, 150, 166, 170, 193, 195
Parker, S. B.   82
Parpola, S.   103
Perry, T. A.   35
Pettinato, G.   47, 88, 120
Philo of Alexandria   14
Plato   9
Podella, T.   2, 145
Poebel, A.   103–104
Pope, M. H.   25, 27, 52, 62, 96, 116, 120–122, 136
Postgate, J. N.   103

Quinn, A.   34

Rad, G. von   3, 74–75, 90
Rainey, A. F.   43, 121
Rendsburg, G. A.   48, 57
Reymond, P.   90
Roberts, J. J. M.   25, 43, 94, 128, 132
Rogers, R. W.   71
Rybolt, J. E.   57
Ryckmans, G.   124

Sachsse, E.   89, 97
Sæbø, M.   90–93, 96–98, 103, 107
Saggs, H. W. F.   145, 156
Sailhammer, J.   69
Sanmartín, J.   11, 96, 121
Sasson, J. M.   146
Schmidt, W. H.   3, 35, 37, 43, 49, 77–78, 80, 90
Schott, A.   101

Scullion, J. J.   62
Segert, S.   17
Shea, W. H.   88
Shimasaki, K.   163
Sjöberg, Å. W.   38, 81, 189
Skinner, J.   49
Smith, G. A.   168
Smith, M. S.   41–42, 55, 118, 120, 122, 135–136, 144–145
Soden, W. von   90, 101, 117
Sollberger, E.   43, 46, 125
Sommer, B. D.   183
Sommerfeld, W.   134
Speiser, E. A.   89–92, 95–98, 101–102, 112
Spronk, K.   191
Stadelmann, L. I. J.   63, 66
Stieglitz, R. R.   138
Stolz, F.   1, 130, 133
Symmachus   10, 26
Sznycer, M.   10, 118, 120

Taber, C. R.   58
Tallqvist, K.   121, 128, 132–134
Theodotion   10
Thompson, R. C.   101
Thomsen, M.-L.   115
Thureau-Dangin, F.   20, 138
Tigay, J. H.   120–122
Tischler, J.   127
Tsumura, D. T.   1, 4–5, 24, 26, 29, 31, 37, 43, 55, 61, 80, 83, 89, 119, 130, 138, 149–150, 154–156, 159, 161–163, 168, 172, 177, 183, 186
Turner, M.   33
Tur-Sinai, N. H.   25, 27, 33

Uehlinger, C.   192
Unger, E.   193

Vanstiphout, H. L. J.   51, 60, 72–73
Vincent, J. M.   64
Vriezen, T. C.   75–76
Vuilleumier, R.   173

Wagner, A.   155

Wakeman, M. K.   36–37, 62–63, 147–148, 175
Wallace, H. N.   113, 115, 137
Waltke, B. K.   13, 49
Watson, W. G. E.   15, 62–63, 159, 166, 182
Weiden, W. A. van der   62
Weinfeld, M.   122, 167, 180
Weiser, A.   156, 161–163
Weiss, M.   157
Wenham, G. J.   3, 13, 34, 69, 78–81, 90–91, 109
Westenholz, A.   40
Westermann, C.   15, 22–26, 35, 37, 40, 78, 90–91, 112–113, 116
Wevers, J. W.   10
Wiggerman, F.   1

Wilcke, C.   74
Wildberger, H.   28, 30, 32
Williams-Forte, E.   54
Wilson, J. A.   74
Wilson, J. V. K.   38, 74, 136, 158
Winckler, H.   99
Wolde, E. van   75
Wright, G. E.   149
Wyatt, N.   136

Xella, P.   126

Young, E. J.   23, 26, 32, 34, 81, 90, 110

Zimmerli, W.   3
Zimmern, H.   36–37, 47, 89, 102
Zurro, E.   47

Index of Scripture

Genesis

1   3–4, 28–29, 34, 36,
    38, 42, 56, 72–74,
    83, 107, 128, 143,
    190, 196
1:1   1, 34, 49, 69–70,
    74–75, 77, 81, 140
1:1–2   69
1:1–3   33
1:1–2:3   34
1:1–2:4   28, 30, 69
1:2   1–4, 9, 12–13, 15–
    16, 18, 22, 26–30,
    32–36, 38–39, 41–
    42, 49–50, 53–54,
    56–58, 64, 69–70,
    72, 74–77, 81, 83–
    85, 107, 111, 127–
    130, 138–139, 143,
    167, 182, 190, 196
1:3   3, 29, 33, 35, 75–
    77
1:3–5   29
1:4–5   49
1:6   49, 70, 131, 138–
    139
1:6–7   112
1:7–8   49
1:8   48, 138
1:9   71, 74
1:9–10   1, 74
1:10   50, 56, 70, 75,
    158
1:11   34, 82
1:14   29
1:24   34
1:26   34, 50, 64
1:29   79
1:30   79
2   3, 82–83, 86, 90–91,
    104–105, 107–109,
    116, 128–129

Genesis (cont.)

2:4   49, 77, 81, 129
2:4–3:24   85
2:4–4:26   77
2:5   3–4, 71, 75, 77–
    82, 110, 129
2:5–6   4, 34, 77–78,
    80–85, 96, 105, 108,
    111–112, 127–128,
    196
2:6   3–4, 50, 80–81,
    85–88, 90–91, 93,
    96–97, 105–108,
    111, 127–128
2:6–7   74
2:7   76–77, 80–81
2:7–8   109
2:8   81, 109, 112, 116,
    125, 127
2:8–9   129
2:10   91, 93, 102, 105–
    108, 111, 127, 129,
    162
2:10–14   129, 136
2:15   83
3:18   78–79
4:17   72
4:18   115
6–7   189
6–8   105
6–11   154
6:11   189
7:11   48, 61, 112, 123,
    127, 138–139, 143,
    189
8:2   61, 112, 123, 127,
    138–139
9:2   50, 65
9:13   172
9:16   172
10:10–12   72
11:1–9   72

Genesis (cont.)

13:10   124
14:19   49
14:22   140
21:15   78
22:17   62
36:39   87–88
49:25   61, 139

Exodus

4:20   171
15:6   190
15:8   63
20:4   50, 64
20:11   50, 64
23:29   31

Numbers

5:21   173
21:17   102, 111
24:17   175
30:14   173

Deuteronomy

5:8   50, 64
11:15   78
32:10   10, 22–23
32:14   162
33:13   61, 139
33:26   68, 167

Joshua

24:27   173

Judges

5:17   153
5:20–21   184
9:13   163

1 Samuel

1:1   10
12:21   22–23

2 Samuel
1:24 116
15:21 27
22:16 131

1 Kings
1:41 162

1 Chronicles
1:50 87, 89
6:19 10
16:15–16 172

Nehemiah
9:6 64

Job
3:8 192
6:18 22–23
9:13 191–192
12:24 22–23, 27
12:24–25 27, 29
12:25 27
20:29 173
26:7 22, 24
26:12 191
30:4 78
30:7 78
35:5 68
36 105
36:27 85–88, 91, 96,
   102, 105–106
38:37 68
41:1 195
41:23 162

Psalms
2:4 159, 190
8:2 162
8:8–9 50, 65
9:5 153
9:6 176
9:7 176
18 5, 148–149, 151,
   155, 196
18:2 83, 151

Psalms (cont.)
18:5–6 150
18:7–15 150
18:8–20 149
18:11 167
18:16 151, 153
18:16–20 150
18:17 151
19:3 173
19:4 173
23:1 83
24:2 165
28:3–9 155
29 5, 31, 129, 152,
   154–156, 163, 168–
   169, 184
29:3 153
29:10 152–155, 171,
   189–190
32:6 188
33:5 64
33:5–7 64
33:6 64, 76
33:6–7 64
33:6–8 64
33:7 64
33:8 64
36:6 68
36:8 116
36:9 125
46 1, 5, 156, 158, 160–
   163, 165, 183
46:1–7 157
46:2 157
46:2–3 156–161, 163
46:2–4 163
46:3 157, 159–161,
   163, 183
46:3–4 165, 183
46:3–5 165
46:4 161–163, 183
46:6 157–160
46:7 176
46:8 157
46:9 157
46:10 157

Psalms (cont.)
49:15 178
52:7 178
57:11 68
60:4 160
65:8 193
66:6 165
68:5 167
68:12 173
68:22 175
69:35 50, 64
71:20 50, 63–64
72:8 165
74:12 193
74:12–14 149
74:13 144, 190, 193
74:13–14 41, 193–194
74:14 144, 190–192
75:8 162
77:9 173
77:17 63
78:23 68
80:12 165
87:4 191
89:9 191
89:9–10 191
89:10 41, 144, 190–
   191
89:26 165
93 145
96:11 50, 64
98:7–8 165
104 143
104:3 167
104:6 70, 143
104:9 70
104:11 111
104:14 78
104:15 163
104:26 41, 144, 195
104:30 76
105:8–9 172
106:9 49
106:20 78
107 121
107:25–27 121

Psalms (cont.)
107:26   61, 139
107:40   22–23
108:5   68
132:12   153
135:6   50, 63–64
137:7   177
139:1   83
146:6   50, 64
148   65–67, 69
148:1   66
148:1–6   66
148:1–7   63–64
148:2–4   66
148:7   50, 64, 66–68
148:7–14   66
148:8   67
148:10   67

Proverbs
3:19   68
3:19–20   50, 64, 105,
   131
3:20   60, 68, 105
8   70
8:22–31   105
8:27   61, 64, 143
8:27–29   64
8:27–32   64
8:29   64, 70
8:31   64
20:1   162

Ecclesiastes
2:6   111
10:19   163

Song of Songs
1:4   163

Isaiah
1:7   31
8:8   177
11:15   165
14:13   25
17:12   162

Isaiah (cont.)
19:5   165
22:2   162
23:1   178
24   24
24:1–3   24
24:4   30
24:10   22, 24
24:12   24–25
27   190
27:1   41, 144, 190–
   191, 194
29:21   22–23
30:7   192
30:28   177
34:11   15, 18, 22, 32–
   33
40:17   22–23
40:22   24
40:23   22–23
41:29   22–23
44:9   22–23
45:8   68
45:18   22, 25
45:19   22, 26, 29
47:1   153
48:18   165
49:4   22–23
50:2   165
51:9   41, 56, 144, 190–
   192
51:10   48
51:15   162
59:4   22–23
62:4   31
63:13   49

Jeremiah
4:23   15, 18, 22, 25,
   27–33
4:23–26   28, 30–31
4:23–28   30–31
4:27   24–25, 31
4:27–28   30
4:28   30–31
4:29   31

Jeremiah (cont.)
5:6   12
5:22   162
6:23   162
12:4   31
23:10   31
31:35   162
32:43   31
33:10   31
50:42   162
51:9   68
51:34   116
51:55   162

Ezekiel
17:7   111
28:13   137
28:19   25
32:2   165
32:6   111
37:1–14   76
37:14   76
38:20   50, 64

Hosea
2:1   27
4:3   50, 65

Joel
4:18   107–108, 111

Amos
1:2   31
1:5   125
7:4   48

Jonah
2:4   161, 165

Nahum
1:8   31, 186

Habakkuk
1:2   176
1:4   179
1:13   179

Habakkuk (cont.)
2:4   29, 179
2:5   12
2:18   173
2:19   173
3   5, 129, 147–148,
    163, 165–166, 168,
    170, 172, 179–181,
    190, 196
3:3–7   180
3:3–15   180
3:5   148, 179–181
3:8   147, 161, 163–167,
    170, 176, 179–181,
    190

Habakkuk (cont.)
3:8–10   148, 165
3:8–11   180
3:8–15   180
3:9   147–148, 154,
    159, 163, 167–170,
    172–173, 180–181,
    188
3:10   49, 61
3:11   170, 180
3:13   148, 174–179
3:13–14   174
3:14   170
3:15   144, 148, 162,
    166–167, 173, 190

Habakkuk (cont.)
3:18   176

Zephaniah
1:3   50, 65
2:4   31

Haggai
2:6   50, 64

Zechariah
8:17   173
9:15   162
10:7   163

Deuterocanonical Literature

Sirach
16:18   64

Index of Ancient Texts

Akkadian Texts

2N-T343 rev. 6   172
4R 26 no. 4:51–52   122

AKA
  223:15   100
  84 vi 59   171
Angim III 35–37   171
AO 6472:16   20–21
ARET
  5, 3:IV:3   126
  5, 4:I:6   46
  5, 6:VII:1–2, 3   46
  5, 6:X:4   46
ARM
  2 22:21   126
  2 25:4, 13   126
  2 140:9   117
  24 11   126
Assyrian Law-code,
    col. III, 93   92
Atra-Ḫasīs (AH)
  I i 7–18   50, 67
  I i 15   46, 51
  I i 15–16   70
  II iv 4–6   19, 83
  II viii 34   31
  III iii 38   31
  III iv 5–6   161, 166
  III iv 6   46
  III v 42–44   31
  S i 7   127
  S iv 49   18–19, 82
  S iv 51   19
  S iv 58   19
  S iv 58–59   18, 83
  S iv 59   19
  S iv 61   19
  S v 1   51, 70
  x rev. i 6   51
  x rev. i 6, 10   46, 70
  x rev. ii 4, 11, 18, 34   46,
    70
  x rev. ii 24, 40   46

BA 5 393 i 34   100

Böhl, *BO* 6 p. 166:4   180
Borger Esarh.
  14 Ep. 7:39   100
  79:4   132
  109 iv 12   100

Creation of the World by
    Marduk   40, 46, 71,
    74, 110
CT
  4 50b:8   93
  12 26, 38128, cols. IV–
    VI, 16   92
  24 16, 23   92
  29 46, 23   92
  39 21:168   25

EA
  74:20   44
  89:47   44
  105:13   44
  114:19   44
  151:42   44
  288:33   44
  340:6   44
Enki and Ninhursag   134
Enuma elish   1, 36,
    38–41, 47, 51–53,
    67–68, 75, 130,
    139, 143–145,
    151
  I
    1–2   74
    1–9   72–73
    3–5   74
    4   133
    6   110
    6–8   74
    10–11   74
    22   44
    71   154
    73ff.   131
  IV   154
    101–4   131
    135ff.   131
    137–38   131
    141–42   138

Enuma elish (cont.)
  V
    62   131
  VI
    5   73
    125   154
  VII
    2   82
Eridu Genesis   134

Gilgamesh
  XI:86   118
  XI:297–98   101

Harab Myth   133
Hirsch, Sargon
  b 1, obv. col. 2: 49–
    55   46
  b 6, obv. col. 8: 32–
    38   46
Hymn to Marduk, line
    27   117

KAR
  153 rev.(!) 10   117
  360.7   127

Lambert, *BWL*, 112–13, line
    6   21
LKA 77 i 29–30   133
Lyon Sar. p. 6:37   99

Maqlu VII 179   100
MEE
  4, 12:V:10   47
  4, 79:rev.III:8′–9′   47, 52

OIP
  2 74:74   100
  2 104 v 70   99
  2 140:7   172

RA
  44 pl. 3 p. 40:22   100
  62 52 17–18   135

SEM 117 iii 15   117

208

STC 1 205:9   122
Streck Asb. 178:2   171,
   180

TCL 18, 103:3   93

UET VI. 61. lines 1′–
   17′   71

VAB 4, 134, 45   46
VE
   1343′   52
   1343′–44′   135
Vocabulary Sb, lines 90–
   91   113

von Weiher, Uruk 2,
   no. 5:7   47
Winckler, *Die Keilschrifttexte Sargons* 44 D
   36   99

YOS 10 25:58   100

**Ugaritic (and West
   Semitic) Texts**

KAI 2.42–43   56

KTU
   1.1   41
   1.1–1.6   42
   1.2   41, 147, 149
   1.2:III   150
   1.2:III:4   45, 51
   1.2:IV   150, 167
   1.2:IV:14–15, 16–17,
      22, 24–25   161
   1.2:IV:15, 16–17, 22,
      25   160
   1.3:II:14   177
   1.3:II:15–16   170
   1.3:III:24–25   59, 68
   1.3:III:25   44, 51
   1.3:III:26   55
   1.3:III:26–28   63
   1.3:III:37–IV:3   144,
      192

KTU (cont.)
   1.3:III:38ff.   42, 55
   1.3:V:7   45, 51
   1.3:V:23–24   175
   1.3:VI:5–6   165
   1.4:I:13–14   45
   1.4:I:18   86
   1.4:I:21   45
   1.4:II:6–7   165
   1.4:III:25   45
   1.4:III:28–29   45
   1.4:III:34   45
   1.4:IV:20–22   45
   1.4:IV:22   45, 51
   1.4:IV:56   86
   1.4:V:6   116
   1.4:V:6–7   116, 118,
      123
   1.4:V:6ff.   61
   1.4:V:7   116
   1.4:V:8   157
   1.4:VII   150
   1.4:VII:29, 31   157
   1.5   149
   1.5:I   150
   1.5:I:1ff.   42, 55
   1.5:I:1–3   144, 192
   1.5:I:1–8   145
   1.5:I:14–16   10
   1.5:I:15   11
   1.5:V:6   166
   1.5:VI:1   45
   1.6:I:33–34   163
   1.6:I:34   45, 51
   1.6:I:42–43   132
   1.6:I:44   45
   1.6:I:45   45
   1.6:I:47   45
   1.6:I:53   45
   1.6:VI   150
   1.16:I:11, 21–22   54,
      61
   1.17:VI:12   44
   1.17:VI:48   45, 51
   1.18:I:10–11   175
   1.19:I:44   86
   1.19:I:45   45, 105, 112,
      122

KTU (cont.)
   1.19:III:12ff.   55
   1.23:30   44–45, 51,
      163
   1.23:34–35   154
   1.23:62–63   45, 67
   1.47   56
   1.82:1–3   148, 179,
      181
   1.82:27   154
   1.92:5   44
   1.100   138
   1.100:1   44, 61
   1.100:3   45, 51
   1.100:62   110
   1.100:63, 64   126
   1.101:1–2   153
   1.101:2   154
   1.101:3–4   148
   1.118:4   25
   1.118:18   151
   1.133:2–5   11
   1.133:4   11

RS
   20.24   51
   20.24:29   56

Ug. 5
   44   25
   58   43, 56
   137   43
   137:I:8′   42
   137:II:1′   16
   137:II:15   22
   137:II:23′   15, 43
   137:II:28′   16
   137:II:36′   43
   137:III:33″–34″   61,
      138
   137:III:34″   43–44, 54
   137:IVb:17   43
   238   95
   559–60   11

Index of Ancient Terms

Akkadian

abālu 31
abarak tiāmtim 39
abūbu 31, 111, 154–155,
 171
abu ilāni 133–134
agû 100
akkadû 104
ālu 19
A.MEŠ-*šunu* 73
apsû 50, 52–53, 110, 136,
 139
arki abūbi 155
ašar erṣetimma 135
awīlū 19
ayabba 44, 56

bānât kalāma 133
bānât šamê u erṣeti 133
bān binûtu 55, 132–133
bān kala 133
bān kullati 133
bānû kalāma 133
bānû nabnīt 55, 132–133
bānû nišē 134
bubu'tu 14
bubūtu 13
būrtu 52
butuqtum 97

ēbir tiāmti 46
edinu 113–114
edû 89–92, 95–106, 114
edurû 124
ekallu 114
enšu 22
enšu ša muškēni 22
eqlu 31
erṣetu 18, 20–21, 59–60,
 80
erṣetu ibbalkat 20
erṣetu ibbalkit 21
erṣetu inūš 21
esigu 99
eṭemmu tiāmat 12

gamertu 31
gipiš 100
giṣṣu daddaru 79

ḫarbu 25
ḫuršan ḫazi 25
ḫuršānu 137

ibbalkat 19
id 89–90, 92–95, 102, 106
idiqlat 115, 125
iḫiqqū 73
ikruṣa ṭidda 110
ilibu 12
ilku 37
inūš 21
isinnu 115
išdu 178

kaššu 100
kiššatu 138
kusa-yāmi 49

lam abūbi 155
libbalkat 19

marāru 157
maṣṣāru tâmti 46
mātātu 72
mātu 19, 21, 80
mayālu ša ᵈNammu 135
meḫûm 99
mīlu 97–98, 100–101, 117
mi-lu₄ ma-'-du 153
miṭṭu 171–172
mummu 133
mummu bān šamê u
 erṣeti 133
muškēnu 22
muṭaḫḫidu 117
muṭaḫḫidu kibrāti 117,
 129

nabalkutu 18–21,
 83
nabalkutum 16–17

naḫbalu tiāmtim 46
nāḫiru 12
nāram 46, 161
nāru 92–95, 102–103,
 106–107
nāšu birqi EN abūbi 155
nišū 83
nūnē apsî 50

pātiq šamê u erṣeti 133
purattu 126

qaštu 171
qû 82

râṭu 102
rēmu 19
rēmu ibbalkat 20
rēmu ul ūlda 20

serrēmu 12
sîsâ ša tâmti 12

ṣēru 80, 114
ṣēru(m) 113

šadî u tâmāti 133
šadû 31, 50
šalgu 121
šamaš 43, 48
šamê 138
ša mê 138
šammu 82
šamšu 48
šamû 60
šamūma 54, 138
šaqû ša eqli 97
šigaru naḫbalu
 ti'āmtim 70
šubat māti ul ikân 21
šu'u 82

tamâte 158
tâmātu 101
tâmta 101
tâmtu 39, 52

tāmtu elītu 137
tâmtum 38, 40, 43–47, 50–
53, 72, 166
tāmtu šaplītu 138
tiamat 37
ti'āmat 75
ti'āmat tu'amtu 137
tiâmta 161
ti'āmtim 70
tiāmtu 39
tiāmtum 43–45, 47, 50–
53, 68
ti'āmtum 38, 53
tīb nakri 21
tuptarrisum 17

ṭaḫdu 117
ṭuḫdu 117

ul ūlda 20
urqītu 82

yamu 44

zārū māti 133

Arabic

'ada 87
'āda 87
'adana 124

bahiya 13, 15
bahw 14

ġadan 123
ġadanu 116, 124

haikal 114
hawiya 11

ḥamr 162

'iyād 86

jannātu 'adnin 124

nġm 124

t'h 10
tihāmat 43
tûh 10

Aramaic

'ănānā' 85, 86

bû'ā' 14
bû'ātā' 14

'dn 117, 124

gwgl nhr klm 117, 129

m'dn 117
m'dn mt kln 117–118,
124, 129

'r' 60
'rq' 60

šmy' 60

Eblaite

AB 120

bù-la-na-tim 126
bù-la-tum 52

ᶦᵗᵘ*ga-šúm* 88

idigra-um 125
ì-du 87
ᶦᵗᵘ*ì-du* 88
ì-túm 88

ᶦᵗᵘNI.DU 88

ṣa-lum 113

ti-à-ma-du 46
ti-'à-ma-tum 43, 46–47
tihāmatum 143
tihām(a)tum 52, 68

Egyptian

b3.w 14
bh3 14
bj3 14
bj3.w 14

p(3)nḥśi 120

śk.ty 120

th3 14

y3d.t 86
yd.t 86

Greek

ἀόρατος καὶ
ἀκατασκεύαστος 9
ἀργὸν καὶ ἀδιάκριτον 10

Βάαυ (Phoenician) 14

ἐπιβλυσμός 111
ἐπιβλύω 111

θὲν καὶ οὐθέν 9

κένωμα καὶ οὐθέν 9

Ματραδ 89

νεφέλην 86

πηγή 85, 111

χαίνειν 13
χάος 13
χασκω 13

Hebrew

'ābĕlâ 30
'abnê-bōhû 32
'ādām 81, 83
'ădāmâ 79–83, 85, 105,
108–112, 115, 127–
128
'ădānîm 125
'ad-ṣawwā'r 177
'akkad 104
'āmartî 26, 27
'āpār 81, 109
'āreṣ 64
'ārôt yĕsôd 177
'aryēh miyya'ar 12
'ayin 23
'āyin 23
'ăzûbâ 25, 31

bā'āreṣ mittaḥat 64
ba'ăšer 27
bal-yô'îlû 23

bammayim mittaḥat
  lā'āreṣ 64
baqqĕšûnî 26, 27
bassēter 26
baššāmayim mimmaʿal 64
bêt ʿeden 125
bĕʿēden miqqedem 110
bĕgaʾăwātô 160
bĕlî-mâ 24–25
bĕtôk 27
bimqôm 27
bimqôm 'ăšer 27
bimqôm 'ereṣ ḥōšek 27
bōhû 13–15

daltê šāmayim 68
dam-ʿēnāb 162
deber 180
deše' 82
dibbartî 26, 27
ʿdn 124
drk 168

'ēd 4, 50, 77, 79–81, 85–
  88, 90–92, 95–97, 102,
  104–111, 127–129, 153
'êd 87–88
*ēdê 96
ʿēden 77, 81–82, 107, 110,
  112–114, 116, 118,
  124–125
'ēdô 85, 91, 96, 104–105,
  114
'ĕlōhîm 4
'ên 'ôrām 29–30
'epes 23
'ereṣ 23, 50, 53, 56, 58–
  60, 63, 65–66, 68, 72,
  80–82, 85, 88, 107–108,
  110–111, 128
'ereṣ ḥōšek 27
'ereṣ midbār 10
'ereṣ wĕšāmāyim 129
ʿēṣ 82
ʿēśeb 79, 82
ʿēśeb haśśādeh 78
'ēš 96

gan 81–82, 108, 110
gĕbûl 70

hā'āreṣ 31, 63–64, 66,
  68–70, 81, 87

hāmîr 157
hammāyim 69–70
hārîm 63
haššāmayim 31, 66, 68–
  69
hêkāl 114
hišqâ 97
hmy 162

ḥāmer 162
ḥănîtekā 170
ḥārēb 25, 31
ḥiddeqel 104, 115, 125–
  126
ḥiṣṣêkā 170
ḥmyʿdn 125
ḥōmer 162
ḥōmer mayim rabbîm 162
ḥōšek 4, 27, 29, 48, 69

ʿîr 23–24
'iššê 96

kālâ 31
kî 78–79
kôkĕbê haššāmayim 62

lammabbûl 152–153,
  155
lāšebet 25
laylâ 48
lĕzeraʿ yaʿăqōb 27
lō'-tōhû 26
lō'-yôʿîlû 23

mabbûl 153–155,
  171
māṭār 105
maṭrēd 87–89
maṭṭôt 169–173
maṭṭôt 'ōmer 173
maʿyān 107–108, 111
mayim rabbîm 151
mʿdnh 125
mê hayyām 64
mĕ'ōrōt 29
merqāḥâ 162
mibbêt 175–176, 178
min 108, 178
min-hā'āreṣ 111
môt 150
mṭh 'lhym 171
mwṭ 159

nāhār 102, 105, 108, 111,
  165
nāhārem 164
nātan bĕqôlô 160
nĕhārîm 161, 163, 165
nĕhārôt 163, 165
nĕšāmâ 76
niblê šāmayim 68
nišmat ḥayyîm 76

'ōmer 147, 169
'ôr 29, 48

pĕlāgâw 163
pĕrat 126
pîw 70

qaštekā 172–173
qaw-tōhû 32
qĕdōš 161
qešet 170
qôl YHWH 155

rāqîaʿ 48, 128, 138
rāšaʿ 175, 178–179
rešep 180–181
rîq 23
rōkēb bāʿărābôt 167
rōkēb šāmayim 167
rō'š 176, 178
rʿš 159
'rṣ 64
rûaḥ 75–76, 139
rûaḥ 'ĕlōhîm 58, 74–76

śādeh 79–81, 111, 115
śîăḥ 79, 82
śîăḥ haśśādeh 78
śmḥ 163

ṣāpôn 25
ṣawwā'r 176, 178
ṣûr 151

šāmayim 48, 60–61, 64,
  139, 143
šammâ 24
šĕbûʿat hā'ālâ 173
šĕbûʿat 'issār 173
šĕbûʿat šeqer 173
šĕbûʿôt 168–170, 172
šĕbûʿôt 'ōmer 173
šĕḥāqîm 60, 68, 167

šeleg 121
šěmāmâ 24, 25, 31
šemeš 43
šibʿat 168
šmym 63
šōham 125
šqh 107

taʾăwâ 11
tadšēʾ 82
tannînîm 67
tēbēl 64
těhôm 2–3, 30, 36–39,
    42–44, 47–50, 53–54,
    56, 58, 61, 63–65, 69–
    70, 72, 75, 77, 107, 127–
    129, 131, 139–140, 143
těhōmôt 63–64, 67–68
těhômôt 49, 60–61, 69,
    105
těhôm(ôt) 49–50, 52–53,
    59, 65–66, 88, 111, 139
těhōmôt hāʾāreṣ 63
těhôm rabbâ 37, 48
thm 68
thwmwt 64
tîrôš 163
tišteh 162
tôaḥ 10
tōhû 10, 12–15, 22–27, 58
Tōhû 10
tōhû baqqěšûnî 26–27
tōhû wābōhû 2–3, 9, 12–
    13, 15–18, 22, 26, 28–
    35, 69, 75, 83–84

ʾumlělâ 30

wā 15
wābōhû 58
wayyîṣer Yhwh ʾělōhîm 77
wayyōʾmer ʾělōhîm 77
wě 80–81
wěhišqâ 111

yām 49–51, 56, 64–65,
    69, 75, 144, 162, 165
yammîm 56, 70, 158
yammîm wěnāhār 161
yaʿăleh 78, 85, 108, 111
yaʿlê 97
yayin 163
yěsôd 178

yēṣēʾ 108
yôm 48
yōṣēʾ 108
yōšěbê tēbēl 64
yšb l- 153
yšb ʿl 153
ʾyš thw 22–23

zěʾēb ʿărābôt 12
zwb 154

Hurrian

Aranzaḫi 126
Arašših 126
aršḫ 126

haikal 114

tapšaḫalše 22
tapšuḫumme 16–17, 21

Old South Arabic

ʿdn 124

hʿdn 124

Phoenician

ʾrṣ 60

šmm 60

Sumerian

a-ab 52
a.ab.ba 44–45, 51–53,
    135
dA.AB.BA 56
a.ab.ba an.ta 137
a.ab.ba ki.ta 137
ab-a 47, 53
abzu 135
ab-zu 52
á-dam 81
A.DÉ 104
a.dé.a 98
A.DÉ.A 89, 91–92, 104
a-kà-dè 104
A-KUL 153
a-kur 153
AN 60–61, 138

anše.eden.na 12
ANTU 44, 138
ANTUM 61

buranun 126

e₄-dé 104–105, 108
e₄-dé(-a) 107
e₄-dé-a 106, 114
edin 113–115
ʿedin 116
EDIN 113
é-duru₅ 124
engur 135
ezen 114–115

gina 126
GIŠ.TUKUL.DINGIR 171–
    172

ḫa-gal 114

íd 102–104, 106–107
díD 92–95
íD 106
uruíd 103
idigna 114–115, 126

KI 60

Lugal-abzu 135
Lugal-id 135

mir 99

dNI.DA.KUL 126

PÚ 52

SIG 22

šár 138
še.a.ab.ba 12

uru 81

Ugaritic

ab adm 55
ab šnm 55
anḫr b ym 11–12
arṣ 45, 51, 53, 59–63, 67
aṯrt ṣrm 45

aṯrt ym 45 ·
aymr 147, 169, 174

bᶜdt thmtm 131, 136
bn ilm 133
bn ᶜnm 175
bny bnwt 55, 132
bn ydm 175
brlt 11
bt 163

dg bym 45
dl 22
ᶜdn 112, 116, 118, 123–
124
ᶜdn mṭrh 116

glṭ 120–123

ǵr 151
ǵrm wᶜmqt 151

hkl 114
hm 11
hm brlt 11
hmlt arṣ 63
hpk 17

ḥmr 162
ḥršn 137

ilm nᶜmm 55
išt 96
ʾiṯt 96

kbkbm 60–63, 68
km db 154
k mdb 154
ktp 175
k ym 154

lbim thw 10
lbim thw(t) 12
ltn 144

lṭpn. w qdš 54, 61

maškanu 22
mbk nhrm 136
mdb 153–154
mdbm 154
mdlk 166
ᶜm(n) 60
mṭ 170
mṭr 122–123
mṭrh 120
mṭrk 166

nhr 147, 161, 164–165
nhrm 51, 136, 147, 163,
165
nᶜm 124
npš 11
nšm 63

qdqd 174
ql . bᶜl 122–123
qn ʾrṣ 56
qrb apq thmtm 131, 136
qšt 170

rbb 122–123
rbt aṯrt ym 45
ᶜr. d qdm 110
rḥk 166
rkb ᶜrpt 150, 166
ᶜrpt 61

ṣmdm 169
ṣpn 25

šḥt 82
šmm 45, 54, 60–63, 67–
68, 143
šmm w thm 61
šmm-w-thm 44, 54, 138
špš 43, 138
šrh 123

šrᶜ thmtm 105, 112, 122–
123

tahāmatu 54, 138
tahām(at)u 48
tahāmu 140
tglṭ thmt 121
th 68
thm 45, 48, 50–51, 61
thm(t) 47, 49, 52–55, 59,
131, 143
thmt 48, 50–51, 54, 60–
63, 112, 123, 127, 136–
137, 139
thmtm 45, 51, 123, 136,
163
thw 10–12, 16
thwt 11
tu-a-bi-[ú] 15–18
tu-a-bi-[ú(?)] 21
tu-a-pí-[ku(?)] 18, 22

ṭkt 120, 122
ṭl 122–123
ṭlg 121
tnn 144
ṭpṭ nhr 160–161
ṭrt 120–123
ṭrt . b glṭ 120

w 11
wnpš 11

yam 48
yd 154
yᶜdn . ᶜdn 116
ygrš 175
ym 44–45, 49–52, 61, 67,
139, 147, 160–161, 163–
166
ytn qlh 123, 157

zbl ym 161

www.ingramcontent.com/pod-product-compliance
Lightning Source LLC
Chambersburg PA
CBHW021957090426
42811CB00001B/62